CHURCHILL'S
Angels

CHURCHILL'S
Angels

How Britain's Women Secret Agents Changed
the Course of the Second World War

BERNARD
O'CONNOR

AMBERLEY

First published 2012

Amberley Publishing
The Hill, Stroud
Gloucestershire, GL5 4EP

www.amberley-books.com

British Library Cataloguing in Publication Data.
A catalogue record for this book is available from the British Library.

ISBN 978 1 4456 0828 0

Typeset in 10pt on 12pt Sabon.
Typesetting and Origination by Amberley Publishing.
Printed in the UK.

Contents

List of Female Agents

Giliana Gerson, over Pyrénées to Lyon, 23 May 1941

'Anatole', landed by a Lysander nr St Saëns, 27 February 1942

Yvonne Rudellat, landed by felucca (fishing boat), nr Antibes, 30 July 1942

Valentine 'Blanche' Charlet, landed by felucca, nr Agay, 1 September 1942

Lise de Baissac, parachuted from Whitley bomber, nr Chambord, 24 September 1942

Andrée Borrel, parachuted from Whitley bomber, nr Chambord, 24 September 1942

Mary Lindell, landed by Lysander nr Ussel, 26 October 1942

Andrée de Jongh, already in Brussels

Odette Sansom, landed by felucca nr Port Miou, 3 November 1942

Mary Herbert, landed by felucca nr Port Miou, 3 November 1942

Marie Thérèse le Chêne, landed by felucca nr Port Miou, 3 November 1942

'Angela', parachuted from a Halifax nr Saumur, Autumn 1942

Jacqueline Nearne, parachuted from a Halifax bomber nr Brioude, 25 January 1943

Beatrice 'Trix' Terwindt, parachuted from a Halifax bomber nr Steenwijk, 13 February 1943

Françine Agazarian, landed by a Lysander nr Marnay, 17 March 1943

Julienne Aisner, landed by a Lysander nr Tours, 14 May 1943

Vera Leigh, landed by a Lysander nr Tours, 14 May 1943

Noor Inayat Khan, landed by a Lysander nr Vieux Briollay, 16 June 1943

Diana Rowden, landed by a Lysander nr Vieux Briollay, 16 June 1943

Sonia Olschanezky, already in Paris

Cécile Lefort, landed by a Lysander nr Vieux Briollay, 16 June 1943

Eliane Plewman, parachuted from a Halifax nr Lons-le-Saunier, 13 August

1943

Beatrice 'Yvonne' Cormeau, parachuted from a Halifax nr St Antoine du Queyret, 22 August 1943

Elyzbieta Zawacka, parachuted from a Halifax nr Warsaw, 9 September 1943

Yolande Beekman, landed by a Lysander nr Vieux Briollay, 17 September 1943

Cecile 'Pearl' Witherington, parachuted from a Halifax nr Tendu, 22 September 1943

Elizabeth Devereaux Rochester, landed by a Hudson nr Bletterans, 18 October 1943

Danielle Reddé, parachuted nr Montluçon, 9 February 1944

Anne-Marie Walters, parachuted from a Halifax, nr Créon d'Armagnac, 4 January 1944

Marguerite Petitjean, parachuted from a Halifax, nr St Uze, 29 January 1944

Madeleine Damerment, parachuted from a Halifax, nr Sainville, 29 February 1944

Eileen 'Didi' Nearne, landed by Lysander nr Les Lagnys, 2 March 1944

Denise Bloch, landed by Lysander nr Baudreville, 2 March 1944

Yvonne Baseden, parachuted from a Halifax nr Gabarret, 18 March 1944

Yvonne Fontaine, landed by gunboat nr Beg-an-Fry, 21 March 1944

Virginia Hall, landed by gunboat nr Beg-an-Fry, 21 March 1944

Maureen 'Paddy' O'Sullivan, parachuted from a Halifax nr Figeac, 22 March 1944

Lucie Aubrac, already in Lyon

Violette Szabó, parachuted from a Liberator nr Azay-le Rideau, 4 April 1944 and again from a Liberator nr Saint-Gilles-les-Forêts, 7 June 1944

Lilian Rolfe, landed by a Lysander nr Azay-sur-Cher, 5 April 1944

Muriel Byck, parachuted from a Halifax nr Issoudun, 8 April 1944

Odette Wilen, parachuted from a Halifax nr Issoudun, 11 April 1944

Nancy Wake, parachuted from a Liberator nr Les Menus, 29 April 1944

Phyllis 'Pippa' Latour, parachuted from a Liberator nr Mont du Saule, 1 May 1944

Marcelle Somers, landed by a Hudson nr Manziat, 3 May 1944

Marguerite Knight, parachuted from a Liberator nr Poinçon-les-Larrey, 5 May 1944

Madeleine Lavigne, parachuted from a Halifax nr Saone-et-Loire, 23 May 1944

Sonya Butt, parachuted from a Liberator nr La Cropte, 28 May 1944

Ginette Jullian, parachuted from a Liberator nr Saint-Viatre-les-Tanneries, 7 June 1944

Krystyna Skarbek (Christine Granville), parachuted from a Halifax nr

Beaurepaire, 6 July 1944

Marie-Madeleine Fourcade, landed by a Hudson nr Egligny, 6 July 1944

Francoise Dissart, already in Toulouse

Elaine Madden, parachuted from a Halifax nr d'Houyet, 3/4 August 1944

Olga Jackson, parachuted nr Brussels, 3/4 August 1944

Frédérique Dupuich, landed by a Lysander nr Genillé, 6 August 1944

Josephine Hamilton, parachuted nr Abberkerk, 10 August 1944

Sibyl Anne Sturrock, parachuted into Yugoslavia, September 1944

Jos Gemmeke, parachuted from a Halifax nr Nieuwkoop, 10 March 1945

Foreword

Between May 1941 and September 1944 over sixty women were infiltrated into occupied Western Europe. They were sent as part of Winston Churchill's plan to 'set Europe ablaze' with missions to work with various resistance movements in France, Belgium, Holland, Poland and Yugoslavia as organisers, couriers and wireless operators. Most left England on moonlit nights from RAF Tempsford, a remote, isolated airfield in Bedfordshire, between Bedford and Cambridge, about fifty miles north of London. Many parachuted from aeroplanes but some were landed in the early hours of the morning in fields or clearings in woods, away from built-up areas. A few were landed by motor boats and fishing boats. Some spent over a year on their dangerous tasks; others were caught as soon as they landed. Having to live in constant fear of arrest, imprisonment, interrogation, torture and execution, they were some of the bravest and most courageous women of the Second World War. Of those who were captured, at least fifteen are known to have been executed. Two were liberated at the end of the war and only one escaped. Two died of natural causes but the others either stayed in their home countries or were successfully brought back to England.

A measure of their contribution to the war effort is the number of awards they were given after the war. Some were honoured more than once and many posthumously. They include one Knight Commander of the British Commonwealth, one Commander of the British Empire, two Orders of the British Empire, nineteen Members of the British Empire, four George Crosses, twelve *Chevaliers de Legion de l'Honneur*, twenty-nine *Croix de Guerre*, nine Mentioned in Dispatches, eleven *Medailles de Resistance*, one *Medaille de Reconnaissance*, one King's Medal for Courage, six King's Medals for Brave Conduct, one *Chevalier de l'Ordre de*

Leopold II, one American Distinguished Service Cross, one United States Medal of Freedom and one Australian Companion of the Order.

Having lived near RAF Tempsford since the mid-1980s, I have researched and published a number of books on the airfield. As I was often invited by local groups to give talks on the subject, often the Women's Institute, I tried to tailor my stories to those of the women involved. Researching accounts of their lives and wartime experiences has been rather like trying to find pieces of a jigsaw puzzle and put them together to produce a picture without having a box lid. Some pieces might not fit exactly and I have to admit that there are many gaps. Using their personnel files in the National Archives, contemporary and modern newspaper articles, obituaries, biographies and autobiographies, specialist history books, personal memoirs, interviews and the Internet, I have attempted to tell their stories. While some of these women have had books written and films made about their exploits, the vast majority have not. What follows is my attempt to ensure that the contributions they made to bringing about the successful conclusion of the Second World War is not forgotten. I will leave it to the reader to picture the reality of their experiences.

I need to acknowledge the help of the staff at the National Archives, formerly the Public Records Office, the Imperial War Museum and the RAF Museum at Hendon. I also need to acknowledge the work of a number of historians: Michael R. D. Foot and Steven Kippax for their work on the Special Operations Executive, Juliette Pattinson and Kate Vigurs for their work on women's wartime history, and Squadron Leader Beryl Escott for her research into the WAAF and FANY. Others whose research and publications contained valuable snippets include Shrabani Basu, Marcus Binney, Bob Body, Freddie Clark, Tom Ensminger, James Gleeson, David Harrison, Sarah Helm, Liane Jones, Rita Kramer, Elizabeth Nicholas, Susan Ottoway, Margaret Pawley, Judith Pearson, Sue Ryder, Martin Sugarman, Tania Szabó, Jerrard Tickell, Pierre Tillet and Hugh Verity. There are many others whose work I have accessed and whose research I hereby acknowledge.

1

Sending Women into Occupied Europe

The body given the responsibility of sending in these women was the top secret Special Operations Executive. Known as 'The Firm', 'The Organisation', The Org', 'The Racket' or 'The Outfit' by those in the know, its official title was the Inter Services Research Bureau with five floors of offices at 64 Baker Street in London. Set up in the summer of 1940, following the evacuation of Dunkirk, it had several objectives. The first was to get information out of occupied Europe. Where were the Germans garrisoned? How many were there? What were their vulnerable points? Who were the people who could be counted upon to actively engage in helping to liberate their country? The second was to send in radios or wireless sets and wireless operators to enable communication between London and the resistance movements. The third was to send in trained agents to help the Resistance in occupied Europe to attack the German forces in whatever way they could. What weapons and ammunition did they need? What other supplies were needed – food, clothing, medicines, money etc.? What training did they need? Locate dropping grounds for supplies and agents. Locate safe houses and identify trusted people who would help. The fourth was to prepare the Resistance to help the Allies when the invasion finally came.

The SOE had sections for each country it sent its agents to, with separate sections for training, buildings, planning, and finance. As well as having to liaise with the War Office and the Foreign Office, it also had to negotiate with the RAF for flights and on occasions with the Royal Navy for sea transport.

Unlike many of Britain's wartime organisations, the SOE had a much more positive attitude towards women. In Michael R. D. Foot's *SOE in France*, he remarked that there are

plenty of women with marked talents for organisation and operational command, for whom a distinguished future on the staff could be predicted if only the staff could be found broad-minded enough to let them join it. The SOE was such a broad-minded staff.

The SOE appointed numerous women to its administrative staff. Squadron Leader Beryl Escott, the Women's Auxiliary Air Force (WAAF) historian, reckoned that about 3,200 out of a total staff of 13,200 were female, whereas the Air Ministry only had 300 women. From April 1942, women started being trained by the SOE for clandestine work in the field. The number of women it took on as agents is uncertain. I estimate about sixty. It needs to be stressed that other Intelligence agencies also wanted women infiltrated in enemy-occupied territory, notably the SIS (Secret Intelligence Service), the American Office of Strategic Services (OSS) and the Soviet Union's *Norodny Kommissariat Vnutrennich Dyel* (NKVD).

There were several reasons why it was decided to send in women. In Kate Vigurs' PhD thesis, 'The women agents of the Special Operations Executive F section – wartime realities and post war representations', she commented that, as women were not part of the German round-ups for forced labour, they could move about the towns and countryside much more easily than men. They could use trams, trains and bicycles for which they needed a permit, whereas men aged between eighteen and fifty would be in constant fear of spot checks and looking conspicuous. It would be completely normal for women to be seen out and about, queuing in shops, visiting the markets and visiting friends. Juliette Pattinson, lecturer in Modern British History at Strathclyde University and specialising in gender, commented in *Behind Enemy Lines* that this not only gave female agents a reason for being out of the home, but also shopping baskets could hide weapons and radio parts: 'messages and packages were concealed in bicycle-frames, shopping baskets, hand-bags, the lining of clothes or round the waist under the clothes'. Items were also hidden internally.

Of the thirty-nine women sent to the area of France controlled by what was called 'F' Section, some had previously belonged to the British Auxiliary Services, the Auxiliary Transport Service (ATS), and the Women's Auxiliary Air Force (WAAF). The SOE's 'F' Section supported the strictly non-political resistance groups under British control. General Charles de Gaulle's Free French Forces organised what was called the RF Section – *Republique Française*. Some members of the WAAF with particular skills, essentially being able to speak French fluently, were transferred into the SOE and trained as agents to be sent into occupied Europe. Others were given honorary commissions in the WAAF in the hope that, as officers in the regular services, their chances of being treated as prisoners of war would be improved. Although many agents were recruited from the War Office, the Admiralty, Air Ministry, Central Registry and Telegraph Office, others were 'introduced' if it was identified that they had language skills. Other skills that would be useful were patience, emotional self-control, and aggression.

Analysis of the SOE records shows that five second officers, six assistant second officers and four flight officers from the WAAF were sent to 'F' Section. Whether any had been at Tempsford beforehand is unknown. Although the Geneva Convention stipulated that women in the Services should not carry weapons, this was not practised by the SOE. Selwyn Jepson, one of the Directorate of Military Intelligence, commented in an interview in 1986 that:

> I was responsible for recruiting women for the work in the face of a good deal of opposition from the powers that be who said that women, under the Geneva Convention, were not allowed to take combatant duties which they regarded resistance work in France as being ... There was a good deal of opposition from various quarters until it went to Churchill.[1]

The taboo of women using arms was abandoned by the SOE when they recognised that women were badly needed in occupied Europe and they needed to be able to defend themselves like any man. Jepson argued that the Geneva Convention did not relate to a modern war that called for the wholesale involvement of civilian populations. As he put it, 'Air raid bombs that demolish homes and kill children bring to every woman by every natural law the right to protect, to seek out and destroy the evil behind these bombs by all means possible to her – including the physical and militant.' He subsequently became SOE's recruiting officer, interviewing potential agents at Sanctuary Buildings, in Westminster, London.

All the women agents were therefore given commissions in either the WAAF or the First Aid Nursing Yeomanry (FANY) in the hope that they would be treated as prisoners of war under the terms of the Geneva Convention and not be sentenced to death without trial. Of the fifteen in the FANY, there were six volunteers, six ensigns, one lieutenant and two of ordinary rank. Fifteen were given commissions in the WAAF and one in the Auxiliary Transport Service (ATS). The reality was that, if they were caught in civilian clothes and found to be agents, they would in all likelihood be interrogated and tortured to get any useful information out of them, and then executed.

What they did not know was the types of torture they might experience if caught. Pattinson examined the testimonies of those who survived imprisonment, which showed that they were beaten with implements, kicked about the body, had toenails extracted, toes trampled upon by boots, were chained to furniture, deprived of sleep, forced to stay awake during many hours of interrogation, deprived of light, food, and medical treatment for wounds, threatened with mock executions, had their fingers crushed, were immersed in water to the point of drowning, burned with hot pokers, heard others being tortured or shot, were subjected to electric currents passing through their bodies, and were kept in solitary confinement. Agents reported numerous injuries, including broken ribs, fractured fingers, teeth being knocked out as well as bruises and cuts. Pattinson's interviews with three of the women who were repatriated found that they were all beaten and badly mistreated, with distinct sexist and sexual overtones.

Sue Ryder commented that, 'All the men and women who trained as agents had to be in top mental and physical condition and possess initiative; they were self-reliant and discreet and capable of standing up to rough and arduous training and work.' The women agents were generally much younger than their male counterparts.

Although there was concern expressed about sending women into occupied Europe on dangerous missions, Colonel Gubbins, the then head of SOE, argued that they would be less conspicuous and find it much easier to get accommodation. Lone men were unusual as, from March 1943, the Germans introduced the *Service du Travail Obligitaire*, compulsory work service. All French men had to register their births. Those between nineteen and thirty-two were sent to work on the Atlantic Wall, in factories in Germany or on the Russian front as many German men were engaged in military duties. Every week, about 20,000 were picked up on the streets of Paris. The Germans expected 500,000 in the first six months.

Forest Yeo-Thomas, a French-speaking British agent sent from Tempsford into France, learned about this compulsory work service and informed London that he feared that the age would be raised to forty-two, then to the middle fifties, resulting in there being no hope ever of forming a Secret Army in France. He suggested that the BBC and SOE use whatever means they could to encourage Frenchmen to avoid conscription by leaving the country or living clandestinely as members of the Resistance. Money needed to be sent, as well as weapons, ammunition, food and forged identity and ration cards so they could survive and defend themselves. He was convinced that these deserters, financed by Britain, armed and trained by SOE agents, would form the nucleus of a Secret Army. The concept of the Maquis was born. The result was that women would be much more visible on the streets than men. It was the ideal opportunity to start sending in women agents. They could invent a hundred cover stories as they could travel extensively and arouse little suspicion. Escott commented that women

> often substituted for a missing husband or brother, as the wage earner of the family. They searched for missing relatives or children. They covered incredible distances hunting for scarce items of fuel or clothing and particularly on a regular search for food to feed their families, with the fierce and protective

care that distinguishes a mother for her children. They were to be found on all the roads – in their locality and out of it – most going about their lawful and innocent duties equipped with the legal and correct passes and papers required of every French citizen. A girl on a bike with a carrier was therefore a common sight everywhere and the Germans had such a stereotyped idea of the role of women that it could take a long time before they would suspect one of being an agent. She was therefore more unobtrusive and less liable to be caught. She might also to be able to use more charm and devious wiles that might hoodwink a questioner. Many trainers objected, but they soon discovered that women could be just as skilful and brave as men and this was soon proved in the field, where they had to overcome the extra obstacle of the ingrained prejudice to women of the people in the countries where they worked, no small task in itself. Thus the most unlikely of agents became assets.[2]

In Foot's *SOE in France*, he expressed the opinion that:

By no means all of F Section's women agents had that ordinary, unassuming air which is so precious an asset for a clandestine; several had the stunning good looks and vibrant personality that turn men's heads in the street. This helped to make them noticed; it was counterbalanced, in the section's view, by making it more easy for them to appear to belong to that leisured class, the comings and goings of which only the surliest policeman is ever going to disturb. It was a mistake to forget how surly some of Hitler's or even Petain's policemen could be.

Exactly how many women were sent into occupied Europe is uncertain. There were some sent from Tempsford by the SIS, but their details are scarce. Their records, if any exist at all, are probably still being held by MI6. In Hugh Verity's *We Landed by Moonlight*, he commented that:

There were a number of different clients, none of whom wanted any of the others to know about their operations. In fact SIS forbade any written matter. Their operations were 'officially inadmissible'.

I have references to over sixty women being sent in. While the majority were flown out from Tempsford, others were sent from Tangmere, Harrington, and in one case Waterbeach, near Cambridge. A few were sent by small boats in the middle of the night. Four were sent to Belgium, three to Holland, eleven to the area of France controlled by de Gaulle and, officially, thirty-nine to the area controlled by 'F' Section. The OSS sent two women to France and the Soviets sent two there as well, one to Austria and one to Germany. Unofficially, there were more. Not all were British. The women were of various nationalities, including Americans, Australians, Austrians, Belgians, British, Dutch, French, Mauritian, Swiss and an Indian-Russian. Several were Anglo-French, their British fathers having married French women after the First World War. Many were married, several had children, one was a grandmother and two were sisters. There were two brother and sister teams and one mother and daughter team among those sent by the RF section. The Soviets planned to send one married couple into Prague but they refused to go. Before joining, the women had been told that their chances of survival were about evens, but in fact something like three agents in four survived. Of those sent to France, thirteen paid the ultimate sacrifice.

There were three women organisers, twenty couriers and sixteen radio or wireless operators in 'F' Section. They all had to sign the Official Secrets Act. Security was supposed to be watertight. Saying anything about the work to one's boyfriend, parents or friends was strictly forbidden. No one was supposed to know anything about the SOE. In fact, the first hint in the British media of these women's role during the war was not until 11 March 1945. The *Sunday Express* included an article on them by Squadron Leader William Simpson, DFC (Distinguished Flying Cross).

WAAF girls parachuted into France
Who are the Waaf officers who parachuted into France to join the Maquis months before D-Day?

This question has plagued Air Ministry officials ever since Sir Archibald Sinclair [Secretary of State for Air] praised Waaf parachutists in the House of Commons last week.

Officially it remains unanswered – for reasons of security. Two only have been named in the press. One Sonia d'Artois (née Butt), is the young daughter of a group captain. She married the French-Canadian officer who jumped with her.

The other, Maureen O'Sullivan, is also young and pretty. She comes from Dublin.

Demure girls
The interesting thing about these girls is they are not hearty and horsey young women with masculine chins. They are pretty young girls who would look demure and sweet in crinolines. Most of them are English girls who speak perfect French. Some were educated in French convents; others attended Swiss finishing schools. A few are French girls who escaped from France and agitated for a chance to go back and work underground. Cool courage, intelligence, and adaptability are their most important attributes. They have to be able to pass themselves off as tough country wenches, and smart Parisiennes.

They were taught parachute jumping in the North of England. They trained with male agents and paratroopers of all nationalities, and leapt with them from fixed balloons and moving aircraft.

But parachuting was a secondary part of their training. They also had to absorb complicated secret details of underground organisation and train the Maquis in radio operating.

After months of intensive training, there often followed weeks of anxious waiting. Then, dressed in the appropriate French civilian clothes of their first role, they were flown by night bomber into moonlit France.

Sometime they dropped 'free' at a pre-determined point. On landing, they fended for themselves; reported to a friendly farmer, then set off at dawn to contact the leader of their resistance group.

Usually however, they landed with arms and food, floating down with the packages and containers. As courier, she went from group to group of the Maquis. It was easier for a girl to pass unnoticed in a France stripped of men by the Germans.

Great courage
Often she was on the spot when supplies were dropped, and helped to unload and hide the containers.

It sounds easy enough. In fact, it is about the most cold-blooded and creepy task that any young woman could choose.

Death and torture are present realities. Atrocity details are well known. There were traitors in the Maquis itself working to betray. Sometimes they succeeded.

But so great was the courage and spirit of these girls that they could afford to send back humorous messages.

One – behind with routine signals – complained that what with washing and darning, and running around with messages, she had little time for routine work!

Another, who had walked for weeks to return to France, had to jump over Kent – due to engine trouble in the bomber which carried her. As soon as she had collected herself, she asked to be allowed to go on with the job the same night.

Behind the veil of secrecy, not yet raised by the Air Ministry, there are great stories of courage and endurance.

For the agent has no status; no friendly uniform or consul to rely on. With her friends she is outside the law – until it catches up with her.

Her first aim
There was one girl I met in Vichy France four years ago. Since then, although not in the Waaf, she has been back and forth many times. Acting as courier and wireless operator, she has also organised Maquis bands. No doubt she has fought with arms, for her first aim is to kill Germans.

Amongst her perilous adventures are included escapes over the Pyrénées into Spain. And she knows the filth, discomfort and despair of Spanish prison camps. But nothing could dismay her. She went on.

All these unknown young girls of the Waaf have proved one thing for ever. The toughest tests of courage and endurance faced by men can be passed with honour by women.[3]

After a selection process the agents were sent on a three-week introductory training and assessment course at Wanborough Manor, near Guildford, if they were in the 'F' Section. After June 1943, they went on a much shorter five-day assessment at Winterfold, near Cranleigh in Surrey. Their trainers' assessment determined whether they would be best used as a wireless operator or a courier. The role of an organiser was generally considered by the SOE to be a man's job. If they were considered suitable they then were sent on a four- or five-week paramilitary training course in Arisaig, north-west Scotland, where they were taught the art of 'ungentlemanly warfare'.

In Susan Ottoway's *The Life that I have*, she quotes Major Aonghais Fyffe, the Security Liaison Officer for the SOE's training schools in Arisaig, as saying:

there was no distinction between the sexes and all suffered the same rigours of Physical training in the early hours of wintry mornings, the same mud, muck soakings in peat bogs on field-craft and the same sore muscles and aching joints from the Arisaig form of unarmed combat. After all, when they were crawling flat to the ground over the peaty marshes of Loch nan Uamh, they were all just bods in battledress.

At the time when SOE first decided to send female agents into occupied Europe, women were banned from carrying weapons in the British armed forces. Special authorisation was needed from Winston Churchill to allow them to be armed. While they underwent the same rigorous training as the men, they soon proved themselves quite capable at subterfuge, using guns, hand grenades, plastic explosives and silent killing.

Apart from those who were going to be sent into the field by boat, all agents had to get their parachute wings. This was done at Ringway Airfield, near Manchester. They stayed either in Dunham House, near Altringham, or in the adjoining estate of Tatton Park. Escott described the training:

They usually did four or five practice jumps, the last one at night and in later years with a leg bag for carrying equipment. Of course the station had its usual complement of airwomen. Having spent about two years at Ringway working on parachutes, 'where most of the time 1,000 troops were dropped day and night', Winifred Smith has clear memories of '... cycling across the tarmac to our section, seeing girls preparing to parachute, complete with lipstick and make-up – otherwise it was hard to tell that they really were girls, what with their parachute suits, crash helmets, and so on. We often watched them waiting to board the plane. It was like follow-my-leader. The girls were towards the back but they were always laughing and we would wave and call good luck. I don't remember more than about three or four together boarding the same plane, in fact often I could only see one.' Trainees sometimes said that they put the girls to jump first out of the aircraft into the grounds of Tatton Park, since they reckoned that the men would not hold back if a woman led the way. As part of her work on modifications to 'chutes and packs, Winifred also went into the training hangar: '... and saw them training on what we called the Fan. They were completely fearless. They were also quick off the mark in getting away afterwards. One had the feeling they didn't expect to come back, so they were living for the moment. When VE Day was over and we could talk more freely, it was agreed by all who had contact with these WAAF, that they had an inner strength and sheer determination which allowed them to do what was asked of them. They were inspired by something greater than the ordinary person.'

Those destined for courier work went to one of eleven secluded country houses in the grounds of Beaulieu, the New Forest. Vigurs pointed out that

This course was aimed at drilling the hard facts of life in France into the trainees, it also aimed to highlight the implications that simple mistakes could carry. It was on this course that agents were trained to think and behave as if they were actually French. Many changes had occurred in France during the Occupation, for example women were not given a cigarette ration, coffee was only available without milk, (so asking for a café noir would raise a few eye brows) and certain foods were only available on set days of the week. Agents had to be aware of these changes which would be second nature to a French person, otherwise a small error could mark them out as different and potentially cost them their lives. Other mistakes that could be ironed out at Beaulieu included teaching an agent not to put milk in her teacup first as this automatically gave her away as English and to look right and not left before crossing the road and not to cycle on the wrong side of the road.

Agents were taught about the two different zones and the demarcation lines, the importance of false documents, papers and cover stories. Agents also learnt to recognise military uniforms, ranging from the Abwehr (Nazi Military Intelligence) the Milice (Vichy paramilitary force) and the Gendarmerie. During the Nazi Occupation France was teeming with collaborators, and agents were taught that no one could be trusted.

Another vital element of training at Beaulieu was the art of clandestinity. Agents were taught various methods of contacting one another through the use of letter boxes, cut outs or dead drops. These were hidden places where messages could be left such as in church bibles, underneath a preordained stone or in between bricks of a wall. It became second nature to them to use passwords when meeting with strangers and if they believed that something was wrong at a rendezvous they were to leave as there could be a trap.

They were taught to write messages on cigarette papers and onion skins and the methods of passing these messages included hollowed out corks, inside cigarettes or hidden inside newspapers. Some of these methods may seem somewhat farfetched and fantastical, but this is the world in which these agents existed and had to become comfortable with, to ensure their success in the field.

All agents, male and female, underwent at least two mock interrogations. Several of the women agents described being woken up by loud banging on the door at some ungodly hour in the morning. An officer would storm in shouting at them to get up and, without dressing, they were ordered downstairs for questioning. Two men wearing long black leather coats and wide-brimmed black hats shouted and screamed at them, asking them questions about their identity and demanding they answer. They had to make sure their cover story was kept exactly to the letter.

As their interrogators were also their examiners, there was double the anguish as they wrote thorough comments on their performance, which were read out during their debriefs at the end of each course. As the interrogation intensified, it became more and more realistic. They used bright spotlights that they shone in their face. Sometimes they were handcuffed so they could do nothing as they were hit about the head, on the arms and had their legs kicked. Some reported being forced to strip in front of the others and stand there whilst they searched her mouth, vagina and backside.

The tension must have been extreme. There would have been the smell, not just of the human bodily odours, but of fear. 'What were you doing at five o'clock? Why did you go out? Why were you at the railway station? Were you meeting a friend? What was his name? What were you wearing? Your accomplices have confessed. We know everything. You're lying. You're lying.' They were very realistic. Far too good perhaps, but deep inside the students knew that this was probably one of the best exercises they could get.

In their debriefing session they were told of agents who had escaped imprisonment in France and got back to Britain. They had been able to provide details of the tortures being used. Being stripped naked, being hung up by the wrists or skewered on meat hooks, having your teeth and nails pulled out with pliers, having cigarettes stubbed out on your skin, being given electric shocks all over your body or nearly being drowned must have filled the women with absolute horror. Most tortures made you semi-conscious after a time. It was said that if you could withstand the first quarter of an hour without 'talking', you probably would not talk at all. One useful suggestion, instruction really, was to count whenever they were under duress. Count into the hundreds and thousands if necessary, especially if they give you an injection. All that would be in your mind under anaesthetic would be numbers. As well as giving them confidence at withstanding interrogation and torture, more importantly it would have motivated them to avoid capture.

The majority of the women agents were trained as couriers. It was thought by the upper echelons of the Dutch section of the SOE as late as 1944 that women were rarely stopped or searched at controls and that they were rarely picked up in mass arrests. That was the case in France early in the war but, as it progressed, most women were stopped and searched as well. What was true was that they made excellent cover while travelling around the country taking messages, papers, money, wireless equipment pretending to be going shopping, foraging for food or visiting friends. It was thought that the Germans wouldn't expect women to be involved in resistance activities. They were expected to be fulfilling the traditional roles of *Kinder, Kirche und Küche* (Children, Church and Kitchen). They were slow to realise that young, attractive women could be politicised and intent on carrying out deadly work. While there were circumstances when a bike was vital for getting around, for long journeys it was recommended that the women travelled first class on the trains, as the Germans were less likely to thoroughly search wealthy middle-class passengers than those in third-class compartments. Big businessmen and Germans who travelled in first class didn't want the police to annoy them. The women were taught to hide incriminating items where they would be least likely to be found – in false-bottomed bags, inside bicycle frames or tyres, under dress belts, under the soles of stockings, inside powder compacts or even inside long hair. These methods offered less chance of detection during perfunctory searches. Should a woman's cover story be doubted, she had to expect a full body search.

Women were also thought to be more resourceful and composed than men and could better talk themselves out of tight spots at checkpoints using their feminine charms. They were also more inventive, conjuring ingenious cover stories. Questions they had to be able to answer were 'Where did you get your laundry cleaned?' or 'Where did you get your hair done?'

Unmarried women would probably have been provided with imaginary boyfriends. Those who were married may well have used an imaginary husband in their cover story. There was almost a husband and wife team in

SOE. While Marjorie March-Phillips's husband was conducting his 'Small-Scale Raiding Force' on various missions overseas, she was recruited by SOE for operational duties. After working as a conducting officer attached to 'F' Section, she underwent parachute training at Ringway with a view to her being sent into France. However, the situation changed when she discovered that she was SOE's first pregnant parachutist [4]

Major Thompson, in his memoirs *The SOE in Belgium*, admitted being an 'accompanying' or 'conducting officer'. With the assistance of a competent secretary, Miss Lee-Graham – later Mrs Koslowska but known only to the agents as 'Mrs Cameron' – he devised ingenious cover stories.

> We considered that most men would look more normal with a little love life and interest, so letters and photographs of girls were provided for men who wished it. The photographs initially provided some difficulty, but one which was solved for us involuntarily by one of our trainees. Unknown to us at the time, a man on leave in London from one of our schools contrived to insert an advertisement in a Quebec newspaper: 'Lonely Belgium soldier wishes to find girl pen friend.' The resulting replies were intercepted by our Security and of course the man could not be allowed to have them. We were, consequently, put in possession of a vast assortment of letters, most of which enclosed photographs of attractive young French Canadian girls, often signed on the back (and we had others signed ourselves!) Of these many were suitable to provide fictitious girl friends for our men, and they could choose from a selection the girl that they preferred. I do not suppose that many French Canadian girls will ever know how usefully they unwittingly contributed to the allied war effort in their youth![5]

There were some in the male-dominated military hierarchy who thought that women were better suited for wireless work. Their nimble fingers, adept at sewing, embroidery, typing and playing the piano, had the dexterous skills SOE needed. Those destined for wireless training spent a few weeks at Fawley Court, Station 54A, near Henley-on-Thames, before undertaking a course at Thame Park, Station 52, near Oxford. Yvonne Cormeau completed hers in sixteen-weeks. Others took nine months, but in some cases, the urgency of the situation meant they only spent a few weeks before being sent into the field to learn on the job. Those students not destined for the field were then sent to the SOE's listening stations at Grendon Hall, Station 53A, near Aylesbury, or Poundon, Station 53B, near Bicester. Wireless operators were expected to lead a solitary existence, able to keep awake until the transmission time was due and to minimise their use of the equipment to less than twenty minutes. As shall be seen, the Germans used sophisticated detecting equipment, which resulted in the life expectancy of wireless operators in the field being only six weeks.

They were made familiar with various codes and ciphers that were in use at the time for communication with agents in the field, and with main stations of the Mediterranean Allied Air Force at Massingham in Algiers or Cairo in Egypt. In Margaret Pawley's *In Obedience to Instructions*, she detailed some of those taught:

> In the early days a code called Playfair was taught. It involved putting messages into rectangular 'boxes' on squared paper according to a numbered order of letters determined by the line of a poem (of which some were original and some borrowed) or sentence from a book. The message was encoded by selecting letters from the opposite corners of the rectangle. The code was superseded by a more secure one, named double transposition. Again, it was worked in 'boxes' on squared paper; it placed the letters of a message horizontally under a 'key' word or words which were put in numerical sequence; a fresh selection was made by transposing them vertically, again in numerical order; the final version was read horizontally. The field operator and base coder would be in possession of the identical poem or novel from which the 'key' word or words would be drawn; the page and line would be indicated in figures at the beginning of the message.

Leo Marks, the Jewish head of codes at SOE, introduced an even more secure code he termed the 'One-Time Pad'. Hundreds of lines of code were printed on silk and, once one had been used, it could be cut off and burnt or, if desperate, swallowed.

> Great care needed to be taken to include two types of 'checks' in every message, a 'bluff' check, to confuse the enemy, and one 'true' check which it was hoped would not be discovered. Many field operators in the heat of the moment left out their checks when encoding messages. At the base, two possibilities occurred to the coder; was this a genuine lapse or had the set been seized by the enemy and was being worked back by them, as happened on several occasions.

In Marcus Binney's *The Women who Lived for Danger*, he quotes Leslie Fernandez, one of the women's trainers:

> During training we attempted to prepare them physically, building up their stamina by hikes through rough countryside. All were taught close combat, which gave them confidence even if most were not very good at it. These girls weren't commando material. They didn't have the physique though some had tremendous mental stamina. You would not expect well brought up girls to go up behind someone and slit their throats, though if they were grappled, there were several particularly nasty little tricks that we handed on, given us by the

Shanghai police.

For many of the women agents, and men for that matter, they had to overcome an instinct instilled in them since birth – they had to look someone important in the face and not tell them the truth. Lying had to become part of their skills while in the field. They had to take on the role of an actor; as in life, some took to the stage much better than others. Escott provided a fitting tribute to them:

> To know what they did and what happened to them can therefore act as a memorial to those who died, and a reminder of the great courage shown by all these remarkable individuals who, in abnormal times, when their world was turned upside down, displayed extraordinary qualities to match their unusual and perilous role.

She went on to say that it was in the spirit of self-sacrifice that most agents undertook this work:

> When deaths occurred it was only for the greater good. On the way, of course, there was excitement, friendship and a gruelling test of the human spirit, but there was also fear, loneliness, hard work and sometimes torture and death.

Wireless operators

Vital to the success of all these secret missions were the wireless operators. A St Neots man recalled how during the war he was posted to Blackpool to run a training course in wireless maintenance and repair in the Winter Gardens. He was struck by one particularly well-behaved group of young women who turned up having just finished a wireless operator's course. They spent most of the time discussing their social life, where they were going that night, who with, and what they were going to wear. Particularly affectionate, they threw their arms round their trainer on finishing the course, telling him that they had been posted to Tempsford. What a surprise! It was only a few miles south of where he lived. Maybe he would see them some time. He didn't. Wireless operators had a dangerous job. It was said that at the beginning of these secret operations, the average life expectancy of a wireless operator in the field was only six weeks. Francis Cammaerts, a French Resistance leader, said that, 'Without your radio operator, you were a pigeon without wings.'

Those who had been in the Girl Guides fared better as they had some understanding of Morse code. It is worth including a few paragraphs from Pawley's *In Obedience to Instructions* as she provides fascinating detail of exactly what their work entailed:

This knowledge needed to be transferred to operating a special key which represented the dots and dashes in terms of short and long sounds. When proficiency was attained, the mock practice key became part of a B2 radio set which relayed the sounds into the atmosphere and could be captured at a distance on a specified wavelength, previously determined.

... at Fawley Court ... a group of twelve girls ... sat at a series of wooden tables, practising their morse on a dummy key day after day. As it became possible to speed up, one moved to the next table, with an instructor sitting at the end. Most trainees would stick at one letter and not be able to overcome the resultant pause for a short period. There was a test once a week, when the atmosphere was really tense. Ann Bonsor recalls going to the cinema and quite involuntarily turning the sign EXIT beside the screen into morse. Probably on this account, wireless operators, like coders, became obsessional; many FANYs have never lost the skill, only some of the speed, fifty years later.

For the last part of their training wireless operators were often posted to Scotland to take part in a scheme called SPARTAN, at Dunbar. FANYs would be based in a mobile signal station, to which agents in training, dispersed throughout the countryside, would work back their sets. Before proceeding overseas, most coders and wireless operators received some experience on an operational station, dealing with live traffic from the field. This would be at Station 53A, Grendon Underwood, or Station 53B, at Poundon. Messages came in from Holland, France, Denmark, Norway and so on. During their earlier training wireless operators would have become familiar with the Q code and the sending and receiving procedures based on this international method of communication; no other means were allowed, never plain language, though some agents in distress, anger or jubilation, might sometimes resort to it.

A FANY operator on duty at her set would be allocated to what was known as a 'sked' (terminology for an expected message at a previously defined time from an agent), with the appropriate frequency, code name and call sign, by the signal master, or other authorised person. She would listen for the three-letter particular call sign of the out-station which should be calling at intervals of one minute, and then listening for one minute. If contact were established, the home operator would send the call sign, followed by QRK How are you receiving me, plus IMI Question mark. The field would answer QSA Your signal readability is, followed by a number from one to five. If it were over three, and therefore fairly audible, the home operator would wait for the field to send QTC I have a message for you. Field messages were always sent first. With numbers less than three, each group of five letters (the invariable number in which signals were sent) would be repeated. The base operator then took down the message in pencil in block capitals on special forms, and then wait until QRU appeared: I have nothing more. If the base operator had messages, the procedure would be reversed. To ask for repeated groups, or QRS send slower, was not well regarded, unless interference was particularly bad, since it would expose the field operator to danger. At the end of a transmission, the base would send VA close down. In the event of sudden enemy attack, the field could send QUG I am forced to stop transmitting owing to immediate danger, whereupon a FANY operator would report this at once to her senior officer. In the event of gross inaudibility, it was possible to ask for help from a second base operator, but this was an exceptional measure in particular circumstances. 'Listening watches' were set up when a field mission failed to respond at its allotted time according to its signal plan.

A specialised training was given to become a signal planner. A small group of FANYs learnt to provide a signal plan for every mission which went into the field. It included a call sign by which to be recognised by the base station, an allocated frequency, obtained by the supply of the appropriate crystals (two slices of quartz cut to a precise wavelength which determined frequency, about the size of a postage stamp) and specific times on a regular basis at which attempts to transmit to the base station were to be made. Trained signal planners who undertook this skilled technical work were given the rank of Lieutenant.

Another technique in which the FANYS were instructed later in the war was that of 'finger printing', i.e. the recognition of morse-sending methods. All who learnt to send morse developed their own individual style. If an agent in occupied territory were captured, attempts would be made to work the radio back to base in England. A FANY operator who could detect a change in field operator would prevent unwise future communications, drops, or reinforcements to that mission.

Not everyone passed the four-month wireless course. They had to reach at least twenty words a minute, much higher than the peacetime requirements of the Services or Post Office. Those who failed to grasp the hang of it all dropped out, and there were many who were transferred to become coders, registry clerks, copy clerks, signal distributors, and teleprinter or switchboard operators. Ryder mentioned that the men and women who were successful in their training as wireless operators included the bravest:

> [For] if they were caught with a set they knew they faced death. To escape detection they frequently had to change the place from which they transmitted messages and, to avoid capture, they often had to disguise themselves – sometimes at barely a moment's notice. German radio-telegraphists were on duty at their listening posts twenty-four hours a day. The Gestapo always had a flying squad ready to go into action immediately to hunt and seize these Bods.

An indication of their work in the field was provided in Frank Griffiths' memoirs of his years as a pilot in 138 Squadron:

The Resistance units in the occupied countries grew and grew until finally some 1,400 independent units were on the books. Initially an agent and his pianist (wireless operator) would be dropped and, in its simplest form, the agent would recruit patriots in small units in various towns and villages. They in turn would select suitable fields for the reception of the drop materials such as guns, ammunition, clothing, money, etc. The agent would, through his pianist, inform London of the place of the reception, give it a code name, a recognition letter and a message which the BBC could broadcast on the day an aircraft was being sent with his supplies. This message would be something in the nature of '*Tartes aux pommes de la tante Helene*' repeated twice each time it was broadcast on the BBC transmission. The first time at 1300 hours. The broadcast of the message would indicate merely that the flight was being planned. The 1800 hour transmission confirmed that the flight really would take place – that is, if the aircraft remained serviceable, the weather didn't deteriorate and if the aircraft didn't get lost or shot down on the way. There were lots of 'ifs' even after all the planning was done.

The SOE Syllabus included advice for all their wireless operators.

a) He should not be used for other work
Other agents should not go to his residence or place of operation. It is even better if they do not contact him direct.
A reserve means of communication with him must be maintained if he has to go into hiding. Only messages which cannot be sent conveniently by other routes should go by W/Tb) Messages must be between 150 – 400 letters
3. Security devices of operator
a) Set disguised as suitcase
b) Bury set on arrival
c) Aerial made of local wire, camouflaged
Must have cover which allows absence at irregular times. Routine job useless unless employer in organisation
Should live with friends as key taps audible, Residence must supply hiding place
d) Should constantly move set and/or aerial
e) Times and length of transmission restricted according to plan

Preparing for the Drop
Once the agents arrived at Gibraltar Farm, the nerve centre of RAF Tempsford their conducting officer escorted them into the barn. Just the same as the men, the women were dressed in a 'striptease' suit – a baggy jumping suit well fitted with spacious pockets, into which went a dagger, hard rations, a flashlight, first-aid equipment, wireless parts, secret maps and papers. Their

ankles were strapped with bandages to give good support and they were given stout boots with rubber cushions under their heels to further reduce the chances of injury on landing. The RAF Air Liaison Officer in charge would refer to them only by their codename. Their passwords, messages and other information were checked to see that they had learnt them off by heart. Checks were made on their clothes and shoes, specially made in SOE workshops, and their other belongings. No British tags were to be on them, no used bus or train tickets, cigarette packets or matchboxes, no initialled handkerchief, etc. Shoes had not to be new so as to avoid arousing suspicion. Their hair had previously been cut in the appropriate style of the country they were going to and even teeth were checked to ensure that the SOE dentist had replaced fillings with the appropriate gold.

A local lady from Sandy reported having to wash some agents' hair before they left. Presumably she used soap from the country they were going to be dropped in as it had to smell right. Whether the Germans had learned to recognise the smell of Lifebuoy or Wright's Coal Tar soap is undocumented.

The cashier would issue agents with foreign documents, enough foreign currency to run a Resistance operation, and a collection of loose change for use on arrival. The serial numbers were never consecutive and notes were often trampled on to give them a slightly tattered look. Heavy canvas jumpsuits were provided, suitably camouflaged with patches of green and mustard brown. They had extra wide legs and arms to fit over the agents' ordinary clothes. A harness was fastened over this and a parachute attached. Many were given a Colt revolver and bullets. Other useful equipment included a jackknife to cut through the parachute rigging should it be snagged; a folding shovel to bury the parachute and be used as a splint if bones were broken; a hip flask full of rum, brandy or whisky; a tin of sandwiches for the flight; and their choice of drugs. Terry Crowdy in his *SOE Agent: Churchill's Secret Warriors* mentioned these drugs:

> 'A' tablets for airsickness; (blue) 'B' pills containing Benzedrine (sulphate) for use as a stimulant (the amphetamine Mecrodrin was also issued); the 'E' pill: a quick-working anaesthetic that would knock a person out for 30 seconds; 'K' pills for inducing sleep and 'L' pills.

'L' pills were lethal cyanide crystals in a thin rubber coating that one could bite through; they were hidden in the top inside part of an agent's jacket, in hollowed-out wine-bottle corks, or in tubes of lipstick. If taken, death would follow within fifteen seconds. Agents were told that the Catholic Church had given them a special dispensation to use the pill 'in extremis'. The final thing was being given a good-luck gift. This might be cuff links, a cigarette case, powder compact or a piece of jewellery – a reminder that SOE was thinking of them. When they ran out of money they were told it could be pawned or sold on the black market.

Some of these smaller items were used to conceal codes, messages and microscopic photographs. Other hiding places included fountain pens, pencils, wallets, bath salts, shaving sticks, toothpaste tubes, talcum powder containers, lipsticks, manicure sets, sponges, penknives, shoe heels and soles, shoulder padding, collar studs, coat buttons, and cigarette lighters. A 2-by-2-inch aluminium cylinder was developed at Aston House as a rectal/vaginal container. It could be unscrewed in the middle and the message inserted. Understandably, no mention of their use appeared in any of the women's stories.

Agents were sometimes given a pigeon to take with them, which they had to release on landing. Basket-loads of carrier pigeons were brought to the airfield from Bletchley Park for the moonlight drops. Each bird had its own cardboard box. Those due to be dropped into enemy territory had a handkerchief-sized parachute attached to the box. Attached to a leg was a tiny container. Unscrewing its lid one would find a rolled up piece of paper and a tiny pencil with request to note down any military information about the Germans. The bird, once released, would then fly back to the loft above the Station Commander's garage at Bletchley Park. One wag suggested mating carrier pigeons with parrots to save having to use the container.

When I was asked at one of the talks I gave on RAF Tempsford whether there was any evidence that Winston Churchill ever visited the airfield, I had to admit that I had come across no documentary evidence suggesting he did. Mont Bettles, a Tempsford farmer, recalled his father telling the locals in the Thornton Arms, the pub at the top of the hill in nearby Everton, that he thought he had seen him. He was driving his tractor up the hill and stopped at a checkpoint to show his pass when a large black car pulled up opposite him. When the rear window was wound down, he saw a large man with a big fat cigar in his mouth who he was sure was Churchill. The locals didn't believe him. John Button, the ex-farm manager, told me that he had evidence that Churchill had been to the airfield as he had seen his initials on some of the doors.

Sue Ryder, one of the FANYs who accompanied Polish agents to Tempsford, commented that:

Though the pre-mission hours were naturally very tense, there was also a wonderful sense of humour and cheerfulness among the Bods. I can't remember any false bravado; on the contrary, it was real wit that came through. No written word can recapture the warmth of the atmosphere throughout the station. Whenever the atmosphere was especially tense or a feeling of dread prevailed, someone in the small group would rally the spirits of the others. They had, too, an extraordinary humility and a religious faith which was exemplified in the way they prepared themselves for their missions, such as making their confessions to a priest who would come to the ops station especially for this purpose.

Captain Haukelid, a Norwegian agent, reported being particularly impressed with the FANYs he encountered. In his book *Skis against the Atom*, he wrote:

> The girls took good care of us in other ways too. They saw that we did not talk to strangers, that we did not catch cold, and that we came home in good order ... when one of our boys took a fancy to one of the prettiest F.A.N.Y.s he would spend the whole day scrubbing the kitchen table – and it needed it. We often washed and scrubbed for hours just to kill time. But however long we kept at it the F.A.N.Y.s were just as amiable – and unapproachable.

Once on board, it was the job of the dispatcher to make the agents comfortable. Wing Commander Pickard was particularly kind to those he called his 'female passengers'. He used to hand over the controls to his co-pilot and go to the back of the plane to sit with them to put them at their ease by chatting. It was often too noisy for lengthy conversations but was appreciated nonetheless.

Tangmere's Ground Control Interception

161 Squadron's missions to France often started from RAF Tangmere, their forward base close to the south coast, about four miles east of Chichester. The proximity to the Continent meant the squadron's range of about 600 miles would take them much deeper into southern France than if they started from Tempsford. Pearl Panton, a WAAF working on Ground Control Interception, recognised immediately when one of Tangmere's special flights set out across the Channel and then later returned homewards. As recorded by Beryl Escott, Panton said, 'They were given quite a different code, plus a special time for the moon to light their way, and they flew very low.' Like all controllers, she kept mum about her work; she never spoke about it, but in her diary wrote:

> It was a full moon last night, an essential factor for the special mission pilots taking off and returning. At 21.30 hours, I was driven from the Officers' Mess to the 'Happydrome'. The officer of the watch gave me my orders. I was to work on the Skyatron radar. A special mission was going out before midnight, due to return just before dawn.
>
> P for Peter 141 took off at 22.00 hours. One of the girls working the watch was startled as she recognised her husband's voice calling to confirm that he was

airborne. She wouldn't have known of this mission, of course. I didn't know her well, but I had met her recently in a nearby café. There she had introduced me to her husband and I remember her delight at a pair of fur-trimmed gloves he had bought her that day. During the night watch she told me she was expecting her first baby.

It was a busy night as usual. P 141 was due to return at 03.00 hours. There was no R.T contact at the scheduled time. I was told to call him and keep calling at regular intervals. He should at least have crossed the French coast. The girl sat next to me, watching the Skyatron, listening intently for her husband's voice. His call would have included a coded message to be passed to Air Ministry. It never came through.

Yvonne George, another WAAF mentioned in Escott's book, said that she liaised between SOE and SIS headquarters, phoning the Intelligence Officer at Tempsford, who – depending on the availability of aircraft and the meteorological report – would decide whether a flight was possible. 'On one occasion I was at Tangmere to see the take off of an aircraft with three agents on board and waited until about 3 am, early morning, for its return. As one of them alighted I caught a strong smell of Guerlain perfume – something we in England had not known for some years!'

Faith Spencer-Chapman, another WAAF, mentioned to Escott that she was in 'Air Ops', which involved dropping agents into Europe, and then in 'Pick up Ops':

> This meant taking agents down to RAF Tangmere and waiting for the Lysander to return with agents who had to be got out of France urgently. Then we had to drive back to London in the early hours and hand them over to be debriefed.

The debrief was the easiest way for the agents to give a clear and personal account of their and their colleagues' experiences whilst they were in the field. Particularly useful was information about interrogation, torture and conditions in prisons and concentration camps. This could be used to advise future agents.

SOE's Liaison Officers

Kathleen Moore was one of SOE's liaison offers, providing the link between their headquarters in London and RAF Tempsford and RAF Harington. According to her obituary in *The Times*, she was born in 1914, the second child and only daughter of Harold Moore, an Irish journalist, and his wife, Katherine Chapman. They lived in Winnipeg, Canada, and following her younger brother and mother's deaths, she had to manage her father's household while she was still a schoolgirl.

Escape came when she went to the University of Manitoba to read French. Her evident gift for the language won her a scholarship to Paris and to the Sorbonne. She stayed on in Paris through the later 1930s, working at the British Embassy until, with the fall of France in May 1940, she along with the rest of the staff was evacuated to London.

There, with Mary Mundle, with whom she had lived in Paris, and Alison Grant, a Canadian friend whom she had met in Paris, she took a flat at 54a Walton Avenue in Knightsbridge. Known familiarly as the Canada House Annexe, it soon became a notable social hub for those on leave from the Special Operations Executive. Each of the three women had become involved one way or another with the clandestine world of Special Operations and Military Intelligence.

Kay had joined the First Aid Nursing Yeomanry (FANY) immediately on her return, but, with her fluent French, soon found herself directly and deeply involved with the RF section, maintaining contact with the Resistance and the Free French, briefing agents before they were sent to France and debriefing them on their return – if they returned.

She rose eventually to become head of Air Liaison, the section that worked directly with the RAF and the USAAF, telephoning them or sending telegrams to arrange flights for her 'Bods'.

It was through this work, or through the social life that spun around it, that she met her future husband, the young Ernest Gimpel. After the fall of France he had joined the Resistance, had been arrested by the Germans but had managed to escape, and in 1942 was one of the few people spirited to England by submarine.

Codenamed 'Charles Beauchamp', he was sent back to France in November 1943, but was soon captured by the Gestapo, brutally interrogated and then sent successively to Buchenwald, Auschwitz and Flossenburg concentration camps. When the camps were liberated by the Allies in the last weeks of the war, he set about finding Kay.

As it happened, she was already in continental Europe, working in a team repatriating prisoners of war. She and Charles were not only soon reunited but, by the end of August, married and on honeymoon, staying with cousins in Ireland at the start of Charles's long recuperation.

2

First Contact with the Resistance:
May 1941 to November 1942

Escott referred to about ninety women being selected for training. Not all were successful, though. Details of those who failed their assessment have not come to light. Freddie Clark's *Agents by Moonlight*, a chronological account of 138 and 161 Squadrons' missions, specifically mentions the names of fifteen women who were flown out of Tempsford. While the others may have been flown out of Tangmere, one of the pilots told me that his crew dropped a female agent into France, but she was not referred to in Clark's book. SOE was not the only agency to have recruited women agents.

Two websites, 'Spartacus' and '64 Baker Street', with sections devoted to female SOE agents, mention several other women who were not mentioned by Clark as flying out of Tempsford. If these online sources are accurate, then it is possible that many of the other women were taken by 138 Squadron Lysanders or dropped from 161 Squadron's Halifaxes or Hudsons and just referred to as 'agents'. It is also possible that a number were sent on missions by the SIS, OSS or other agencies.

The first agents infiltrated into France were two Frenchmen working for Charles de Gaulle's Intelligence Service, Maurice Duclos with John Mulleman as his wireless operator. They were parachuted near Saint Cirq in the Dordogne on 13 February 1941. Over the rest of 1941 a further seventy-three men were sent, some landed by sailing boat, some by ship, but most parachuted from Whitley bombers or landed by Lysander. By the end of May 1942 a further eighty-three were sent in, some going by submarine and motor gunboats. They included more French Intelligence officers but also SOE and SIS agents. Whilst some were sent on intelligence gathering missions, others on sabotage missions, many were sent to liaise with members of the Resistance, identify their needs, locate drop zones and arrange for them to be supplied. Some were sent to support existing escape lines and establish new ones in an attempt to bring back to England escaped prisoners of war, downed pilots and aircrews as well as military and political figures who London considered important for the war effort. Once permission was given for women to be sent into occupied Europe, the SOE arranged for wireless operators and couriers to be sent in to help with this work, and, in one case, a woman to establish her own network.

Giliana Gerson

The first woman claimed to have been sent in by the SOE was Chilean-born Giliana Balmaceda. A beautiful young actress, she was working in theatres in Paris in the 1930s and married Victor Gerson, a wealthy British rug and carpet dealer who had settled in the capital after fighting in the First World War. His first wife had died and his son had been killed in a road accident. Following the German invasion of 1940, Victor and Giliana fled to England, where Victor had transferred most of his stock. Settling in London, they both were thought potentially useful to the SOE.

In Cookridge's *Inside SOE*, he mentions Victor Gerson suggesting to a Mr Humphreys that he and his wife could help set up an escape route, helping get people across the Pyrénées into neutral Spain. Giliana volunteered to use her Chilean passport and valid travel documents to return to France, crossing the frontier legally from Spain. Whether she was flown out by one of the Special Duties Squadrons was not documented.

On 23 May 1941 she made her way north to Vichy, where, as well as spying on Petain's government, she collected documents such as ration cards that could be reproduced by the SOE for its undercover agents in France. She also met several Spanish ex-Republicans who were prepared to help with the planned escape route.

In Squadron Leader Beryl Escott's *The Heroines of SOE*, she states Giliana acted like a visitor, pretending to be lost and asking innocent questions and being forgiven because of her brilliant smile. 'With her sharp eyes and the retentive memory of an actress, she wandered unrebuked into forbidden areas.' She learned what passes and papers people needed to have in their possession every day. She made a note of all the train and bus controls there were and built up a collection of timetables and information on different forms of transport being used. She managed to find out about the different ways of crossing legally and illegally between the Occupied and the Free Zone and what formalities there were staying at hotels and boarding houses. She found out the times of the curfew and what penalties there were for breaking it. She made copies of ration cards and notes the different prices for daily foodstuffs and noted what shortages there were. 'In the cafés she tested the reactions of the French to the German occupation and cultivated useful contacts for the future.'

In mid-June she left the country and went first to Madrid, presumably visiting a contact in the British Embassy, and then to Gibraltar, from where she was returned to London on 24/25 August 1941, bringing back valuable information for SOE.

A few months after her return, on 6 September 1941, her husband was dropped by parachute near Châteauroux and he went on to set up groups of resisters in the Lyon and Perpignan area and what became known as the 'Vic' escape line. Lyon was the centre of the Vichy government during the years of France's occupation and many diplomats and correspondents from around the world were based there. Under Victor Gerson's firm leadership and tight security, despite his line being infiltrated on three occasions by the Gestapo and him being arrested on a train between Paris and Lyon, his cover story convinced his interrogators and his organisation helped numerous people escape into Spain until France was liberated.

'Anatole'
In Hugh Verity's *We Landed by Moonlight*, he mentions what is thought to be the first female agent to be parachuted into France. Who she was and what she did remain a mystery.

> For operation 'Baccarat' Murphy took off at 2145 on 27 February (1942). He found solid cloud cover over the French coast at 1,000 ft and only 3,000 yards visibility below. Failing to fix his position near Abbeville, he flew north-west until he could get a radio fix from base. Then he found Abbeville and set course for St Saëns where, at midnight, he landed one passenger and picked up two, including Rémy.
>
> The new arrival in France was an unknown young woman called 'Anatole'. Rémy reported: 'She laughs, very happy to be back in France. I understand that she totally vanished.'

However, on Pierre Tillet's list of infiltrations into France he mentions the passengers as G. Renault, aka Rémy, and Pierre Julitte. Freddie Clark did not mention 'Anatole', but added that Murphy carried out 161 Squadron's first Lysander SIS operation. One hopes that one day MI6 will declassify and release their documents of the women they sent into occupied Europe.

'Anna Frolova' – Francine Fromont
On 3 March 1942, the first Soviet woman agent was sent out of Tempsford. There had been two other women sent from the Soviet Union as part of a secret agreement between Churchill and Stalin whereby Britain agreed to send their agents, codenamed Pickaxes, into occupied Europe. As German troops occupied much of Eastern Europe, the Soviets were unable to re-

establish links with their existing agents in Western Europe. The distance was too far and the chances of their planes being shot down were too great. SOE was given the task of liaising with the NKVD, the Russian secret service, looking after the agents while they were in Britain and negotiating with the Special Duties Squadrons to fly them out. Their stories are detailed in my book, *Churchill's and Stalin's Secret Agents: Operation Pickaxe*.

Yvonne Rudellat

SOE records show that the first woman agent they sent into France was forty-five-year-old grandmother Yvonne Rudellat. Born Yvonne Cerneau on 11 January 1897 at Maisons Lafitte, near Paris, she was one of ten children. Her father, a horse-dealer for the French Army, died when she was in her teens and, unable to live with a domineering mother, she moved to London. She worked in a variety of jobs until 1920; whilst working as a salesgirl at the Galeries Lafayette in Regent Street, she married 41-year-old Alec Rudellat, an Italian waiter who had worked as an undercover agent. In the *Daily Herald* journalist James Gleeson's book, *They Feared No Evil*, he mentioned her marrying an Italian antique dealer. Escott described her as 'a vivacious, dainty character with dark hair and hazel eyes, whose air of fragility was deceptive, but being an incurable romantic, erratic and completely irresponsible, the marriage eventually failed, though she did have a daughter, became a grandmother and was on good terms with her ex-husband'.

When her daughter went to school, she managed a decorating business in West London and in 1941, bombed out of her husband's lodging-house, she became a receptionist in Ebury Court Hotel near Victoria Station. Gleeson described her as the manageress. One of her guests was in the SOE and, impressed by her calm efficiency, recommended her to the organization.

Colonel Maurice Buckmaster, the head of SOE's 'F' Section, wrote about her in an article published in *Chambers' Journal* after the war. In it, he called her Christiane.

> The revolving-doors of the hotel clicked merrily round. It was a busy hour, and the foyer was full of men in uniform and men who looked as if they wanted to be in uniform: for, in the early months of 1940, permission to fight as a soldier, sailor, or airman for Britain was almost as difficult to obtain as entry to an exclusive club.
>
> Behind the reception-desk Christiane was dealing courteously but firmly with the more obdurate would-be clients, who refused to believe it possible that all the rooms in the hotel were really booked. She was no longer young, and the years behind the reception-desk had brought lines in her forehead and a rather weary stoop to her shoulders. Her steel-rimmed spectacles gave her an old-maidish look, belied only by her strong, straight chin and direct glance.

Christiane was tired; tired of this artificial life of 'No, Madam, I'm afraid the hotel is full until after Easter, or '*Oui, Monsieur, je ferai l'impossible. Demandez de nouveau demain*'. There was generally, even in pre-war years, a fairly large French clientele at this London hotel: now, in March 1940, members of French missions thronged the salons and competed for the few available rooms. 'It's a pity the War Office doesn't take the whole hotel over', thought Christiane, as the desire for freedom, the right to express her patriotism in more direct fashion, again overwhelmed her.

Hers was a double patriotism, arising from her parentage: a French father and a British mother had each given her a share of their ardent love for their country. Her own volatile temperament, confined by circumstance into the cramping occupation of hotel receptionist, threatened every now and again to boil over, as it once had when she fell in love with, and married, a young Englishman whom she had met in the 'other war'. She was widowed now and her daughter was expecting to be called up at any moment.

As she answered the persistent ring of the house telephone and the buzzer, Christiane realised with a sigh that she had ambitions which she saw no chance of gratifying. She wanted the active life which lay before her daughter; she wanted the life of any of these hard young men in uniform who were still untried in war, but who promised to give a good account of themselves when the fighting started; she wanted to use her perfect knowledge of French – the thought of clandestine work flitted through her busy brain, but she dismissed it as hopeless; she wanted to break away from the monotony of this drab existence, but she had not the faintest idea how to make the break. She knew many people, some V.I.P.s, but she knew them in her capacity as a hotel receptionist. They would be faintly amused – and the nicer ones more than a little sadly sympathetic – at the whim of an old maid, for such she seemed, seeking to fight for her country, her countries. She was not really tied, since she had put aside, with French frugality, enough to ensure her against hardship in her declining years, and her daughter was capable of earning her living. Yet Christiane felt almost helpless as day followed day and the papers on her desk still had to be dealt with, and the clients became more and more disgruntled.

When summer came, and the disasters in Flanders culminated in the capitulation of France and the armistice which Christiane found shameful she decided that the time had come for drastic measures if she were to retain her self-respect. '*Cela ne peut pas être,*' she said to herself of the armistice. 'It just can't be so. At least one Frenchwoman', she thought, 'will refuse this dreadful pact with the enemy.' She sought out the Manager of the hotel and told him she wished to leave. It was not nearly as easy to get away as she had thought, and she was obliged to drag on at her job until a bomb in April 1941, lucky for her, unlucky for some of the guests, solved the problem by partially destroying the hotel.

Calling on a close personal friend of mine, who had often used the hotel in the past when he left his home in Paris for a brief visit to London, Christiane explained her desires to him. He sent her on to me, since he knew, more or less, what I was doing and thought that Christiane might be of help in the office. When I spoke to my friend on the telephone about Christiane, I too thought she would be a good addition to the office staff, and it was for that reason that I fixed up a rendezvous with her.

But Christiane had other ideas. She was a good enough psychologist to let her ideas percolate through to me slowly, to avoid the risk of a curt refusal which it would be difficult to retract. She put out a feeler or two, made light of her age, and finally, with a sincerity which I found completely disarming, begged to be allowed to serve her countries more actively. I had to temporise; there was no other way. We made the usual routine inquiries, we interviewed her several times, and ultimately we agreed to start her training. She was radiant; the years seemed to drop from her shoulders, and she insisted on going through the physically tough courses as well as the purely theoretical ones. She was one of the happiest and most enthusiastic students we ever had, man or woman. Nothing came amiss to her, and she devoted to the acquiring of the finer arts of lock-picking, for instance the same studious attention as she had accorded to the preparations of a client's accounts in her hotel.[1]

She had thought of joining the ATS when her seventeen-year-old daughter signed up, but work for SOE took precedence. Her personnel file in the National Archives shows that, after passing the assessment course in Wanborough, aged forty-five, she went on the first women's paramilitary training course in Arisaig in May 1942, staying at Garramor (STS 25A). This was one of ten shooting lodges requisitioned by the SOE. She spent all the time 'clad in borrowed battledress or khaki denim overalls'. Her first training officer was not impressed, describing her as a 'little old lady'. Back in London she joined the FANY as an ensign in July 1942 before going to Beaulieu, where she stayed at The Rings (STS 31) with twenty-two-year-old Andrée Borrel, forty-four-year-old Valentine 'Blanche' Charlet and fifty-two-year-old Marie-Thérèse le Chêne.

According to Stella King's biography *'Jacqueline': Pioneer Heroine of the Resistance*, Yvonne was told not to tell anyone that she had been to Arisaig.

To overcome the problem of three of them being considered too old to parachute into France, the SOE negotiated a sea passage with a specially trained Royal Navy crew. At the end of July 1942, Flying Officer Thomas Russell of 138 Squadron flew in his Whitley down to Portreath in Cornwall, where he picked up Yvonne and three other agents, Nicholas Bodington, Henri Frager and Harry Despaigne. After refuelling, he flew them down to Gibraltar but on the way the plane was attacked by two German fighters, who destroyed one of the plane's engines. Russell managed to reach the colony flying at fifty feet above the water. From Gibraltar they were taken secretly in *Seadog*, a specially adapted felucca – a 40-foot-long, narrow-beamed, 20-ton wooden sailing boat – to the south coast of France, successfully evading an Italian patrol boat on the way. Feluccas have been described as having one tattered sail, a malodorous engine, the flags of half a dozen South American republics in the locker, a Polish skipper, some whisky, a revolver, some camouflaged depth charges and as many secret agents as happened to be going their way. Equipped with hidden guns and a powerful engine, they were able to evade inquisitive Italian patrol boats.

They were landed on the beach at Antibes, near Monaco, on 30 July. Yvonne made her way by train on her own from Cannes to Lyon to pick up some false papers from Virginia Hall, an American agent, then smuggling herself in a steam train's coal bunker she safely crossed the demarcation line between the Free Zone and the Occupied Zone and rendezvoused at a safe house in Paris. She went to see her mother, but only to catch a glimpse; there was no way she could know she was back in France working for the British.

From Paris, she caught the train to the industrial, university town of Tours to work as a courier for Francis Suttill, the Anglo-French barrister's PROSPER network, which covered much of north-western France, but in particular between the PHYSICIAN and MONKEYPUZZLE networks in the Île de France. She used a variety of aliases and codenames, including 'Suzanne', 'Jacqueline Viallat', 'Mme Gauthier (née Cerneau)', 'Soaptree' and 'Leclair'.

Before she was sent into France with a pistol strapped to her leg, she admitted being prepared to kill. According to King, she is reported as saying:

> If a German or anyone stops me and tries to search me, there is only one thing to do. I will have to shoot him. I don't want to do that. It would be difficult to bury him. The ground is so hard ... If it happens, I hope it is near an asparagus bed where the earth is soft and sandy.

Buckmaster noted that, once Yvonne had found her safe house, she was to search for suitable fields for receiving containers and other agents.

> [To] this end, she acquired a bicycle on the black market and installed herself in an inconspicuous little cottage in the Touraine. Her immediate chief was a French commandant, and through him she was in touch with Prosper, about whom I have already written. I think Christiane was thoroughly happy during this time. She had plenty of scope for action, plenty of excitement, and was in great danger. She enjoyed the affectionate esteem of all those men and women who knew what she was doing, and the amused tolerance of all those others

who had not this knowledge.

Only the French Commandant knew that in her bicycle basket, each day as she set off on her excursions, lay a stock of explosives and a hand-grenade, for Christiane always hoped to come across a really worth-while target, and it would have been too provoking to have, say, Hitler's car at her mercy, without the means of destroying it. If anybody at all wondered what was in the bicycle basket, carefully concealed with a scarf or some newspapers, they probably assumed that this eccentric middle-aged lady was engaged in petty black-market deals, buying eggs from the farms, or harmlessly gathering mushrooms in the woods.

To Christiane there was nothing exceptional in trundling about with enough explosive to blow up a house: she was in a war to do a job and she was not going to be content with half-measures. She and her commandant got on together splendidly; they were both single-minded people, whose sole preoccupation was to speed up the task in hand. They didn't worry about non-essentials. The parachute operations which they arranged were admirably carried out, both being invariably careful over details, and their group amassed quite a store of weapons and explosives. Occasionally Christiane would go to Paris to take a message to Prosper from her chief. After such visits Prosper would inform us by radio that Christiane had been in, and we would know all was well.

According to Gleeson, her first organiser reported her to London as having gone over to the Germans. Unable to believe it, they sent another agent to ascertain the truth. He quickly vindicated her and she started an 'explosive' career which led to consternation and death in the ranks of the occupying Germans.

By March 1943, Yvonne had not only bicycled across hundreds of kilometres of the Loire countryside but also organised parachute drops and took part in various sabotage operations. She helped blow up the 300,000-volt electricity cables of Chaigny power station, south of Orléans, and two locomotives in the goods station at Le Mans.

On 21 June she drove off in a rarely used Citrôen for Beaugency on the Loire, with Pierre Culioli, her new organiser, and two recently arrived Canadian agents, who they were to take on the train to Paris. When they drove through the village of Dhuizon in the wooded area of Sologne south of Paris, they found it full of German troops. Stopped at a check point, Pierre and Yvonne's papers managed to pass inspection but the Canadians were taken to the Mairie, the town hall, for further questioning. When they drove there, she and Pierre went in to have their papers cleared but discovered their comrades' accents had made the police suspicious. They left, deciding to make a getaway, but were called back. They accelerated away but were followed by three German cars. Once within range, they were fired on. Yvonne was hit by two bullets, one in the back of the head, which knocked her unconscious. According to the Wikipedia entry for Yvonne Rudelatt:

> Pierre saw the amount of blood coming from the wound, and since Yvonne was unresponsive, he decided to kill himself rather than be taken and tortured. He slammed the vehicle into a ditch and then the side of a cottage, but the two woke up in a hospital at Blois hours later. Yvonne was told that her injury wasn't life threatening, and that the bullet hadn't pierced her brain, but that it would be unsafe to remove it.

David Harrison's SOE website gives the date as 18 June 1943, while another source gives 21 August. The Citrôen was impounded and in the boot were found the radio set and all the Canadians' messages, letters and equipment. This led to mass arrests in the PHYSICIAN network and incriminated many in the ADOLPHE network.

Culioli was taken to a military hospital, stripped, chained to a bed and left to suffer before being taken for interrogation at the Gestapo headquarters on Avenue Foch in Paris. From there he was sent to the grey, fortress-like Frèsnes Prison, a few kilometres south of the capital, near what is now Orly airport. Subsequently, he was sent to Buchenwald concentration camp on the Ellerberg, near Weimar in Germany and was one of the lucky ones to survive.

Yvonne was sent to a civil hospital in Blois where the doctor decided to leave the bullet in her brain. To avoid her being interrogated, the nuns kept her unconscious. Her colleagues in the Resistance planned her escape but she was transferred to another hospital in Paris before they could manage it. Yvonne was taken for interrogation at the Gestapo headquarters, where she exaggerated her confusion and memory loss. In September 1943 she was also imprisoned at Frèsnes. According to Andy Forbes's now defunct 64 Baker Street website:

> [She] used the name Jacqueline Gautier, which was whispered to her by a fellow prisoner when she could not remember her own, due to amnesia after her wounds. She was then transferred to Ravensbrück, arriving on 21 April 1944. She was subsequently moved on to Belsen, where she died after contracting typhus on or about 23 April 1945.[2]

Buckmaster's article provided a different ending. He claimed that she recovered from her wounds but was physically in bad shape after a long time in solitary confinement. When the camp commandant found that she was unfit to work, he had no compunction in sentencing her to the gas-chamber. It was 'the Führer's will' – and it caused less trouble that way.

Christiane had no illusions when the wardress ordered her to the baths. She knew what awaited her, but she had no regrets. She knew that her work was well done and that the flame of resistance, lighted by the patriots, would not fade. She was happy that she had done something useful, but she had no inkling of the fact that her name would be forever honoured in France.

Ravensbrück, eighty kilometres north of Berlin, was built in a beauty spot, noted for its lakes and secluded villas for wealthy city-dwellers. Its site was on marshy ground, often infested with malarial mosquitoes. There were enclaves outside the camp for working parties doing factory or heavy agricultural work in the community, as well as a *Jugendlager*, or youth camp, where those too ill or unfit for work were accommodated. Escott gave a long account, which is worth including to provide an idea of the conditions many of the women agents had to endure.

The main camp surrounded by high walls was built for about 6,000 prisoners. Inside were wooden huts for living quarters containing three tiers of bunks, a few brick buildings for kitchens, showers and a concrete cell block. Cinder paths divided the huts in front of which blossomed flowers in profusion. But there, all semblance of cleanliness and proper conditions stopped. The place was in fact known to the French as *L'Enfer des Femmes*, the Women's Hell.

Nearly all the prisoners were civilians, both young and old, from conquered countries either as slave labour or on suspicion of involvement with the Resistance, all being imprisoned without trial, though this did not prevent them being cruelly tortured during questioning in the camp's political department. During the war years over 50,000 women, at the lowest estimate, died in this camp from dirt, disease, overcrowding, squalor, starvation, overwork and ill-treatment, apart from those who were shot or gassed or sent to die elsewhere.

When Cécile Lefort was admitted in 1943, she spent her first days in the quarantine hut, where new arrivals were kept for three weeks to ensure they brought no new infection to the camp. After being checked in, though weary from the long train journey, she had to stand several hours before being admitted to the bathhouse, where she was told to strip and her former clothes were taken away. Here she waited naked in the cold for a further few hours under the tiny hole in the ceiling where the shower worked, and that was only for a few minutes. With a sliver of soap and a pocket handkerchief of a towel she had to clean herself. Again a long wait and then a shock. Two men came in, one to look at her teeth and one to give her a cursory medical examination, which revealed something was wrong.

Then she was issued with prison clothing, thin and inadequate for the advancing winter, and dispatched to the quarantine hut. There, no one was to be allowed outside, though all were awakened well before dawn for bitter acorn coffee. They were crowded at the window watching while the other women lined up five deep in front of their huts, in the freezing cold and rain, the living and the dead together, and stood for the hour-long 'Appells', where they were counted and appointed their work for the day. Some were detailed for gardening, some for sewing or knitting, some for corpse, rubbish or coal collecting, some for road mending, cleaning latrines, tree-felling or potato picking, women being used instead of horses to drag the heavy carts. Work went in shifts of 10 or 11 hours each, day and night, lights out coming at about 9 pm. Food, mainly vegetable soup and half a loaf of bread a day, was not sufficient for such heavy work. This was the life that awaited them when quarantine was finished.

Pattinson mentioned that, while in the camp, Yvonne tried to colour her grey hair with a boiled onion skin that she had found, but her thick hair, which had become brittle from persistent dying, would not change colour. Instead, she had to resort to masking her grey hair by wearing a piece of cloth like a turban.

On 2 March 1945 she was transferred to Belsen, where 75,000 prisoners died, mostly from neglect. In Foot's *SOE in France*, he noted that typhoid and dysentery were widespread in the concentration camps:

> Unnoticed amongst the hundreds of prisoners suffering from both these diseases at once was a Frenchwoman who called herself Mme Gauthier, who had arrived from another camp six weeks before. Her only close friend in Belsen was separated from her in the middle of March by the iron circumstances of that insensate world; she was then as well as anyone could be amid the prevailing lack of food, fuel, clothing, decency, privacy, what civilised communities call 'the necessities of life'. She 'was not in bad health, she suffered occasionally from loss of memory, but she remained in good morale and she looked neither particularly drawn nor aged'. But she soon fell dangerously ill. When the camp was captured, she was too far gone from her diseases, or too steeped in her own cover story, or both, to mention to a soul what she had been; unnoticed to the last, she died on St George's day or the day after, and her body was huddled with twenty thousand others into one of the huge mass graves. Her name was Yvonne Rudellat.

Yvonne was awarded the Member of the British Empire medal (MBE) by King George and the *Croix de Guerre* by de Gaulle's new government. Escott mentioned that it was her successes in France that led the SOE to send in more women.

It was not until 1946 that details of what happened to Yvonne and other captured agents started to find their way back to Britain. In some cases, it was not until much later. Vera Atkins, the secretary of 'F' Section, made it her duty to find out what happened to all those she had sent in, particularly the women. She was born Vera Rosenberg and, being Jewish, changed it to Atkins, her Scottish mother's maiden name, when she arrived from Romania in 1937. The *Dictionary of National Biography* describes her as 'a handsome grey-eyed blonde, some 5 feet 9 inches tall'. Given her involvement with SOE, she took it upon herself to see off all those women destined for France. She had made arrangements with them to send already written letters to their families and relatives on designated dates to help lessen their worrying while their loved ones were out of touch. She took charge of the wills that the women made up before they left and ensured their personal possessions were looked after.

There were some nights when her long hours at Baker Street, Portman Place, Tangmere and Tempsford meant that she didn't return to her flat in Bayswater. Her mother, whom she shared the flat with, suspected she was having an affair with a married man. Described as the 'heart and brain' of 'F' Section, with an eagle eye for detail, some suggest that Vera was the model for Ian Fleming's Miss Moneypenny in his James Bond novels and that 'M' was Sir Maurice Buckmaster, her boss.

Vera's role included overseeing all aspects of agents' preparation for entering enemy territory, from the latest work and travel regulations to what clothes they should wear, and what they should carry at different times of the year and in different regions of the country. She even advised them about what they should eat and how they should eat it. Although she didn't accompany them on their training courses, she liaised with their trainers and met up with the women, often at West End restaurants, which allowed them a safety valve to express their anxieties and their hopes for their missions.

It was a particularly difficult task given the secret German policy of disposing of enemy agents in what they called '*Nacht und Nebel*', in France '*Nuit et Brouillard*' and what Atkins understood as 'Night and Fog'. The parents of those missing must have gone through enormous stress, not knowing what had happened to their sons or daughters but probably fearing the worst. Other sources suggest the date of Yvonne's execution was 24 April.

Valentine 'Blanche' Charlet
Much of the following detail was not discovered until 1946 and afterwards. Comparatively little detail has emerged about the second woman sent into France. SOE records show that the forty-two-year-old, small, dark-haired and attractive Valentine 'Blanche' Charlet was landed in the same way as Yvonne on Rade d'Agay beach, to the south of Antibes, on 1 September 1942.

According to Escott, the captain very generously gave her his cabin and later admitted that he was quite disturbed by her tantalizing presence. 'If we both acquitted ourselves creditably, that was all due to her.' Being so close to so many women must have been quite awkward during the voyage. The boat returned to Gibraltar with Major Nicholas Bodington (an SOE agent who organised many of the pick-up operations), Andre Gillois, Gillois's wife and two Belgians.

Born in London on 23 May 1898 to Belgian parents, she managed an art gallery in Brussels before the war and built up a wide range of clientèle. Although she could speak several languages, her English was only described as 'passable'. During the invasion in May 1940, she fled the country and joined the Women's Transport Service (WTS) in London. She stayed in Ebury Court Hotel, where she presumably met Yvonne Rudellat. Like Yvonne, her language skills, and having lived in Belgium, brought her to the attention of the SOE. Escott described her as being a natural recruit with fluent French, maturity, lively manner and quick understanding.

After a successful interview, she was given a commission in the FANY as an Ensign and underwent training with Yvonne Rudellat, Marie-Thérèse le Chêne and Andrée Borrel. In view of Blanche's and the two former women's ages, SOE decided not to send them for parachute training.

Blanche's cover name in France was Madame Sabine Lecomte, known by her wireless codename as 'Christianne', and in the Resistance as 'Berberis'. Her mission was to work with the DETECTIVE and HECKLER networks in the Lyon area. Put up in a seaside villa until morning, she made her way alone to rendezvous with a contact in Cannes. On arriving, she found that he had been arrested the day before. Unable to find other contacts over the next few days, she made her way north to rendezvous with Virginia Hall in Lyon. There had been a plan for her to replace Virginia but increased German activity meant she was ordered to join Philippe de Vomécourt's VENTRILOQUIST network. He wanted her to be his courier and locate safe houses for twenty-two-year-old Brian Stonehouse, a new wireless operator, codenamed Celestin. This proved difficult, as the Germans were on the look-out for Resistance activity, but eventually she found him one house in Feyzin, about ten kilometres south of the city.

Stonehouse, described by Pattinson as one of the SOE's few homosexual agents, was dropped blind, with no reception committee, and had difficulty retrieving his wireless set which had been caught in a tree. The set proved difficult to operate and before he got it working, he caught dysentery and needed looking after by Virginia Hall. It was some time before he could transmit.

Foot stated that her work involved arranging contacts, recommending who to bribe and where to hide, supervising the distribution of wireless sets, and soothing the jagged edges of agents in the run. In Escott's *The Heroines of SOE* she states that when Blanche met Stonehouse and discussed the situation, they both wanted to change networks, concerned about how disorganised Vomécourt and his assistant Lieutenant Jean Aron were, their comments that SOE was incompetent, and that they only wanted arms and money.

On 24 October 1942 she went to pass Stonehouse an urgent message Vomécourt wanted sending to London. According to SOE records it was 1 November and she had only been in operation a month. On arriving at the house in Feyzin, in the grounds of Château Hurlevent, she was concerned seeing two caravans or trailers by the side of the road. She put the papers she had brought in an outside shed and went in to see if everything was OK. Everything was normal so she fetched the papers and went up into the attic to find Stonehouse busy transmitting. Even though she said she needed him to send her urgently, he insisted on finishing his first. She therefore started encoding Vomécourt's messages. Suddenly, the light went off. Stonehouse stopped and called out 'Danger'. She picked up her papers and he carried the set down the back stairs to the basement where they hid them in some soft sand behind the lift shaft. When they went out by the back door, they were stopped by an armed policeman who arrested them.

In an interview after the war, Stonehouse gave a slightly different account of their arrest:

I'd been at the château on the air for several hours and I'd been spotted by the vans that follow the beam to the transmitter. Château du Hulverent was about thirteen kilometres outside Lyon, in the country. Monsieur Jourdan had been keeping an eye open for any strange faces in the vicinity and he'd seen someone so he immediately turned off the mains. That was the pre-arranged thing with me if something fishy was going on outside. 'Christiane' was sitting with me when this was turned off. She was feeding me messages, coding or decoding messages, and she said, 'My God, it's the Germans,' and I said, 'What do you mean the Germans?' she said, 'I forgot, I walked past them on the way here.' That was pretty awful, because, if she'd told me when she arrived that she'd passed these Germans, we'd have had plenty of time to pull my aerial down and escape, because the castle wasn't surrounded by then. She wanted to kill herself, she told me, because she felt so awful about that.

I pulled the aerial down, but inadvertently left a little insulating porcelain thing hanging from the ceiling, and hid the transmitter at the bottom of a lift shaft and Monsieur Jourdan put the lift down and jammed it there. 'Christiane' and I tried to get out of the back of the château, which overlooked the garden and the valley of the Rhone. We got out on to the back terrace and sat down pretending to make love, because we'd seen a man come around the far corner of the château. Then another came with a gun and we were caught.[3]

In Blanche's debrief after the war, she recollected him being in his dressing gown and they 'sat down and started kissing like mad, pretending we were having a thing'. It didn't work as they searched the house and found the wireless set and papers. In the car while being taken to Petit Depot in Lyon, she claimed that she hid her address book under the seat. Whilst waiting to be interrogated, they had only a few minutes to agree their cover stories. She was going to say she didn't know what a wireless operator was and that she was a married man's mistress and didn't want to give his address away for fear of embarrassing his wife.

During interrogation by French police, she kept to her cover story and they helped her as a French citizen by suppressing some of the evidence against her but they discovered that Stonehouse was English, along with her codename. When the Germans interrogated her, they were much harsher. When she was asked if she really was Christianne, she pretended to faint and, when she recovered, pretended to play the part of a stupid woman who had wanted to play her glorious part in the Resistance but knew nothing about it. The questioning took place over several days, during which time she was kept in the women's block, though she did manage to let Stonehouse know what she had said.

On 13 November 1942, after twenty days behind bars, enough evidence was obtained and they were transferred to the prison in Castres, near Toulouse. This was a prison from which guards took out men and women and shot them following attacks on German troops. With only half an hour's exercise a day and poor food, her morale was low. She shared a cell with three other French women but was careful not to talk too much for fear of one of them being a 'stool pigeon', an informer. However, discipline was not strict and cell doors were sometimes left unlocked. Befriending a Yugoslav cleaner, she learned that other prisoners had acquired duplicate keys and pistols and that, when the guards were having an evening meal, there was a plan to escape. It worked.

On 16 September 1943, many of the guards were overpowered and a total of thirty-seven to fifty-one inmates got out in groups of two or three. With the assistance of a young boy, she and Suzanne (Warren) Cherise, one of the imprisoned Resistance members, tried to meet up with the others. When the boy got lost, Blanche and Suzanne set off on their own. After several hours' walking, at six o'clock in the morning, they stopped at a church and asked the priest for help. He gave them the name of a nearby farmer, who let them sleep in his barn. Suspecting he might betray them, they decided to move on. After two more days without food or shelter, they found a Benedictine monastery in Dourgne, where they were taken in by the monks and provided with accommodation in the guest house.

After two months they were put in touch with an escape network who took them to the Pyrénées. Despite two attempts, they had to turn back because the icy weather and deep snow drifts made the crossing impossible. They returned to the monastery and, at the beginning of January 1944, agreed to work as couriers and escorts to and from Paris. Blanche was sent to Lyon, but she was afraid people might recognise her. After a month, she moved into the Jura mountains and in April 1944 the SOE arranged for her and Suzanne to escape.

Instead of a Lysander pick-up, a large group were to be brought back by motor gunboats. Gleeson reported how, when the message '*Patrick fait toujours pipi au lit*', came through after the nine o'clock news one night, they were taken in the back of a bread van with other evaders to a remote bay on the Normandy coast. Blanche had brought a bottle of Chanel No. 5, but it broke in her bag and there was great worry its smell would attract attention. About two in the morning, lifeboats picked the group off the beach and took them to boats waiting offshore. Despite being shot at by German boats lying in wait, the gunboats out-raced them and she was brought safely back to England on 20 April 1944, the only woman SOE agent brought back by the Royal Navy. Like Yvonne Rudellat, Blanche was awarded the MBE by King George VI 'for services in France during the enemy occupation'.

Lise de Baissac

It was the following moon period when Clark refers to the first FANYs to be flown out of Tempsford. On 23 September 1942, a mission to occupied France was aborted due to the 'wrong reception'. The pilot did not get the correct letter code flashed to him by the people on the ground.

> There was little time wasted in mounting this operation again and the following night, the 24/25th, F/O Wilkin in Whitley Z9428 (NF-W) took off at 20.50 in an endeavour to complete this operation. It was a straight forward trip leaving the UK at Bognor and crossing the French coast at Pte de la Peree at 22.34 hours flying at 2,500 feet. Flying south they pinpointed Orléans and the Loire and made their way down to the target area reaching it at 00.35. They were now flying in low broken cumulus with a ceiling of 500 feet. The DZ was found without trouble but instead of a triangle of red lights, as expected, they were white, but the flashing light was OK. Making two runs over the target at 01.00 hours the drop was made from 500 feet, the dispatcher reporting 'agents jumped when told – everything OK'.

One of Flight Officer Wilkin's passengers was petite thirty-seven-year-old Lise de Baissac, a major in the FANY. She was born to French settlers at Curepipe on the island of Mauritius and was thus a British subject. At the outbreak of war she was working in Paris with her brother Claude. Because he would have difficulty getting official permission to leave, he made his own way to Gibraltar. Lise went to the Dordogne and, ashamed by the Armistice, helped escaped prisoners of war to make the journey to the Spanish border. Desperate to follow her brother, she managed to get exit papers from the American Consulate and made her way to Gibraltar via Spain and Portugal. Imagine her surprise to discover her brother was on the same ship.

Knowing someone at SOE, Claude was accepted but Lise, disappointed not to have been invited, found an office job in London. Within months her language skills attracted her to the SOE, who by that time were keen to recruit women. She told Gleeson, 'When they told me that they wanted me to be something like a spy I objected. Being a Mata Hari did not appeal to me at all. However, they said that it was not really spying but merely going into France and organizing and doing what I could for the Allies, so I agreed.'

In November 1943 she joined the second all-female training course and was commissioned as a captain in the FANY. One of her colleagues was twenty-two-year-old Andrée Borrel, a member of the French Resistance and a lieutenant in the FANY, codenamed 'Denise'.

Given that Lise was the oldest of the second group of women agents to attend the 'finishing school' at Beaulieu, one of her instructors commented that 'she was very much ahead of her fellow students and, had she been with others as mentally mature as herself, she would have been even more capable'. The SOE commandant who prepared agents for clandestine life said she was 'quite imperturbable', a woman who could 'remain cool and collected in any situation'. Described by Escott as small, slight, with black hair, light eyes and a very confident manner, her trainers found her 'exceptionally intelligent, strong-minded and decisive, with a definite flair for organization and better working on her own as an organiser.'

They were dropped at Boisrenard, just outside the village of St Laurent Nouain, close to the town of Mer, north of Bordeaux. After they were met by Culioli's reception committee, she reported needing some tea but was disgusted to discover that someone had replaced the tea in her hip flask with rum. After sleeping in a hut in the woods until the night-time curfew ended, Culioli took them by horse and cart to a safe house. After a few days, which allowed her to acclimatise to wartime France, Andrée went north to work in the PROSPER network in Paris while Lise, codenamed 'Odile', stayed for a few days before moving south to Poitiers to run a reception réseau for incoming agents with the ARTIST network.

The SOE wanted her to gather information on everyday life under German occupation; whatever she could find out about rationing and the use of ration books; what food shortages there were; what it was like using the trains, what restrictions there were on movement and what passes and permits were needed. She also had to locate suitable parachute drop zones and landing grounds and attempt to build up a network of reliable and trustworthy helpers.

Helped by a local auctioneer, she rented first a two-room basement apartment near the railway station and then another right next to the Gestapo headquarters in Poitiers. There she played the part of Madame Irene Brisse, a quiet widow who was seeking refuge from the tension of Parisian life. Without a wireless set, she had to make trips to Paris to send and receive messages and receive funds. On other occasions, she went out on her bicycle looking for flat drop zones while posing as an amateur archaeologist. Stopping to look at ancient monuments or to pick up and examine a stone became part of her everyday behaviour. In Tours, she found shelter in Yvonne Rudellat's room; in Paris she met Francis Suttill once, her main contact being Andrée Borrel. Through her trips to Bordeaux, she became friendly with Mary Herbert, her brother's courier. In the evenings at Poitiers, according to Escott, 'she sometimes entertained friends for a meal, excellent cover for night-time visiting agents, who then drew little attention when leaving late. Of real friends she had few, except the auctioneer and a university professor giving her Spanish lessons'.

Interviewed after the war by James Gleeson, she told him how two months after she arrived she received a message on her wireless set that a new agent was being sent. She had to meet him in the early hours of the morning, take him back to her house and brief him on all she had learned so that he could carry out his mission more safely. For almost a year, that was her main task, being the reception officer for thirteen new agents and arranging for agents, Resistance leaders, important political, military or business figures and sometimes their wives and girlfriends, to be returned to England in a Lysander or Hudson. The latter was much larger plane which could carry ten passengers, but needed a longer landing strip.

During the nights of the full moon, she slept little, often helping to unpack the containers, dispose of them and the parachutes, and transport the supplies and arms to safe houses.

She described to Juliette Pattinson how once in a train she asked a German to help put her suitcase on the rack above her head. 'I had things in it. But I mean it was part of ordinary life. It was not important.' What she had inside she didn't specify, but on one occasion Lise was given 250,000 francs (about £1,400) to carry.

Sometimes she went across to Bordeaux, where she met her brother Claude, who had been dropped by a Halifax three months earlier. He was building up the SCIENTIST circuit, which had an estimated 11,000 men, organised sabotage missions, and provided reports on submarine and shipping movements to the SOE. Over the next few months Lise acted as liaison officer between the SCIENTIST, PROSPER and BRICKLAYER networks, and is reported in her obituary in the *Daily Telegraph* to have taken part in attacks on enemy columns.

This work entailed her becoming adept at looking the part. She told Pattinson that for her there were not many opportunities to dress up. 'In France, they were wearing very old things. Everybody wore all sorts of things and not particularly elegant. Old clothes were taken out of cupboards. Clothing was in very short supply, rationed and expensive.'

In June 1943, the PROSPER network was penetrated by a double agent, which led to the arrest of numerous agents, including Andrée Borrel. In Maurice Buckmaster's wartime autobiography *They Fought Alone*, he told of one female agent who was arrested when an astute Gestapo agent observed her accidentally looking right before she looked left and stepped into the road. The traffic braked and she unwittingly became the centre of attention.

When word reached London, Lise was instructed to return to England. There followed a period of nervous tension until the flight was arranged. 'It is a bit of nerves, you know, will the plane come, will it? As I say, I'm not a nervous person, anxious ... It seems to me, it's part of the work, of life.'

On the night of 16/17 August 1943, Squadron Leader Hugh Verity landed his Lysander in a field two kilometres east of Couture-sur-Loir and seven kilometres west of Vendôme to bring Lise, her brother Claude, and Major Nicholas Bodington back to England. Within days of her escape, the Gestapo swooped and arrested many in her network, killing some of her friends. According to Foot, some in the SOE were suspicious of Bodington because of his friendship with Henri Déricourt, the Air Movements officer for the SOE in France. Déricourt was thought to have passed sensitive information to the Abwehr, the military intelligence organization, in return for money and protection.

After being debriefed, Lise had a well-earned rest before being sent on a refresher course at SOE's training schools, where she attended the parachute jumping course at Ringway with Yvonne Baseden and Violette Szabó. They jumped well but Lise broke her leg. She told Gleeson that parachuting was the only thrill of her work. Although she loved all sport, she thought jumping was best. 'I thought I knew everything but I didn't.'

During the enforced wait she acted as a conducting officer but, with the approach of D-Day and the arrest in early 1944 of many agents and Resistance members, there was an urgent need for replacements. When asked if she would be prepared to return to France, she agreed. On 9 April 1944 it was again Hugh Verity who landed her safely at Villes les Ormes, north-west of Châteauroux. He reported bringing back little French presents for his wife. At three in the morning one day, he woke her up by emptying a bag of lipsticks for her on the bed.[4]

Using the same cover as a 'widow', she travelled as Madame Janette Bouville, but was also known by the codenames of 'Marguerite' and 'Adele'.

Arriving in the early hours of the morning, her reception committee provided her with a bicycle to get to her safe house, but, as she was still recovering from her broken leg, she couldn't keep up.

> I was a right long way back and I had to follow them ... they had turned right or left. I couldn't see. Luckily, I turned right and it was there that I found them. Had I turned left I don't know what would have happened to me ... But that was really frightening. I still remember that ... Perhaps, it's the most difficult moment of all my missions. Should I turn right or left?

Initially, she worked with the PIMENTO network but considered them to be militant socialists with political aims under the control of someone in Switzerland, not London. She requested a transfer to join her brother's new SCIENTIST II network in Normandy. When the SOE agreed, he appointed her as second-in-command. Whilst part of her work involved reconnoitring large landing grounds that could be held for 48 hours while airborne troops established themselves, her main task was as an arms instructor. There was also another responsibility, using her diplomatic skills at managing some awkward members of the group who were keen on uncoordinated attacks on the Germans, rather than following SOE's orders. Between April and May 1944, at least thirty receptions on Claude's drop zones provided 777 containers and 300 packages of arms, ammunition and other supplies. On 1 May, they were joined by Phyllis Latour, another wireless operator who had only been partly trained as the need was so great.

After D-Day, Claude divided his growing network in two. Lise and others in her group moved to Orne, where she saw disciplined German soldiers moving to the front. Weeks later, she saw them as demoralised stragglers. Based in a room in the back of a schoolhouse, she had to continue maintaining her façade as a widow when troops took over the school as their headquarters. Whilst dispatch riders arrived at the front with their messages and reports, her colleagues arrived on bicycles at the back to supply her with theirs. On occasions, she added what she noticed from the flags on the German maps on the wall of their control room, useful intelligence about their troop movements.

She had a lucky escape when the Germans told her that they needed the whole school building and that she would have to move out. Hurrying back to her room, she found it already occupied with her belongings scattered on the floor. One of the soldiers was sitting on her sleeping bag, which, having disobeyed orders, had been made out of parachute silk. 'I tried to keep my dignity but inside I was very frightened. When I asked the man to get up and let me take my bag, I was really anxious to leave the place.' Escott mentioned that she was more nervous about her bag of English sweets being found in a kitchen cupboard.

Captain Blackman, the leader of a Special Air Service (SAS) team that parachuted behind enemy lines in July 1944, received lots of help from Lise. He recommended her for an OBE, praising her work during which she risked her life daily. Cycling sixty or seventy kilometres a day carrying compromising material like batteries and crystals for Phyllis Latour's set and secret documents meant that she would have been shot without trial if she had been caught.

Another British army officer claimed later that 'the part she played in aiding the Maquis and the British underground movement in France cannot be too highly stressed and did much to facilitate the Maquis' preparations and resistance prior to the American breakthrough in Mayenne.' A note in her SOE file said that, 'She was the inspiration of groups on the Orne and by her initiative caused heavy losses to the Germans with tyre bursters on the roads near St Aubin-le-Desert, St Mars, and as far as Laval, Le Mans and Rennes. She also took part in several armed attacks on enemy columns.'[5]

Living in constant fear for their lives put pressure on all the agents. Pattinson refers to Lise reminiscing about her experiences to Summerfield after the war. She said, 'You know that you're in danger all the time but you always think that you will go through. I have never been afraid really that I should be caught. It never occurred to me. I think that we're all like that. If you're frightened you can't do anything.' However, she did confess to feeling nervous on a few occasions.

With the Germans retreating, they were anxious to take with them anything of value. One soldier stopped her and demanded her bicycle. She refused, telling him that she knew his Commanding Officer and would report him for theft immediately at the school. Thinking better of it, he walked away swearing. On another occasion, she slapped a young soldier across the face for trying to take her bicycle by force and got away with it.

There was another lucky escape when, in summer 1944, Lise was cycling from Normandy to Paris carrying spare parts for wireless sets. They were fastened around her waist under her dress. When she was stopped at a checkpoint, the German guard thoroughly frisked her.

> He searched me very carefully. I knew he could feel the things I was carrying. But he said nothing. Perhaps he was looking for a weapon like a revolver; maybe he thought it was a belt. I do not know ... I was very, very frightened. He touched everything and he let us free. That was once when I really was frightened.

Within two hours of the Germans leaving, the Americans arrived to liberate the village. Going out to the *Mairie* to meet them, she gave them quite a surprise. There was Lise, dressed in the FANY uniform she had especially packed expecting this occasion. One amazed soldier asked where they had come from. 'Out of the sky!' shrugged another, completely ignorant of how accurate he was. Other villagers expressed their astonishment. They had thought she was just an unobtrusive widow and there she was being handed over control by the Americans. She spent the next few weeks mopping up arms and ammunition, which she had stored in the surrounding countryside, and locating the graves where men and women of the Resistance had been interred. She also acted as judge and jury for the villagers rounded up and accused of collaborating with the enemy.

Lise was lifted out of France for the second time on 16/17 August, yet again by Verity in a Lysander, landing at Tempsford at 0400 hours, despite flak over Caen on the Normandy coast. Like Yvonne Rudellat and Valentine Charlet, Lise was awarded the MBE and *Croix de Guerre*.

After the war, she worked for the BBC in London as a programme assistant for the Overseas service, translating news from English into French and also being a news reader. She later married a Monsieur Villameur and went to live in France. She told Gleeson:

> Films and novels have made people think of an agent's work as glamorous. But believe me, our job was, above all, sheer hard work. What was needed was cold-blooded efficiency for long, weary months rather than any bursts of heroism. Looking back I find my strongest emotion was acute loneliness – the loneliness of a secret life. Even the relief of talking to other agents was the rarest luxury – for our own safety we were only supposed to contact one another when strictly necessary ... They didn't catch me. In that serious game of hide-and-seek I won. I am rather proud of that.

Following Lise's death in 2004, Jean-Paul Salomé, a French film director, read her obituary in *The Times* and decided to make *Female Agents*, a film released in June 2008 that is loosely based on Lise's wartime experiences. He wanted to pay tribute to the role played by women agents in France.

> When the war was over, General de Gaulle accorded little importance to the role women played. Out of more than 1,000 Liberation Crosses that were awarded, only six went to women ... It is this slightly macho view of the Resistance that excluded women.[6]

The reader can decide from what follows whether they think the other women included here deserved similar honours.

Andrée Borrel

On 24 September 1942, Andrée Borrel, mentioned earlier, parachuted with Lise de Baissac from F/O Wilkin's Whitley into a field near St Laurent Nouan, on the Loire about twenty kilometres south-west of Orléans. It was their second attempt as the original flight the previous evening had to be aborted. She was returning to France after escaping several months earlier and receiving SOE's training.

Born on 18 November 1918 to working-class parents, she grew up on the outskirts of Paris and, described by her sister as a *garçon manqué*, a tom-boy, she enjoyed bicycling into the countryside, hiking and climbing. To help her widowed mother, she left school at fourteen and worked in a bakery and then as a shop assistant. Her socialist sympathies encouraged her to fight in the Spanish Civil War. By this time, she was described by Escott as 'a small, dark-complexioned, stocky young girl, very quick, athletic and determined'.

With General Franco's army defeating the International Brigades, she went to Paris. When war broke out, she moved her mother to Toulon on the Mediterranean coast, trained with the *Association des Dames de France* and looked after wounded soldiers at Beaucaire Hospital, St Hippolyte du Fort, a Vichy-government-run internment camp near Nimes. There she met Maurice Dufour, a supervising officer in the camp who had been recruited by Albert Guérisse, a Belgian doctor. Guérisse had joined the Royal Navy when he escaped from Dunkirk in 1940, using his Australian friend's name: Pat O'Leary. After being sprung from prison, he was recruited by the SIS and used his contacts and training to establish contacts with London through Switzerland. They provided funds and wireless operators for what became known as the PAT line, which ran from Belgian to the Spanish border.

Maurice Dufour, an officer in the RF Section who worked with Andrée, thought she was 'a free spirit, this was wartime and inevitably they shared both a bed and a passionate desire to liberate their country'.[7] When the hospital was closed, they helped with the PAT line until it was betrayed in December 1941. Andrée and Maurice were forced to hide in Toulouse. Later she stayed in Hotel du Tennis, the last refuge of evaders before the border. As the network began to expand again, Jack Agazarian was parachuted in as another wireless operator, with his wife Françine as his courier. Maurice and Andrée established a villa at Canet Plage outside Perpignan, the last safe house before the hard and dangerous route over the Pyrénées into Spain.

Over her time on the PAT line, she helped Jews, SOE agents, and an estimated 600 Allied airmen shot down over France to escape by felucca or over the Spanish border and back to England. Gleeson described her as 'a tough, intelligent girl with a love for adventure, a preference for sweaters and slacks and enjoyed nothing better than a good sabotage operation like blowing up an important railway bridge or some German officers' cars.'

Eventually, following a large number of arrests, they escaped over the Pyrénées themselves and made their way by train and a British diplomat's car to Lisbon in Portugal. Maurice was shipped back to England but Andrée stayed, working at the Free French Propaganda Office at the British Embassy.

Andrée stayed in Portugal until April 1942, when she too went to London. On her arrival she was interrogated at the Royal Patriotic School in Wandsworth. Many immigrants to Britain were said to have spent a few days at the school for 'questioning'. Once cleared by MI6 she volunteered to help de Gaulle's Free French. As she would not tell them about the PAT line, they were unsure whether she was a double agent or not. Whether Andrée knew or not is uncertain, but Maurice was suspected by the RF section of being a German agent and was brutally tortured in the converted coal cellar underneath 10 Duke Street, the headquarters of the Free French. According to Dufour's obituary in *The Times*, they had threatened to kidnap and gang rape Andrée. After being sent to the Free French camp at Camberley, between Reading and Aldershot, he escaped and made his way to Andrée's lodgings. However, desperately worried that Maurice's escape and his High Court writ would name de Gaulle and others in the RF Section, SOE 'shut him up', put him into a safe house, gave him £2,000 and promised he would be able to stay in Britain. Maurice and Andrée never saw each other again.

Known to have strong socialist views, Andrée was subsequently recruited by the SOE in May and became a lieutenant in the FANY, receiving £3 a week in pay. Her training officers considered her tough, self-reliant and absolutely reliable. Buckmaster thought she had the utmost courage and coolness but the other women on her course found her intense and rather frightening. Escott reported Yvonne Rudellat being shocked when Andrée told her that the best way to deal with a sleeping German was to stab his brain with a pencil through the ear. Marie-Thérèse le Chêne 'saw through her assumed sophistication to the innocent beneath and tended to mother her'.

Andrée and Lise got out of the Lysander onto a field belonging to the *maire*, the local mayor, and brother-in-law of one of the reception committee. Being so close to the river Loire had made it easy for the pilot to locate. Her mission was to make her way north to Paris to work as a courier in thirty-five-year-old Francis Suttill's PROSPER and PHYSICIAN circuits. Tall, athletic and beautiful, she was often to be seen wearing a fur coat and rolling her own cigarettes. With the codename 'Denise' she became more than a messenger, posing as Suttill's sister. 'He let her do the talking, and she played to perfection the harassed country girl taking her farmer brother to the market in the local town'.[8] She travelled around northern France with him, organising networks and training Resistance members in the use of weapons and explosives supplied by 161 Squadron. In her personnel file is a citation for an award, which stated that she 'took part in several coups de mains, notably an operation at Chevilly power station in March 1943. She distinguished herself by her coolness and efficiency and always volunteered for the most dangerous tasks'.

During their training in Arisaig, both men and women were taught how to use the Sten gun, Bren gun, Thompson sub machine gun, PIAT (Projector Infantry Anti-tank) and hand-held revolvers such as the Colt .32 and Colt .45, Flaubert, Browning, Luger and Mauser. She also helped arrange drop zones and the escape of downed aircrew and SOE agents. According to some sources, she was the lover of Gilbert Norman, the wireless operator.

Suttill was so impressed with Andrée that, despite her being only twenty-four, he appointed her second-in-command in March 1943. In a note to the SOE, he said that Andrée 'has a perfect understanding of security and an imperturbable calmness ... Thank you very much for having sent her to me'. She also worked on the MONKEYPUZZLE network in Brittany and used the codenames 'Monique', 'Whitebeam' and 'Denise Urbain'.[9]

To give an idea of what Andrée was doing, Shrabani Basu, in her book *Spy Princess: The Life of Noor Inayat Khan*, said that in April 1943, Suttill's group had carried out sixty-three acts of sabotage, derailing trains, killing forty-three Germans and wounding 110. By June the group covered twelve *départements*, had thirty-three DZs and received 254 containers of supplies. They picked up 190 containers in June alone and more attacks were planned.

However, lax security and betrayal led the Germans to arrest her in Paris on 23 June, along with Suttill and Norman. All three had been inseparable. Rita Kramer's interviews with Andrée's relatives revealed that she managed to smuggle messages out of prison. Written on cigarette paper, they were folded and hidden in her lingerie and sent to her sister to be washed. Some were laundered in ignorance and it was a sympathetic prison matron who alerted the sister of their existence. Most messages were to reassure her mother and request items like a sweater, notebook and hairpins, ending with lots of kisses. Others indicated that she had been betrayed by Gilbert Norman. Buckmaster said the messages Andrée sent to him were full of courage and the unshaken belief that she would escape. According to Foot, several Germans testified that she never talked at all and treated them with fearless contempt throughout her captivity.

She was sent first to Karlsruhe in Germany and then to the Natzweiler-Struthof concentration camp in the Vosges mountains, about fifty kilometres south-west of Strasbourg. Escott described how between 2130 hours and 2200 hours, about a month after D-Day, she and three other female SOE agents were taken out of their cells one-by-one to a room with eight beds. Ordered to lie down, Andrée was given an injection of phenol, carbolic acid. After she lost consciousness, a doctor declared her dead. She was stripped and taken to the furnace in the crematorium. Witnesses later told how she was still conscious as she was dragged to the ovens. Crematorium workers heard one girl call out *'Pourquoi?'* and the guard replying *'Pour Typhus'*. Fighting to the last, she was said to have scratched her executioner's face.

Andrée was awarded the MBE and 'Mentioned in Dispatches' as well as being given the King's Commendation for Brave Conduct, the *Croix de Guerre* and the *Medaille de Resistance*.

Mary Lindell

During the moon period following Lise and Andrée's drop, forty-seven-year-old Mary Lindell, codenamed 'Marie-Claire', was Lysandered into France. No details of her or her mission were recorded in the SOE records. The reason why is revealed in Barry Wynne's biography of her, *No Drums, No Trumpets*, and on Christopher Long's Royal Air Force's Escaping Society website. Born in Sutton in Surrey in 1895, Mary was described as 'a very remarkable English woman, impeccably English in upbringing and manner, extremely resourceful, courageous, strong-minded and used to getting her own way'.[10] During the First World War, she served as a nurse but was sent home for hitting a matron with a bedpan brush. Joining the *Secours aux Blessés Militaires*, a division of the French Red Cross, she won medals for gallantry under fire. The last Czar of Russia awarded her the Russian Order of St Anne and the French Prime Minister awarded her the French *Croix de Guerre* with Star.

After the war she married a French nobleman, Count de Milleville, and settled in Paris on the rue Erlanger. When the Germans invaded France in May 1940, she worked as a nurse, wearing her British ribbons on her Red Cross uniform. As her work allowed her to ferry sick children over the demarcation line into the Unoccupied Zone, she had the requisite passes. With the help of her three children, she hid escaped Allied soldiers who had not managed to get out with the other troops at Dunkirk in her home and then drove them through the night to safety in Limoges.

> Later, Mary, by sheer bluff and boldness, managed to get petrol permits, and permits for herself, a nurse and a mechanic to travel freely on humanitarian missions. These were obtained via the German commander in Paris, General von Stulpnagel, and also Count von Bismark. Earlier, General von Stulpnagel had in fact signed an order, stating that men found helping evaders would be shot and women sent to concentration camps. This order was posted throughout France. He had now given Mary petrol and permits in disobedience of his own orders.[11]

One of her daughters had an affair with a German officer, but whether Mary knew about it is unknown. Mary, then in her mid-forties, ensured that many evaders were smuggled to safe houses where they would be met by guides, brave young men and women, who escorted them to Marseille. There they were helped by the Pat O'Leary escape line in crossing the border into Spain and then getting back to England, either via Gibraltar or Lisbon in Portugal. Christopher Long's website records that:

> Despite Mary's success her methods were amateurish and it was only a matter of time before the Gestapo were on to her. Arrested by the Paris Gestapo, Mary was interrogated and kept in solitary confinement for nine months. The Gestapo were now waiting for further instructions to detain Mary, but with the help of a friendly wardress, Mary walked out of Frèsnes prison and kept on walking without looking back. Making arrangements for her children first, Mary travelled to a safe house at Ruffec and, disguising herself as an elderly governess, followed the escape line to Spain and England.

A telegram containing news of her escape reached the office of Airey Neave and Jimmy Langley, MI9 officers working in the War Office in London. With the assistance of the SOE, they were supplying escape lines with funds, agents and supplies. They were told of a woman dressed in French Red Cross uniform, with a British passport in the name of Ghita Mary Lindell. Their contact in Barcelona told them that the American Vice Consul in Lyon had obtained her travel visa for her and the Vichy government had issued her with an exit permit after she had informed them that all her money and papers had been stolen.

In Neave's *Saturday at MI9*, he described her arriving at his flat in London dressed in the royal blue uniform of the French Red Cross.

> She had dark brown eyes and chestnut hair, and her face was finely proportioned. Her figure was slight, and her uniform well-cut. She seemed very feminine, but in her expression there was an intensity, a stubbornness which somehow did not fit with her smart appearance.

Although the powers that be would not hear of it, she demanded to be sent back to France. They argued that people known to the Gestapo should not return. It was too great a risk. She argued that she still had many contacts in Ruffec, near Angoulême, who were able and willing to help and, being a long way from Paris, she would not be recognised. Her strong personality eventually prevailed and she was allowed to return. Neave said that she had a crash course in coding and a course in night landing in the little Lysander aeroplane:

> This involved the training of agents in the laying out of flare paths and signals

to the pilot. It needed considerable discipline on the part of the 'reception committees', many of whom had only the most primitive equipment. Agents had to be taught how to place the flares correctly and pass on these procedures to others in the field. Since Lysanders were fitted to hold only two passengers, they also had to be trained to warn the pilots of approaching enemy fighters.

Neave gave her a final briefing and drove her down to RAF Tangmere. This was the Special Duties Squadron's forward base. Lysanders flew low by moonlight across the Channel and, avoiding anti-aircraft batteries, used pinpoint navigation to identify their drop zone. Neave gives the date as 21 October 1942 but, checking Freddie Clark's *Agents by Moonlight*, an account of the Tempsford Squadron's operations, there was no mention of her. Eight of the nine missions that night were to France but Mary didn't appear in the records.

In Hugh Verity's autobiography, *We Landed by Moonlight*, he gave a different date of 26/27 October, saying that Mary was flown by Pilot Officer Bridges to Thalamy Airfield, east of Ussel, with Ferdinand Rodriguez, a wireless operator. Clark mentions the Flight Officer flying on SIS operation ACHILLES that night but gave no additional details. Officially, pilots weren't meant to know who their passengers were but, according to Neave,

> When we reached Tangmere, the Squadron Commander took us to the briefing room. The reception committee organised by the SOE was at a point sixty miles south-east of Limoges and fifteen from the small town of Ussel. Before take-off, there was a moving incident when she was introduced to the pilot of her aircraft. He was a Canadian, a slight young figure, and a Battle of Britain hero, and with several decorations. He took both her hands and said: 'I just wanted to say thank you for going over there. I can't tell you what we feel about it, but all the boys have tremendous admiration for what you're doing.'

Although MI9 wanted her to have a wireless operator, she refused, saying she couldn't work with the person they had chosen. Using her original Red Cross pass and a forged French one and known as Comtesse de Moncy, she moved into a room at the Hôtel de France in Ruffec and set up what became known as the Marie-Claire escape line. Not long after her arrival, Mary was said to have been deliberately knocked off her bike by a car thought to have been driven by collaborators. Thinking her to be dead, the patriotic villagers carried her to a remote farmhouse and had begun to dig her grave. A friendly chemist arrived, pronounced her alive and refused to sign the death certificate. She ended up in hospital with five fractured ribs, a serious head wound and injuries to her arm and leg. The Gestapo arrived shortly afterwards, having been informed that there was 'an English agent' there.

They searched the wards without success. She had been hidden in a cellar, behind a pile of wood. Although still very ill, she had to move and was taken to Lyon shortly after Christmas 1942. The Christopher Long RAF Escaping Society website states that, in her absence:

> Many more evaders were moved along Marie-Claire line, two of whom were Major C. Hasler and Cpl W. Sparks. This pair were the two survivors of the Operation Frankton raid on shipping in Bordeaux harbour (otherwise known as the Cockleshell Heroes). Lack of a wireless operator prevented Mary knowing of the raid. But the commandos, who had to make their way inland to contact an escape line, had been briefed to make for Ruffec and the Café du Paris. This was unusual practice but on this occasion the only way to return was via an escape line. The Café du Paris was not found, however. Both men entered a small café and were helped by the owner, eventually finding themselves with 'Marie-Claire'. Of the eight Commandos only two survived. The remainder were captured and executed.

It was her youngest son, twelve-year-old Maurice, who took Hasler and Sparks to a safe house in Lyon. When Mary met them there, her first reaction was to hand Hasler a pair of scissors and order him to cut off his magnificent blond moustache. She then lectured him, saying:

> We've only got one rule for Englishmen in our care – NO GIRLS. From past experience we know that once they meet a pretty girl everything goes to hell. So we shall take care to keep you away from them.

Before long the Gestapo were back on her trail. Both her sons were arrested to try to find out where their mother was. They didn't talk. Maurice was released after being badly beaten, but Oky was deported to a concentration camp and never heard of again.

Mary spent time out of circulation, recuperating in Switzerland, then, despite the pressures, returned to Ruffec and continued her important work, financed with money brought in by agents dropped regularly from Tempsford. Downed aircrews from different parts of France were accompanied in stages to safe houses she had located in Ruffec. Once a group of between five and eight had been gathered, Mary would take them herself to the Pyrénées and hand them over to mountain guides. In early November 1943, she and four 'helpers' took five airmen by train via Toulouse and Foix to Andorra. Before they got to their safe house she learned that the line had been blown, so they all returned to Ruffec. Another route was planned, this time via Limoges, Toulouse, Tarbes, Pau, Oleron and Tardets, and then on foot over the Pyrénées.

This route proved to be a success and the group crossed the Pyrénées towards the end of November 1943 in winter conditions. On the 25th November 1943 Marie-Claire was waiting to meet a courier called Ginette who was escorting airmen from Ruffec to Pau. The weather was very cold and it was snowing. The train arrived at Pau station without Ginette and the airmen. Marie turned to leave and was confronted by two Gestapo men. Later, after initial interrogation, Marie-Claire was taken by train to Paris. Whilst under escort by two Gestapo guards she feigned sickness, made her way to a toilet, saw an opportunity and threw herself off the train. The guards immediately started firing and she was seriously wounded in the head and neck. She was returned to the train and taken to a German hospital. A German doctor rebuilt her neck and saved her life in a 4½ hour operation. Despite being extremely ill and running a high fever, Marie was deported to Ravensbrück concentration camp. Two things were in her favour and probably saved her life: firstly, she was moved into the hospital at Ravensbrück initially, and secondly, as a trained nurse, she remained in the hospital and survived.[12]

After the war, she became the Royal Air Forces Escaping Society's representative in France. A film of her war experiences was made by ITV in 1991; it was called *One Against the Wind* and starred Judy Davis. The story of her life is told in Barry Wynne's book *No Drums, No Trumpets*.

Odette Sansom, another of the lucky few to survive imprisonment at Ravensbrück, told Rita Kramer in an interview after the war about meeting seven other captured women when she was taken to Avenue Foch, the Gestapo headquarters, in an exclusive part of Paris near the Champs-Élysées. Odette recalled one hot day thinking that the building was so beautiful that she might as well enjoy her time there and asked the guards to bring her some English tea. They got it in proper china cups. None of them had seen anything like that in a long time.

They shared one of the girls' lipstick and talked about their experiences of being captured. Several of them, including Odette, believed that they had been betrayed by an informant.

We were all young, we were all different, but we all had the feeling in the beginning that we were going to be – helpful. That was why we went into it. And to have impressed the people around them as they did is almost enough. They impressed everyone – the Germans, their guards. They behaved extremely well, those women.[13]

After interrogation they were sent to Frèsnes Prison. Almost a year later, the Germans transported Odette and several other captured SOE agents – Andrée

Borrel, Vera Leigh, Diana Rowden, Sonia Olschanezky, Yolande Beekman, Eliane Plewman and Madeleine Damerment – to the civilian women's prison at Karlsruhe, north-east of Strasbourg. Exactly a month after the D-Day landings, on 6 July 1944, Andrée, Vera, Diana and Sonia were taken to the Natzweiler concentration camp in the Vosges Mountains of Alsace. An eyewitness account was provided by Brian Stonehouse, one of the very few prisoners who survived. The Spartacus website includes his evidence to a military court in the spring of 1946:

> There was one tall girl [Andrée Borrel] with very fair hair. I could see that it was not its natural colour as the roots of her hair were dark. She was wearing a black coat, French wooden-soled shoes and was carrying a fur coat on her arm. Another girl [Sonia Olschanezky] had very black oily hair, and wore stockings, aged about twenty to twenty-five years, was short and was wearing a tweed coat and skirt. A third girl [Diana Rowden] was middle height, rather stocky, with shortish fair hair tied with a multi-coloured ribbon, aged about twenty-eight. She was wearing a grey flannel short 'finger-tip' length swagger coat with a grey skirt which I remember thinking looked very English. The fourth woman of the party [Vera Leigh] was wearing a brownish tweed coat and skirt. She was more petite than the blonde in grey and older, having shortish brown hair. None of the four women were wearing make-up and all were looking pale and tired.[14]

The women were taken out, injected with phenol, carbolic acid, and put in the crematorium furnace. Andrée was only twenty-four. After the war she was posthumously awarded the Knight Commander of the British Commonwealth medal (KCBC), the *Croix de Guerre* and the *Medaille Republique Française*.

Andrée de Jongh

Andrée de Jongh was not directly involved with RAF Tempsford, but her work helping Tempsford personnel is worth mentioning here. She helped set up Comète, similar to the Marie-Claire escape line, but operated with SIS help from Belgium. When Belgium's King Leopold capitulated to the occupying German forces three weeks after their invasion in May 1940, twenty-four-year-old Andrée de Jongh ('Dédée') was working as a commercial artist in the Sofina company in Brussels. The director, Baron Jacques Donny, was financing the shelter of escaping British soldiers in various safe houses in the city and Andrée got involved in nursing these men. Along with her sister Suzanne, her father and many other brave Belgians, she helped about four hundred Allied airmen and soldiers get out of the country to safety via neutral countries of Switzerland and Spain.

On several occasions, she accompanied groups across the Pyrénées to give them a second chance to fight the Nazis; some of these groups were flown out of Tempsford. Using a traitor, the Gestapo arrested her father and then her and other colleagues. She was one of the few who survived interrogation and imprisonment at Ravensbrück and after the war was awarded the George Medal by the British, the Medal of Freedom by the Americans, and the *Croix de Guerre avec Palme* by the Belgians. She was also created Chevalier of the French Légion d'honneur and awarded the Belgian Order of Leopold. Her biography, *Little Cyclone*, was written by Airey Neave, her SIS controller, who described her as 'one of our greatest agents'.[15]

Odette Sansom

Odette was one of the few to survive imprisonment. Born Odette Brailly in Amiens on 28 April 1912, she lost her father, a bank manager, when he was killed at Verdun in the First World War. Educated at the convent of St Thérèse, Escott reported them finding Odette difficult. Suffering from various diseases as a young girl including temporary blindness and rheumatic fever, in 1926 her mother moved the family to Boulogne on the Normandy coast to benefit from the sea air. In 1930 this small, vivacious, pretty eighteen-year-old girl with light hair and eyes, married Roy Sansom, a hotel worker and son of a British soldier who had been billeted with her family during the war. In 1932 they moved to London and, when her husband joined the Army and was posted overseas, she was living with her three daughters, Françoise, Lily and Marianne, in a village in Somerset. She joined the WAAF as an assistant second officer and, one evening, after listening to the news on the radio, she was intrigued by an appeal for photographs of the French coast. As she had some snap-shots of Boulogne, she added details on the back and sent them to the War Office. It was a mistake. She should have sent them to the Admiralty. When her letter was opened, it was passed on to SOE, one of whose methods for attracting recruits was by placing an advertisement for translators in the papers. Her knowledge of France made her a potential candidate.

She later admitted that, during her interview with Selwyn Jepson, the recruiting officer, she had lost her temper when she found out that he had made enquiries about her life in England and France.

> 'Well, what do you mean? Why did you have to make enquiries about me? What do you think I am?' I was told, 'Oh calm down, we're going to explain to you why. We train people here and we send them to the country of their origin, or if they speak a foreign language well we send them to that country where they can use it and be useful for the war effort.' I could see that. I agreed with all that. I said, 'Yes, of course. I can see that.' Then I was told, 'Well, we think women could be useful, too.' 'Yes,' I said. 'I think women are very useful.' And that did it. I was told, 'So glad you think that way because we're going to ask you to do it.'[16]

In Jepson's interview file, also in the Imperial War Museum, he acknowledged that

> Odette was a shrewd cookie and she knew at once what it was about. She guessed and said, yes, she wanted to do it. And I said, in effect, 'Wait a minute, what are your domestic circumstances?' she said they wouldn't bother her. She had a husband and a couple of children but the husband didn't come into the matter very much and the children would be looked after by an aunt. When could she start?
>
> I was rather doubtful about her capacity. Although she had perfect French and knew France, her personality was so big that I couldn't quite see her getting away with it. However good the cover story we gave her, I couldn't see her passing unnoticed. I had a little form that I wrote names and addresses on and, for my own guidance, made a comment on the bottom on the question of suitability. I remember very clearly on her piece of paper I wrote, 'God help the Germans if we can ever get her near them, but maybe God help us on the way' – because she has such a huge personality and will dominate everybody she comes in contact with. Not necessarily because she has a dominant nature, but because she just can't help it.[17]

She had been separated from her husband, so she arranged for her three daughters, aged seven, nine and ten, to be sent to a convent boarding school in Brentwood and to be looked after during the holidays by her two 'splendid aunts and devoted uncle' while she was 'working in Scotland'. In an interview after the war by the Imperial War Museum, she said that

> I used to say, well, I've got children and they come first. It's easy enough to go on thinking that way. But I was tormented ... Am I going to be satisfied to accept this like that, that other people are going to suffer, get killed, die because of this war and trying to get freedom for my own children. Let's face it. So am I supposed to accept all this sacrifice that other people are making without lifting a finger in any way?[18]

Over the following months, she underwent SOE paramilitary training with the second group of women in Scotland, parachute training at Ringway and clandestine warfare training at Beaulieu. In Jerrard Tickell's biography *Odette*, he commented that when she was asked by one of her training instructors how she might handle an assailant, she responded by saying that she would run and, if he pursued and caught her, she would pinch him and pull his hair. The instructor was said to have replied, 'Ladies, it will be my unwelcome and embarrassing duty to teach you other and less refined methods of disabling would-be aggressors ... I have never before had to teach such things to ladies.'

Whilst doing a jump at Ringway, she smashed her face on the side of the hole as she was jumping out of a basket, sprained her ankle on landing and was sent to an ophthalmic outpatient clinic.

The SOE decided not to send her in as a courier or wireless operator, but, like Lise de Baissac, as an organiser in the area around Auxerre in Burgundy, north-central France. Her mission was to establish herself there, locate a safe house to provide temporary accommodation for newly arrived agents and recruit people who would help.

Once briefed, suitably clothed and supplied with the wherewithal for her mission, she taken to Tempsford, checked over and put on a Whitley bomber destined for Gibraltar. From there she would be taken by felucca and dropped on the Mediterranean coast of France. As the plane was taxiing up the runway another plane landed and crashed into it. Odette was lucky to have escaped uninjured.

Another flight was arranged the following week, this time in a Lysander. Once settled in the passenger seat, a messenger ran across the runway to tell the pilot to abort the mission. A message had come through saying that there would be no reception committee as they had all been arrested by the Germans.

A week later, she was taken to Plymouth harbour and boarded a Sunderland flying boat. Before the plane took off, a storm blew up causing the flight to be cancelled. Desperate that she be sent on the next available plane, the following week she boarded a Whitley bomber, but was only in the air a few minutes before it crashed a few feet from a cliff edge. Not to be outdone, she was sent to Greenock in Scotland to board a troop ship, which succeeded in dropping her at Gibraltar.

Like Yvonne Rudellat, Odette was dropped by a felucca, landing at Port-Miou, near Marseille on the Mediterranean coast, on 4 November 1942. Landed with her were three male SOE agents, an SIS agent and two lieutenants in the FANY: Mary Herbert, who went to work in the SCIENTIST network, and Marie-Thérèse le Chêne, who went to work in the PLANE network.

Tickell detailed how, codenamed 'Lise', she rendezvoused as planned with 'Raoul', Peter Churchill, in the back room of a beauty salon. Peter was a British agent who was on his third mission in France. He was in charge of the SPINDLE network, operating between Cannes and Marseille and, when he met Odette, he took to her in a big way. Too busy to arrange her trip to Auxerre, he wanted her to act as his courier and asked SOE to agree. Posing as Madame Odette Metayer, her cover story was that she was a widow whose husband had died of bronchitis. She wanted to escape the rude and boisterous nature of war-torn Amiens and live a quiet life in the beautiful lake country of the Jura Mountains. In reality, she and her companion 'Arnaud', Captain Adolphe 'Alec' Rabinovitch, selected drop zones for the containers of arms and other supplies that were delivered by Tempsford crews. According to Tickell, Peter

> ... put her down at about twenty-five. Her name was Lise and from her mop of light-brown hair, swept back to reveal a rounded forehead, down to a pair of discerning eyes, there emanated a distinct aura of challenge that was only intensified by the determined set of her chin below a somewhat colourless face. A fearless look suggested that not even the thought of the prisons held any terrors for this girl; so much so that, in the flash of time he gave to this snap judgement of her, it even occurred to Michel that she might not bother to take all the precautions she should to avoid capture.
>
> But what took and held his gaze above all else were the hands; hands such as he had never seen before in his life. They were long with slim, capable fingers and, as the left one held the wine-glass and the other broke off pieces of cake, he observed the telltale expanse between thumb and forefinger, denoting extravagance, generosity, impetuosity; the ambition in the index fingers; the unusually wide gap between them and the second fingers, showing independence of thought only matched by the independence of action that almost cried out from the gaping valleys that lay between the third and little fingers. At the moment, the second and third fingers of the left hand were overlapped in a shy gesture, as though seeking each other's company – or was it to hide the platinum wedding ring that had not escaped his eagle eye? If the occasion arose he would take a surreptitious look at the lines of her palm and see whether or not they confirmed the already extensive disclosures of the general view.[19]

Once Peter managed to get permission from Baker Street that Odette was 'indispensable', he sent her on a mission to Marseille. When she didn't return on time, he arranged for the trains to be watched, eventually replacing the man sent to keep watch at the station himself. He and Arnaud were both in awe of her.

In his autobiography, Peter related how one of the rendezvous he had sent her on involved meeting a Dr Bernard, who, concerned about her, found her a room for the night in what he considered the safest house in town – a brothel. She spent a nerve-racking and sleepless night because the place had been raided by the German Military Police in search of *réfractaires*, men who had avoided being called up to go and work in German factories in France or Germany. The only reason her room wasn't searched was that the madame – a patriot – told the police that her niece was sleeping in that room and that she had got scarlet fever. On another occasion she was stopped by German soldiers after the curfew. When the sergeant called for the duty officer, Odette explained that she was in a desperate hurry to get to Cannes to see her daughter, who she had been told was seriously ill. Adding a few tears worked. When several contacts in the Resistance were arrested, Odette and Peter had to make themselves scarce, moving to Arles for the winter. On the train journey there, she astounded her friends by taking a request for two francs for the 'Winter Relief Fund' to a German general sitting in the restaurant car, suggesting that he ought to contribute as it was his army that had caused the distress. To avoid creating a commotion the general paid it, but Peter advised her to keep her exuberance within limits. She didn't, as in his second book, *Duel of Wits*, he recalled that she

> put the cat among the canaries by placing a broom-stick against a German Colonel's door in an occupied hotel where we had once stayed. How she had chuckled when he had opened the door and it had struck him in the face.

While Peter and Odette were together, arms drops were arranged for several thousand poorly armed *réfractaires* camped out on the Plateau de Glières.

When Peter was ordered to return to England for a conference, 'Arnaud' arranged a Lysander pick-up. In the early hours of the morning, they were waiting nervously for the plane. When they eventually heard its engine, Peter was about to flash his recognition letter to the pilot when suddenly a searchlight flooded the landing strip. German soldiers, informed by a traitor in the network, approached from the bushes. Splitting up, they ran off. Not having not got the agreed signal and probably seeing the commotion, the pilot swung his plane around and returned to England. Running through the darkness, Odette heard dogs coming after her. Remembering her lessons on evasion techniques, she made for a river, waded through the icy-cold water ,and reached the other side. Luckily, she got away. Peter also managed to escape.

When another DZ was suggested, the SOE's Liaison officer suggested another because it had already been designated for the RF, de Gaulle's Resistance groups. Consequently, they moved back to Cannes in the spring. But it was not for long. Following the arrest of two of their close contacts, they moved north into the Jura of the Haute Savoie and stayed in the Hotel de la Poste in the little village of St Jorioz, about forty kilometres from Geneva. Odette had an 'authentic' medical certificate stating that she had consumption and needed to stay above 400 metres.

There was a Resistance group based sixteen kilometres away in Faverges for which they arranged supplies. Arnaud stayed up the mountain and arranged a successful pick-up. Peter left Odette in charge while he went back to England for a debrief and rest. Within a few weeks, Arnaud received a message that Peter was to return on 16 April and, according to Peter, she sent a message back saying she had been visited by 'Henri', identified later as Hugo Bleicher, a sergeant in the Abwehr, the German Security Office. He promised her the release of the two prisoners if she could arrange a Hudson pick-up for him to go to England. He wanted her to arrange for a wireless set to be sent and claimed that he represented a group of Nazis who were planning a coup against Hitler and were keen to arrange a truce and end of the war. The message she got back told her that Bleicher was 'treacherous' and not to be trusted. She had to dissolve her network, cut contact with the Annecy group and move immediately to the other side of the lake.

When 'Arnaud' found another safe house and set up his transmitter, he received a message saying Peter was coming back and a safe DZ needed finding. The site they chose was the snow-covered summit of Mount Semnoz, about five kilometres south of Annecy. They had paced out 100 metres to the right and left to ensure there was enough room for a drop and prepared a bonfire the day before. Despite London telling her not to be part of the reception committee, she went anyway. When they heard Flight Officer Legate's 30-ton Halifax bomber approaching, the bonfire was lit with a bottle of petrol and they flashed the letter 'F'. Legate reported that at 0052 hours on 16 April 1943, he dropped the agent at 800 feet at an airspeed of 140 mph, closely followed by five containers.

According to Gibb McCall in his *Flight Most Secret*, Odette did not know that Peter had been ordered not to get in touch with her. She had been compromised. He was singing the Marseillaise, the song of the Resistance, when he landed in her arms. As they came down the snow-covered slopes above Lake Annecy in the pitch dark, she slipped and fell ten metres down an almost vertical gulley, knocking herself out. X-rays taken after the war show she had shattered her fifth vertebra. Overcoming the pain, she whisked Peter off to a room in the hotel, saying that he was her husband. She did not think 'Henri' would be back for four days.

A few hours later, Odette was awoken by the hotel owner. There was a man downstairs who wanted to see her at once. Unsuspecting anything untoward, she went down to the lobby to find 'Henri' and other men standing there with pistols. She was marched back upstairs with a pistol in her back.

According to Peter Churchill, his room was burst into by 'Henri' and a contingent of Alpini, Italian soldiers who were controlling that part of south-east France. Some in the French Resistance say they were still in bed together when they were captured. During the commotion, Odette managed to hide Peter's wallet – containing telephone numbers of some of his contacts and 70,000 francs – and pack some warm clothes. He had previously passed on half a dozen new radio crystals, half a million francs, two Belgian automatics, a Sten gun, 200 blank identity cards and dozens of ration books. Dressed in her one and only dark-grey suit, with silk stockings and square-toed shoes, she was taken to an Italian prison.

Three weeks later they were taken by train to Paris. During the journey she managed to share a few moments of conversation with Peter and pass him her tiny crucifix. Incarcerated in Frèsnes Prison, she managed to save the fresh bread she was given, only eating the stale so that she might pass on bits when she saw Peter on the occasions 'Henri' allowed them to be together. There were days when she was taken to Avenue Foch, the Gestapo headquarters, for interrogation. Dr Mark Baldwin, an SOE historian, reported that, to protect Peter, Odette insisted to her interrogators that she was the organiser of the group.

Churchill recalled in his third book, *Spirit in the Cage*, how on one occasion, when their convoy had just arrived back from an interrogation session,

> I found myself in a large open pen where the whole group was herded together under the eye of a guard whilst waiting for the next move. I slipped up close to Odette and as she spoke to me with her back to the sentry, a girl I had never seen before, but who was patently English to her finger tips, stood between me and the guard so that he would not see my mouth moving. Despite my anxiety not to miss a second of this golden opportunity to speak with Odette, I was nevertheless instinctively conscious of this girl's unselfish act which included a delicacy of feeling that made her turn about and face the German so as not to butt in on our privacy. I could not imagine what this refined creature with reddish hair was doing in our midst.
>
> 'Who is she?' I asked Odette.
>
> 'Diana Rowden,' she replied. '... One of us.'

To occupy herself while confined, Odette worked in the sewing-room. While there, as the guards were wearing a new style of Africa Korps cap, in the ones she made, on the piece of cardboard that stiffened the peak, she wrote the words 'Made in England'. She jammed her scissors into the holes of the power point to blow the fuses and cut the electric wires so that she could get the guards to fetch the most hungry prisoners on the pretext that they were electricians and they could be given extra food while 'on the job'. Spare cloth she saved to make children's toys like rabbits and dolls.

In his *Spirit in the Cage*, Peter said that

> her moral courage and fearlessness were like a fountain of strength upon which I was to draw on many a future occasion of black despair ... Odette's morale was sky-high. It was where she had put it and maintained it through her own optimistic personality, and it had devolved on other prisoners and guards alike. I began to understand what Paul Steinert meant by the regard in which he said she was held. But what I did not and could not understand was the principal reason for these words, since neither he, nor Odette, nor Henri ever told me of

the sufferings she had undergone, for it was her intention that I should never know and she had sworn those who knew to silence.

In Elizabeth Nicholas' book *Death Be Not Proud*, she claims that Bleicher penetrated a number of the 'F' Section SOE Resistance groups. As a result, not all the drops from Tempsford went as planned. She believes that the first vital penetration of SOE was in autumn 1941 by Mathilde Carré. Termed affectionately by Bleicher as 'La Chatte' because she often curled up contentedly in large armchairs, Carré was a member of Inter-Allied, a very early Resistance group founded by some Polish groups stranded in France after 1940. She was arrested but, unwilling to accept life in prison, was seduced into becoming Bleicher's mistress. He had her installed in an establishment called 'The Cattery', where she continued to work her wireless, sending German-inspired messages to London.

Rita Kramer's *Flames in the Field* details the penetration and deception, the double and triple crossing that was going on on both sides. She explained how, following the Gestapo's successful penetration of the Dutch Resistance, the head of Netherlands Section sent, to the person he thought was his agent, contact details of a PROSPER agent in Paris who would help Dutch agents to escape through France. With this information the Germans were then able to send a double agent to penetrate PROSPER and capture numerous radios and their operators. Those men and women who succumbed to German persuasion allowed the Nazis to play the same game with Baker Street.

Pretending that she was Peter's wife and saying that he was Winston Churchill's nephew may have kept her alive. Tickell claims that, during Odette's interrogation, one of the assistants

> began leisurely to unbutton her blouse. She said, 'I resent your hands on me or on my clothes. If you tell me what to do and release your hands on me, I will do it.' 'As you wish, unbutton your blouse.' Having already been burnt by a hot poker on her spine, she was then told to take off her stockings and her toenails were extracted. 'To be tortured by this clean, soap-smelling, scented Nordic was one thing. To be touched by his hands was another.' Before her fingernails were removed, a higher ranking officer stopped the interrogation, but she was warned, 'If you speak about what has happened to a living soul, you will be brought here again and worse things will happen to you.' [Though] she had kept silent, she was filled with sickness and fear for she had heard of some of the other things that the Gestapo could do to women's bodies.

She was said to have had fourteen interrogations, during which she refused to give any information about her friends.

I could have told them what they wanted to know, just like that. They wanted to know where our radio operator was; they wanted to know where another British agent who had arrived some time before had been to, and now was. I'm not brave or courageous, I just make up my own mind about certain things, and when this started, this treatment of me, I thought, 'There must be a breaking point.' Even if in your own mind you don't want to break, physically you're bound to break after a certain time. But I thought, if I can survive the next minute without breaking, this is another minute of life, and I can feel that way instead of thinking of what's going to happen in half an hour's time, when having torn out my toenails they're going to start on my fingers.

Bleicher told her that, if she was prepared to work for him as a double agent, she would be well treated. When she refused, she was told that she was condemned to death as a British spy. Never knowing when the execution was to take place, every time the door of her cell was opened, she expected the worst.

On Armistice day, when I had been in prison since April, at ten o'clock in the evening I was taken out of my cell and taken down to the courtyard of the prison. There was a car waiting with two men in uniform and the man who tortured me, who was not in uniform, said, 'Well, as you are so devoted to your country, I thought you'd like to go to the Arc de Triomphe on 11 November and see the German guard standing there.' We went, believe it or not, round and round the Arc de Triomphe. I said to him, 'You like what you are doing, the job you are doing. You are a sick man. You like doing this.'

To keep up appearances she used margarine as face cream, turned up the hem of her prison skirt an inch every day so as not to let the worn part show, and used rags from her stockings every night to act as rollers in her hair. Interviewed by J. Pattinson about her time in concentration camp, she said, 'I used to put them on every evening religiously in case they would fetch me the next morning to put me to death. I wasn't going to be seen going to my death without my curls.' Machine-gun turrets, search lights, Alsatian dogs and electric wires surrounded the compound, thereby limiting any chance of escape. In Mavis Nicholson's *What Did You Do In The War, Mummy?*, Odette admitted that during her solitary confinement she visualised the routine domestic chores undertaken by wives and mothers and imagined making clothes and decorating the rooms of her three daughters.

I imagined what I wanted them to wear, then I would get the pattern, then the material, lay it out, cut it out and stitch it. Every single stitch I'd sew until it was all finished. Then I would refurnish all the houses of people I'd known, starting with walls, carpets, curtains.

On 12 May 1944, she was collected in a van, taken to a beautifully decorated room in Avenue Foch, and locked in with seven ill and miserable-looking women, whom she discovered were SOE agents. Provided with cigarettes and tea and milk in nice China cups, they were allowed to chat. No doubt the room was bugged. From there they were taken by train to Karlsruhe civilian prison. Not allowed to be together, they shared a cell with two or three German women prisoners, including anti-Nazi activists, black marketeers and prostitutes.

On 18 July 1944, she was put on one of the 'death trains' and sent first to Frankfurt, then Halle, and finally to Ravensbrück concentration camp, eighty kilometres north of Berlin. Gleeson reported that on the way, one of the guards thumped her hard in the mouth, saying 'I give you that for Winston Churchill – with my compliments'.

Ravensbrück was a forced labour camp where medical experiments, like testing gangrene injections, were undertaken. Her underground cell, where she was again kept in solitary confinement for three months, was within earshot of the execution yard. When the guards switched the light on to bring her rations, it blinded her. She was given a cup of watery ersatz coffee and a slice of black bread, later a bowl of thin soup made from unwashed vegetable scraps, and lastly another coffee. During the hot August days the central heating was turned on full blast. Depending on the moods of her sadistic guards, she was starved and subjected to extremes of light, dark, heat and cold. Although burnt on her back, she never broke her heroic silence.

As the Allies approached Berlin, Fritz Sühren, the commandant of the largest women's camp ever known, believing Odette's story that she was the niece by marriage to Winston Churchill and Geneviève de Gaulle was the niece of the French president, drove them in his white limousine as hostages to the American lines to give himself up. It was 29 April 1945. Tania Szabó, in her book *Young, Brave and Beautiful*, an account of her mother's life, tells how Geneviève, ill with pleurisy, described Odette as a 'terribly gaunt woman who seemed very old. A few stray hairs had grown again on her shaven head.' Both were still in their twenties.

When Sühren told the Americans that Odette was a relation of Winston Churchill and that she had been a prisoner, she told them Sühren was the commandant of Ravensbrück. He was arrested and, although a physical and nervous wreck, she managed to seize his Walther PPK pistol and returned to England with it. Along with two dolls she made out of scraps of material, it can be seen on display at the Imperial War Museum.

Speaking to the Museum in 1986, Odette described her first night of freedom from the camp.

The first night of my release was unforgettable. It was a glorious night, full of stars and very cold. The Americans wanted to find me a bed for the night but I preferred to sit in the car. It was so long since I had seen the night sky.[20]

When she returned to England, reunited with her daughters, she learned that her husband had died whilst she was in prison. She was awarded the MBE in 1945 and in 1946, the first woman to be awarded the George Cross by King George VI. De Gaulle's new government awarded her the *Chevalier de la Légion d'Honneur*. In 1947 she married Peter Churchill and following their divorce in 1956, she married George Hallowes the same year. She died on 13 March 1995.

There have been disputes and debates about the veracity of her accounts, with Foot suggesting that her stories about being tortured were fabricated to sensationalise her story. Odette claimed to have made these statements, including identifying double agents in F Section, but the relevant pages in her personnel file are missing. Either she made it up or the pages were removed. In Kate Vigurs' thesis, she provides a fascinating analysis of the post-war accounts of Odette's and other agents' biographies and autobiographies as well as their coverage in newspapers, in films and on television.[21]

Mary Herbert

The next woman to be sent was Mary Herbert, born in Ireland on 1 October 1903, the youngest daughter of Brigadier Edmund Herbert of Moynes Court, Chepstow. After attending the Slade School of art, she studied at London University and was fluent in German, Spanish, Italian and French. She added Arabic at the University of Cairo and Russian after the war.

Known to her friends as Maureen, Escott described how, in the 1920s and 30s, she worked as an escort for children at Farm Schools in Australia and then in passport control at the British embassy in Warsaw. When she returned to England, she worked in the Air Ministry as a civilian translator in the Intelligence section and joined the WAAF in September 1941 and was stationed at RAF Innsworth. In fact, she was the first WAAF to volunteer for SOE work in March 1942, with a Section Officer commission pre-dated to 15 January 1941.

In Escott's *The Heroines of SOE*, she included a quotation from Claudine Pappe, a relative: 'Mary was a tall, slender, fair-haired woman, who was naturally courteous and considerate of other people, generous and trusting, and in some ways naïve. She was attractive with an engaging smile, made and kept friends easily and her knowledge of art, literature and languages made her an interesting companion.'

After training with Odette Sansom, Lise de Baissac and Jacqueline Nearne at Beaulieu – the second batch of female agents – thirty-nine-year-old Mary,

'1.7 metres tall, slim, with short fair hair, pale face and inconspicuous' was taken to a flying boat in Plymouth harbour. The flight was cancelled at the last minute so, two days later, she, Marie-Thérèse le Chêne, Odette Sansom, Marcus Bloom and George Starr, were taken by submarine to Gibraltar. Starr was to become the organiser of the WHEELWRIGHT network in south-west France, with Bloom as his wireless operator. According to Gleeson, the flying boat took her to Gibraltar but the felucca didn't appear so they were returned to London to wait. When she went back a few weeks later, it was by submarine.

On 31 October 1942, they were landed by felucca at Port-Miou, between Marseille and Toulon, from where Mary had to make her own way by train, bus and bike to Bordeaux. Using the cover name Madame Marie-Louise Vernier, and codenamed 'Claudine', and sometimes 'Mariel', she waited until the curfew was lifted and caught the train to Tarbes and from there towards Bordeaux. Nervous, despite having cleverly forged identity papers, on 10 November she illegally crossed the demarcation line between the Free Zone and the Occupied Zone. The following day the Germans took over the south of France, following the Allies landing in North Africa.

In December 1941, earlier than expected, she met her organiser, Claude de Baissac, in Bordeaux and started work as his courier. Escott commented:

> Mary was probably not what Claude had been expecting. She was well educated with training in art and a degree, had travelled widely and like Claude, was of a very good family. She was tall, slim and fair-haired, but at 39, four years older than he. Apart from being highly intelligent and sincerely religious, she had one useful characteristic born from experience, in that she could merge into a crowd without attracting attention, an enormous asset for an agent who always wanted to be inconspicuous. However, her peculiar status in a small mostly male circle, combined with her special closeness to her chief, and being the willing recipient of the compliments and courtesies paid by all true Frenchmen to any female, brought her more vividly to life in the coming year.

As courier for the SCIENTIST network, she carried messages, documents, money and radio parts. She also acted as post box for de Baissac, located safe houses, identified potential recruits and helped escaped prisoners and downed aircrews down the escape line to the Pyrénées. In her dealings with Claude, she was very security conscious, never talking to him when he was talking to someone she did not recognise. Her network successfully attacked German positions in and around Bordeaux, shattering the radio station at Quatre Pavillions from which Admiral Dönitz communicated with his U-Boat fleets out in the Atlantic. The Luftwaffe airfields near Marignac were crippled and the anti-aircraft batteries and radar establishment at Deux Potteaux were put out of action when the power station at Belin was blown up. This was timed to sour German-Spanish negotiations over trains running between Spain and Bordeaux. The cutting of railway lines, blowing up of road bridges and bringing down of telephone lines made the Gestapo even keener to find and punish the perpetrators.

Mary's travels brought her into contact with her boss's sister, Lise de Baissac, who organised the ARTIST network in Poitiers. Contrary to all the security rules, they became close friends. On one of her visits to Paris, she successfully located Francis Suttill and returned with a replacement transmitter for her organiser.

As the size of the PROSPER and the SCIENTIST networks grew, there was the fear of infiltrators and double agents. As she had been in the field for about a year, the SOE thought she should be Lysandered back with Claude but, as his sister Lise was in great danger of being arrested, she went instead of Mary. In June 1943 the Gestapo swooped. André Grandclément, Claude's replacement, had succumbed under pressure to collaborate with the Germans, evening showing them the location of arms caches. Many hundreds were arrested and, under torture, some supplied vital information. 300 were killed. One of Mary's comrades had been caught with a list of all the members' addresses. When Mary heard about this, she changed her disguise, moved to a new apartment, and started using a new identity card.

When she learned that it was too dangerous for Claude to return, she was left to hold together what was left of his network. She was also very concerned because, over the time she had spent with him, their relationship deepened and, as far as my research has revealed, she was the only agent to become pregnant. According to Gleeson, Claude told HQ that he was going to marry Mary and asked if they would put the marriage banns up in an English church. This was done and they got married and had a honeymoon under the eyes of the Gestapo. According to Escott, they did not marry until Mary was back in England.

Inconsolable at being separated, she was in no fit state to continue her clandestine work. Robert Landes, the replacement organiser, arranged accommodation for her at a private nursing home in La Valence, a Bordeaux suburb, and provided her with enough money to meet her needs, ensuring she cut all links with the Resistance.

A request to HQ arrived asking for the right kind of gear to be dropped. The FANYs at Thame Park took to their knitting needles, Vera Atkins visited the right kind of shops, and a container filled with nappies, vests, tiny socks, cardigans, gripe water, safety pins and other baby items of varying colour and sizes was dropped to her reception committee.

Baby Claudine was born by Caesarean operation in early December 1943. Without telling anyone, Mary slipped away and hid in the apartment of her 'sister-in-law' in Poitiers. Although being a mother halted Mary's clandestine activity, it didn't stop the Gestapo arresting her and all the other residents in the apartment building on 18 February 1944. When they found her in bed nursing her baby, they asked her if she was Madame Brisse, Lise's cover name. When she denied it, they asked her if she knew her whereabouts. She did not know.

Telling her that she would have to answer other questions, she had to leave baby Claudine with her maid. While Mary was in prison, the baby was taken and looked after by French Social Services. In her debrief after the war she made no mention of physical torture but commented that she was put in solitary confinement for looking out of the window. There was no bed, just a stone slab with no blankets or chair. After being there for a day, she said she felt very ill. Under interrogation, she kept to her cover story when questioned about her life history and her relationship with Lise. When shown photographs and asked to name people in them, she claimed that did not recognise any of them. Her queer accent, she explained, was due to fact that she was visiting from Alexandria in Egypt and that speaking a mix of Arabic, Italian, Spanish, English and French was enough to upset anyone's pronunciation. She didn't know the woman who was in the apartment before her and argued with them that a woman with a baby was hardly likely to be a British agent.

She was released on 9 April 1944, Easter Sunday, for lack of evidence after two months. She was told that she would be re-arrested if she spoke to anyone about what she had seen or what questions she had been asked. Her belongings were returned, except a ring, which they claimed they had misplaced. She returned for it the following day and her interrogators apologised. After arguing with the nuns at the orphanage that she had been wrongfully arrested, she was reunited with her daughter and hid in a small country house near Poitiers. There she began a new life with her daughter.

By September 1944 Bordeaux had been liberated. Lise and Claude were now free of their SOE responsibilities, so with Buckmaster's permission, borrowed a car and went looking for Mary. An accidental acquaintance eventually put them in touch with the family who owned the house where she was staying.

Although they all returned to London and the marriage took place at Corpus Christi Church on 11 November 1944, the relationship did not last. He left her to go to Africa to work with General Koenig and Mary took Claudine to live with her father, initially at Moynes Court, and then in a large country house in the Wye valley. According to Wikipedia, she committed suicide by hanging herself on a crab-apple tree in her garden on 23 January 1983.

Marie Thérèse le Chêne and Madame Petit

Marie-Thérèse was born in Sedan in the Ardennes on 20 April 1890, the eldest of three children. She grew up in France but moved to London when she married Henri le Chêne, a British hotel manager. When war broke out, they were both recruited by the SOE and Marie-Thérèse attended the first women's training courses before being landed by felucca on 31 October 1942.

Her original mission was to join her husband's PLANE network in Lyon and act as his courier. Using a new identity as Madame Marie-Thérèse Ragot and codenamed 'Adèle', she made her way to the capital of Vichy France. Virginia Hall had found her a safe house on the outskirts of the city but, as the Germans took over what had been the Free Zone and flooded Lyon with troops and wireless detection units, many in the Resistance had to change plans.

Henri had been dropped in April 1942 and had built up an extensive network between Périgueux and Clermont-Ferrand. He concentrated on sabotage and propaganda and had acquired a large number of women between fifty and sixty to act as his couriers. At that age, he considered them less conspicuous. Escott commented that when he learned that his wife was being sent to help him, he was reported to have been displeased. He was later reported to have said that he joined the SOE to get away from his wife but that she had followed him into it.

Her new role was distributing anti-German leaflets and tracts and taking bags and parcels of messages. She spent a lot of time travelling by train, sometimes as far south as Marseille, where she developed links with an escape line and made contacts in the CARTE network in Cannes, Toulon and Antibes. Passing through Clermont-Ferrand, she watched the Michelin Rubber Works, where workers sympathetic to the Resistance were deliberately producing inferior tyres which needed more regular replacement as well as distributing her propaganda leaflets. Building in obsolescence guaranteed them work and reduced the chances of them being sent on forced labour in Germany.

Her work in the wooded hills and valleys of the Dordogne was more pleasurable. There was a good DZ, drop zone, near Domme, which supplied much of the local Resistance's arms and ammunition. As the hills were riddled with caves, they proved invaluable to hiding supplies until they were needed for D-Day.

In Lyon, railway workers distributed her leaflets in the marshalling yards and engine works as well as on the trains themselves. On a trip to distribute tracts in Paris, she visited her sister-in-law who expressed surprise to see a small, grey-haired, determined old woman with a market basket on her arm. Marie-Thérèse expressed surprise that Jews and Communists, whilst not agreeing with the propaganda of her leaflets, were prepared to put aside differences to ensure the liberation of France.

In December 1942, she learned that Pierre le Chêne, her brother-in-law, who had also been recruited into the SOE, had been parachuted after Henri to work as a wireless operator. Through her contacts in Robert Boiteux's SPRUCE network, she learned that he had been captured with his set. Arrests followed and Henri, concerned when members of his network started being arrested in January 1943, decided to cease operations and flee to England.

Marie-Thérèse, exhausted by the strain, was unable to escape over the Pyrénées with Henri, so he found her a safe house with good friends where she could recuperate. When she recovered she went to Paris to see if she could arrange a Lysander pick-up. Henri Déricourt, SOE's Air Liaison Officer, promised to let her know when one became available. Returning to Lyon, she met Robert Boiteux, who had taken over the SPRUCE network, and asked if she could do some courier work for him. She had useful contacts and knew the area well. After undertaking sabotage work on the local railway and canal, Boiteux asked her to arrange a flight back to England for all the agents in his network. This required a Hudson pick-up. Once she located a suitable landing string, she arranged for the co-ordinates to be sent to London.

After the nine o'clock news on 19 August 1943, a message was included in the *messages personnels*, which indicated their flight was on. All ten assembled on a field north-east of Angers, about one kilometre south-east of the village of Soucelles, where they had to avoid a large herd of bullocks that stampeded past them in the mist when the plane arrived. Marie-Thérèse and her companions were safely returned to England the following morning, to be welcomed by a breakfast of bacon and two eggs. Reunited with her husband, who had returned to England safely after crossing the Pyrénées, she learned that her brother-in-law survived imprisonment.

'Angela'

Sometime in the autumn of 1942, one of 161 Squadron's pilots flew eighteen-year-old Derrick Baynham and a younger FANY wireless operator/courier out of Tangmere to a landing strip in the unoccupied zone of France, near Saumur, south of the Loire. Intriguingly, Derrick's name has not appeared in the mainstream SOE literature and neither has that of his accomplice. According to his obituary in the *Daily Telegraph*, he had been awarded the George Medal for bravery when he was only seventeen. Fifty years later, in his short pamphlet-style memoir of his recruitment, training and SOE mission, entitled *'Never Volunteer' Said My Dad*, he referred to her as Angel but admitted towards the end that many names he used were fictitious to protect their identities. They met at Thame Park, one of the SOE's country houses, where they had intensive wireless training courses.

The previous day a young FANY called Angela had come up to me in a very anxious state saying that she had answered an advert for a bilingual secretary, and was now being trained as a wireless operator in Morse, and in various subversive activities. She had no idea of what she was being trained for. I told her that I had no idea either. I did not mention the German Uniforms in the QM Stores ...

We were then moved to a similar country house – Chicheley Manor – near Newport Pagnell. Here we had further wireless training, including setting up various Spy sets in the nearby country and transmitting back to base, using one time pad codes ...

I was told to choose a Wireless trained courier to go with me. This was because as a man it would be difficult for me to move around without being noticed, and although my French was reasonable, it would not have fooled a French Gendarme for long. I decided to ask Angela, as she had been educated in France, and her morse was brilliant. Also I had grown rather fond of her, which seemed to be mutual. Not a very professional approach, but she readily agreed, and I was given permission to brief her on the details of my mission, or at least the part of it that would affect her.

Later that day I began to have misgivings. She was not eighteen yet and would have been described in my day as 'stunning'. It was certainly a very dangerous mission and the chances of getting back to UK were evens at best. I suggested that she talked it over with the Senior FANY, and postpone her decision until the following day. She said that she would not change her mind, but would do as I said. The following morning the Senior FANY asked to see me in her office. She said that she had told Angela that she would be in good hands, and after all that is what we had been trained for. If she wanted to change her mind, she could be a UK Operator and nobody would ever blame her. She then said that Angela was quite sure of herself, and trusted that I would look after her and not get her into any trouble. I replied that we were both very well trained and would know what to do. She said 'That's not what I meant' and she had the courtesy to blush!!!

I went off to find Angela, and thanked her for her confidence in me. She threw her arms around my neck, kissed me, and said that she was quite sure that we would be lucky. A bit overcome, I said that we should not rely on luck but on our training ...

We were to fly in a Westland Lysander by night from RAF Tangmere in a few days' time. We were then kitted up in civilian clothes, but something had to be done about Angela's striking good looks. Such treatment was deemed unnecessary for me!! When she reappeared some hours later with a schoolgirl's haircut she looked about fifteen at the most, and would have been classified in the Army as 'Jail Bait'.[22]

Their mission was to report to Baron Philippe de Vomécourt's VENTRILOQUIST network operating around Limoges and find out what had happened to three missing agents; to investigate if a wireless operator who had included errors in his messages was being forced to send under duress; to see if there was an informer in the circuit and to eliminate him or to arrange his elimination; to spot new talent in France to be returned to UK by Lysander for training; to 'recce' and report on new small industrial enterprises being relocated from cities to make weapons components; and to plant bogus information to entrap informers.

Things didn't go quite according to plan. When they landed, the expected agent they were supposed to meet had already been arrested.

That night we took it in turns to keep awake with torches at the ready, guns loaded. When my turn to be awake came, around 3 a.m., Angela woke me up. I could see that she had little tears running down her cheeks, she apologised and said that she was cold and frightened. I said cheerfully I hope, 'you need not apologise – I am not too happy myself – so join the club'. I wiped her tears away and stroked her poor shorn hair until she drifted off to sleep. In fact there were a number of options available to us, but I would discuss them with her when we were both awake. I suddenly remembered that we both had a half bottle of Navy rum with our goodies. What better time as I thought it must be the 'Dog Watch'. Life was not so bad after all!

Despite help from the local farmer and his wife, they didn't manage to make contact with VENTRILOQUIST and only narrowly escaped capture by the Milice, the Vichy government's security police. While Derrick set up his radio in a pigsty, Angela went to the local market with a message. Suddenly,

I heard a noise behind me. I thought that it was Angel – it was a member of the Milice holding a pistol in my direction. I had made an elementary mistake; I could not reach my own weapon! He told me to stand up and keep my hands in the air. Suddenly, there was a loud shot, I thought at first that I had been hit, but it was he who folded up and fell to the ground. Then in tripped Angel as I was about to finish him off. 'Don't fire' she said, 'there is another one and you might alert him'. In fact he was already dead. She appeared to be quite pleased with herself; and told me that I was supposed to be looking after her, and in future she would be my Nanny. She then went on to say that she saw a van arrive, which was parked in the farmyard. There were two Milice in it, one of whom was still sitting in the front reading a paper. The other had gone off to have a look around, first to the copse where we had spent the night and then to the pigsty. She carefully followed him, and when she came to the pigsty, she quickly took in the situation, and shot him through a window.

We had to get rid of the other one. So Angel acted as bait, and lit a small fire, to heat up some water, in full view of the van. The unfortunate occupant had not heard the single shot, and when his accomplice had not appeared back, got out, and looked up on the hillside. He saw Angel about 800 yards away, and set off to investigate. As he approached Angel, I was hidden behind a hedge about 15 yards away and shot him before he had even had time to say anything. All this might seem to be rather cold-blooded, but we could not take prisoners, these were the rules of the game in SOE. We carried him up to the pigsty, and laid him out next to the first victim, I went through their papers and found that their names were those of two of the worst bullying Vichy collaborators in the Town, with a history of arrests and shootings.

When the bodies were found, a search of the surrounding area ensued, which discovered the hidden radio set they had brought with them. The locals told them that two men were keeping watch, waiting for their return. Rather than killing these men, Baynham decided to knock them out for twelve hours with an injection. He claimed this had been supplied by the RSPCA and that he had been a fully paid-up member ever since.

I beckoned Angel to come up by my side, and checked that her pistol safety catch was not on. We slid forwards on our stomachs until we were almost up to the spot where I had seen them on my morning recce. I suddenly recognised two bodies lying only a few feet ahead – my heart was pounding – I nudged Angel who was wide eyed with anticipation before the penny dropped. They were both asleep, and their weapons were lying on the grass. I stood up over them gun in hand, and told Angel to quietly wake them, up, but not to shoot unless I did. As they woke up and realised their predicament I made them lie face down, limbs outstretched. They pleaded for their lives as Angel frisked them for any arms – they both had pistols which Angel removed. I was pretty sure that they had been drinking but their panic soon brought them around. I called up the two helpers and supervised the tying up operation which was probably overdone, even to the extent of attaching lines to their feet and wrists between two separate tree trunks so that they could not attempt to untie each other. Angel then injected them in the thighs, we assured them that the jab was just to put them asleep for a few hours until they got relieved. We did not gag them, as we did not know how to do it without risk of suffocation. How to tie up people was not on the syllabus in my SOE training!

The tense circumstances of their mission threw them together in a way which led to the inevitable question as to whether they should develop their relationship.

However, when I woke up at about noon she had put her arms around me, pressed her cheeks which were wet with tears against mine while quietly sobbing. I did not quite know what to do – I just asked her to talk to me. She said that as we approached the Milice she had a fear that almost paralysed her. She had felt that we would most certainly be killed, and we would have died without having shared ourselves with each other when we had the chance. I forget what my responses were, but they were to the effect that when we had got through our mission our time would come, and would be all that more precious for waiting. It's hard for me to explain now – I loved and adored Angel – we both expected that we would be caught eventually to be tortured and executed, but maybe we would get back one day to England, marry and have a little family together. The stakes were too high to risk wrecking our future by giving in to immediate satisfactions, Angel had to be my prize when we had accomplished whatever was required of us.

Not long afterwards they moved to Perigeux, where Angel developed a chest infection. Quite seriously ill, Baynham arranged for her to be looked after by Roman Catholic nuns in a convent, where she stayed until 1945. When he returned to England, he was commissioned into the Royal Signals corps and was wounded by a grenade while serving overseas. He was briefly taken prisoner but escaped and was 'Mentioned in Dispatches', a military award for gallantry. When he returned to England after the war he made enquiries after Angel, only to discover that she had managed to get back, had married and had two children. He kept her identity secret even on his deathbed in 1999.

3

Sabotage Operations Begin in Earnest:
January 1943 to October 1943

As has been mentioned, the SOE had several training schools for their agents but they also had specialist courses for sabotage. Whilst the women sent on these courses were chosen to be mostly wireless operators and couriers, they all underwent paramilitary courses, which involved weapons training and handling explosives. Some had to add training groups of Resistance in blowing up railway tracks, trains, canal gates, electrical installations and factories and delivering weapons, ammunition and what was called *plastique* to the Resistance groups. One was sent into Poland to help with resistance work there. Those women sent into France were to face a much more dangerous environment than those sent in beforehand. Following the Allied landings in North Africa, the Germans took over the Free Zone of southern France in November 1942. Aware that there were agents being infiltrated into France, supplies were being dropped and sabotage being undertaken, the Abwehr, the Nazi Military Intelligence, and the Gestapo stepped up their operations. Agents were captured, some with their sets. Those who succumbed to harsh interrogation and torture, and sometimes financial rewards, agreed to talk and some agreed to send German-inspired messages back to London. These radio games led a number of agents to be captured by a Gestapo reception committee. They also increased their Direction Finding teams, aiming to locate the wireless transmissions. Offering large rewards for information leading to the arrest of resistance members and foreign agents appealed to some collaborators. Tight security was therefore vitally important for the women about to be sent.

Jacqueline Nearne
Twenty-six-year-old, dark-haired Jacqueline Nearne, a volunteer FANY, was,

according to Clark, the next SOE agent to be flown out of Tempsford and parachuted into France. Details of her life and wartime experiences were published in several accounts of SOE's women agents. Her Anglo-Spanish family moved to Boulogne-sur-Mer in 1923 and later to Nice on the south coast. When war broke out, her brother Frederick went to England and joined the army RAF and the rest of the family moved to Grenoble in the French Alps. Her job involved travelling around the south of France as a sales representative for a firm of office and furniture suppliers. In June 1942, desperate to escape the possible German occupation, Jacqueline carefully planned her and her younger sister Eileen's escape through Spain, Portugal, and Gibraltar to England.

After being debriefed about their experiences, desperate for work, they registered with the Ministry of Labour. Rejected for a job with the Women's Royal Navy Service as she had no experience of driving on the left-hand side of the road or of driving in the blackout, she was invited to an interview by SOE. She was accepted for special duties, given a FANY commission and sent to work in Buckmaster's 'F' Section as a liaison officer with the French Resistance movement. She joined the second group of women to receive paramilitary training with Lise de Baissac, Mary Herbert and Odette Sansom. During her parachute training, she was known as 'Jackie Red Socks' as she had been told not to take British-made socks into France. Buckmaster started his article 'Travelling Saleswoman', an account of Jacqueline's wartime experiences, with the following:

> In a room in a country-house a girl was sitting alone. The blackout curtains were drawn back, and the only light, that of the moon, nearly full and serene in a clear sky, fell upon her face. It was a young and beautiful face, in which courage and steadfastness showed clearly, but a close observer might have noticed traces of stress.
>
> As on previous occasions, she was spending her leave in this country-house. To her hostess she was just a F.A.N.Y. on leave from the daily round of normal and perhaps monotonous duties. But in the girl's mind thought followed quickly upon thought. 'The moon will be full tomorrow night, and the weather should be clear. Shall we take off, and will the flight be successful this time?' Her thoughts returned to those other flights, fraught with danger, when she had set out, strung to concert pitch, to fly over France and descend by parachute upon enemy soil, only to suffer the dreadful anticlimax of the return flight because conditions had proved unfavourable for her descent. That long cold wait in the aircraft, that return to another spell of waiting in England; how many more times must I endure them? Thought ran on unceasing.
>
> It was the winter of 1942, and France was occupied by the Germans. The only convenient way for British liaison officers to get there was by parachute.

And even this way was not, strictly speaking, 'convenient'.

In the early years of the war few aircraft were assigned to special operations of this type, and the weather, especially in winter, was not often suitable for landings by parachute. Liaison officers might have to wait for weeks possibly months, before their hazardous journey could be undertaken. Even then the pilot might well be unable to find the small field perhaps 400 miles (640 km) from his base, where the 'reception committee' flashing feeble torches, awaited his passenger.

False alarms, abortive and dangerous flights menaced by enemy night-fighters and 'flak' were even more unnerving for the passenger, who had his mission before him, than for the crew of the aircraft. We used to reckon that three months waiting or two abortive attempts were about as much as an officer could be asked to endure, unless he or she had particularly strong nerves. But Jacqueline, the girl in the moonlit room, certainly had strong nerves. She had to wait from September until December and make several unsuccessful flights before the night arrived on which she made her parachute descent, yet she remained as calm and collected as one could wish ...

Jacqueline's name was given to me because of her perfect knowledge of French; after a brief interview she was enrolled in the F.A.N.Y., and seconded to my department for special service. She quickly obtained her commission and started training. But her French education and long residence made difficult to her problems which would have been easy for a girl with English upbringing. She became nervy and depressed; whereas at the first interview she had been confident of her ability to go back to France to live an underground life, now the very complexity of her training shook her self-confidence. She became thinner, and was obviously worrying about her ability to take on the job.

It was at this stage that I saw her for the second time. The training authorities had just issued an unfavourable report on her, and I thought that perhaps I had been over-optimistic about her qualifications. I went to see her at the school. There was no doubt about her being worried; but in the course of half an hour's talk she unburdened herself of her worries, and when I realised that her preoccupation was purely with the mechanics of what she was learning, I had no hesitation in advising her to go on with the course. She worked fantastically hard; she was determined to master the theoretical as well as the practical side of the job. That she succeeded is proved by her magnificent record, which owed much to the high standard of security which she maintained throughout her area of operations.

In October 1942 Jacqueline was invited to see Buckmaster who gave her a small present before her flight. It included a necklace, gold watch and a hundred thousand francs, which she put in a cloth belt tied around her waist. Afterwards, she and her organiser, Squadron Leader Maurice

Southgate, were driven up to Tempsford for the flight. Once over the drop zone the pilot reported not seeing the lights of the reception committee so the mission was aborted. Another flight was arranged which was aborted when the fog proved too dense for the pilot to see. On the third attempt there was yet again no reception committee and on the fourth, the aircraft's engines failed to work so they never took off. One imagines that she and Southgate were looked after at Gaynes Park whilst they waited for the next flight and worried about what problems there must have been with the reception committee.

Finally, on 25 January 1943, they were dropped blind, just over a kilometre north of Brioude, in the Massif Central. Buckmaster's article stated that

> During the last and successful flight there came again that tense feeling, those speculations upon the immediate and perilous future. Now they were near the place, and she made the final preparations; the green light indicating that she should leave the aircraft showed; a last contact of friendly hands helping her out of the aircraft, and she was falling ... She thought: 'I must make a good landing, I hope I don't get caught in a tree. Who will be there to meet me? Have the enemy been warned?' She landed, and as she collected herself perceived a shadowy figure approaching. Was it a German? She drew her pistol and waited.
>
> The figure approached, also with drawn pistol, but all was well, and she was welcomed, and taken to safety for food and rest.

According to Gleeson:

> Jacqueline, choosing to go first, jumped and made an excellent landing from five hundred feet. Sitting on the ground she watched the aeroplane turn and begin its journey home. It was a beautiful clear moonlit night. She folded her parachute before starting to look for Maurice when suddenly she saw two silhouettes in the moonlight – one of them was pointing a revolver at her. 'I felt it very unfair to be caught so quickly,' Jacqueline told me. 'I couldn't think what to do next. I just walked up and down trying to ignore the man and thinking to myself what should I say. I had done nothing wrong and my papers were in order – and then the man whispered my name. it was Maurice and the other silhouette was a stump of a tree.'

Southgate's mission was to take over the leadership of a new STATIONER network that stretched from Châteauroux to the foothills of the Pyrénées. Jacqueline must have had her heart in her mouth when, very shortly after landing, he asked a female cyclist the way to Brioude – in English!

It was not a problem and they managed a four-hour walk to the village arriving at 0600 hours. To her amazement, Maurice spoke to the first man she met in English, a mistake which made them both doubly sure it would never happen again.

Once on the train, she sat down in a compartment and suddenly realised she was sitting opposite a German soldier. Pulling out her paper, she ignored him and safely reached Clermont Ferrand.

Codenamed 'Designer', Jacqueline worked a courier between several SOE groups operating around Paris. Her new identity was Madame Josette Norville and her cover was that she was a chemist's sales representative. Escott explained that this allowed her to travel freely everywhere and 'despite being shy, she began to gain confidence. She was small, dark and slight, with a rather chameleon appearance, fitting in unobtrusively wherever she went. Jacqueline's life as a secret agent was filled with constant danger. The threat of being exposed as an SOE agent or being betrayed by a comrade must have created tremendous tension. Despite this, she travelled on long and arduous train journeys to maintain contact with agents, wireless operators and the neighbouring HEADMASTER network run by Sydney Hudson, forming a vital link between several other SOE networks operating in Paris, Clermont-Ferrand, Toulouse, Pau and Poitiers. She also carried spare parts for radios, found drop zones and organised reception committees for newly arrived agents. In Pattinson's book, *Behind Enemy Lines*, she included a transcript from the film *School for Danger* in which Jacqueline starred after the war.

CAT   The police were searching luggage at the station. They made me open my suitcases.
FELIX Gosh – what did you do?
CAT   I tried sex appeal.
FELIX Did it work?
CAT   No, it was a complete flop! I had to open it.
FELIX What about the WT set?
CAT   I told them with a sweet smile that it was an X-ray machine.
FELIX It must have been a very sweet smile for them to have swallowed that!

Part of her work included escorting downed British airmen along the escape line south to the Pyrénées. 'Were they pretty glad to see you?' Buckmaster asked her on her return to England. 'Well yes, but of course they had no idea I was English; I didn't tell them who I was'.[1]

In September 1943, she was joined by Pearl Witherington, who took on similar courier work in her network. Although sabotage was not given high priority, she liaised with Resistance members in their attacks on the aluminium factory at Lannemezan, factories in Limoges, munitions factories in Tarbes and Montluçon, and several small-scale attacks on the Michelin

Rubber Works in Clermont-Ferrand.

As shall be seen later, her sister Eileen was also dropped into France to work as a wireless operator and when Jacqueline learned of her sister's capture, she was told to return to England. Instead, she gave up her seat in the Lysander for a political refugee.

After fifteen months in the field, her life had been one of constant train travel. London eventually became concerned about her health so they arranged for Jacqueline to be picked up by Flight Lieutenant Taylor in a Lysander in April 1944. Chalked on the side were the words 'Jacqueline must come'. She had to leave knowing Eileen was unlikely to get back. Buckmaster told of how,

> In the spring of 1944 we received information that the wife of a well-known and popular French general (who had escaped to England) was actively being sought by the Gestapo. We ordered Jacqueline to get in touch with her, and arrange to bring her out by a Lysander aircraft which would be sent to fetch her. While these arrangements were being made, we learned that Jacqueline herself and another officer were in imminent danger, owing to the arrest of a member of her organisation. Quick action was essential. The operation was scheduled at once, but the problem of space in the aircraft arose. We knew that Jacqueline would not readily consent to leave her post until 'Madame la Générale' was safe. It was therefore necessary to issue a definite order. The way we did this was to chalk on the side of the aircraft an order of priority for the passengers, which the RAF pilot called the 'batting order'. To our regret we had to leave Madame off the list. But all was well, since Jacqueline had arranged for a safe hiding-place for whichever of the women had to be left behind, and we brought Madame to safety a few weeks later. It was as well we did bring Jacqueline first, for a few days later her Chief was arrested and Jacqueline's photograph figured on the notice boards as: 'Wanted. Reward offered for the capture dead or alive of individual known as Jacqueline or Josette.'

After the liberation of Paris, Buckmaster took Jacqueline, dressed in her FANY uniform, back to her old haunts. When they went into a bistro, her old headquarters,

> The manager's face, as he bustled forward to receive the British military visitors, was wreathed in smiles of professional welcome. When he recognised Jacqueline, his surprise was almost pathetic, and although he stoutly protested that he had 'known it all along', his look of incredulous amazement had betrayed him. Jacqueline was immensely popular. Not only has she great beauty and charm, but her sense of comradeship and her kindliness are delightful. She made many friends, whose affection and admiration for Britain

are unbounded. The personal example of a girl like her is worth more than the finest political speeches.

Southgate was one of the lucky few to survive imprisonment at Buchenwald. For his work he was posthumously awarded the MBE and the *Croix de Guerre*. She too was awarded the MBE for her work in France. In 1944 she and Harry Rée, another returned SOE agent, took part in an RAF film unit documentary, *Now It Can Be Told*. It told the story of a man and woman team of F Section agents doing undercover work in France and was released later as *School for Danger*. After the film, Jacqueline went to work in the United Nations' Protocol Section in New York and died in London on 15 August 1982.

Beatrice 'Trix' Terwindt

In Michael Foot's *SOE in the Low Countries*, he mentions three women being sent to Holland and two to Belgium. The first was thirty-one-year-old Beatrice 'Trix' Terwindt. The seventh child of a Belgian mother and a Dutch father who ran a stone quarry, she acquired English, French and some German at an English convent school in Bruges. She worked for some years as an air stewardess for KLM, the Dutch airline, but when Holland was invaded and the Germans closed down civil aviation, she was given a desk-based job.

What sparked her to leave Holland is unknown, but it is possible that she had made acquaintance with people involved in the Pat O'Leary escape line, which helped downed Allied pilots, crews and agents get back to England via Belgium, France and then east into the Swiss Alps or south over the Pyrénées into Spain and then Gibraltar. Accompanied by a young Dutch student, she walked out of Holland, through Belgium and into France in March 1942. While the customs official on the border at St Julian looked the other way, they ran across into Switzerland. Perhaps with the assistance of MI9, the secret organisation supporting the escape routes, she got a flight to Lisbon and from there to England.

There she was introduced to Airey Neave, an intelligence agent with MI9. He had been wounded and arrested at Calais and eventually imprisoned in Colditz Castle. After a daring escape, he managed to get into Switzerland and then along the Comète line through France into Spain and Gibraltar, arriving in England a few months before Trix.

Recognising her potential working with the PAT line, Neave arranged for her to undergo 'F' Section's paramilitary training at Wanborough Manor. After weeks at Beaulieu she underwent parachute training at Ringway. In Neave's autobiography, *Saturday at MI9*, he admitted considering but then rejecting the option of using plastic surgery to reconstruct her facial features. As there were no other volunteers, he escorted her to Tempsford on 13 February 1943, helped her into her parachute harness, and handed her some Dutch guilders and forged nurse's identity papers. He also warned her about two collaborators, Poos and Slagter.

Having overcome her fear of flying, Trix was the first female agent to be dropped into Holland, along with several containers, one of which included her wireless set. Codenamed 'Chicory' and also known as 'Felix', she had the mission of helping support the PAT line in getting agents out of the country. Unbeknownst to her or the pilot, the Germans had arranged everything. They had captured a wireless operator and their set and coerced them to send messages to London, who did not pick up on the missing security codes. So began the *Englandspiel*, whereby the Germans made arrangements for the SOE to send agents, supplies and money straight into their hands.[2]

She jarred herself badly when she landed in fields near Steenwijk, a small farming community about twenty kilometres south-west of Groningen, but was helped by the welcome committee, including Poos and Slagter, who, as it was raining, sheltered her in a nearby barn. The collaborators checked her identity papers, suggested they were inadequate, and recommended she wait until they could supply her with new ones. As she had been unable to make her first rendezvous with one of the genuine Resistance figures, they managed to coax it out of her. According to Foot, they explained that London was often out of date with its addresses and they could not take responsibility for letting her continue with her mission until they had checked it out for her.

Suddenly, someone threw a blanket over her head. Thinking she was having her nerves tested like when she was rudely awoken at Beaulieu and subjected to brutal interrogation 'practices', she didn't resist as forcefully as she had been trained. She was grabbed from behind and handcuffed before she could manage to get her poison pill into her mouth. Taken to the Abwehr headquarters in Driebergen, she was interrogated without a break for four days. According to Neave, she was surprised at how much more her captors knew about the SOE than she did and was perturbed that the Germans couldn't understand why the British had sent a lone girl who evidently was very poorly briefed about her organisation. Apparently, they didn't realise she was from another covert operations department.

She never knew until much later that the wireless set dropped with her was retrieved and used to send messages back to London. C. J. Smit, her rendezvous, and his friend were arrested at the address she gave them in The Hague. They were shot the following year. The plane that dropped her was shot down on its return journey. Given the amount and density of anti-aircraft artillery in the Low Countries, very few planes returned. Orders were issued to shoot at them on their return flight so their passengers and contents could be dropped safely.[3]

Nel Lind, a fellow prisoner, said she had got the impression that the Germans wanted to keep Trix alive. They even gave her a wireless with which she could listen to the BBC while she was in solitary confinement for eighteen months, apart from a brief spell during which they unsuccessfully planted a spy in her cell.

Diet Eman, in her book, *Things We Couldn't Say*, recalls her time in prison when she met Trix who, she said,

> wore a tiny piece of fur round her neck that resembled a (pine) marten. She called it 'Freddy' and sometimes spoke to it and stroked it ... Her eyes seemed kind of wild and nervous, very sunken, and her facial features were pulled tight. She was very anxious.
>
> That night, after the others had gone to sleep, I stayed awake because something inside me told me that this woman was special. Although I'd never met her before, my instincts told me I could trust her, and I knew there was more to her than the little she'd told us. We sat on the floor against the wall, just the two of us, and we talked the whole night while the others were asleep. She told me her story that night in cell 306.
>
> She was from a very well-to-do family, so rich that she didn't have to have a job. Before the war she had studied at university, but she became bored with going to school, she said. Air travel had just begun at that time, and she became one of the KLM airline's first stewardesses. She said that she flew only to challenge herself: she had been deathly afraid of flying, so she challenged herself to get on an airplane by becoming a stewardess, of all things.
>
> When war broke out, she'd made her way to England and was working for the Dutch intelligence service. When she arrived, Queen Wilhelmina invited Beatrix over for tea! It's difficult for Americans to understand loyalty and love for the crown, but I always loved our royal family. That night, when Beatrix told me that she had had tea with the queen, I was nearly overwhelmed with admiration for her!

Eventually she was transferred to Ravensbrück and then Mauthausen concentration camp in Germany, from where she was eventually liberated by American forces on 5 May 1945. The experience ruined her health. Neave's postscript of her story reads:

> She has never indulged in any recrimination and bitterness. She has treated her nightmarish experience as one of the fortunes of war. It was this quiet faith and serenity of spirit which brought admiration from her captors. Thanks to her refusal to talk, she was one of the few survivors of 'Northpole' [one of the German radio games] who escaped death. As she wrote to me afterwards: 'I was an amateur but in war risks have to be taken. I played a game of cat and

mouse with the Gestapo with the only difference that I was caged and the cat was free.'

Trix died on 7 April 1987.

Françine Agazarian

According to SOE records, between 18 March and 17 June 1943, six more women were taken to France by Lysander. Françine Agazarian, a French volunteer FANY, was the first. Born Françoise Andre on 8 May 1913 to French parents, she was working as an English-speaking secretary when France was invaded. According to Escott, in order to get to England, she used a marriage of convenience to a Sergeant in the Signals Corps, who claimed he was an escaped prisoner of war. Arriving in London in September 1941, it transpired he was a bigamist. With the marriage annulled, in late 1942 she married her former fiancé, Jack Agazarian, and followed him into the SOE.

Concerns were expressed about her in her training. In Pattinson's *Behind Enemy Lines*, she mentioned that one of Françine's instructors didn't think highly of her, reporting her as 'temperamental, might blow the gaff in a fit of jealousy, might be indiscreet in a fit of pique, sometimes exhibited temperament and caprice. Moody, jealous and unattractive to men.' She must have impressed others as she completed her training and went out by Lysander on the night of 18/19 March. She landed south of Poitiers, a few kilometres north of Marnay where, with identity papers in the name of Madame Françine Fabre and codenamed 'Marguerite' and 'Lamplighter', she joined her husband Jack. He had been parachuted in on 29 December 1942 with a mission to work as a wireless operator in Francis Suttill's PROSPER network. Her mission was to be a courier with this and the PHYSICIAN networks, passing and collecting information and delivering money, forged documents and weapons to members in the Paris area. According to Escott, it was felt she would work well with her husband despite her frail appearance and temperamental personality. The Spartacus website includes her post-war comment that:

Although in the same network, my husband and I were not working together; as a radio operator he worked alone and transmitted from different locations every day. I was only responsible to Prosper (Francis Suttill) whom we all called Francois. He liked to use me for special errands because, France being my native land, I could get away from difficulties easily enough, particularly when dealing with officialdom. Francois was an outstanding leader, clear-headed, precise, confident. I liked working on his instructions, and I enjoyed the small challenges he was placing in front of me. For instance calling at town halls in various districts of Paris to exchange the network's expired ration cards (manufactured in London) for genuine new ones. Mainly I was delivering his messages to his helpers: in Paris, in villages, or isolated houses in the countryside. From time to time I was also delivering demolition material received from England. And once, with hand-grenades in my shopping bag, I travelled in a train so full that I had to stand against a German NCO. This odd situation was not new to me. I had already experienced it for the first time on the day of my arrival on French soil, when I had to travel by train from Poitiers to Paris. A very full train also. I sat on my small suitcase in the corridor, a uniformed German standing close against me. But, that first time, tied to my waist, under my clothes, was a wide black cloth belt containing bank-notes for Prosper, a number of blank identity cards and a number of ration cards; while tucked into the sleeves of my coat were crystals for Prosper's radio transmitters; the crystals had been skilfully secured to my sleeves by Vera Atkins herself, before my departure from Orchard Court. My .32 revolver and ammunition were in my suitcase. The ludicrousness of the situation somehow eliminated any thoughts of danger. In any case, I believe none of us in the field ever gave one thought to danger. Germans were everywhere, especially in Paris; one absorbed the sight of them and went on with the job of living as ordinarily as possible and applying oneself to one's work. Because I worked alone, the times I liked best were when we could be together, Prosper (Francis Suttill), Denise (Andrée Borrel), Archambaud (Gilbert Norman), Marcel (Jack Agazarian) and I, sitting round a table, while I was decoding radio messages from London; we were always hoping to read the exciting warning to stand by, which would have meant that the liberating invasion from England was imminent.[4]

When Françine got to Paris, she rendezvoused with Julienne Aisner, who had an office on the Champs Élysées. After spending a night in her studio apartment, she moved to another in Rue de Colonel Mol, which Julienne had rented for her. Jack spent time there when he was not transmitting from other safe houses. To prevent the concierge making too many enquiries, she was told that they were escaping a jealous husband. On her travels she grew familiar with the German and French police controls, check-points, stops and searches. Suttill sent her to various *Mairies* to take cleverly forged time-expired ration cards or local papers to exchange them for the real thing.

Gleeson reported how she was very nearly caught by the German's 'Northpole' radio game. Having captured wireless operators and their sets, some were coerced through torture and bribes to collaborate. Messages were then sent through to SOE requesting arms, ammunition, money, the latest wireless sets, money and more agents so that the Germans knew exactly when and where they would arrive. They sent two Gestapo agents pretending to be British down one of the escape lines from Holland, through Belgium into France. When they approached one of the network in Paris, without having their credentials checked, they were given the name of a café near the Sacré Coeur in Montmatre. They were introduced to the Agazarians, Andreé Borrel and two members of the Resistance playing poker. Accepted as genuine agents, they infiltrated their network and arrests followed.

When people started to disappear, arrangements were made for Françine, Jack and some other members of the Resistance to be lifted out. The prospect of being caught and her constant travelling had worn her down. She lost weight and became pale and nervous. Although she felt that she ought to continue her work, the SOE insisted that she return.

On 17 June 1943, when the two Lysanders landed, Diana Rowden, Noor Inayat Khan, Cécile Lefort and Charles Besnard got out. Françine, Jack and three others were safely returned to England where her gallantry was 'Mentioned in Dispatches'. Her husband went back, was captured along with Suttill and Borrel, survived six months of interrogation, torture and solitary confinement and was eventually executed alongside Dietrich Bonhoeffer, the Lutheran pastor, at Flossenburg concentration camp.

When Françine learned of her husband's death she was with a group of FANYs stationed at Paradiso, ME 54, the SOE's forward camp near Brindisi in Italy. From here containers were being dropped into northern Italy, Yugoslavia, Albania and Greece. Margaret Pawley, one of the other FANYs, recalled her out in the gardens of the house they shared, kicking the gravel, trying to come to terms with her loss. Just as the boat passed the Scilly Isles on Françine's return to Blighty, she was asked what she was going to do. Her reply was that she was going back to France to see if she could find out who betrayed her husband.[5]

After the war Françine was Mentioned in Dispatches for her actions in France, as was her husband, who was also posthumously awarded the *Croix de Guerre*. She died in 1999.

Julienne Aisner

There is confusion in the records over the next women sent into France. Hugh Verity refers to landing twenty-eight-year-old Julienne Aisner in his Lysander in March 1943. Other records state it was May. Born in Anglure, near Troyes in 1900, the daughter of a policeman, according to Escott, she grew up to be 'an exceedingly beautiful and attractive woman, small and full of energy with a round face, softly curling hair and large liquid dark eyes.' She married Lieutenant M. Lauler of the US Marine Corps in about 1924 and moved to Miami. A few years after her son was born, her husband was killed in a car crash so, in 1929, she went to live with her parents in Lebanon. When her father retired, the family moved to Hanoi in Vietnam and joined her sister, whose father-in-law owned a chain of cinemas. The tropical climate made Julienne ill so, in 1933, she returned to Paris and worked as a script writer. Two years later she married Robert Aisner and, using her connections in Hanoi, became a partner in a small film company with an office overlooking the Champs-Élysées.

From her windows she witnessed the arrival of German troops, the shooting of hostages and the rounding up of French citizens for work in German factories. When her husband joined the army, she sent her son to live with his aunt in America and, in November 1941, began to help thirty-three-year-old Henri Déricourt find seven safe houses for SOE agents in the PHYSICIAN and FARRIER networks in and around Paris. Slapping a German officer in the face for making improper suggestions led to her being held in Cherche-Midi prison for two months. Divorcing her husband in 1941 left her with the film business, and this cover helped her in welcoming and acclimatizing new agents. She also became Déricourt's mistress.

On 18 March 1943, he sent her to Poitiers for a double Lysander pick-up, and returned with Françine Agazarian, who had been sent to work as a courier. On seeing Jack Agazarian, she arranged to have a chest X-ray retouched to show him as having an ulcer, and acquired a forged hospital certificate for him to ensure that he wasn't picked up for forced labour by the Germans.

Recognising her as an efficient helper, Déricourt arranged for her to be sent to England for SOE training. On 16/17 March, having told her business partner and staff that she was going on a month's holiday, she was picked up by Hugh Verity from a field one kilometre north-east of La Chatre sur-le Loir and forty kilometres north of Tours.

After a month's training to work as a courier in the reformed INVENTOR network, Verity landed her by Lysander at Azay-sur-Cher, near Tours, on 14/15 May. Accompanying her in a double operation was forty-year-old Vera Leigh. Both were described as volunteer FANYs. Verity returned with Suttill.

On getting back to Paris, using a new identity as Madame Marie Clemence, codenamed 'Claire' and, depending on whom she met, 'Jeannette', 'Dominique', 'Eminente', 'Ploye' and 'Compositor', Julienne carried messages between various members of the Resistance in and around Paris. She also worked with Charles Besnard, a barrister in the FARRIER network west of Paris, with whom she developed a relationship. It appears that she was aware of the suspicions about Déricourt being a double or triple agent. Nicholas Bodington, another SOE agent involved with Déricourt, bought the small Bistrot Mas in Place St Michel for her to run. It was to be used as a contact point for agents seeking to escape from France and also to evacuate RAF pilots or Resistance members who needed taking to England. Noor Inayat Khan transmitted from this café when she was evading capture in Paris in August 1943.

One awkward task she had was ensuring that Madame Felix Gouin, the wife of one of General de Gaulle's ministers, was sent to England with all her luggage. On the night of 19 July 1943 she had to hire three velotaxis to take her to the Azay sur Cher drop zone and squeeze her and the luggage into Flight Lieutenant McCairns' Lysander.

Suttill's arrest in August 1943 sent shock waves through numerous Resistance networks but Julienne avoided capture. A number of people suspected Déricourt, so the SOE ordered him to return for questioning. According to Verity, he picked up Déricourt and his wife on 9 February 1944. She had come on a shopping trip to London and was described as short, plump, having brassy hair and travelling in a very expensive-looking fur coat. Déricourt expected to parachute back with her within the week, despite her having had no training nor taken an active part in the war.

He was returned to France, but not until after the war, to stand trial as being a German agent responsible for the arrest, torture and death of numerous French and British agents. He was released through lack of evidence. It is now acknowledged that he was in fact working for MI6 and used his SOE role as a cover. He claimed at his trial that the SOE allowed agents to be captured to distract the Germans' attention from the Allies' invasion plans. There was a rumour that the Germans had paid him four million francs for his information and that, after the war, the plane he was flying over Laos crashed in mysterious circumstances.

At the beginning of March 1944 Julienne received a telegram from London asking her to come back. Just after she received it, the barman at the bistrot in the Rue St Andre des Arts told her that two strange men had come in, used the correct passwords and demanded to see her. They refused to give their names and although rather shabbily dressed, he reported them having an 'air policier' about them. As they were insistent, he told them that the proprietor was ill and couldn't see them.

Julienne noticed people keeping watch on the bistrot. Besnard was convinced that he was being followed. Warned by a colleague that he faced arrest, he went to see Julienne, discussed the problem with her and came to a decision. They would both return to England. However, with Déricourt already gone, she had to get a message through to Buckmaster in London. She went to see André Watt, codenamed Geoffroi, her wireless operator. He encoded her request for an urgent pick up.

When the reply came back, it was positive. Watt had been ordered back as well. She closed the bistrot and told the concierge of her apartment that she was going away for some time and gave instructions that it should be looked after until she returned. Besnard sorted out his affairs and they both waited. Once London sent though the flight details, they agreed to leave Paris and take separate trains to Tours. They were not arrested at the controls at the stations or during the identity checks on the train and, once out of the station, they made their own way to a safe house in the suburbs.

As well as Julienne and Besnard, there were four other passengers who were due to be returned in a double Lysander pick-up. Given the widespread arrests, other agents whose safety London was concerned about were told to leave.

Late in the evening of 5 April, they all made their way out of town to another field, codenamed Grippe, one and a half kilometres east-northeast of Azay sur Cher and about thirteen kilometres southeast of the city. The RAF favoured flat land away from built up areas. There was plenty on both banks of the River Cher.

When Flight Lieutenants W. Taylor and G. Turner landed their Lysanders, four passengers disembarked, including Andrée Studler, an OSS agent sent to prepare for D-Day, and Lilian Rolfe, a wireless operator destined for George Wilkinson's Historian network. Julienne and her colleagues boarded with their luggage and were safely brought back to Tangmere.

Given her close relationship with Dèricourt, there were suspicions that she had been working for the Germans. Interrogated closely during her debrief, she acknowledged that others were concerned that he was a double agent, but she had no evidence of it. She provided details of all those in her network and the contacts she had made.

Three weeks later, she married Besnard and, once Paris was liberated, they returned to settle down there. She died from breast cancer on 15 February 1947. In acknowledgement of her work, she was awarded the King's Medal of Commendation. The citation for her Croix de Guerre stated that, 'For one and a half years she sheltered more than fifty officers British and French being sought by the Gestapo, taking daily risks in cold blood.'[6]

Vera Leigh

According to Escott, Vera Glass was born in Leeds on 17 March 1903 and adopted shortly after birth by Eugène Leigh, a wealthy American racehorse trainer who raced in the United States and in Europe. As his wife was English, Vera grew up in England but became an accomplished horsewoman, practising at his stables in England and at Maisons Laffitte, near Paris. Although she had wanted to become a jockey, after completing her education she worked as a dress designer for the Reboux fashion house in Paris. In 1927, aged twenty-four, she went into partnership with two friends to establish a *'grand maison'* known as Rose Valois in the Place Vendôme. When war broke out, her father's American citizenship enabled her to claim neutrality. She fled south to Lyon and joined her long-term fiancé Charles Saissaux, the managing director of a Portuguese film company. They planned to escape to England but when Vera met Virginia Hall, she ended up working for the Pat O'Leary network, helping downed Allied airmen and escaped prisoners of war to get over the Pyrénées.

When American women in France started being interned in September 1942, she managed to cross into Spain herself but spent several months imprisoned in Miranda de Ebro internment camp. A British embassy official managed to help get her out, into Gibraltar and back to England. There, aged forty, she volunteered to join the SOE, whose trainers described her as 'confident and capable with all weapons ... about the best shot in the party' and 'dead keen'. However, according to Escott, an acquaintance in London described her as 'not very pretty and less of a Parisienne than she believed herself'.

On 14 May 1943, Vera and Julienne Aisner were landed by McCairns' Lysander in a field, codenamed Grippe, near Azay sur Cher, thirteen kilometres south-east of Tours. At three o'clock in the morning, leaving the men to deal with fourteen suitcases, they cycled ten kilometres across fields to the railway station to catch the train to Paris. She stayed first at one of Julienne's apartments in Neuilly-sur-Seine and then at one on Rue Lauriston. Unknown to her, it was near the headquarters of Bony-Lafont, an underground spy gang working for the Germans. Later, she found her own apartment in Rue Pergolese, not far from Avenue Foch, the Gestapo headquarters, and very close to Sergeant Bleicher, the Abwehr investigator.

Using identity papers in the name of Madame Suzanne Chavanne, codenamed 'Simone' and also known as 'Almoner', she worked as Sidney Jones's courier with the INVENTOR network north-west of Paris, and with DONKEYMAN south-east in the Ardennes. Ignoring SOE rules, she met up with her almost every day and they became very friendly. According to Gleeson, Vera knew the risks she was taking on returning to Paris. Many people knew her but she could not be sure whether they were Pétain sympathisers. 'She made no attempt to disguise herself, she remained the well-groomed, fashionable, well-to-do Parisienne of old. In spite of the wartime shortages and restrictions, the ladies of Paris kept up their traditional couture to as high a standard as was possible.'

On one occasion she saw her brother-in-law in the street. Trying to avoid him failed and he recognised her. It transpired that he was running a safe house for Allied airmen as part of an escape line. She decided to help accompany them through the streets of the capital. Unbeknownst to her, the Germans knew of her activities. Although she changed apartments regularly, she, Sidney, and his bodyguard were arrested when they met in the Café Mas in the Place des Ternes in Paris on 30 October 1943. Gleeson reported her spending five months carrying out her duties 'extremely efficiently, bravely and successfully'.

In Foot's *SOE in France*, he reported Bleicher as saying that 'she had lodgings quite near me. For months I would watch her tripping along the pavement in the morning, so busy, so affairée. She was of no interest to me; so long as she kept out of my way; she could play at spies'. Whether this was true, Foot said, was uncertain; but he admitted that 'she did choose apartments right on the Gestapo's doorstep'.

By October 1943 Vera was receiving information suspecting Déricourt of treachery. Warned that she might be arrested, she took no notice. When a doctor's visit diagnosed her as having suspected tuberculosis, she did not turn up for the X-ray examination. On 30 October she was sitting in Café Mas when Bleicher arrived and arrested her and the bodyguard of an SOE agent.

After imprisonment, interrogation and torture at 84 Avenue Foch, the headquarters of the Security Police, she was transferred to Frèsnes prison. The Gestapo appeared to know all about her activities, as she had made too many mistakes. From there she was sent with other 'F' Section women to Karlsruhe jail. On 6 July 1944, forty-one-year-old Vera was sent to Natzweiler-Struthof concentration camp, where she was kept in solitary confinement. Escott mentioned a fellow inmate recalling her calling out for a pillow, and believing she was brutally whipped and probably raped. Shortly after her arrival, she was injected with phenol and placed in the crematorium furnace. A remembrance plaque originally stated that she was murdered, but this was replaced with 'died for her country'. It can be found on the wall of the Holy Trinity church in Maisons Laffitte. Although nominated for the George Cross, the powers that be only awarded her the King's Commendation for Brave Conduct.

Noor Inayat Khan

The next to be sent in were twenty-seven-year-old Noor Inayat Khan, forty-three-year-old Cécile Lefort, twenty-eight-year-old Diana Rowden, and Charles Skipper, in a double Lysander operation. Noor was a particularly beautiful Indian princess whose life story has attracted considerable attention. According to her biographer, Shrabani Basu, her great-great-great-grandfather was Tippoo Sultan, the Tiger of Mysore and last Moghul emperor of southern India. Her father was a popular Sufi mystic who was resident in the Kremlin in Moscow in the early twentieth century and who had married an American woman. Born on 1 January 1914, Noor's privileged background meant that she travelled widely around Europe and was enrolled at the Sorbonne in Paris.

Her name means 'Light of Womanhood'. However, its burden started when her father died when she was thirteen, which meant Noor had to look after a grieving mother and two younger brothers and a sister. She became a children's writer in France and published *The Tales of Jakarta*, stories of the Buddha. When Paris fell to the Germans in 1940, she fled to

England with her mother, sister and brother. The bombing and strafing of lines of innocent evacuees convinced her that the German regime needed to be fought against. Calling herself Nora Baker, she joined the WAAF, where she was trained in wireless operation at Harrogate, telegraphy at Edinburgh, and signal training at Forth and Medhill before being promoted to Aircraftswoman 1st Class at Abingdon. Despite being described as petite, her training officers were impressed by her quiet determination to be sent back as an agent. A deeply spiritual person, she believed she had to resist Nazism and wanted to be in the front line.

Being fluent in French, she was soon spotted by the SOE. Selwyn Jepson, SOE's interviewer and recruiter, commented afterwards:

> I see her very clearly as she was that first afternoon, sitting in front of me in that dingy little room, in a hard kitchen chair on the other side of a bare wooden table. Indeed of them all, and there were many, who did not return, I find myself constantly remembering her with a curious and very personal vividness which outshines the rest... the small, still features, the dark quiet eyes, the soft voice, and the fine spirit glowing in her.[7]

In Jepson's interview file in the Imperial War Museum, he acknowledged questioning her about her loyalty.

> She said, 'My first loyalty is to India.' I said, 'I can understand that.' She said, 'If I had to choose between Britain and India I'd choose India.' I said, 'At the moment we have to choose what you feel about the Germans,' to which she said, 'I loathe the Germans, I want to see them lose this war.' So I said, 'Right, would you like to help to that end?' That was the only time when a loyalty was not directly British.[8]

Early 1943 saw her being posted to the Directorate of Air Intelligence, seconded to the FANY, and then sent for SOE training at Wanborough Manor with Yolande Beekman and Cécile Lefort. One instructor commented that she was 'exceptionally reliable and unselfish'. In Patrick Yarnold's book *Wanborough Manor*, he quotes Lieutenant Tongue describing her as being 'in good physical condition' and Lieutenant Corporal Gordon commenting that 'she is a person for whom I have the greatest admiration ... she is not quick, studious rather than clever. Extremely conscientious'.

After paramilitary training at Arisaig in Scotland, an earlier operation meant that she did not do parachute training. Instead, she was sent to Thame Park, the first woman to attend the SOE's course on radio and signals training. By April 1943 her Morse speed of 18 wpm (sending) and 22 wpm (receiving) was the fastest of any trainee operator. After that, she attended the intensive course at the Beaulieu 'Finishing School'.

During her time off, Noor visited her mother and her friend Jean Overton Fuller, who went on to write her biography. In Rita Kramer's *Flames in the Field*, Noor's escorting officer is reported as saying that Noor found her mock interrogation during her SOE training 'almost unbearable ... she seemed absolutely terrified ... so overwhelmed she nearly lost her voice', and that afterwards, 'she was trembling and quite blanched'.

Foot, in his history of the SOE, quoted one of Beaulieu's staff officer's reports on her that she was 'not overburdened with brains but has worked hard and showed keenness, apart from some dislike of the security side of the course. She has an unstable and temperamental personality and it is very doubtful whether she is really suitable to work in the field'. In the margin beside her report was a note which said she was 'completely unpredictable, too clumsy, too emotional and too scared of handling weapons'.

Buckmaster, the head of SOE's 'F' Section, wrote beside it, 'Nonsense.' As a Sufi Muslim, Noor was a pacifist and it is said that she left her pistol behind when she left.

In Leo Marks's *Between Silk and Cyanide*, he stated that SOE blamed Noor's mystical upbringing for teaching her that the worst sin she could commit was to lie about anything. When she was startled by an unexpected pistol shot she went into a trance, emerging from it to consult the Bible. On one of her exercises while at Beaulieu, she was cycling to a safe house to practise transmitting when a policeman stopped her and asked her what she was doing. She told him that she was training to be a secret agent and showed him her radio to prove it. After a mock interrogation by the Bristol police, the superintendent told her instructor not to waste his time with her. 'If this girl's an agent, I'm Winston Churchill.'

Yvonne Baseden, a fellow trainee, described her as a 'splendid, vague, dreamy creature, far too conspicuous – twice seen, never forgotten', who had 'no sense of security and should never have been sent to France'.[9]

Her friends called her 'Bang Away Lulu' because of the loud clackety-clack of her Morse key tapping – said to be the result of fingers frozen from chilblains. However, Buckmaster was rather taken with her, describing her as a 'sensitive somewhat dreamy girl' whose French would be far more useful to the Resistance in France than it ever could be to the RAF.

SOE records show her as being given a commission as an assistant second officer in the WAAF. Her salary of £350 per year was paid into her bank account quarterly. Squadron records show she was Lysandered out with Jacques Courtard on 21/22 May, but had to return as there was no reception committee.[10] Basu mentions that her file says she was on a 96-hour scheme in Bristol from 19 to 23 May, so the squadron records are out by a few days.

The situation in Paris was increasingly desperate and a new wireless operator was needed urgently. She, Cécile Lefort, and Diana Rowden, other French Section agents, were sent to Chalfont St Giles, probably to Roundwood Park, one of SOE's requisitioned country houses near Chorleywood. Here agents had to go over cover stories, check codes, learn maps of the area where they were to be sent, improve radio skills and await instructions. Noor's cover story was that she was twenty-five-year-old Jeanne-Marie Renier, a children's nurse from Blois who was now a governess looking for a job.

Pierre Raynaud, a French agent, recalled coming across Noor before she left, sitting and poring over a railway timetable. In an interview with Kramer, he told her that Noor had no idea what it was all about, what she was going into. She gave him the impression that she thought that the trains would still be running on the pre-war schedules. In fact, he was convinced that it was intended that she be caught.

On her final visit to her mother, she shocked her by informing her of her engagement to a British officer. The officer was not identified, except it was said that he had a Norwegian mother. Noor had broken an earlier engagement while in France so hoped to marry on her return. Her mother's last words were 'Be Good!'

As she had to wait until the next full moon, she had a session with Marks to improve her coding. In his *Between Silk and Cyanide*, Marks revealed his infatuation with her and how impressed he was with her coding. He insisted she use a transposition key of at least twenty letters. If she used eighteen, he would know that she had been captured.

On 16 June, Vera Atkins drove Noor in what some agents jokingly called 'the hearse', a large station wagon, to RAF Tangmere. According to Basu:

> It was nearly evening by the time they reached Tangmere in Sussex and stopped outside the little ivy-covered cottage just opposite the main gates of the RAF station. It was partly hidden by tall hedges and could hardly be seen from the road. Though it was a summer evening, all the doors and windows were shut and the silence was almost eerie. But as the two women stepped inside, they found the hall was full of smoke and they could hear men's voices.
>
> Tangmere Cottage was a seventeenth-century house with low ceilings and thick walls. On the ground floor were two living rooms and a kitchen. One of the living rooms was used as an operations room for the crew and there was a large map of France on the wall, a table, and a map chest. There was an ordinary telephone line and a scrambler phone line for confidential conversations. The second living room was used as the dining room and had two long trestle tables where agents and pilots often had their supper before they left. Upstairs there were five bedrooms for the pilots.

According to Verity, after a hearty farewell supper, 'when they were upstairs waiting for the bathroom, she spotted a paperback by a pilot's bed. It was called "Remarkable Women". That book will have to be rewritten after these girls have done their stuff. The only sign of nerves she said was in a slightly trembling cigarette'. As a farewell present, Vera gave her a silver bird brooch from her own jacket lapel to give her luck.

It was a double Lysander mission, piloted by Jimmy McCairns and Bunny Rymills. Vera Atkins waved goodbye to Noor, and forty-three-year-old Cécile Lefort, a courier, in the first, and Charles Skepper, the organiser of the MONK circuit, and Diana Rowden, another courier, in the second. Rymills told Verity that 'Cécile looked like a vicar's wife. Her French did not seem to me to be all that hot. Noor Inayat Khan was wearing a green oilskin coat'.

Henri Déricourt was there to welcome them when they landed with their luggage in a field at Le Vieux Briollay, seven kilometres north-east of Angers, near the confluence of the Sarthe and the Loire. Among the five returning passengers were Françine Agazarian and her husband Jack, and three political figures, Pierre Lejeune, Victor Gerson, and Madame Pierre-Bloch, who recalled that while they were waiting they had all had a delicious *poularde à la crème*. Jack Agazarian had been transmitting for twenty-three different agents in Paris and needed to get out before being captured.

It was not as perfect a landing as they had hoped. Raynaud, another SOE agent, commented that a container dropped earlier had exploded on landing, drawing the attention of the authorities to the DZ. The Germans had already captured two Canadian agents and their radio and were playing a radio game back to London that they called 'The Canadian Circuit'. Details of the intrigue, double and triple crossing, can be read in Kramer's *Flames in the Field*.

Skepper and Cécile headed south; Diana headed for Dijon and, codenamed 'Madeleine', Noor first buried the pistol she had been given in case she was attacked on landing and cycled to Angers, the nearest railway station. She was to work with the CINEMA-PHONO Resistance group as Henri Garry's much-needed wireless operator in Paris and the Le Mans area. Escott detailed how, when Noor arrived at Garry's apartment, where he was living with his fiancée, she expected to meet an old lady. She made errors with the passwords so that it was some time before they eventually met. It was an intense time as, within ten days of her arrival, the Gestapo made mass arrests in the Paris Resistance groups she was working with.

Basu details how on several occasions Noor was reprimanded by Madame Balachowsky, the wife of a professor at Grignon Agricultural College, for pouring the milk in everybody's teacup the English way, milk last, toasting bread in front of the fire, and openly handing over a map to an agent in the street. However, needs must and she was allowed to transmit from Gilbert

Norman's set in one of the greenhouses while the gardener kept watch. On another occasion, he picked up her folder containing her security codes from where she had left it on the hall stand by the front door.

In Overton-Fuller's *Madeleine*, she identified further mistakes. Despite being told not to make contact with people who might have recognised her from before the war, she visited her old harp teacher and some old neighbours to see if they might know of any safe houses from where she could transmit. Telling them that she was a British agent and getting a friend to help her encode and decode messages were not considered best practice, neither was leaving messages with her landladies and asking them to give them to whoever called for them. Fellow agent Roland Lepers warned her about leaving her exercise book open with all her messages in it. If the Germans caught her, they would capture the book as well. She ignored him.

While she was at the Agricultural College, two sisters in the Resistance, Germaine and Madeleine Tambour, were arrested. She was probably involved in the negotiations for their release. Suttill offered a million francs to a German colonel, tearing them in half, saying the other half would be handed over when the girls were safe. The women released weren't the Tambour sisters and the Germans demanded a further half million, annoying Suttill. He was arrested on 21 June, leaving Noor on the run with France Antelme, with whom she developed a romantic relationship.

In her citation for the *Croix de Guerre* there is reference to her wounding or killing some Germans when they went to search the Balachowskys' house at Grignons, but Basu found no mention of it in her report.

According to the Spartacus website, for five months she was always on the run, having to change houses as part of her mission to help Allied airmen escape and send back vital information about German troop movements. Between July and October, she is said to have sent over twenty messages in extremely difficult conditions, assisted thirty downed pilots to escape, and ensured that arms and money were delivered to the right people. She pinpointed positions for parachute drops as well as arranging flights to get agents out. When the SOE eventually realised that the PROSPER, CHESTNUT, and BRICKLAYER networks in northern France had completely collapsed, Noor ignored their instruction to return home in the Lysander sent for her.

In August she was the only one of SOE's wireless operators still at liberty in Paris, with 6,000 francs as expenses from Antelme, 1,000 from Déricourt, 40,000 from Garry, as well as 400,000 for Robert Gieules, an administrator at the *Compagnie Générale des Conserves*. There were descriptions of her posted at all the stations and radio detection units were out to pick up her transmissions. When Roland told her that the clothes she wore and the way she walked looked typically English, he bought her new clothes. Dyeing her hair red and then blonde and back to brown eventually made it coarse and stiff but, along with wearing dark glasses, it helped Noor evade capture, as did carrying her set around with her in a violin case and using numerous safe houses.

Colin Gubbins, the head of SOE, said that she occupied 'the principal and most dangerous post in France'. When stopped by the Gestapo as she cycled with her wireless in the front basket, she did not tell them the truth. She persuaded them that it was the latest cinematic projector.

Escott narrated another occasion when she managed to get a German soldier who was living in the same apartment building to help her to loop the aerial wire to the branches of a tree outside without him suspecting her. When he had done it, he bowed politely and was reported as saying, 'At your service Mademoiselle.' Luckily for her, she met an old friend who was working for RF Section. He agreed to drive her round in his car so long as she included some of his messages when she was transmitting.

Knowing the immense risks she was taking, Buckmaster ordered her back to London. She refused until she could be guaranteed a replacement. According to Escott, she sent London a list of the captured agents and was getting increasingly stressed. Running around when she was not cycling meant that she lost weight and began to look as if she was being hunted. 'A feeling of impending disaster drove her to seek the solace of her old house in Suresnes and some former friends, though she warned them of the danger of harbouring her. Once she broke down in tears saying, "I wish I was at home with my mother", and she was deeply touched when one London message ended, "May God bless you".'

Three times Déricourt tried to get her on flights during the August and September moons, but each time they were either cancelled or someone else got the seat. When she was assured there was definitely a Lysander coming in the October moon period she agreed, then went off air for ten days.

Raynaud told Kramer that he has evidence he thinks may indicate that she was ready to leave on one of Henri Déricourt's flights but was left behind at the last moment. When she came back on air on 18 October with a new batch of messages, the transposition key was eighteen letters long. She had been betrayed. According to Marks, Renée Garry, the sister of her circuit leader, Henri, was paid 100,000 francs (£560) for giving Noor's address to the Gestapo. This was only a tenth of what they usually offered for information leading to the arrest of British 'terrorists'. Basu suggests Renée had been in love with Antelme who, since he saw Noor, showed no further interest in her.

Although she agreed to be Lysandered out on 14 October, she was finally arrested the day before at an address that had been cancelled as a safe house before she left England. In a post about German radio games on the Special Operations Executive website, it was claimed she went to a rendezvous with, unbeknownst to her, a German agent, Karl Heldorf, who spoke with an American accent. It appears that the Gestapo knew exactly who she was and what she was doing. Whether she evaded those who tailed her, hoping she had led them to other members of the Resistance, is unknown.

Escott says she fought so viciously, biting the wrists and clawing the eyes of the man at the door that, despite his gun, he needed assistance from Gestapo headquarters. Her wireless, codes, and notebooks were found in her bedside table, which gave the Germans a list of all her wireless messages sent and received. Kramer wrote that she kept them in a school exercise book 'as a result of a misunderstanding on her part of the phrase in her operational orders instructing her to "be extremely careful with the filing of your messages"'. She had ignored the instruction to destroy them once they had been sent. The Gestapo then used this information to send more false messages to London. Despite Marks suspecting she had been arrested, Buckmaster refused to believe it and the radio game was played for three months. Supplies, agents and money were sent straight into the hands of the Germans, 8,572,000 francs to be exact – but probably counterfeit.

Despite interrogation, the former head of the Gestapo in Paris said that Noor never told them a thing. Escott, in her *Twentieth Century Women of Courage*, claims that they never used torture, 'finding that kindness drew more out of her, of which she was unaware since directly questioned she would give no information. Her main interrogator considered her utterly unworldly and truly good'.

She made one escape attempt by claiming that she needed a bath and then climbing out of the fifth-floor window. Her plan was thwarted when she realised that there was no way down without jumping. A later escape attempt failed when she managed to remove the bars from the ceiling window in her cell and got onto the roof. An RAF air raid alerted the guards, who discovered her escape and caught her before she could get down.

Following this, she was held in chains in solitary confinement as she refused not to make any more escape attempts. After six weeks, on 26 November she was transferred to a prison in Pforzheim, the first British female agent to be sent to Germany. She was given a change of clothes once a week and lived on a meagre diet of potato peel or cabbage soup. After surviving almost a year, she was driven to Karlsruhe, where she met Eliane Plewman, Madeleine Damerment and Yolande Beekman in the Gestapo HQ. The four of them were escorted the following morning, first to Stuttgart, then Munich and then to Dachau. On the journey they were free to chat and reminisce.

Heinrich Himmler, the overseer of the Nazi concentration camps, had decreed that all the Führer's enemies had to die, but only after torture, indignity and interrogation 'had drained from them the last scintilla of evidence which should lead to the arrest of the others'.

Basu thought Noor might have been raped the night before her death. All four were locked in separate cells, perhaps to see if they would talk. According to the 'scrapbookpages' website, 'A. F', a former Dutch prisoner, witnessed her execution on 12 September 1944 by Willhelm Ruppert, a sadistic SS guard.

> The SS undressed the girl and she was terribly beaten by Ruppert all over her body. She did not cry, neither said anything. When Ruppert got tired and the girl was a bloody mess he told her then he would shoot her. She had to kneel and the only word she said, before Ruppert shot her from behind through the head, was 'Liberté'. She was 30 years old.[11]

SOE records the date as 13 September. Ruppert was tried for war crimes after the war and executed by the Americans. A square in Noor's home town of Suresnes, Paris, was named in her honour and a blue plaque is placed outside her London residence of 4 Taviton Street. Noor was 'Mentioned in Dispatches', awarded the MBE, the *Croix de Guerre*, and was one of only three wartime women who were given the George Cross. Part of her citation for the honour, quoted on the Spartacus website, reads:

> She refused to abandon what had become the principal and most dangerous post in France, although given the opportunity to return to England, because she did not wish to leave her French comrades without communications, and she hoped also to rebuild her group.

A bust of Noor, sculpted by Karen Newman, was erected in Gordon Square, London, where she used to take a book and sit reading on one of the benches. It was only a few minutes' walk from 4 Taviton Street, where she stayed before being sent on her mission. It is the first for an Asian woman in this country and stands for peace and religious harmony, the principles Noor Inayat Khan believed in.[12]

Diana Rowden

Also landed with Noor was Diana Rowden, one of the female agents featured in Rita Kramer's *Flames in the Field*. Diana, codename 'Paulette', went to work as a courier with John Starr's ACROBAT network in the Jura Mountains of south-east France. Born in London on 31 January 1915, she was a Scot, brought up by an English mother at Cap Ferrat, a villa on the French Riviera. She spent most of her time sailing or running wild with her two brothers. The yacht her mother rented was called *Sans Peur*. When she was thirteen, her mother sent her to boarding school in England, which curtailed her freedom but taught her Spanish and Italian. Escott noted that she was rather stocky, of medium height with red hair and pale complexion. Despite becoming self-contained and withdrawn, she remained poised and sophisticated. When she was seventeen, she enrolled at the Sorbonne, like Noor, and took up a career as a journalist. In the confusion and panic at the outbreak of war, she volunteered for the ambulance corps of the British Expeditionary Force and remained in unoccupied France after the armistice. During the confusion, she lost contact with her mother, who escaped to England in a coal boat. She stayed, helping prisoners of war to escape and make their way back to Britain. In mid-1941, when the authorities became suspicious, she managed to use the same escape route over the Pyrénées into Spain and made her way back to England.

Diana promptly enlisted with the WAAF and served for a time with Air Intelligence in the department of the Chief of Air Staff before being promoted to Intelligence Officer at RAF Moreton-in-Marsh. Following a minor operation, she was sent to Torquay to recuperate in a convalescent home. There she met Squadron Leader William Simpson, a pilot shot down over France who had managed to escape. They struck up a friendship and, as he worked in the French Section of SOE, he arranged for Diana to be interviewed. She impressed them, saying she was 'very anxious to return to France and work against the Germans'. Against her mother's wishes, she joined and, although her training report said she wasn't very agile, she had plenty of courage and was physically quite fit. Her grenade throwing was very good, she was a very good shot and did some excellent stalks.

On landing, Diana was met by Henri Déricourt and, using the cover name Madame Juliette Rondeau, stayed in a dark back-attic room in the Hotel Commerce in Lons-le-Saunier, where the proprietor did not worry about customers' registration. Despite the relatively safe accommodation, Starr thought her accent might give her away so he insisted she moved in with him at the beautiful Chateau Andelot at St Amour, near Switzerland. She travelled constantly by bicycle up and down mountainous roads and forest tracks, locating dropping grounds and landing strips, assisting in reception committees and delivering instructions and taking messages back to Starr. Occasionally she took the train to rendezvous with agents in Marseille, Lyon, Besançon, Montbéliard and Paris. To avoid a German police check of her forged papers, she locked herself in the toilet on one trip and got away with not being searched.

Some of the plastic explosive delivered from Tempsford to the ACROBAT network was used in an attack on the converted Peugeot car factory at Sochaux, near Montbéliard. Harry Rée, known as 'César', worked with

Diana, Starr, and John Young, their Scottish wireless operator, before taking charge of the neighbouring STOCKBROKER network. The factory was now manufacturing aircraft engine parts for the Luftwaffe, and tank turrets, tank engines, and tank tracks for the Wehrmacht. It had been targeted by the RAF in mid-July 1943 but many of the bombs fell on the heavily populated residential area near the railway line, killing hundreds of civilians.

Rée suggested to SOE that precision sabotage would be a more efficient and less risky way of putting the works out of operation. Using an inspired tactic, he contacted Rodolphe Peugeot, the boss who was thought to be sympathetic to the Allied cause, and propositioned him. When the RAF attacked again, there was no way of estimating how much damage they would do. Should he co-operate with the Resistance, a well-placed explosion could cripple production but not destroy the plant. To prove his own credentials, Rée arranged through Diana's messages for the BBC to read out a special *avis* or *message personnel*.

It worked and, in Buckmaster's 1992 obituary in *The Daily Telegraph*, it was said he used photographic evidence of Rée's success to convince 'Bomber' Harris at Bomber Command HQ that the SOE were capable of blowing up targets which Harris had maintained were better left to his air crews.

Rée was Lysandered out with Jacqueline Nearne; they both returned safely and starred as SOE agents Felix and Cat in the 1944 RAF film *Now It Can Be Told*, which detailed some of their operations in France. There was a plan to go with the propaganda film unit to France but the bad weather meant they had to shoot the action in some fields in Bedfordshire, probably close to the airfield as several shots were of RAF Tempsford. There are also shots of Wanborough Manor, where the agents were trained; Brickendonbury Manor, where industrial sabotage lessons were given; Gibraltar Farm, where the agents got their parachutes and final briefing; and planes on the runway at Tempsford Airfield.

Rée recalled in an interview in the Imperial War Museum that:

The first sabotage was about the beginning of November and they decided they'd blow up a whole transformer house where all the electricity came into the factory. About five men were involved, Frenchmen who worked in the factory. They had their pistols in the pockets of their overalls and they had their explosives, plastic blocks with room for a detonator, in their pockets too. There was a wonderful carelessness about the whole thing. They were playing football with the German guards outside the transformer house – somebody had forgotten to get the key – and in playing football one of them dropped his plastic block of explosive and one of the German guards who was playing football pointed it out to him. 'You've dropped something, sir, I think.' He put it back in his pocket. That was absolutely typical. The transformer house blew up and after they went on throughout the whole of the rest of the war fixing these magnetic blocks to machines and enormously reducing production. They also arranged for production figures to be produced which we sent back to London.[13]

Barely a month after Diana's arrival in France, Rée was arrested, betrayed by a double agent. Escott's *Mission Improbable* provides a detailed account of Diana's mission. Knowing that her details would be circulated by the French authorities, she dyed her hair, changed its style, got rid of her old clothes, borrowed more modest clothing, assumed another identity, and moved to work in a bistro and shop in Epy, a small hamlet a few kilometres away. She stayed there for three weeks before joining John Young, the wireless operator, in the sawmill of the Chateau Andelot. On one occasion she was arrested on suspicion of being in the Resistance but managed to convince them she wasn't. The Juif family she was staying with suggested she change her appearance. She changed her codename to Marcelle and pretended that she was their cousin recovering from a serious illness.

Her courier work took her to various groups working in south-east France along the Swiss and Italian frontiers. In the middle of November, Young got a message from London informing him that a new agent, codename 'Benoit', was coming. He arrived on the 18th with instructions hidden in a matchbox and a letter from Young's wife. Diana went with him to pick up his suitcase from the dropping ground at Lons-le-Saunier and had a drink at the local Café Strasbourg, one of the network's mail drops. She took him back to the sawmill, unaware that he was flashing a torch behind him. At about six in the evening, three cars drove up and the doors were flung open just as dinner was being prepared and the Feldgendamerie, the German military police, stormed in. With no time to react, the agents and the family were handcuffed and taken away for questioning. Diana had hidden the wireless crystals in the baby's cot mattress.

The mail drop may have been identified; they could have been followed, but the fake 'Benoit' was said to have returned to the house to search for the wireless set and crystals. In Cookridge's *They Came from the Sky*, he claims that Maugenet, one of the agents dropped on 15/16 November, was captured by the Gestapo shortly after he arrived, and he was then impersonated by an English-speaking French agent who successfully identified Diana.

She was taken initially to Lons police station and put in a cell where she could hear Young being tortured. On about 20 November, she was taken to Avenue Foch, the Gestapo headquarters in Paris. On one occasion whilst she was being interrogated, she was introduced to Starr, her former organiser, apparently free and employed by the Germans. Two weeks later, on 5 December, she was transferred to Frèsnes Prison, where she met Odette and other female SOE prisoners. Less than a month before D-Day she was sent to Karlsruhe and, in early July, taken with Vera Leigh, Andrée Borrel and Sonia Olschanezky to the Natzweiler concentration camp. Around 2200 hours on 6 July 1944, she was called out of her cell, escorted towards a large hut by two guards and told to lie down on a bed for a typhus injection. It was not. It was a massive dose of phenol. Her body was then taken to the crematorium and incinerated. Escott reported that she was wearing a short grey flannel skirt, a finger-tip swagger coat and her short, fair hair was tied up with a tartan ribbon when she was executed.

In honour of her work for the Resistance, Diana was awarded the MBE but, according to Escott, it was withdrawn when it was discovered after the war that her death had pre-dated the award. However, she was 'Mentioned in Dispatches'. The French recognised her better, awarding her the *Chevallier de la Légion d'Honneur* and the *Croix de Guerre*.

Sonia Olschanezky

Although not one of the agents sent out from Tempsford, Sonia Olschanezky has been mentioned as one of the women executed alongside some of SOE's agents. The Spartacus website reveals that Sonia was a German Jew, born in Chemnitz on Christmas Day 1923. Her father ran a lingerie shop in Paris during the 1930s, but Sonia did not want such work. Her ambition was to be a dancer, but she had to work as an au pair. When war broke out, aged only nineteen, she joined one of the Resistance groups in the city as an *agent de liaison*. In June 1942 the Vichy government started implementing the Nazi order to round up the Jews in France. Sonia was held at Drancy internment camp with about 2,000 others waiting for transportation to Germany. Her mother managed to obtain her release after providing false papers suggesting that Sonia had 'economically valuable skills' and after paying a bribe to the appropriate German official.

Codenamed 'Tania' and also known as 'Suzanne Ouvrard', she worked as a courier for the JUGGLER network between Châlons-sur-Marne and their headquarters in the rue Cambon, near the Place de la Concorde. Engaged to Jacques Weil, the second in command, she was promoted to *sous-lieutenant* in November 1943, when the organiser managed to escape into Switzerland. She evaded the round-up of contacts in Chalons-sur-Marne and worked in Paris as well as she could until she was arrested in the Café Soleil d'Or and taken to the Gestapo Headquarters on Avenue Foch on 22 January 1944. After a time in Frèsnes, she was taken to Natzweiler, where she was injected with phenol and cremated with the other women on 6 July. She was only twenty-one.

Cécile Lefort

The first of two Irish agents sent into France was Cécile Lefort. Born Cécile Mackenzie in London in 1900, she worked as a surgeon's receptionist in Paris in the 1920s. In 1925 she married Monsieur Lefort, a respected Parisian doctor who had a large villa outside the village of St Cast, near Dinard in Brittany. There she enjoyed sailing and became an accomplished yachtswoman. When war broke out, all British nationals in France were advised to leave. Accordingly, she left her husband to his practice and returned to England. Despite being over the age limit, she was accepted by the WAAF as a policewoman but, as with Noor, her knowledge of French brought her to the attention of the SOE and she joined in 1943.

Escott mentioned that, while in training, Cécile told a friend about her villa and the friend in turn told a fellow agent in de Gaulle's RF section who was looking for a safe beach to use as an escape route to England. She gave him her antique Irish ring, telling him to show it to her maid at the villa, who would then let him stay. Thus started what became known as the 'Var' escape line, taking Allied airmen back across the Channel when there was a rising tide on moonless nights, when a rowing boat would land and take the thankful passengers to a waiting fishing boat.

Yarnold mentions Lieutenant Tongue as doubting that Cécile had the ability to achieve much and Lieutenant Gordon commenting that she was 'very ladylike and very English'. Her supreme fitness allowed her to complete her training with ease.

According to Escott, Bunny Rymills, the pilot who flew her across the Channel in a Lysander from Tempsford, accidentally left on his transmitter and the pilot of the following plane could hear his conversation:

> 'Now madame, we are approaching your beautiful country – isn't it lovely in the moonlight?' Back came an answer in soft accented tones, 'Yes, I think it is heavenly. What is that town over there?' He replied, and continued pointing out all the local landmarks as they passed over them, a running commentary for which the listening Germans, if there were any, would have been most grateful.

After landing, she made her way south to work as a courier for Francis Cammaerts in the JOCKEY network. Codenamed 'Alice', she worked up and down the Rhône valley.

After a brief trip to Paris with Noor, during which she in all likelihood broke security rules and met up with her husband, she made her way south by train to Montélimar. There she met Cammaerts, who had her accompany him on his visits to organisers and agents in Toulouse, Clermont Ferrand, Agen, Lyon and Digne. Escott commented that she carried out her errands conscientiously. She lived every day with the spectre of capture, whether in shelter or on the route, at rest or at work. She knew that any small slip of hers or those around her might give her away. She lived with fear. Timid by nature, she always bore in mind the risks not only to herself, but also those with her and the far wider network of helpers in her own and other circuits. Poor Cécile! How often must she have recalled her comfortable past. Did she ever regret her decision to take on such dangerous work? Was her love for her husband – still out of her reach – a sufficient motive? It was a hard and unforgiving life and at 43 years she was not as young and resilient as most of the others who undertook it. To her organiser she was a rather quiet, secretive, shy person, with a perpetually surprised look about her and to a young man she seemed old.

Cammaert's network, using explosives dropped in containers by 138 Squadron, blew up railway lines, power stations and industrial targets. The attack on the hydro-electric power station on the River Durance near Largentière halted production in the factories making aluminium for German planes. Consequently, there was a search for the saboteurs.

Having only been in France for three months, on 15 September 1943, Cécile was betrayed while she was visiting a 'blown address', a whitewashed villa belonging to Raymond Daujat, a corn merchant and Resistance leader in Montélimar. The constant travelling and nervous strain had made her so exhausted that she was desperate for a comfortable bed for the night. Two carloads of Gestapo officers arrived early the following morning. Daujat escaped by climbing through a window but, according to Escott, she was caught in the cellar and brutally interrogated at the Gestapo prison in Lyon. In theory she would not have known Cammaert's whereabouts, as he kept tight control over his network's security. When he was told of her arrest, he set about an escape plan but it had to be abandoned when he discovered she had been taken to Lyon. Instead, he ordered all his network to lie low to avoid being captured.

Cécile's arrest and that of the other two women who arrived by Lysander in June made Escott suspect betrayal. All arrangements, she noted, had been made by Henri Déricourt.

It is also strange that of *all* the WAAF who landed in this way, none survived. Were they betrayed before they landed and were they living on borrowed time before they were taken? Had the Germans first let them go, hoping to be led to more important agents? If so it was a foolish gamble and the German plans must have misfired, as they could not have realised the amount of harm that could be done by leaving the girls on the loose, added to which they almost certainly lost track of each of the girls for some time, although there was always the likelihood that one might later be recognised, as may have happened to Cécile. Noor and Diana were only caught by being betrayed. It shows therefore that either the German intelligence service was remarkably inept, or that the girls had learned their security drill in Britain very thoroughly to stay free for so long.

From Lyon she was transferred to Avenue Foch in Paris and then transported to Ravensbrück. During quarantine, she was diagnosed as having cancer of the stomach, was operated on successfully by the camp doctor and allowed to recuperate in the hospital block on a diet of vegetable soup and a type of porridge. However, following the Allied bombing raids and invasions of Poland and France, the prison staff became more brutal. Sometime in early 1945 she was allocated work duties at the Judenlager, where she was expected to work on a diet of acorn coffee, turnip soup and a little dry bread. Overcrowding meant that there were five or six women to a bed. Clothing and mattresses were infested with lice, and typhoid and dysentery were widespread.

Escott mentioned that Mary Lindell, the former Red Cross nurse and escape line organiser, tried to get Cécile transferred onto a knitting group back in the main camp. Mary signed a form authorising three women's return but, when one refused to go, Cécile stayed behind to persuade her to go. When she went to join the others, they had gone. She was left behind. It is believed, Escott suggests, that she died from an overdose of a white 'sleeping' powder, often issued by a fellow inmate. Otherwise, like many of the others, she was gassed later that month. There was no trace of her body when the camp was overtaken at the end of the war. It was presumed to have been cremated with the others. Afterwards she was 'Mentioned in Dispatches' and awarded the *Croix de Guerre.*

Eliane Plewman
There were suspicious circumstances surrounding the dropping of the fifth female agent Clark mentions as having been taken out of Tempsford. On 13/14 August 1943, Flight Lieutenant Cussen of 161 Squadron flew into the Jura Mountains on operation MESSENGER. On seeing a flashing 'K' to the south-east of Lons-le-Saunier he dropped a package, closely followed by twenty-five-year-old Eliane Plewman, a French SOE agent and member of the Resistance.

Born in Marseille on 6 December 1917 to a Spanish-French mother and British father, Eliane Browne-Batroli was educated in England and Spain and worked in an import-export company in Leicester when she finished college. She handled business correspondence in Spanish, English, French, and German which, when war broke out, allowed her to take up work in the British embassies in Madrid and Lisbon. By July 1942 she was working for the Spanish section of the Ministry of Information in Kensington and her brother Albert was working for SOE.

That summer she married Tom Plewman, a British army officer, but, following his return to his regiment, she too was recruited to work in the SOE as a volunteer FANY. He couldn't deter her from undertaking her training and returning to France. Escott commented that she was 'a vital brilliant woman, with a heart-shaped face, dark hair and eyes and a fair skin, whose presence lit up the room wherever she went. It is hard to imagine anyone who looked less suited to war work. Her devotion to France, her intelligence and her cool, balanced attitude made her an obvious choice for SOE'.

A note in her personnel file showed that the SOE officers rated her highly, describing her a 'very tough woman with unexpected charm. She was obviously most capable and acted with discretion. She was calm and nothing rattled her. We have much esteem for her'.

Her brother was parachuted into France with Robert Benoist, a retired Grand Prix racing car driver. On her training course she met Bob Maloubier, a French agent, who recalled in an interview with Pattinson that he warned her that:

> If you're too good you'll be taken on as a radio operator. Radio operators usually don't do anything at all. They stay in, in hiding. The others do some type of sabotage, they go round, they form reception committees for parachute. Basically [if you become a radio operator] you'll be in a remote place. It's very dangerous too.

Eliane was driven to Tempsford and flown out towards the Jura Mountains, but had to be returned when the pilot aborted the drop. Despite shattered nerves, she was determined to try again. The next flight was more successful but not perfect. On 14 August 1943, Flight Lieutenant Cussen reported that the reception was laid out about two kilometres south-south-west of the agreed DZ at Lons le Saunier, but that Plewman agreed to be dropped near the package. According to Escott, she landed thirty-two kilometres away from the DZ. Her parachuted drifted over a farm and a dog kept barking at her as she dropped. Trying to avoid it, she sprained her ankle badly on landing. As no one was there to meet her, she buried her parachute and hid her briefcase in some bushes. No wonder. According to Clark, it contained one million francs (£5,600) of SOE money designated for Charles Skepper's MONK network. Rather than start out limping across the countryside, she laid low for a few days until her ankle improved. The reception committee presumed she was lost. Eventually, she made her way to locate her contacts, only to discover they had all been arrested.

Using the identity of Madame Eliane Prunier, codenamed 'Gaby' and sometimes known as 'Dean', she travelled south to meet Skepper. He wanted her to live in Marseille and work as his courier. As she had lived in the city for some years before the war, she was concerned that some of her old acquaintances might recognise her. Instead, she located a safe house in the countryside, where twenty-year-old Arthur Steele, a London music student and the network's wireless operator, joined her so he could transmit more safely.

She travelled by train or *gamogenetic*, a charcoal-powered Ford truck, between Marseille, St Raphael and Roquebrune, arranging parachute drops, teaching about arms and explosives and undertaking sabotage operations. Sometimes, on the way back from a drop, her truck driver used to stop and give lifts to German soldiers who sat unknowingly on boxes of arms and ammunition in the back.

Following the Allied invasion of North Africa, 240,000 German troops were sent into what had been the Free Zone. Gun emplacements and artillery batteries were set up along the coast in case the Allies attempted to land on the Mediterranean coast. There was also a concerted effort to curtail Resistance activity.

This didn't deter Eliane. According to Gleeson, there was one occasion in Marseille when, carrying a heavy suitcase laden with explosives which she was planning to use, she bumped into her brother Albert. He carried it on and off the train for her and helped in the operation, but he thought that she was being pushed too hard. He and his wife were kind to her, but she was concerned about their lack of security. In January 1944 her network damaged thirty trains, de-railed the train to Toulon in a tunnel, and destroyed the first break-down train sent to repair it, halting all traffic on the line for four days. This increased German security on the rail network but the MONK network damaged thirty more lines in March.

There was a tense moment on one train journey reported by Escott in *The Heroines of SOE*:

Eliane was standing in the corridor packed with German soldiers. As she also spoke German, during a conversation with the German officer beside her, he asked for a light for his cigarette. Eliane was in a dilemma. She had two boxes of matches in her bag. One carried a message from a resistant – the reason she was on the train – but they both looked identical. She had just lit her own cigarette from one, so she couldn't deny having any. Reluctantly she handed one over to him and then with his cigarette alight, he pocketed the box. Did he know? She was surprised to leave the train undiscovered. Back at base, with shaking hands she poked at the matches in the remaining box. Nothing! It dropped to the floor and a twist of paper fell out. The message. All was well. Such heart-stopping incidents were part of daily life for an agent.

On another such occasion she was afraid that she had mislaid her handbag with money, identity cards, ration books, and keys. A fellow resistant let her climb onto his shoulders to reach her open apartment window, where she was lucky to find them.

As one of her network had a special diet, she undertook to get him food on the black market. However, the man who provided her with what she wanted shared a mistress with a man in the pay of the Gestapo. On 23 March 1944, this was claimed to have led to Skepper being arrested. Unaware, Eliane and Steele called at his apartment the following day with messages for him. On seeing two German soldiers outside, they took out their revolvers to challenge them but other soldiers rushed from the building and overpowered them.

Being a small network, news travelled fast, but before a plan to rescue them could be implemented, they were moved to Les Baumettes Prison, near Marseille. She is said to have had the amazing courage to hint to her German interrogator that, if he took her out for a good dinner, she might be amenable to telling him more about the network in which she was employed. Having eaten the dinner, she calmly announced that she had changed her mind. The torture used by the Gestapo included being prodded between the eyes with a very powerful electric current. According to Escott, Eliane was so beaten about the head and tortured that her swollen face made her almost unrecognisable.

After three weeks of physically tough interrogation, through which she claimed that she only admitted that she was Skepper's mistress and sang to herself every night, she was transferred to Frèsnes Prison. Steele was hanged at Buchenwald and Skepper was executed in Hamburg.

On 13 May 1944, the Germans transferred her, Yolande Beekman, and Madeleine Damerment to a civilian women's prison at Karlsruhe from where, on 10 September, they were transferred to the Gestapo HQ to meet Noor Inayat Khan. The following morning they were transferred to Dachau, where they were locked in separate cells. Within hours of arriving, they were dragged past the barracks, forced to kneel by the crematorium and executed with a single shot to the head. Escott suggested that they all knew too much about the Gestapo's infiltration of the PHYSICIAN network to be allowed to live and tell the Allies. Like many of the other women, Eliane was awarded the MBE, the King's Commendation for Brave Conduct and the *Croix de Guerre*.

Beatrice 'Yvonne' Cormeau

On the night of 22 August 1943, Squadron Leader Ratcliff of 161 Squadron took off in his Halifax on a double mission. His first was to drop thirty-three-year-old Beatrice 'Yvonne' Cormeau with eight containers near the hamlet of St Antoine du Queyret in the Gironde, about 120 kilometres east of Bordeaux.

Escott's research showed that she was born Yvonne Biesterfeld on 18 December 1909 in Shanghai, where her father was a British consular official. Following his death when she was nineteen, the family moved around Belgium, France and Switzerland, where, after completing her education, she worked as a secretary to the legal adviser in the British embassy. She married Charles Cormeau, an army officer, before the war and had a daughter. According to her obituary in *The Times*:

> In the catastrophe of May 1940, her husband was killed in action. Her mother, who stayed in Belgium, was packed off to Ravensbrück, from which she never returned. Yvonne managed to get to England with her two-year-old infant, and decided, on reflection, that it would be better for her child in the long run if she went away to help to defeat Hitler, horrible though the thought of separation was. She joined the WAAF in the autumn of 1941. She was able to pass for a Frenchwoman, and so moved into the Special Operations Executive a year later. After passing the paramilitary and security schools, she was trained as a wireless-telegraphy operator as well as a parachutist, codenamed 'Annette', and dropped into France on August 22–23, 1943, to work for Colonel George Starr, codenamed 'Hilaire', a principal figure in the Resistance in south-west France.[14]

Her four-year-old daughter Yvette, whom she had to leave behind, was initially sent to a nursery school in Bristol but, when that was disbanded, Yvonne decided that, rather than lose contact with her daughter if the next boarding school was evacuated or closed, she put her in a country convent of Ursuline nuns near Oxford.

Identified early as a potential wireless operator, Yvonne was sent to Thame Park in Oxfordshire, another of SOE's large country houses. According to Escott, 'her sensible attitude, quick wit, and intelligence were coupled with plenty of strength and independence of character, which all helped when she started training as a wireless operator alongside Noor Inayat Khan and Yolande Beekman'. The course included physical training; using, diagnosing faults in, and repairing radios; learning how to encode and decode messages; mastering Morse code; typing at between eighteen and twenty-two words per minute; and memorising all the security checks necessary during transmission. An operator at the General Post Office only averaged twelve. Escott commented that when Yvonne was in the field, she was so accurate, sensible and careful that there was rivalry among the FANY at the home station as to who would get her messages, and the Resistance members would not let her have anything to do with explosives because her fingers were so vital for contacting London.

In Liane Jones' *A Quiet Courage*, she quotes Yvonne as being 'the only member of the party who seemed to have sex-appeal for the male members but it was exerted in a very quiet way'. Although she showed talent with the wireless set, her training instructor at Beaulieu was not impressed with her clandestine skills. His report in her personnel file said that she had 'very little personality or aggressiveness ... intelligent and quick-witted without being intellectual ... seems to live on her nerves and might become rattled in a difficult situation'. Despite this negative report, Buckmaster decided to send her anyway.

In an interview recording held at the Imperial War Museum, she revealed her motivation for joining the SOE.

> After my husband was killed I joined the WAAF, the Women's Auxiliary Air Force. Well, going into the forces, one had to fill in a great number of questionnaires and when they asked, 'What have you as special qualities?' I put down my knowledge of German and Spanish and bilingual French. After a while this got through to the Ministry, of course, and then, as they were looking for people for SOE, I was interrogated. I received a telex from London asking that I should come down to town as soon as possible to see a certain Captain Selwyn Jepson. He asked if I was pleased with my work that I was doing and then he spoke about France. France at that time was divided into two parts, the northern part was completely occupied by the enemy and the southern part was so-called unoccupied, so we talked about that and he suddenly asked me if I would return to occupied France. I replied in the affirmative. I thought this was something my husband would have liked me to do, and, as he was no longer there to do it, I thought it was time for me to do it.[15]

The interview went on to shed light on the instruction the SOE provided for women during their training, and on Yvonne's experiences when she landed on French soil again.

> They gave us some ideas about living and operating in France but they said, 'You've got to judge when you're on the spot. Things might change by the time you're there. All we can tell you is that there may be certain days of the week when you can't have certain drinks or foods in certain cafés, so don't ask, just try and see what is on the menu and advertised for those days. Please don't do too much dyeing of your hair or have very noticeable make-up and things like that because you'll fall foul at some time or other. Try and dress as they do

locally as much as possible. If you're going to live in the country, don't have a manicure, don't have this, don't have that ...'

Slowly but surely my chute opened and I didn't even feel the jerk on my shoulders. It was only three hundred feet so it wasn't a long drop. I took off my jumpsuit immediately and handed it to the French people who were meeting me. I only had a handbag, with my money in, which was strapped behind my back, cushioning the lower vertebrae of the spine so that the shock wouldn't damage anything. I was dressed in what I thought was normal for France: a black coat and skirt with a silk blouse and black shoes. My ankles were bandaged, as I was in shoes and not jump boots.

Her destination was very rural but, as it was the first time an agent had been dropped in that area, many people came out to welcome her, making her very worried that it might attract unwanted attention. She collected the three wireless sets in fake suitcases that had been dropped with her. The crystals and codes were hidden in the false lining of her briefcase. As soon as she could, she acquired a bicycle and moved to her safe house in Pujols to begin transmissions.

Before long, she was called to go south to work as a wireless operator for George Starr's WHEELWRIGHT circuit. He was a friend of her husband whom she had met in England before the war, but, according to Escott, Starr did not want a woman. He had specified he needed someone over 35.

Using the codename 'Annette' and 'Fairy' and 'Sarafan' as aliases, dark-haired, green-eyed Yvonne had her base in a farmhouse in Castelnau sur L'Auvignon, a remote hilltop village in the south-west of France with no electricity and no running water, just a well. Only one of the three radio sets dropped with her was workable, so she had to carry the twenty-pound set around with her whenever she wanted to transmit. This was much lighter than the thirty-two-pound set earlier operators were given. Her work impressed Starr and very quickly he began to recognise her worth, not just as a wireless operator but also as a courier. The only thing he insisted on was that she did not carry her revolver with her. In her interview at the the Imperial War Museum she admitted that there were German soldiers in the area but most 'were too old, too young or too injured to be any threat, but after D-Day the SS were sent in. there was always a Gestapo presence, always informers willing to fulfil a personal vendetta for cash ... We were more frightened of the Milice, they were very politically dedicated'.

In order to avoid the German detector teams getting a 'fix' on her transmissions, she had been instructed to locate suitable safe houses for her transmissions, never staying in the same place for more than three days and never sending them from the same loft, barn or field. Being such a rural location meant that there were many isolated farm buildings and the vineyards proved useful, as she could hide her seventy feet of aerial between the rows of grapes.

Her travels took her to the Dordogne, Gascony and the foothills of the Pyrénées. Vera Atkins had told the women before they left 'not to do too much dying of your hair or have very noticeable make up of things like that as you'll fall foul at some time or other. Try and dress as they do locally as much as possible'. According to Escott, Yvonne had several disguises, such as a district nurse, a children's nurse and, for a very short time, a cow minder. During the hot summer of 1942, she spent time relaxing when she was looking after a herd of cows. When she took them back to the cowshed to be milked, she discovered an extra cow. An irate neighbouring farmer accused her of stealing, so she was sacked.

When she went to the Pyrénées she would transmit from the edge of a wood, avoiding the leaves, which deadened the transmission. This made it virtually impossible for the German *gonios*, radio detection vans operated by the *Funkhorchdienst*, to pinpoint her.

George Starr ran SOE's largest network, for which Yvonne arranged 140 arms and supply drops by 161 Squadron. She was said to have never had a day's leave or rest. During her time in France, Yvonne trained two local men, a butcher and a former wireless operator in the disbanded French Air Force, but they were not provided with her ciphers or other secret material. Although described as 'a first-class operator' sending some 400 messages 'without a single mis-code' during the thirteen months she was in the field, 'very nearly a record', Foot claimed that she broke a cardinal rule by transmitting them from the same location. In an interview with Gleeson, she admitted transmitting from the same house for two months and that the Germans knew about it and that it was a woman operator. They could tell by her 'fist'. 'On three occasions I was betrayed, once by a Spanish communist but they never found me.' She was lucky as there were eight Castelnaus in France.

Escott reported her travelling widely, sometimes up to sixty kilometres a day, carrying her set in a basket on the front of her bicycle covered with vegetables or other items of shopping, and transmitted from bedrooms, the back rooms of shops or cafés, in a loft, a barn or an outhouse. When she first started transmitting, it was three times a week. During the invasion in June 1944, it was as often as three times a day.

It was her good fortune that instructions were shortly given from London to the effect that the former fixed times and wavelengths of messages that all operators had been instructed to keep and called 'skeds' (schedules) were to be made far more flexible and varied, so that the German detectors would find it harder to focus on any regular pattern of signals. Incoming messages were also grouped at night, a practice that was far safer if more disruptive of sleep. Additionally, agents were instructed not to transmit for longer than 15–20 minutes – shorter if possible and never more than 30 minutes at the maximum. In the early days many operators had been caught beside their sets because of the long, wordy messages upon which their organisers had unwisely insisted. Yvonne had shorter material and she did not start putting it into cipher by the double transposition method until an hour before her call. The key to her cipher was drawn from a sequence of figures, cut from a jumbled assortment printed on a silk handkerchief, which she preferred to use rather than one-time pads, as these were both bulky and difficult to hide and transport. Silk slips and messages were then burned as soon as transmissions were completed, so that nothing remained if she were subsequently discovered. The same went for any incoming traffic, which she promptly decoded and passed to her organiser or gave the instructions to those concerned. She was meticulous about the security of her messages, her set and her location, her care paying dividends.

She was lucky. Such was the success of the *gonios,* the radio detection teams, that the average time before capture of SOE's wireless operators was only six weeks. The Germans knew that someone was transmitting in that region but had been unable to locate her. They hoped to attract someone to inform them of her whereabouts with a reward of five million francs, half of that offered for Starr.

Buckmaster, in his book *Specially Employed,* reported how, in the summer of 1943, the RAF dropped some leaflets near Condom. The following day Yvonne sent a vigorous protest:

ORDERED BY BOCHES TO CLEAN UP LEAFLETS FROM OUR BEST PARACHUTE GROUND. SPENT ALL SUNDAY PICKING UP. LUMBAGO VERY PAINFUL. TELL RAF TO DROP LEAFLETS IN SEA NEXT TIME.

The strain of her work, cycling everywhere, and lack of good food and sleep led to her health declining. Her weight dropped to just over six stone (42 kg) and she suffered from insomnia.

She never carried the pistol she was given, arguing that if she was found with it at a check point, she would be arrested. Carrying a radio would have meant arrest, interrogation and almost certainly torture. 'You had to be very steady. You couldn't afford to feel exhilarated. After I'd come through a difficult check, I would feel washed through. I felt the strain – I couldn't help it.'

Beside her set she had a pair of field glasses through which she could look out over five kilometres of countryside, which was closely guarded by Spanish members of the Maquis. There was also a contingent of Starr's men based in the village, who had been specially trained and were ready for action.

> The identity they gave me, with cards and all that, was quite good, but as soon as I arrived and showed these papers to my boss, he told me, 'Look, the quality of the paper is far too good. I'll get you some new cards.' So those were changed. I went out with ration cards, too, but again the paper was a bit too good. Paper had deteriorated in France.
>
> I'd left my wedding ring and engagement ring in England but my finger was unfortunately marked by the wedding ring after a certain number of years. One very observant woman told me, 'There's a shiny line on your finger.'
>
> I must admit to butterflies floating in my tummy the whole time. You had to be careful. You had to have eyes in the back of your head. The life was totally different to anything I'd experienced previously ...
>
> You never knew, man or woman, who was prepared to give information to the Gestapo. Sometimes it was a personal vendetta between two families. Other times it was just for money.
>
> One day I met 'Hilaire'. I'd gone to meet him, to give him messages, instructions from London. And as we got near a very small village, cycling, we saw on the shutters of a house, which served both as the schoolroom and the town hall, two identikit-type drawings of ourselves. So we looked at them, looked at each other, we didn't say anything and we split up. I went back north and he went south.

Despite having to lead a fairly solitary life as a wireless operator, she quickly noticed that every local woman wore a necklace, bracelet or other ornament. She duly bought a selection but then discovered that peasant women didn't wear any. In her debrief after returning to England she said, 'I was asked to look after the cows, take them out in morning and bring them back at sunset ... Before going, the farmer's wife had told me, "Don't wear a watch. No woman who looks after cows would be able to afford a watch."' Like many British women in the 1940s, Yvonne was a heavy smoker and found it so difficult in Castelnau to find any tobacco – except on the black market at exorbitant prices – that she had to give it up.

Yvonne had an outstanding record, especially when 'Wanted' posters appeared in her neighbourhood with an accurate sketch of her appearance. She even survived a bullet tearing through her skirt and being shot in the leg. On one occasion after keeping a rendezvous with Starr, their car was stopped at a road block.

> We'd been told the Germans were coming on the roads to the east and west so we took one due south, hoping to escape them. We hadn't gone fifteen kilometres when we were face to face with a personnel carrier. We were stopped

and told to get out of the car, then they put us in a ditch with two soldiers. Both had a pistol, one in my back and one in Hilaire's back. The *feldwebel* was telling somebody on the radio that he'd stopped a tobacco inspector and a woman, the woman had a district nurse's card on her, what was he to do with them?

My perspiration was coming down and flies were sticking in my perspiration and I couldn't move, because if I'd moved they would have shot me immediately. Waiting, waiting. Then the crackle came. 'Get in the car' – which we did at once. Suddenly he asked me what was in the case, which had been thrown on to the back seat, which, of course, was my radio set. I opened it. I knelt on the seat and showed it to him. He asked me what it was. I said, 'Radio,' which in German, means X-ray as well as radio-set, and, in view of the fact that I was meant to be a district nurse, he thought it was an X-ray set, he said, 'Go,' and we got out very fast. The engine was already running.

On another occasion, she managed to jump out of a back window and escape into the countryside, pursued by gunfire, when the Gestapo made an early morning call.

After the nine o'clock news on 1 June 1944 came the phrase '*Les sanglots lourds des violins d'automne*'. It was the long-awaited 'A' message, to let the SOE agents know that D-Day was imminent and that when the 'B' message was heard, it meant D-Day was the following day. On 5 June it came: '*Bercent mon Coeur d'une languer monotone*'. These were lines from Paul Verlaine's popular poem *Chanson D'Automne*, where one word in each line had been deliberately altered. Translated the 'A' message reads: 'The heavy sobs of the autumn violins' and the 'B' message 'Lull my heart with its tedious monotony'.

Following the 'B' message, 300 other messages were read out, each one an instruction to Resistance groups across France to commence their actions against the Germans. Yvonne, Starr and his courier, Anne-Marie Walters (referred to later), had to become much more mobile as the 2nd Panzer Division stationed in Toulouse had been mobilised to journey north to defend Normandy against the invasion. She was involved with a small group, which blew up the power station in Toulouse, brought down power lines and cut telegraph wires causing severe communication problems for the Wehrmacht Group G garrison. Bridges, tunnels, and points along the railway lines were blown up, forcing the troops to use the roads. Trees were cut down to fall across the carriageway and booby trapped to deter them being moved. Explosives, camouflaged as stones, bits of wood, and animal droppings, were placed at strategic points and tyre bursters were thrown on the road. These and hit-and-run tactics targeting the troop carriers ensured the Division did not reach Normandy for seventeen days.

Yvonne distinguished herself by keeping meticulously to the transmission times. When a spotter plane was seen over Castelnau and a large German force approaching, Starr ordered the evacuation of his headquarters. Collecting her equipment, she made her way down the hill through the fields, assisted by a doctor carrying his medicine bag. It was needed as she was shot in the leg. Finding a farmhouse, she sent London the information about the attack. It was later reported that about 800 Germans and 150 members of the Resistance were engaged in the battle, with 240 Germans and twenty French killed.

Yvonne made her way to meet up with Starr's men, who, with the assistance of some Jedburgh teams and other Allied troops, formed the Armagnac battalion. Over the following weeks, they attacked the retreating Germans and on one occasion, trapped on the Lannemezan plateau, continued to transmit despite being under attack by machine guns and aircraft bullets. According to Escott, 'she never took unnecessary risks, but her courage and coolness saw her through'.

When Toulouse was liberated on 20 August 1944, the occasion was one of great celebration. Escott told how the crowds dropped to the ground when a loud bang rang out from the middle of the procession. It had not been a sniper but the tyre on their car bursting. When the crowd realised, there were laughs and smiles and the car was lifted bodily onto the shoulders of the Resistance, carrying Yvonne and Hilaire into Place Wilson, the main square.

According to her obituary in *The Times*, like Hilaire 'she was soon dismissed back to England by a furious General de Gaulle, who could not abide any resisters who were not under his own direct command'.

One of the last messages she received was an instruction to rendezvous with the Chief Test Pilot who had been specially flown in from Farnborough. She had to help him find and bring back to England the black box and a wheel from the latest German Heinkel Bomber. With the help of her contacts, they located the items and she accepted the proffered lift home on 23 September 1944.

In November, Yvonne, accompanied by senior members of SOE's F Section, went on the Judex mission. Over a period of several months, she toured the main centres of Resistance activity in France, trying to investigate the work and fate of the SOE agents and the French who had helped them. Awards and compensation were arranged and equipment recovered which could be used in the continuing war in the Far East. Escott noted that Yvonne was pleased by the results in her area,

> where from a centre set up there she helped to identify those who had suffered most, and whose distress gifts of money, clothing and, particularly in agricultural areas, farm implements and seed, would serve to alleviate.

Finally, she returned to England and *The Times* article reported:

> After the war, she and her daughter were reunited, and she settled down to
> the job of bringing up the girl. She was one of the earliest members of the
> Special Forces Club, served for many years on its committee, and formed in
> and around it many new friendships. She became a British citizen, and was
> appointed MBE. The French were more generous with honours, awarding her
> both a *Croix de Guerre* and membership of the Legion of Honour. She was
> tireless in promoting Anglo-French friendship.[16]

She died on Christmas Day 1997.

Elyzbieta Zawacka

In David Oliver's *Airborne Espionage*, he mentions Elyzbieta Zawacka,
the first and, according to my research, the only female agent sent from
Tempsford into Poland. On the night of 9/10 September 1943, Squadron
Leader Krol and his Polish crew flew their Halifax and dropped her,
two other agents, and their stores before returning safely to Tempsford,
a round trip of over eight hours. Thirty-four-year-old Elyzbieta was a
mathematics teacher in the 1930s and an instructor in the *Przysposobienie
Wojskowe Kobiet*, Polish Women's Military Training Organisation. When
war broke out, she became a commandant in the Union for Armed
Struggle and, codenamed 'Zelma', undertook courier work in Warsaw and
became a deputy of Zagroda, the Department of Foreign Communication
in the Home Army. In February 1943 she made her way overland across
Germany, France and Spain to Gibraltar, from where she was flown to
England.

In Ian Valentine's *Station 43: Audley End House and SOE's Polish Section*,
he narrates her

> taking a suitcase of dollars from Berlin to Silesia in 1942, having to jump from
> a moving train at night to avoid the Gestapo. Her sister was interrogated and a
> colleague arrested and beheaded in Katowice in the same year. Under arduous
> conditions she and other couriers carried information intended for the Polish
> Commander-in-Chief in London. The information they carried was incredible
> in their diversity and included intelligence concerning U-boats in the Baltic,
> German troop movements, V-1 jets and V-2 rockets, Auschwitz, photographs
> for forged documents, escape routes, German industry, munitions factories,
> sabotage, information and plans of enemy aircraft and armour, Jewish ghettos,
> cooperation with the Resistance in Hungary and Germany, extermination of
> Poles and Jews, particularly in the parts annexed by the Reich.

She undertook a training course at Audley End, near Saffron Walden, Essex, sharing a room with Sue Ryder. Having completed that, she underwent parachute training and, codenamed 'Zo', parachuted back into Poland to join her colleagues. She took part in the Warsaw uprising before moving to Krakow to continue her underground activities. In 1945, she joined an anti-communist organisation but quit after the war ended and became a teacher. Her honours include the highest Polish state distinction – the Order of the White Eagle – as well as the British Veterans' Badge.

Yolande Beekman

According to the SOE records, the next woman sent out was Yolande Beekman, a Swiss citizen. Yolande Unternahrer was born in Paris on 28 October 1911 to a Dutch mother and Swiss/French father who had adopted British citizenship. She moved to London to be educated at Hampstead Heath and later went to a finishing school in Switzerland. By the time she had finished her education, she was fluent in English, French and German. Escott described her as a short, plump, good-humoured, kind and rarely ruffled, dark-haired woman with a surprisingly homely English appearance.

She worked in children's clothing stores in Camden and Highgate but, when war broke out, she joined the WAAF and trained as a wireless operator at Thame Park. While there, she gained a reputation as a great sock darner and fell in love with Jaap Beekman, a sergeant in the Dutch Army who was also training there. She was recruited to the SOE in February 1943 and trained at Wanborough with Yvonne Cormeau, Noor Inayat Khan and Cécile Lefort. Their conducting officer was Mrs Jean Sanderson of the FANY.

In Patrick Yarnold's *Wanborough Manor*, he records Lieutenant Colonel Gordon's description of Yolande as 'a nice girl, darned all the men's socks, would make an excellent wife for an unimaginative man, but not much more than that'. He was unaware she was married, as all recruits were given false identities during training. Lieutenant Holland's report at the end of her course stated that 'she shows any amount of determination in mastering the intricacies of W/T'. Nigel Perrin pointed out that:

> Her self-assurance and determination soon shone through, as did her cheerfulness and idealism, being motivated by 'the "good of the cause" and devotion to duty.' Her time at SOE's finishing school at Beaulieu underlined the same qualities – popular, practical and dependable, her pace was a deliberate plod rather than a gallop: 'full of common sense and resource ... the stolid type.'
>
> In August Yolande began training as a wireless operator at Thame Park in Oxfordshire. She found coding and transmitting hard work but she became a great favourite with everyone, not least with a recruit for SOE's Dutch section,

Jaap Beekman, who fell in love with her. Their schedules only allowed for a brief engagement, and they married in London later that month. Even as they celebrated plans were underway for Yolande's first mission, and early in September she saw off her husband at King's Cross station, for what would prove to be the last time. Beekman took part in a mission to Holland in August 1944, and returned to England before the end of the war.[17]

Buckmaster[18] acknowledged that a good deal of thought went in to deciding where she was to be sent and who was to be helped.

[We] decided on Yolande, a girl of Swiss extraction sent to us by the W.A.A.F. Her French was perfect; the trace of Swiss accent was a positive advantage, as it diverted attention from her rather typically English appearance. She was quiet and homely – she had gained immense popularity at the wireless school by taking over the unofficial duties of sock-darner for the men – and her unruffled cheerfulness and good humour were great assets. She quickly developed an easy camaraderie with Guy [Bieler], which promised well for their future activities.

Guy had an amused tolerance for the women engaged in our work, which some might have faintly resented. But Yolande took no offence at his attitude, and her very unaffectedness and simplicity won his esteem and admiration.

The time soon came for the two to leave on their mission, and I went down one November evening to see them off from the special aerodrome which we used. It was fairly rare in November for flying conditions to be good enough to risk a parachute operation involving 'bodies', but that night the moon was nearly full, there was a little cloud, but not too much, and there was no fog forecast. The messages announcing their departure to the waiting 'reception committee' in France had been put on both programmes of the B.B.C.: '*Georgette aime les roses*,' the French announcer had said in that polite, cool, unemotional voice which he reserved for the 'personal messages'. '*Georgette aime les roses*' meant to the listeners who had arranged the message: 'Guy and Yolande are leaving tonight and will be dropped on your ground'. It meant a lot more. It meant: 'And we in England know that you are preparing for your fight to oust the invader. We will help you by sending you the tools, so that you may finish the job. These two British officers have volunteered to make your link-up with the Supreme Command, so that your efforts may be co-ordinated with the general Allied effort'. But we didn't need to tell them that; they knew.

Guy and Yolande were very cheerful as they got into their parachute harness, and watched their packs being stowed away in the bomb-racks of the aircraft. They cracked a joke with the skipper; they embraced, both of them, the F.A.N.Y. driver who had taken them down to the aerodrome; they let themselves be hoisted into the fuselage of the aircraft with much jest and merriment, and they waved a cheery farewell as the pilot taxied off, leaving me standing in the dispersal bay in the deepening dusk.

A month after her marriage, 17 September, thirty-one-year-old Yolande, codenamed 'Mariette', with identity papers in the name of 'Yvonne de Chauvigny', a war widow, landed in France. Buckmaster stated that Guy Bieler had fallen heavily on landing and dislocated his spine, so appointed Yolande to deputise for him.

Verity claims Yolande was landed in a double Lysander mission. Wing Commander Bob Hodges and Jimmy Bathgate of 161 Squadron flew out on 17/18 September, landing her and three others at Le Vieux Briollay, three and a half kilometres west-north-west of Villeveque, which was north-north-east of Angers. This was the same field that Henri Déricourt arranged for Noor Inayat Khan, Cécile Lefort and Diana Rowden's arrival. According to Perrin:

> Reception organiser Henri Déricourt gave them each a bicycle, which Yolande apparently had trouble riding, and when the morning curfew had lifted he shepherded them into the city. On the way she fell off at her first sight of a German patrol, but they were able to reach the station safely and split up before boarding the first train to Paris. This party was lucky: unknown to them, Déricourt had been helping the Gestapo for some time, and other agents arriving at his landing grounds were followed to their destinations.
>
> The next day they met up briefly with Déricourt at a café near the Arc de Triomphe, before they went their separate ways.

Her contact in Paris gave her a message from Baker Street, cancelling the original plan for her to work for Captain Trotobas in Lille and telling her instead to go south to St Quentin in the northern Aisne department. She stayed in the homes of a schoolmistress, a farmer, a pharmacist and then in a room above a café. According to Escott, three times a week she would let herself in with a key, lay down on a wide, brown velvet divan, her head cradled in mittened gloves, and await her transmission time. It was so cold in the attic at night. Disregarding instructions, Foot stated that she was imprudent by transmitting from there at the same time on the same three days of the week for almost early three months. However, according to the Spartacus website, her unaffectedness and simplicity evoked the esteem and admiration of Gustave Biéler, the Canadian head of the MUSICIAN network. The messages she decoded for him included instructions to attack the lock gates at St Quentin, which was at the heart of the French canal system that was being used to carry submarine parts from the factories in Rouen, where they were made, down to the Mediterranean. The Allies didn't want them being used against their forces pushing up Italy towards France. Yolande helped arrange the parachute drops of explosives and other supplies and, on a very dark February night, limpet mines were attached to waiting barges and a timing switch to the lock gates. The operation was a success, closing the canal system for a few months until it could be cleared.

With increased German activity, her friends had reported seeing wireless detection vans in the neighbourhood, even on Christmas Day. When one passed the house, her friend ran upstairs to warn Yolande. She broke off her transmission with a warning signal, put the set and the aerial in its case and moved to another house. Yolande still managed to continue her transmissions and, to avoid being recognised, dyed her hair blonde and used different identity papers with a new cover story.

One of the venues she used to meet up with members of several nearby Resistance networks was the Moulin Brûlé, a café on the outskirts of St Quentin which she thought was safe. Kramer thought it was the weakest link in the chain of security forged in the early days of clandestine activity. An overenthusiastic conversation was said to have been overheard, which led to the *gonios* successfully locating Yolande's transmissions. On the morning of 13 January, she came downstairs for a pre-arranged meeting with Biéler, the café owner, and another man. Buckmaster[19] narrated how

> two feldgendarmes rushed in on her before she could draw her revolver, and was taken into custody.
>
> Even when she was beaten into unconsciousness, she resolutely kept her lips closed, and forced her mind to obliviousness of Guy's whereabouts. When they gloatingly told her that he was captured she betrayed no emotion. They did not know whether she believed them or not.

In Foot's *SOE in France*, he mentioned German claims that their D/F vans had pinpointed her house as the source of transmission and observed it. Escott was of the opinion that she hadn't been located by the radio detection teams but either a traitor in the circuit had betrayed her or someone had passed on information during torture. There had previously been hundreds of arrests in Francis Suttill's PROSPER network. The arrest of the organiser and wireless operator together meant the end of the MUSICIAN network.

Yolande was taken a few days later to the local pharmacist, who the Gestapo believed was holding money for the network. The owner denied knowing anything about it, but could tell that she had been tortured from her badly swollen face.

Other members of the network attempted a rescue bid, but it failed. Biéler was transferred to Flossenbürg prison camp, where following further interrogation he was shot. Yolande was transferred to Avenue Foch in Paris, where it was hoped that she might play her radio set back to the SOE with German-inspired messages. The plan failed and she was sent to solitary confinement in Frèsnes Prison.

On 13 May 1944 the Germans transported her and seven other captured SOE agents – Eliane Plewman, Madeleine Damerment, Odette Sansom, Diana Rowden, Vera Leigh, Andrée Borrel, and Sonya Olschanezky – to a civilian prison for women at Karlsruhe in Germany. She was confined there under horrific conditions until 11 September, when she was suddenly transferred to Dachau concentration camp with fellow agents Madeleine, Noor and Eliane. After being beaten and badly treated, at dawn the following morning, they were taken to a small courtyard next to the crematorium and forced to kneel. They were then shot through the back of the head and their bodies cremated.

At the end of the war, Yolande Beekman's heroic work was recognised by the French government with the posthumous award of the *Croix de Guerre*. Yolande's mother referred to her as someone who was gentle and quiet but made with a core of steel, and was said to have stated that Yolande was already pregnant at the time she was sent on her mission. She had hoped her daughter would return with her grandchild. A note in her personnel file states that SOE knew nothing about her pregnancy. One wonders whether she had the baby. There was no mention of it in Escott's *Mission Improbable*.

Her gallantry was also 'Mentioned in Dispatches'. She was remembered by her friends as laughing, pretty, and unafraid.

Cecile 'Pearl' Witherington

Five days after Yolande's drop, twenty-nine-year-old Cecile 'Pearl' Witherington, a Flight Officer in the WAAF, was parachuted into France. Born in Paris on 24 June 1914 to British parents, Pearl didn't go to school until she was thirteen. Her father, described as an alcoholic of expensive tastes and unstable means, died when she was sixteen so she had to help her mother look after three younger sisters. Four others in the family had died.

When the Germans invaded France in May 1940, she was working as the personal assistant to the air attaché in the British embassy in Paris, and had fallen in love with Henri Cornioley, a young French lieutenant. They planned to get married, but when she learned that he had been captured, her problems were acute. Not being a diplomat, she was not evacuated with the consular officials, so, on 9 December 1940, she moved with her widowed mother and three sisters into the Unoccupied Zone. The following day the Germans arrived at their apartment to arrest them.

In an interview with Gleeson, she described how:

After having slipped through their hands the four of us boarded a train and left the Gare de Lyon station. We had no idea at all how we could cross the demarcation line ... But in the carriage we spoke to a man who said he was an escaped prisoner of war and had been free for some time and frequently crossed and re-crossed the line. We were not sure that we could trust him, but we had to take a chance and in the end he proved to be quite genuine. We followed him off the train at a small station at 4.30 a.m. It had been pouring with rain and the ground was muddy and slippery. We started out on our trek across country in the dead of night, not knowing where we were going. There was the man, with his bicycle, Mummy, Mimi, Jackie, and myself. We splashed through a farm and Jackie lost her shoes in the mud – but we could not wait to find them because we had to be across the line by 6 a.m. to catch a bus to the nearest town. We met a German sentry and we all dived, face down, into a ditch. Mummy spread a rug she was carrying over the bicycle and he did not spot us as he passed by. We went on. When we got near the end of 'No Man's Land' our guide told us to wait and he went ahead to see if the coast was clear. It was and he came back and told us to run. Run! Our legs were giving way.

They made it and, after three months in Cherbourg, where Pearl helped with an escape line that was passing thousands of escaped prisoners of war, they eventually found accommodation in Marseille. When faced with internment, with the help of the Resistance she managed to escape across Spain and Portugal, and eventually reached Britain with her family on 14 July 1941.

Her two sisters immediately joined the WAAF but Pearl used her connections and joined the Air Ministry as a personal assistant to the Director of Allied Air Co-operation and Foreign Liaison. Furious at what was happening in France, she was desperate to join the SOE. Her school friend, Maurice Southgate, was working in the same office and he had successfully applied. Her boss was against it but when she appeared in the office one day dressed in a FANY officer's uniform, he could do nothing about it.

She recalled in an interview after the war, 'Deep down inside me I'm a very shy person but I've always had a lot of responsibilities ever since I was quite small.' As her father died when she was sixteen, she 'thought, well, this is something I feel I can do ... There's this question of being so mad with the Germans and anyway I didn't like the Germans. Never did. I'm a baby of the 1914–18 war. There is the question of trying to do something useful for the war. But it was also, the biggest part of it was, I think, this fury that I had against the Germans 'cos I was really mad with them'.[20]

Buckmaster[21] claimed that it was Pearl who interviewed him in June 1943 rather than the other way round. In his presumably censored article published after war about some of the agents he sent into France, he commented that:

Pearl struck me as a trifle diffident when I first met her. I know now that she was worried about her family, and perplexed by a most difficult decision: whether to follow her instinct and take the work for which she was suited and which attracted her, or to remain in England doing the dull chores of a household which her genius for organisation alone kept in order. She chose the job which was next to her heart, and never regretted the decision. Once it was made, she was a new person. She had been exacting and a trifle pernickety about the work and what it entailed, but now she threw herself with zest into her training and proved herself an unexpectedly muscular and athletic young woman. Her revolver-shooting was extremely good, and she enjoyed it. I can't help thinking how very much surprised her staid Air Vice-Marshal would have been to see her on the Sten gun range, or crawling up to 'attack' an electrical sub-station.

All this outdoor life changed her mentally as well as physically. When she joined us, she was pale and tired from office work and the strain of the sleepless nights of the London Blitz. I doubted if she would pass the doctor, she looked so drawn and anaemic. Tall and fair, she had classic features, but she wore a mask of reserve and seemed withdrawn into herself.

When I saw her in action at the school after a few months of training, I could hardly believe my eyes, for here was and outstandingly good-looking young woman, bronzed and sturdy, with the handshake of a backwoodsman. The reserve was gone, the mask dropped. Self-reliance blazed in her eyes, her voice was firm and sure. When she gave an order it was obeyed; she radiated confidence. She was a born leader and the intricate 'schemes' in which she took part gave infinite scope for that blend of intellectual prominence and innate leadership which made up her strong personality.

When her period of training was completed, she came up to London for briefing in her mission, because we took the utmost care to see that the men and women who were selected for liaison work in France received the fullest possible instructions in the methods to be employed, as well as information regarding conditions prevailing in the territory where they were to work.

Pearl worked hard at her briefing; she went into every question in the greatest detail and would not leave it until she was satisfied that she had grasped its smallest implications. She learned much by heart, but, not content with this, she acted her part to herself continuously until it became her nature to adopt it. By the time she was ready, I was convinced that she would make an ideal representative.

Not only had she a perfect command of French and a very good knowledge of the weapons she and her men would be called upon to use, but she grasped with easy competence the full import of a most delicate mission.

After passing the initial assessment, she was said to have missed out the paramilitary training in Scotland and attended a special explosives and weapons course. Such courses were held at Brickendonbury in Hertfordshire. According to her obituary in *The Times*, one instructor expressed doubt about her potential during her training: 'Not the personality to act as a leader ... best employed as a subordinate ... She is so cautious that she seems to lack initiative and drive. She is loyal but has not the personality to act as a leader, nor is she temperamentally suited to work alone'.[22]

Not everyone agreed. Juliette Pattinson recorded an interview with Pearl after the war in which she said, 'PT was at half past seven in the morning and they expected me to run ... I refused and they said, "What are you going to do if the Germans get you?" and I said, "I'll deal with that when it comes [laughs] but you're not getting me running at 7.30 in the morning." No thank you. [laughs] I couldn't stand it.' Maybe she decided to show just what she was capable of because her final assessment reported that 'this student, although a woman, has got leader's qualities. Cool, resourceful and extremely determined. Very capable, completely brave ... An excellent student for the job. Knows what she's in for and anxious to get on with it'. The comment on her demolition work was that she was 'extremely keen on this and would like to specialise'. Her firearms instructor added that she was 'Outstanding. Probably the best shot, male or female, we have yet had'.

Despite this, she was reported in Margaret Rossiter's *Women in the Resistance* as not wanting to engage in any violent acts against the enemy, asserting, 'I don't think it's a woman's role to kill.' Her major weakness was Morse code, so she was pleased she wasn't asked to train as a wireless operator.

As she had promised her mother that she would not return to France, to stop her from worrying, Pearl told her a white lie that she had been posted to North Africa. The SOE sent monthly letters enclosing some of her £350 annual salary.

The flight on 3 September 1943 was the third attempt in as many days. Imagine her tension. On the first attempt there were no lights from the reception committee, so the pilot aborted the mission and the plane returned to Tempsford. On the second there was still none. The weather was so dreadful that they didn't even drop the pigeons. On the third, the Halifax pilot, Flight Sergeant Cole, made a successful drop of fifteen containers and five packages about thirty kilometres south-east of Tours. Sixteen minutes later, he dropped Pearl at a flashing 'D', about seventeen kilometres south-south-west of Châteauroux, south-east of Tours. She landed in strong winds, slightly off course, between two lakes and was met by Maurice Southgate, the leader of the STATIONER network. The suitcases carrying her equipment were nowhere to be seen.

Vera Atkins had prepared a surprise for Pearl when she landed on 23 September 1943. She had arranged that her boyfriend, Henri Cornioley, would be in her reception committee. They had had been engaged to before the war but the chances of a future together were dashed when he was captured by the Germans. After escaping from a prisoner of war camp, he was leading a underground camp of men loyal to de Gaulle.

Unfortunately, it being a windy night, she landed sixteen kilometres away from the drop zone so it was a few hours before she held him in her arms. One wonders whether she used her real name or her new identity as Marie Jeanne Marthe Verges. Codenamed 'Marie', she also used the name 'Pauline'.

According to Gleeson, she was in the thick of battle within a few days, joining Jacqueline Nearne, Southgate's courier, and Amédée Maingard, his wireless operator, organizing drops and reception committees, taking messages, teaching the Resistance how to use the arms that were dropped as well as the *plastique* – plastic explosives. Her cover story was that she was a travelling sales representative for Lancray Beauty products. Using night trains, often very cold, she visited such cities as Paris, Lyon, Poitiers, Châteauroux, Limoges, Toulouse and Tarbes. She acquired a first-class season ticket and for the first three months slept on unheated trains often too full of people for her to stretch out. At night there were fewer German and Vichy police checks, so she surrounded herself with pro-German magazines and wore her hair in a plait in German style. In an interview held at the Imperial War Museum, she said that:

> The job of a courier was terribly, terribly, terribly tiring. It was mostly travelling by night. We never wrote and we never phoned. Any messages were taken from A to B and the territory we were working on was really very big, because apart from Paris, we had Châteauroux, Montluçon, down to Toulouse, from Toulouse to Tarbes, up to Poitiers. It meant mostly travelling by night and the trains were unheated.
>
> One of the jobs I did regularly was going from Toulouse to Riom near Clermont-Ferrand. I'd leave Toulouse at seven o'clock at night and get to Riom at eleven o'clock the next morning absolutely frozen stiff to the marrow and having had nothing much to eat. Then I went into the safe house, to the people who received me, where there was no heating either ...
>
> I was terribly, terribly careful and very much awake to what was going on around me because you never knew, wherever you were, in a train or a restaurant, if anybody was listening. An occupation is really one of the most awful things because you're just not at home. You have to be careful of everything.[23]

Sometimes it was arms and explosives she was carrying. All she was given was the location of a rendezvous to deliver and pick up messages. In Escott's *The Heroines of SOE*, she claimed that this proved dangerous on occasions.

Three weeks after she arrived, Southgate was lifted out and taken back to Britain, leaving Pearl to deal with a truculent and unfriendly colonel in the Maquis. According to Gleeson, Maurice considered her a shrewd and diplomatic person and, in time, his men acknowledged her as a highly respected leader. When Maurice's expected fortnight stay was extended to three months, Pearl's responsibilities increased, having to liaise with various figures in the Resistance, many hard-line Gaullists and some Communists.

Buckmaster[24] narrates how her mission was to persuade a French colonel to accept the requirements of the the Allied HQ rather than acting independently. He was won over by her promise of regular parachute drops of supplies.

> It was not an easy assignment for a girl, but I felt sure that Pearl could do it. Where a man would probably have pointed out bluntly that only an officer with the facility of radio contact with London could procure the arms and equipment necessary to turn these Maquisards into an efficient fighting force, Pearl secured the same result by tact and charm in half the time and with no hard feelings on either side. When I met the French colonel later on, the obvious devotion in his eyes as he looked at her and the way he told and re-told the story of the battle at Romorantin proved that she was no mean diplomat.

Christmas 1943 she spent in Paris, but it was spoilt by an attack of neuralgic rheumatism, the result of so many cold nights on the train. Shortly after Octave Chantraine was captured, she had to send a vital message to London but, with no wireless operator, had to cycle to another sector, a long and arduous ride. She also took a large sum of money for the leader but had not been given a password. It took many tense minutes trying to convince 'Roger' that she was from Octave Chantraine's group before she was accepted. She had been told to rendezvous with 'Robert' but no-one knew anyone of that name. The other men were ready to shoot her as a German spy. At another time at Poitiers, had she not been stopped by the concierge of the building, she could have walked straight into the arms of the Gestapo.

In Terry Crowdy's *SOE Agent*, he mentioned that one, Colonel Villiers, who commanded a large Maquis group, was impressed by her successful sabotage of the Michelin factory in Clermont Ferrand. Knowing that Peugeot had been successfully persuaded to have their factory sabotaged instead of bombed by the RAF, Pearl made a similar offer to Michelin's management. Although they agreed initially, they refused to co-operate. On 11 March she wrote to

HQ, telling them:

I regret to inform you that the proposed sabotage of Michelin has completely fallen thro' in spite of repeated attacks. The management, after agreeing to the proposed instructions, refused to collaborate and still do so. Villiers' sabotage leader has been arrested; he tried to set fire to the M. factory by putting thirty incendiaries in one workshop; he did not take into consideration the working of the '*dispositif de sécurité d'incendies*'.

I wish to put on record the management's attitude vis-à-vis the sabotage plans. They refuse to believe the R.A.F. will have time to bomb Clermont Ferrand before an Allied landing: in the meantime they are working, turning out material and making money whereas if the sabotage had taken place when proposed they would be doing none of these today. They are playing for time.

If it is decided to destroy Michelin by bombing the factory, the R.A.F. could also bomb Bergougnan where they are turning out material exclusively for the Huns.

There is very little defence around Clermont Ferrand and what there is, is mobile.

I hate to suggest the bombing of M. but Villiers and I think it would give the management a lesson and force Villier's hand if Clermont Ferrand was bombed.

An addendum dated 5 April 1944 pointed out:

Michelin was pinpointed and destruction complete in main factory. People in Clermont say many of the incendiaries were dud. Casualties: about 16 killed and 20 injured. Sanatorium damaged by the blast, no casualties or damaged material.

When she discovered that about 40,000 tyres destined for German military transport vehicles were burnt, she didn't reckon that a great success as she felt more ought to have been destroyed. Whether the Bougourgnan tyre plant was also destroyed is unknown.

In April 1944 Southgate and Jacqueline Nearne were ordered to return to England. They were Lysandered back on 9 April. Pearl was put in charge. Concerned that the stress of being second-in-command was taking its toll on Maingard, she organised a May-Day picnic and a swim. Shortly after, Southgate returned, bursting with new ideas, and walked straight into a trap in Montluçon on the same day. He forgot to check for a danger signal and was arrested, interrogated and eventually taken to Buchenwald concentration camp.

When they discovered that Southgate had been captured, Maingard informed London. The network was split in two. Maingard kept the area south-east of the Indre and Cher valley and renamed it SHIPWRIGHT. She was put in charge of the area to the north, in the triangle between Valençay, Issoudun and Châteauroux. This new network was called WRESTLER. Immediately, Pearl and Cornioley moved to the guard house in the grounds of Château Les Souches.

She divided the increasing number of men and boys who flocked to join her network into four, appointed an appropriate leader for each, and allocated each a specific area to work. She instructed them to harass the Germans crossing their section and then retreat, hit-and-run tactics rather than an all-out battle. Finally, after repeated requests to London, she was sent a French Commander with whom she liaised so well that her standing amongst the men increased. Escott quoted her as saying, 'it was not my official mission to command guerilla fighters, but events were beyond me and I had to make the most of my modest capabilities'. Known as Lieutenant Pauline or their mother, the men would crowd around her bicycle when she arrived. 'She was an excellent, clear-headed organiser with such personality, leadership, and skill that she could manage most situations to her advantage. She could also rely on the support of Cornioley and the new military commander'.

Over the months she was in France, the STATIONER network was financed to the tune of about 750,000 francs (£4,200) a month, money dropped by the SOE. With 150,000 francs for her personal use and the help of Cornioley, she concentrated on arming and training over 2,700 members of the Resistance. She arranged for them to be supplied by Tempsford's 138 Squadron. Their attacks on the Germans led to, according to one estimate, over 1,000 dead. Desperate to capture her, the Germans offered a million franc reward for her arrest, the equivalent of about £500,000 today.

In the heat of the summer of 1944, pedalling with messages to various Maquis groups, she would often stop at a farmhouse, hot, dusty and thirsty, and ask for a glass of water. At first, the local farmers insisted that she drank wine, but it resulted in her not being able to stay upright, let alone pedal straight. With the memory of a drunken father, she became equally determined to refuse their offers, sometimes quarrelling with them in order to get the precious water. Using her bicycle so often, she wore a hole in her only skirt.

On one occasion she had to wade waist-deep through a freezing river (Cher) with her bike slung across her back as a bridge she needed to cross was unexpectedly being guarded. Her network cut the Paris–Toulouse railway line over 800 times in the Indre district, thus delaying the German reinforcements getting to Normandy after D-Day. The telephone lines her teams cut were not repaired until the Germans left France. Her closest shave came on 11 June 1944 when, holed up with Henri in the attic of the gatehouse to the chateau in Valençay, they were woken by German troops. They thought there was a large garrison of Maquis hiding there. In an interview quoted in Kate Vigurs' PhD thesis, she stated:

It was 8.30, on a Sunday morning ... I hurried over to the place where we put some arms that had arrived, at least there was something. I sat down on my own. I did not have time to look at the things at all, the hand grenades and the Sten magazines until a chap came up and said 'you'd better get moving, they're coming up the alley'. Well, Henri had arranged with me to meet at the Miller farm if something happened, it was through the woods and I went there and there were five or six of us including the wife and daughter of the farmer, I thought I saw a German coming up the alley and he took a pot shot and he hit the head of whoever, I do not know, six or eight Germans were there and they were so mad that this chap had been killed that they started firing. I thought they're not going to catch me in a house, not in a thousand years so I left through the back of the barn and into a wheat field. I thought I can get out of the other end and into the woods, in June it was a lovely sunny day, it was hot. It was there I stayed from about 11 a.m. ... until 10.30 at night. I could not move, because up and down this country road there were lorries full of Germans and I wouldn't have had time to get out of the field and into the woods which I thought I was going to be able to get to ... I thought I shall never see my life again, it is impossible, we were completely surrounded, it was bang, bang, bang all day, and in fact we lost one chap and the communists lost six, it was their own fault, silly asses, because they were in a farm.

According the 2002 Channel 4 documentary *Behind Enemy Lines: The Real Charlotte Grays*, she and 150 men held off 2,500 enemy troops for fourteen hours before escaping through a three-foot-high cornfield with her group's cash box. She hid there in the blazing sun for four hours while the Germans occasionally fired into the field, only moving when the wind rippled the corn. Eventually, she made a run for it and found another farm to shelter in, but had to leave behind the wireless set, weapons and stores. Twenty-four of her colleagues were shot in the raid, but she met up with Henri. It was some time before she managed to inform London and arrange sixty plane-loads of supplies.

With the majority of French men seeing women's role as very much secondary, Foot stated that Pearl's position as a female and foreign network commander was somewhat invidious. However, 'not the sort of person to be put off by a point of etiquette... she found a complaisant local Colonel to mouth the orders she composed'. This way, he suggested, her decisions were respected, because they seemed to come from a man. According to Buckmaster:

Commanding her 2,600 men, armed with Bren guns, Sten guns, and hand grenades, she determined to harry the enemy's crossing. The battle raged for the whole of a summer's day. Houses were looted and burned down; men were locked in groups grimly fighting for their lives. Pearl was everywhere, encouraging, ordering, sending up reinforcements, food, and ammunition. When the Germans brought up tanks, it was she who gave the order to let them through and to attack the following column of thin-skinned vehicles from the rear. It was she who watched the ambushes to make sure that fighting was broken off before the enemy could deploy overwhelming force. A great day for Pearl.

It is difficult for us to picture her as she must have been at the end of that great day, when the noise of battle died away and the German troops swarmed like locusts into the little villas of the unfortunate villages that had been in the battle line. Like ghosts the Maquisards took to the woods, whence their flying-columns sallied forth again to lay fresh terrors in the path of the Germans' advance next morning. There was no sleep for Pearl that night; messages from London had to be read and replies sent. Instructions had come through about the reception of new officers. 'What a bore,' she thought, 'to have new officers now. They'll be too late for everything except the mopping-up – and the victory march.' But there were the orders, and wrenching her weary mind back to her job, she gave instructions for the new arrivals to be received on the parachute ground, safely housed, fed, and sent on their way.

Soon the sweep of General Bradley's army along the Loire came to her relief. 18,000 Germans, caught by the patriots in this area, surrendered to the Americans at Chateauroux, and Pearl, in obedience to her orders, reported back to London. She didn't stop in Paris, because she felt she must first report to her Headquarters; there might be more work for her in Eastern France. When she landed at the English aerodrome, she was just a W.A.A.F. officer, one of thousands travelling on their official duties. She looked no different from any of them; or was there, barely perceptible, a particularly firm tilt to that determined chin, an unusually appraising glance from those fine eyes? I thought so, but then I knew her secret …

The colonel was not the only one to hold Pearl in high esteem. I spent an afternoon in September 1944 at Châteauroux barracks, while she was feted by the officers. It was amusing, yet in a way pathetic. The mess looked like a schoolroom in which the senior boys were celebrating the visit of a very popular master. They had brought out their best fare; there were elaborate table-cloths, fancy cakes (fancy cakes in the France of September 1944 needed 'organising') and of course champagne, much champagne. Pearl was surrounded by the 'boys' all talking at once, recollecting this or that incident, living again the fighting of June and the dangerous, tortuous underground work of the preceding eighteen months. And she was congratulating, praising, promising to come back again, just like an indulgent teacher with a precocious class. But when she said goodbye and they wished her luck, she confessed to me that those were her happiest days.[25]

Gleeson added that during her time in the field, apart from the railway sabotage, a thousand Germans had been killed in four months and a further twenty thousand were forced to surrender. However, unlike other organisers, she was opposed to killing. In the same interview she stated that:

> I didn't go out and fight with a gun. I don't think it's a woman's job that, you know. We're made to give life, not take it away. I don't think I could have stood up and coldly shot somebody ... I didn't actually go in for full blowing-up. I didn't use explosives, neither did I use arms and neither did I kill people ... The last thing I felt like was a terrorist.

Details of her return to England are to be found in Escott's *Mission Improbable*:

> When we got back to London all the heads of circuits were there; they were all men, and I was the only woman. The head of it all said 'Gentlemen!' And he turned to me and said: 'That applies to you, because you've done a man's job!' I'm the only woman who's ever done such a thing: going from a courier to military commander!

In her debriefing report, Pearl mentioned that her men killed over 1,000 Germans in five months and wounded many more. When she married Cornioley in London in October, the SOE gave her an £8 postal order as a wedding present. Having only completed four parachute jumps rather than the usual five when she was at Ringway, she was refused her wings.

Although recommended for the Military Cross, she was ineligible as she was a woman. Major General Colin Gubbins, the head of SOE, wrote that 'her control over the Maquis group to which she was attached, complicated by political disagreements among the French, was accomplished through her remarkable personality, her courage, steadfastness and tact'. When she was awarded what she termed the 'puny' MBE (Civil), she returned it with a note saying that she did not deserve it as she had done nothing remotely civil.

> The work which I undertook was of a purely military nature in enemy occupied country. When the time for open warfare came we planned and executed open attacks on the enemy. I spent a year in the field and had I been caught I would have been shot, or worse still, sent to a concentration camp. I consider it most unjust to be given a civilian decoration. The men received military decorations. Why this discrimination with women when they put the best of themselves into

the accomplishment of their duties.

However, she did accept from de Gaulle the *Croix de Guerre*, the *Croix Legion d'Honneur* and the *Medaille de Resistance*. In 2006 she received the insignia of the CBE from the Queen and, two years later, her much more coveted parachute wings. She died on 24 February 2008.

Elizabeth Devereaux Rochester

SOE records mention Elizabeth Devereaux Rochester and Danielle Reddé as being the last two women agents sent out in 1943. Born in New York on 20 December 1917 to an English mother, Elizabeth was educated by governesses until she was sent to Roedean girls' school in England where she enjoyed golf, tennis, sailing, riding and hunting. Later she went to finishing schools in France and Austria. When her parents divorced, her mother married Byron Reynolds, an American businessman, so her two daughters were given his surname. As a wealthy American, she had lived an affluent lifestyle in the 1930s, travelling in style around much of Europe and developing excellent contacts within the European aristocracy. At seventeen, her step-father took her to Berlin on one of his business trips. Whilst he admired the Germans, the visit opened her eyes to Nazi policies and turned her violently against them.

In her autobiography, *Full Moon to France*, she tells how she was on vacation in Greece when war broke out. Rather than return to the United States, she jumped ship at Marseille, lying to the American officer that she was desperate to buy some sanitary towels. Catching the train to Paris, she joined the American Hospital Ambulance Corps as a driver and was involved with taking food to prisoners of war.

After the Japanese attack on Pearl Harbor, the United States joined the Allies. As all Americans in France were considered enemy personnel, Elizabeth's mother was interned in Vittel concentration camp. Rather than lose her friends and leave her beloved France, Elizabeth and Bridget, a British girlfriend working with the French Resistance, moved to Chalon-sur-Saône, near the French Alps, helping get Jews, Allied airmen and young French men wanting to avoid forced labour in Germany across the border into Switzerland. Hiding in ditches, avoiding guards in the early hours of the morning, sleeping rough and living simply with sympathetic French peasants was a big change for her. She buried her American passport but kept her French identity card.

After reaching Geneva, the American consulate suggested she return to the United States. She refused, expressing an interest in helping in the war effort. Within days she was approached by the British to work for them. They wanted her to return to France and continue working on the escape route. She agreed.

After a few more journeys the local gendarmerie were on to her. The young officer sent to arrest her was successfully bribed with a large bag of oranges she had just brought back. Rather than make things difficult for the peasant family she was staying with, she decided it was time to leave France. In spring 1943, accompanied by Blanc, a fellow Resistance worker, she made her way south, first to Carcassonne then to Perpignan. Her mission was to set up a new escape route across the Pyrénées and take important requests to the British consulate in Barcelona, asking for a wireless operator, weapons, ammunition, food, and blankets for the Maquis.

Having to leave her grey suit and a book by Colette, she wore all her jumpers, and her haversack contained only toilet articles, a blouse, some handkerchiefs, pyjamas and a pair of shoes. Using aspirin to counter the effects of an infected wisdom tooth and mumps, she was taken by a Catalan guide over the pass used by the Spanish Republican Army when it escaped into France. She told Gleeson that it was the most awful experience of her life.

After a month or so working in the British embassy in Barcelona, she got her *salvoconducto* – a cardboard travel pass, new identity cards and a mission to escort nine men to Gibraltar. By early summer 1943 she was back in England. After being debriefed at the Royal Patriotic School, she joined the Women's Transport Service and was soon identified as a potential agent by the SOE. According to Escott, the Americans, presumably the Office of Strategic Services, disapproved of her as she was too easily recognised and had been too closely involved with the British Secret Services, with their interest in escape lines and potential secret agents. Having passed her interview and assessment at Wanborough, she was trained at Arisaig, Ringway and Beaulieu.

Gleeson described her as 'the best of her group, taking up unarmed combat in her magnificent stride, sabotage, shooting and detonating explosives came easily to her, rock-climbing, mountaineering and forced marches over the difficult Scottish countryside delighted her, she was good at sports and an excellent skier'.[26]

Her fear of parachuting was not a problem as, on 18 October 1943, twenty-seven-year-old Elizabeth was flown out of Tempsford in a Hudson. Accompanying her were Richard Heslop, her organiser; Owen D. Johnson, his radio officer; and J. Rosenthal, one of the MARKSMAN Resistance leaders. It was Johnnie Affleck's first Hudson mission. He touched down at 0030 hours in a field at Lons-le-Saunier, four kilometres west-south-west of Bletterans, after clipping a belfry tower and ripping the upper branches of some tree tops. This was the same drop zone as Eliane Plewman. In *Full Moon to France*, Elizabeth described what happened:

> We flew an hour or more over the dark and tranquil countryside, the shadow of our plane gliding along to keep us company. Then, when the dispatcher came and took our mugs of coffee, I knew we were almost there.

The pilots who flew these missions, whether in big planes or in tiny Lysanders, were the crack airmen of the RAF. They had to be because setting down their machines in fields lit only by flare paths cast by flashlights or bonfires required the most extraordinary skill. This time, perhaps because the other plane had already landed ahead of us and was taking off as we approached, our pilot missed his landing. Instead we hit the church belfry. The shock was tremendous, sending cases falling all over the place. What it did to the belfry I don't know. Monsieur le Curé would certainly have a lot of explaining to do.

'You'll have to jump. I think my landing gear is jammed.' The impersonal voice came over the long-com.

Suddenly the dispatcher was there, fitting a parachute harness on Paul while the plane veered. I started to feel sick as I drew my rucksack towards me, preparatory to having it strapped to one of my legs. The suitcase would follow later. God only knew where.

'Christ! All the Germans in the sector must be on the alert.'

'It's all right! She's out. Stand by for landing. Hurry! Hurry!'

And hurry we did. So much so that I sprawled on my face in the mud of France.

Just as well. My mac was too clean anyway.

I returned to France by the moon of October. There was a nip in the air and the sky was studded with stars. It was not a winter sky nor yet a summer one. A farewell and hello one, disputing the mellowness of summer, heralding the sharpness of winter.

The reception committee were said to have been surprised to see a tall, fair-haired young woman with a long aristocratic nose get out of the plane. McCall said that Elizabeth was accustomed to men's attention.

She looked a typical product of the girls' public school she had attended in southern England. She was in fact American, but showed no trace of her background. Heslop had been reluctant to take her because he felt even the most dim-witted policeman would be unable to mistake her for anything other than British.

Within minutes of landing she learned that Stephen, one of the circuit's leaders, had been arrested. Her initial safe house was a chalet she rented up in the mountains in Albigny, near Lake Annecy, where she hid her suitcase containing plastic explosives in the cellar. Her task was to help Heslop, codenamed Xavier, in an Anglo-French mission called CANTINIER, to work with French Gaullist J. P. Rosenthal. Initially it involved helping arrange the arming of the Maquis of the Ain, the Jura and the Haute Savoie. To give an idea of what it entailed, I include a few extracts from her autobiography.

Back at the house, I clattered down the steps of the cellar, my ski boots ringing against the stones. Behind a heap of empty bottles I found the suitcase. From a separate cardboard box I took the detonators and time pencils, carefully wrapped in cotton. Laying everything out on a board stretched across two barrels, I began to make up my charges, not noticing I hadn't any waterproofing until the primer was wedged in the plastic explosive. Although there was no necessity for the charges to be waterproof, I needed a dark material to wrap them because, once they were clinched by magnets, they would show up lighter than the locomotives. I remembered a navy blue scarf I had. It would be just right ...

Much later the four boys turned up, and when they filed in, brushing off the snow and blowing on their chapped hands, I knew I was committed. The thing had to be done.

I drew out Stephen's plans and briefed them step by step. Then I opened the suitcase and handed out the Sten guns. For myself I kept nothing. I was carrying the charges; that was enough.

The next day it snowed till eleven. Afterwards the sun came out and everything was crisp and fresh-looking. As I went down the hill, the lake was like a sheet of blue. I had planned the operation for nine, intending to wait in the house of a friend until then. When I hit the road and started towards Annecy, one of the boys tagged along behind. I was precious now. I was carrying the charges.

I left ten minutes before the rendezvous. Everything was quiet in the streets – the dimmed-out lamps casting long shadows on the snow. Only my footsteps made a ringing noise on the frozen sidewalk.

I turned off the secluded street into a busy thoroughfare and a shadow stepped out behind me. In front of the station it and I turned into a dark alley. I was to meet the others in an abandoned warehouse, and as I walked through the cavernous building, I heard the scraping of rats. Once the shadow behind me whispered: 'Careful Mademoiselle! The flooring is bad.'

Through the dirty, broken windows came a glow from the snow-covered station yard ... Finally the time came for us to move. My guard went first. I followed some paces behind. As I left the shelter of the warehouse, my back felt nakedly exposed. We walked slowly, stopping only once – when we reached the tracks ...

It only took a few minutes to clamp the first charge on the bearing rod. The second was equally easy, but, walking around to the third, I stumbled against a steel girder. The noise was frightful, and to my horror, a flash of light shot up just beyond the snub nose of the locomotive. I stood petrified while behind me my guide slid up and I felt the hard barrel of his Sten gun straining against my thigh. It didn't reassure me at all ...

Back in the warehouse I made the boys dismantle their Stens and stow them away in a rucksack. They were feeling so pleased with themselves I feel they would have walked through the streets of Annecy just for the heck of it. The whole operation had taken just fifteen minutes ...

I think I made the chalet in record time that night. I know I was puffing when I leaned against the gate. The air was now so clear that I could see down to the lake. I tried to think of anything, anything but three charges wrapped in dark material clamped to a bearing rod. Maybe I'd forgotten to crimp them. It sometimes happens in the excitement of the moment. But no, I'd done it before placing them in the primer. I was close to tears when I thought about my instructors back in England. A hell of a life for an American who happened to have been brought up in France. I should have let the Germans intern me. Time now, I snarled between my teeth, gripping my watch. Yes, time ladies and gentlemen. Time ... A vision of beer in pewter mugs and hot, happy faces in the pub. Time. ... It must be ...

Bang! ... It was sharp and clear and sweet music on the cold air.

Grinning, I opened the gate and trudged across the yard. I had my hand on the door when the second charge went off. Almost immediately after, the third exploded. For once I didn't swear when I fumbled with the matches to light the paraffin lamp; later, when I added a few drops of water to the violet, I was very happy.

David Harrison listed her as having worked as a courier for Lieutenant Colonel Richard Heslop, an RF agent in the MARKSMAN circuit in the mountainous region of south-east France, where she used the codename 'Typist' and the name 'Elizabeth La Grande'. Having an excellent memory, she could memorise a message verbatim, which saved her having to carry it around on pieces of paper.[27] Her training in 'ungentlemanly warfare' meant that she was as adept with handling explosives as she was with her hockey stick. In whatever situation she found herself, she was said to have

had a dignified bearing, a haughty arrogance which was once the hallmark of the English gentlewoman abroad.

She became a familiar sight in the Haute-Savoie and Jura, striding along the hilly roads between villages, her rucksack slung across her back, for all the world like an English eccentric on a walking holiday.

Her greatest attribute was a phenomenal memory. She rarely had to carry written messages. She could recite them carefully, memorise them, then repeat them verbatim when she arrived at her destination.[28]

George Millar, author of *Horned Pigeon* which describes his work with the Resistance, recalled meeting her in a remote farm. She was dressed in 'a handsome costume of brown tweed, extremely well-cut with a divided skirt. In her rucksack, slung on her back, was a magnificent dressing case with gold fittings and containing gold-backed brushes and combs – it was worth then about a million and a half French francs'. Whether she had taken it with her from England or acquired it in France was not mentioned.

Having located landing sites for Dakotas to take Allied personnel back to England, she helped Heslop run what was known by those who used it as the 'Xavier's Air Express Service'. In a comment to George Millar, a former *Daily Express* correspondent and another SOE agent sent to France, she complained that most of the American and British pilots – whom, among her other duties, she helped to repatriate – seemed so common.[29] Heslop was very impressed with Elizabeth and commented in his autobiography, *Xavier,* that she

> looked as English as her name – but was American. She was tall, with a prominent nose, and she did not walk, she strode. When you saw her coming towards you in the mountains, you automatically expected to see a couple of Labradors at her heels, and that her first words would be 'Had a bloody good walk, yer know, nothing like it for keeping fit'. I thought SOE were mad to send her to France, as she stuck out like a sore thumb, but when I raised the question they said she was a fully trained operative and knew the Savoie well. I liked her too, and my reluctance to take her was only based on her English looks. She did a fine job, for she had guts and imagination ...
>
> I was very fond of Elizabeth, for she seemed so English and appeared my only link with home at that time ...
>
> She had worked very gallantly for me and was always on the search for work. She never liked to sit about and if she had to stay in the command post for any length of time she would pester me to give her a task to get her moving again. But as the weeks went by I had more and more discreet and diffident inquiries about her. A person would say: 'Ah, Elizabeth, what a wonderful girl she is and how well she's liked. But doesn't she look English.' ...
>
> I didn't want to sack her because of the great assistance she was to me, and anyway I did not have the heart to. I took the coward's way out and asked London to recall her, having explained in my cable the growing concern about her Englishness.
>
> When the cable arrived ordering her to return to SOE, Elizabeth asked me why she had been recalled, but I was evasive and embarrassed and made some poor excuse. She then pleaded to stay, but I told her it would be folly as her mother was under constant surveillance by the Gestapo and the French police as she was known to be a foreigner. Reluctantly Elizabeth agreed to stay away and finally she left me.

She did visit her mother, though, who had been released from prison due to bad health. Almost as soon as she arrived, Elizabeth was arrested but kept to her cover story and was released.

When the Germans sent two divisions to attack the Resistance in the Haute-

Savoie, she managed to escape. Had it not been for forgetting her bag and delaying her departure, they would have arrived in a village which was wiped out by the Milice. Skiing through the mountains for two days helped them to escape to safety in Ambérieu.

As well as training men, on one occasion she was forced to help in a sabotage operation. The leader of a mission had been arrested so, according to Escott, she went to a railway shed in Annecy and set up the primers, time pencils and *plastique* on three railway engines herself.

> She planned to do this before the curfew at 11 o'clock, a job that could have been done in about 12 minutes. By bad luck, it snowed heavily that day and the men did not arrive until late. Nevertheless, she carried on as planned, handing out Sten guns and carrying the charges herself. It was done, though not without further delays and incidents, but they got away with it, with no-one killed.

Sometime later in 1944, Jean Helfer was claimed to have flown his Hudson out from Tempsford on a mission to pick her up from a former Luftwaffe airfield at Ambérieu. Heslop had decided that, as she was 'too conspicuous', he wanted to send her back to England, partly for her own sake and partly for those who were worried about her. She pleaded to be allowed to finish the job but he was adamant. So was she. She was desperate to get to Paris to see her invalid mother before flying back on 29 October. Instead, she was arrested on 20 October at a Swiss friend's apartment where she had left her bicycle, which she needed to get to her safe house in a convent. She wasn't sure if the telephone call she had made had been intercepted or whether she had been betrayed by her friend's friend, who had an Austrian brother-in-law.

A black Citroen took her to Rue des Saussies, where many arrested Resistance members and other criminals were held. In her Canadienne jacket she found a packet of RAF matches and a sixpence. She was being framed. The former she ate and the latter she slipped behind the skirting board.

To avoid her watch being taken she came up with an idea. 'Fortunately it was not too large and fairly flat. If my rectum would take it, it seemed the best place, but even that was no guarantee. I would have liked to smile at the idea of a timepiece playing hookey in my ass, but I didn't. I was just too worried about keeping it in there.' Two pairs of panties helped for a while but it was all in vain as the watch was eventually confiscated when she was put *au secret* – in solitary confinement for trying to escape by removing the bar from her cell window. Despite managing to unscrew the door lock from her cell, she gave up the idea of escape until she was transferred to Frèsnes Prison. An iron splinter from the bed didn't draw enough blood when she tried to commit suicide. Her will to live was too strong. Details of her captivity and interrogations can be found in her autobiography.

She stuck to her cover story that she was a US citizen who had only recently returned to France from Switzerland, having sold most of her jewellery to do so. While in prison, friends sent her food parcels and during interrogations, the Germans were never able to link her with the SOE.

Shortly after the D-Day landings, she was tried before a judge attached to the German army and accused of being in possession of a fake identity card. In fact, it was the real one she had been issued in 1940. According to Escott, the judge revealed the name of the person who betrayed her, someone she had suspected who was in her circle of Ambulance Service friends. Both Elizabeth and her Swiss friend were released and, being American, they were sent to the Vittel internment camp. When the Germans pulled out of Paris, she was freed by Allied forces. Heslop said of her afterwards that she had done 'a fine job, for she had guts and determination', but blamed London for recruiting someone who looked so un-French. In appreciation of the work she did, she was awarded the *Croix de Guerre* and the *Chevallier Legion d'Honneur*. According to Wikipedia, she never married and died in St Malo between 1981 and 1983.

4

Mass Arrests & Torture of SOE Female Agents, January 1944 to D-Day

The Abwehr and the Gestapo's counter-intelligence operations had successfully broken some Resistance networks and many hundreds had been arrested, imprisoned, taken to concentration camps and executed. Having suffered heavy losses, more agents were needed to create new networks and ensure the surviving Resistance groups were prepared for D-Day. Rather than encouraging independent attacks, the Resistance needed co-ordinating, and there was a special need to ensure the growing numbers of people opposed to German occupation had the wherewithal to resist. Plans were put in place to make sure that the Allied landing not only remained secret but also that German reinforcements be stopped from reaching Normandy. With so many wireless operators and couriers being caught, there was a vital need that they be replaced. In some cases, the urgency of the situation meant that training had to be curtailed.

Danielle Reddé

Danielle 'Eddie' Reddé, according to the World War Two Escape Lines website,[1] was a telephonist who joined the Resistance in Lyon in 1941. When the Australian Tom Groome (Georges de Milleville) was parachuted into France in October the following year to act as Pat O'Leary's wireless operator, Danielle worked as his courier, helping to get escapees and evaders into Spain.

In Neave's *Saturday at MI9*, he mentioned her taking his decoded messages to room 202 in the Hotel de Paris at Toulouse at 1430 hours and returning with O'Leary's reply for transmission to London.

On 11 January 1943, she, Tom, and some of the men they were wanting to get out of the country were arrested at a house in Montauban. He had failed to set a look-out while he was transmitting and was caught by

German direction-finding equipment. The English called them 'D-Effers' and the French 'Gonios'. Taken to the Gestapo HQ at Hotel Ours Blancs in Toulouse, Tom jumped out of a window trying to escape. Although he was recaptured, Danielle managed to escape in the commotion and crossed the Pyrénées in March with Nancy Wake, an Australian, and several others involved in the French Resistance. Her codename was 'Camille Fournier'. After arriving in England, she joined the BCRA (*Bureau Central de Renseignements et d'Action*) on 14 June. This was de Gaulle's Free French Intelligence Bureau on Delphin Square. Using the name Edith Daniel, she was trained by the SOE as a wireless operator for RF Section.

Codenamed 'Morroccin'/'Marocain', she was said by Harrison to have been parachuted into France on 1 January 1944 to work in the Lyon area.[2] Clark says that the winter of 1943 was so severe that many missions had to be cancelled. As there was none from Tempsford that night, it's possible that Danielle was flown in from Massingham, SOE's forward base in Algeria. Whether she had been flown out of Tempsford earlier is unknown. Tillet gives the date as 9 February but the only detail was that she was dropped near Montluçon.

As well as sending radio messages, she acted as a courier and was also known as 'Maria Kermarec'. After the American and French Forces landed on the Mediterranean coast in August 1944, their northern advance eventually overran Danielle's area.

The *Mémoire et Espoirs de la Résistance* website mentions her arriving back in London on a ship from Calcutta on 3 May 1945. What she was doing in India is unknown but the SOE was active in the Far East at that time. Before long she accepted another mission, this time as Sous-lieutenant Simone Fournier, to work with the SOE in liberating Allied prisoners of war held in Japanese camps in Indochina. On 22 August, this time codenamed 'Edith Fournier', she and Lieutenant Klotz parachuted into Thakhek, Laos, just over the border from Thailand. She was to work as his wireless operator. While she was away, de Gaulle awarded her the *Médaille du Combattant Volontaire de la Résistance*, the *Médaille commémorative des services volontaires dans la France Libre*, the *Croix du Combattant*, the *Croix de Guerre avec Palme* and *Chevalier de la Légion d'Honneur*.

In commending Danielle for the *Croix de Guerre des théâtres d'opérations extérieurs avec Etoile d'Argent*, Colonel Roos and Capitaine Goudry said that on 14 December 1945 Danielle parachuted with her radio into what they described as a very dangerous part of Laos with no reception committee. Despite being wounded on landing and surrounded by hostile forces, she showed calm and composure. Thanks to her constant efforts and devotion, she saved numerous human lives and participated in the evacuation of all the French from the province where she was working and transmitted vital military and political messages. However, the wound she got on landing resulted in her being hospitalised in Bangkok.

Once recovered from her injury, she was assigned to Saigon on 29 March 1946. This mission involved dealing with all the social problems raised by repatriating the French women and children who had been interned in Shanghai, separate from their husbands. For her work in the Far East, Danielle was awarded a *Citation à l'ordre du Corps d'Armée*. The British awarded her with the Medal of the British Empire as well as an honorary Colonial Medal. In 1953, she was given the *Médaille en Argent du Million d'éléphants (à titre militaire) dans l'Ordre du Règne du Laos*, the *Médaille militaire*, and the *Médaille des Evadés*.[3]

Anne-Marie Walters

The first flight of 1944 from Tempsford was not until 4 January, when Pilot Officer Buchanan flew his Halifax on operation WHEELWRIGHT 50 to France. The Squadron records note that he was suspicious when a twin-engined aircraft was spotted with its navigation lights on near Angoulême. The navigator pinpointed Langon in the Gironde and, ten kilometres from the target, picked up a Rebecca transmission. He descended in good visibility in the clear moonlit sky to about 700 feet and dropped fifteen containers, four packages and two agents: Claude Arnault, an explosives expert, and twenty-year-old Anne-Marie Walters.

According to her autobiography, it was a marshy field on the edge of a wooded area of the Landes, not far from Condom. While she was sipping acorn coffee in a decrepit farm, deep in straw and manure, a two-oxen cart picked up the packages that were dropped with her.[4]

Born in Geneva on 16 March 1923 to a father who was Oxford don and Deputy Secretary General of the League of Nations, and a French mother, Anne-Marie was raised in Switzerland speaking mostly French with some English. Many of her holidays were in the south of France with her parents and younger sister, Cici. Attending an International school, she became politicised on hearing about events in the Spanish Civil War. When war was declared, her father drove her, her sister, her mother, and their dog in his Humber car to safety in Hendaye, via Narbonne. Several days later they caught a P&O liner at Verdon-sur-Mer which took them to Glasgow. Micky, her dog, had to be left behind at the harbour.

The following year, despite the disapproval of her mother, seventeen-year-old Anne-Marie, like many of the other female agents, joined the WAAF. As an Assistant Second Officer, she worked in the RAF Fighter Command headquarters at Bentley Priory, near Stanmore. Here, as an 'itinerary plotter', she helped plot all enemy raids on wall maps, blackboards and the large 'Ops' table, using information provided by WAAFs listening to messages through telephone headsets. Different-coloured counters representing the Luftwaffe formations were moved across the map using magnetic rakes.

Although dismissed for indiscipline, she was taken on by the SOE on 6 July 1943. SOE recognised that her knowledge of French would prove a valuable asset. Her personnel file in the National Archives includes comments from the instructor for the Student Assessment Board while she underwent training at Winterfold, near Cranleigh in Surrey. Dated 29 July 1943, the document records her General agent grading as F, Intelligence Rating 9, Aptitude for Morse AVERAGE, Mechanical AVERAGE, with the remark that she was:

> A keen, very intelligent girl with a realistic practical sense. Ample courage, determination and a sense of humour. She has marked latent possibilities but is at present immature, inexperienced and not sufficiently in control of herself for subversive work. With maturity she should prove a girl of exceptional qualities.[5]

Similar concerns appeared in her instructors' report while she was on the paramilitary training course in Meoble Lodge, Inverness-shire, between 2 August and 13 September. During her parachute training at Ringway, she admitted that she only jumped because the boys expected the girls to be scared and refuse. Rubbing their hands with glee in anticipation of a good laugh, they said, 'Ha ha. We just cannot wait to see you shake like a jellyfish and howl with terror on the edge of the hole.' When it came to it, they were just as scared as she was, but she made herself equal to them by jumping. Afterwards, she went to the SOE's 'Finishing School' at Beaulieu. The instructor there showed a similar awareness of character. His report, dated 26 October, stated that:

> She is well-educated, intelligent, quick, practical and cunning. She is active minded, curious, and has plenty of imagination. She is keen and, on the whole, worked hard, displaying outstanding initiative. Nevertheless she is erratic and was inclined to be inattentive when she was not particularly interested. She has a very strong character, is domineering, aggressive and self-confident. She is vain and rather self-conceited. She has been badly spoilt and is always 'agin the government'. She is rather an exhibitionist and hates being ignored. She resents discipline or any attempt to thwart her wishes. She is irritable and impatient of the mistakes of others less quick and intelligent than herself. She is inclined to get over-excited and is slightly hysterical. She is rather more immature than the other members

of the party, but it was not, on the whole, beneficial. She tended to make them discontented and to distract their attention from their work. It is doubtful whether she is aware of what she is undertaking, especially in its relation to others. She has a strong personality. At times she is charming. All too frequently, however, she is rude and tactless. She is restless and lacking in repose. She would make as many enemies as friends. She will not hesitate to always make use of her physical attractiveness in gaining influence over men. In this respect she is likely to have a disturbing effect in any group of which she is a member. This influence was clearly discernible here. She has the brains, and to some extent, the character to do valuable work. Nevertheless it is doubtful whether she should be employed. As an individual she is likely to be conspicuous. She would almost certainly resent occupying a subordinate position, yet she does not appear to be temperamentally suited to have authority over others. She will probably exercise an unsettling influence upon many with whom she comes into contact. Codes: routine practice only required.

Desperate for more agents, Buckmaster overrode these concerns, and allocated twenty-year-old Anne-Marie a courier role in a quiet, rural area of south-west France. 'She is going to the field with a very limited job which will not endanger the security of any other agents.' On 6 November, she was appointed an assistant senior officer in the FANY, her salary being paid into her bank while she was in the field.

The first attempt to drop her was on 16 December, but the mission was aborted because of the bad weather. The signal letter was flashed but the pilot couldn't make out the red landing lights. Returning to England was traumatic because of dense fog everywhere. Approaching Woodbridge on the Suffolk coast, the pilot communicated with the airfield. The Commanding Officer asked permission of the Commanding Officer of Tempsford to have the passengers bail out. This was refused. On the fourth attempt to land, the Halifax crashed, killing the pilot, navigator and either the engineer or dispatcher. The other crew members were wounded, one sustaining broken ribs, another a broken arm and the third a broken leg. According to her personnel file, Anne-Marie was lucky. A padded helmet, parachute and padded jumpsuit protected her so that, apart from shock and concussion, she only had a cut on the scalp and a bruise behind the right ear. Claude had an abrasion over his right eye and slight sprains to his ankles. They were driven down to London, where Anne-Marie was provided a safe house with Mrs Winser, 17 Devonshire Close, W1. Both were described as 'in high spirits and expressed a wish to be able to return soon to their jobs'.

The second attempt, on 4 January, was successful. She and Claude parachuted safely in a marshy field, just missing a canal, at Créon d'Armagnac, near Gabarret, a small village about forty kilometres east of Mont-de-Marsan in the wooded Landes. Taken by the reception committee to a nearby farmhouse, it seemed that everyone knew who she was and where she had come from, welcoming her with wine which she felt it impolite to refuse.

Codenamed 'Colette', Anne-Marie worked as a courier for George Starr's WHEELWRIGHT circuit but used the alias 'Paulette' in her autobiography. Her identity card was in the name of Alice Davoust, with a cover story that she was a Parisian student recovering from pneumonia. Needing the air, she was based in Castelnau-sur-l'Auvignon, a small hilltop community in rural Gascony, which was considered safe from German eyes as it had no electricity and no running water. The toilet was the bushes behind the hen house. Developing a hacking cough and fever shortly after arriving helped her cover when the doctor was called. Yvonne Cormeau was already working there as Starr's wireless operator, and as he was building up his network, he needed more help. Escott narrated one of Anne-Marie's first tasks in her *Mission Impossible*.

> She learned to drive in the hair-raising French style, mainly in vehicles with charcoal powered 'gazo' (for *gazogéne*) as the French mockingly nicknamed any makeshift power source which they were forced to use for their transport, since only the Germans had petrol for their Citröens. She used cars, trains, her bicycle, and crowded buses. She sometimes had to chase far afield after busy members of the circuit to deliver and pick up her messages. She met people of all kinds, shapes, sizes and walks of life who were members of the Resistance – a butcher, a spare parts shopkeeper, a womanising spiv, a communist, a second-hand clothes dealer, a wine merchant, a girl whose husband had escaped to England, and a Jew.

Her first important mission was to meet twenty-one escapees from the central prison at Eysses, near Toulouse, and accompany them to Fourcés. After a 160-kilometre trip in the back of a truck to Tarbes to find guides to escort them over the Pyrénées, she and Starr had to find them safe houses until the weather was right for a crossing. They also had to avoid a detachment of SS troops sent in to get retribution for an attack on some of their numbers. More of her adventures can be read in Escott's book.

> Another escape mission was to accompany a French police inspector to the Pyrénées. He had worked for the resistance in Paris, Grenoble, and Agen, but now the Gestapo net was closing around him, so he had to be sent to safety as he was endangering not only himself but also the circuit. On the way to

the railway station he confessed to concern over the fact that he carried a gun and two identity cards. One was a false civil card to show the Gestapo, the other was his true police card allowing him to carry arms, which he could use at French controls. In their first train he dozed and all went well, but in the second from Toulouse to Montréjeau, sitting opposite each other in an empty compartment, they were interrupted by a ticket collector. Before looking at their shared ticket he started asking Anne-Marie searching questions and then studied her companion's civil papers. From where she sat Anne-Marie saw the policeman grow pale and she remembered the incriminating revolver. She grabbed her bag and started fumbling in it, drawing the ticket inspector's eyes to her. Still looking at her he handed back her friend's papers and left the compartment without another word. As she relaxed, the policeman warned her to be still and slipped his gun behind the seat. Then two men in turn passed along the corridor, watching them out of the corner of their eyes, a frequent trick of the Gestapo who hoped to catch suspects relaxing and taken off their guard. The police inspector's brother had been caught like this. Nothing more happened, however, the journey was completed, and the policeman was delivered to a safe house ready for onward transmission to the Pyrénées guides.

Other missions included carrying important messages from 'Hilaire', BBC messages, demolition orders, A and B messages (coded orders for before and after D-Day), money and letters between Montrejeau, Mazeres de Neste, Tarbes and Agen in Gers, as well as to places in the Dordogne, Paris, and Brittany. Despite her suggesting it, 'Hilaire', did not send her on any risky jobs. In fact, 'The main fighting I did was getting into buses, which was no small enterprise!'

In Jacques Poirier's *Giraffe Has a Long Neck*, he said that on Anne-Marie's first bus journey she made an almost fatal error at the ticket office by saying:

'A single to Brive, please.' '*Que dites-vous?*' [What did you say?] demanded the woman behind the window. I quickly pulled myself together. '*Un billet pour Brive, s'il vous plait, madame.*' And to think I'd just spent nearly six months learning the tradecraft of a secret agent!

On one occasion she had to go to Paris. Aware that she might be stopped and searched at any time, she had in her mind what had happened to a seventeen-year-old boy in Agen. During the first week of her time in France, he was arrested by Gestapo and died the same day following torture. As it turned out, she survived the trip.

In her autobiography, *Moondrop to Gascony*, Anne-Marie admitted feeling like she had 'British agent' written all over her face but, after a while she 'lost the sensation of being an outlaw' and never had a dull moment. When she had to go to large towns she had to modify her appearance. 'I discarded my beret, it was all right in a small town like Condom, but in Agen women wore high, complicated hairstyles and even more complicated ear-rings.' Starr advised her that her hairstyle needed changing as it was inappropriate for rural communities. 'You'd better not do your hair swept up across the back like this. Women in country towns round here wear it very high in front and down at the back ... Your clothes are not very suitable for this region either.' He also warned her not to smoke in public as so few women smoked in that area that she would be picked out right away.

It worked, as during her work she brushed sleeves with the Gestapo, arranging for wanted men to leave France, waiting on lonely fields for an incoming plane bringing arms and ammunition and sharing with unflinching bravery the hardships of underground life. While there she became 'romantically involved' with Claude, which also caused concern for Starr. As a present for her twenty-first birthday, he arranged a beautifully decorated cake with twenty-one lighted candles – the latter being impossible to find in occupied France. He had cut some detonating fuse and painted it pink, which caused her friends to evacuate the room.

After D-Day, the Germans launched an attack on Castelnau-sur-l'Auvignon. Escott detailed how she acquitted herself bravely, unpacking and distributing grenades. As hand-to-hand fighting got closer, she was ordered to take the groups' records and hide or destroy them. While a small band of men fought off their attackers, she had time to bury the box in a cave beneath the village church. She also had time to rescue some SOE money from the Mayor's house, where Starr lived, but could not retrieve her identity cards. As she was running away, she heard the houses being blown to pieces when their arsenal exploded in the church tower. Once out of danger, she got a lift to Condom to be reunited with her friends. For several weeks she helped the Armagnac Battalion receive more parachute supplies and 'Jed' teams.

The 'Jeds' or 'Jets' were a team of three fully uniformed and trained French, British, American or Canadian officers who were sent into France by parachute on and after D-Day to liaise between the Allies and the Resistance, direct sabotage missions, and ascertain the need for supplies, money and ammunition. One of the team was a wireless operator who would contact London and arrange parachute drops. They sent a strong message to the local people that the Allies had arrived to help liberate them, a great boost to morale.

However, having been identified to the Vichy police by an informer,

Starr ordered her to go to Lannemezan. On the morning of 29 June she rendezvoused with US Major Horace Fuller, codenamed 'KANSUL', Captain Guy La Roche, and Sub-Lieutenant Martial Siguad, both French. They were the Jedburgh team of BUGATTI, parachuted into the Hautes Pyrénées from Blida, in Algiers.

In Hewson's postscript to the republished *Moondrop to Gascony*, he quotes from an undated confidential letter Anne-Marie wrote to Buckmaster. In it she told him that, when she returned to Avéron-Bergelle at midnight on 25 July 1944,

> I was pushed into a room by Buresie (Hilaire's *'garde de corps'* – a Russian ex-legionnaire) and shown a paper declaring textually: *prière d'arrêter et d'incarcérer Mademoiselle Colette dès son retour* ... I was thrown into prison with the captured Miliciens and collaborators (including their fleas and lice) and a guard was ordered to sleep at my side ... The whole Maquis knew of this and decided I must be a Gestapo double-agent ...

The following day she was taken to Hilaire's command post, where he accused her of having an affair with a member of the battalion, spreading scandalous stories about him having relations with another female agent, and of being undisciplined. She vigorously denied his accusations.

> I brought KANSUL to HILAIRE, who wanted to try and explain the various political entanglements of the region to him. From then on I continued liaison with them, mainly on bicycle.
>
> On July 28th, HILAIRE decided to send me on to LONDON with a report on the various political difficulties in the S.W. He gave me no contact for one of our escape lines, and I am convinced that he had none. KANSUL put me in touch with guides. He also asked me to go on a mission for him to Major Champion, at 1ssU6, Algiers – which I was glad to. Started out on August 1st, lost ourselves four times: left from the Col des Arts, west of Aspet, climbed the Pic du Gard, passed near Boutx and Mollo and arrived well east of Canejan on August 4th ...[6]

Accompanying her were US Major Fuller, the leader of the Jedburgh BUGATTI team, Captain La Roche, a wireless operator, and Leslie Brown, a downed RAF pilot who had joined the Maquis and fought bravely with a Bren gun at Castlenau. They were all taken into custody by the Spanish police and transported via Sort to Vielha. After four days behind bars, the British Consul arranged their release and onward journey to Barcelona to meet Colonel General Harold Farquar, described by Hewson as a solid supporter of the SOE.

Under the guise of 'Miss Fitzgerald', Anne-Marie made her way to Madrid, where she had to wait another four days before getting the necessary papers to allow her to get to Algiers with Major Fuller's message.

> I was at 1ssU6 Algiers on September 1st; there I saw Major Marten instead of Champion. He suggested that I should go back to France for the Jedburgh section and work with a party under his command. I was to help rounding up the Jeds which I could easily do in the S.W. and help in their debriefing. After that was done, we were to start a new plan of re-contacting all the contacts we had (both the F Section and the Jeds) in order to build up, from that very solid basis, new and better post-war relations between the French and the British. We had a long talk with Col. Anstey [?] about it; he agreed to take me on and suggested we should start back to France right away. I was very attracted by this job as I had always been interested in Franco-British relations and because I had worked for seven months and failed to see the conclusion of all our efforts, being away during the big Allied victories. Unfortunately, London refused to allow me on this job and I had to return.

Getting back to England by the end of July 1944, she was upset not to have had three suitcases of luggage forwarded to her and to only be offered a £15 clothing allowance. When she contacted SOE, they told her that the contents of her cases had been bought with SOE funds so didn't actually belong to her.

With the help of US Captain Millet, one of 'F' Section's training officers, she and FANY officer Suzanne Warren managed to get onto another parachute training course at Ringway. Her visit at the end of October caused quite a stir. Sergeant Kenworthy, the External Security Officer at Ringway, commented in his report that she showed complete disregard for personal security during the course.

> The usual precautions taken to hide the sex of FANYs performing parachute descents were put into effect, but from the first they were nullified by her behaviour on the dropping ground at Tatton Park. The following are examples of what happened during the week:–
>
> Immediately on landing, she invariably removed her protective helmet, and shook her hair out, thus advertising the fact that she was a woman to everyone in sight. This happened on at least one occasion when Paratroopers were also on the field. She appeared to make a point of conducting a conversation either on the field or in the air with someone at least fifty yards away ensuring that her voice attracted the attention of anyone who had not previously seen her. Following a descent she and her colleague

Right: 1. 1944 photograph of RAF Tempsford, the airfield from which most of the women agents were flown. (Courtesy of East Anglian Aviation Society) *Below*: 2. Undated photograph of a Lysander, the small plane used to land many of the women agents sent to France and return passengers to England. (Freddie Clarke, *Agents by Moonlight*)

3. Undated photograph of Short Stirling bombers which had to be specially modified to carry containers and parachutists into occupied Europe. (Courtesy of wwiivehicles.com)

4. Undated photograph of Handley Halifax bomber used to parachute agents into occupied Europe. (Courtesy of wwiivehicles.com)

5. Undated photograph of a FANY driver, often employed to bring the women agents to their airfield and pick them up when they returned. (Courtesy of Bill Bright)

6. Agents being checked to ensure there was nothing to indicate they were from England on their clothing. (Courtesy of Harrington Aviation Museum

7. Undated photograph of agents kitted up and preparing to board the plane. (Courtesy of Harrington Airfield Museum)

8. One of the agents receiving her last kiss before boarding the plane. (Courtesy of Pierre Tillet)

Above: 9. WAAF Sergeant 'Tottie' Lintott chalking up details of the missions for that night on the board inside Gibraltar Farm, the nerve centre of RAF Tempsford. Dated between 31 March and 28 April 1944. (Courtesy of Ken Merrick)
Right: 10. Anne-Marie Walters parachuted into southwest France in January 1944 to work as a courier in George Starr's WHEELWRIGHT network. (*Le Battalion de Guerilla de l'Armagnac 158e R.I.* 1997)

Left: 11. Violette Szabó, codenamed Carine, dropped in France on 4 April 1944, returned by Lysander on 30 April and returned on 7 June. Arrested three days later, she was executed at Ravensbrück concentration camp in early 1945. (Courtesy of Harrington Aviation Museum)

Below: 12. One of RAF Tempsford Westland Lysanders. Known as 'Lizzie' or the 'Flying Carrot', it was used by 161 Squadron to take two or three passengers to occupied France and bring others back. Pilots could land in a field the size of a football pitch and take off in less than five minutes. Note the ladder on its side to speed up operations. (In Freddie Clark's *Agents by Moonlight*)

Above: 13. Eileen Nearne or 'Didi' as she liked to be known, worked as a wireless operator in the Paris area. After capture, interrogation and torture she was sent to prison camps in Germany and was one of the very few to escape. (Courtesy of Odile Nearne)
Right: 14. Jacqueline Nearne, Eileen's sister, worked as a courier in South West France and was returned to England in 1944. (Courtesy of Odile Nearne)

15. Eileen and Jacqueline's brother, Francis Nearne, who was recruited by Jacqueline in May 1943 to work as a courier and Lysandered back to England five months later. (Courtesy of Odile Nearne)

16. Eileen Nearne (left) and Odette Sansom at the 1993 (she was Odette *Hallowes* by this date) unveiling of a plaque commemorating those who died at Ravensbrück concentration cam. They were two of the few survivors. (Courtesy of Odile Nearne)

would remain on the field without their helmets, watching other descents. When spoken to by the Medical Orderly whose duty it was to get them off the field unnoticed, she replied in a rude fashion. In the presence of two M.T. drivers (and I believe among other students) she talked freely of actual operations in which she had taken part. Any effort by her Instructors to make her conform to the Security rules were received with ill-grace; her attitude being that the need for it had passed.[7]

Without her knowledge, Starr had sent a message back to 'F' Section saying that he had had to send her back to England because, despite his efforts to train her since her arrival, she was, according to a note in his personnel file,

> Undisciplined, most indiscreet, man-mad, also disobedient in personal matters, She constitutes a danger to security, not only her own but of everyone. On the other had she does not lack courage, never hesitated to go on any mission. Totally unsuitable for any commission. She should not be sent back to France to work for our organisation.[8]

Back in England, she got off to a bad start. In a note in her personnel file, an RAF pilot training instructor commented on her being somewhat indiscreet. He had noticed her standing on the departure platform for the Manchester train at Euston station. Nothing untoward, but she had caused quite a commotion wearing her blue parachute wings on her FANY uniform. After being spoken to, she resigned her commission. Notes in her file indicate that a planned job working for the Free French fell through, so she made plans to work for *News Chronicle*, one of the British daily papers.

What follows is a transcript of an interview she had with the BBC in early March 1945. The blocked text had to be deleted before transmission.

CUE MATERIAL FOR PARACHUTE GIRL

On March 5th, Sir Archibald Sinclair revealed for the first time in his speech to the Commons that members of the Women's Auxiliary Air Force have been to the fore in helping the Resistance groups in Europe before the landing on D-Day, either as Liaison officers, or couriers or radio operators.

We have in the studio today a girl who was parachuted into France many months before D-Day [and] remained several months after fighting with the Maquis. This WAAF had an English father and a French mother and was brought up in Geneva and she begins this interview with Vera Lindsay by telling how she was chosen for this special work.

[BLOCKED]

PARA.GIRL: Well I was in the WAAFs and as I'd always made quite a lot of noise about being able to speak French and wanted to do some work having to do with the Free French and I had been on the list for transfer of jobs for some time.

LINDSAY: Tell me – how long did you train for this special work and was the training very difficult?

PARA.GIRL: Well I trained quite a long time, and the training was extremely interesting and very useful to me but I'm afraid I cannot talk at all about that right now.

LINDSAY: Were there other women training with you?

PARA.GIRL: Yes, there were a number of other women training with me. Quite a number trained after I left and went later too.

LINDSAY: But were they English girls who spoke French?

PARA.GIRL: Some were French but most of them were English girls speaking absolutely fluent French. Actually French like a native woman.

[BLOCKED]

LINDSAY: But in those days just before you left were you able to see ordinary people? I mean your friends in London?

PARA.GIRL: Well the only people I knew and frequented so to speak were my friends who were doing the same job as I was and my family didn't know anything about it and we had worked out all our stories to the last details. Whenever they came at home they never mentioned anything of the work we were doing. My parents knew I was doing secret work but they didn't know at all, they didn't have any idea what it was. And my friends played up to the game very well.

[BLOCKED]

LINDSAY: And just before the jump – what was the feeling? Were you afraid?

PARA.GIRL: No, I wasn't afraid. In fact it was the only time in all the jumps that I have made that I really wasn't afraid at all. There were so many things to think about and it was our second trip. The pilot had circled some time in the region before being able to contact our people on the ground and we had a horrible moment that we should have to go back once more. And when the pilot declared that he had contacted the people and we were to go to action stations and jump – I felt so relieved at the idea that we wouldn't have to go back again to England it was really quite a pleasure. [BLOCKED]

LINDSAY: ... they've never learned what your work was?

PARA.GIRL: Oh no, they never found out.

[BLOCKED][9]

Starr, when he met de Gaulle in Toulouse on 16 September 1944, was given just days to leave the country. The new President of France didn't want a British military figure running affairs. Desperate to get back to France herself, Anne-Marie managed to get appointed as assistant to the American Press Attaché in Toulouse. A report, dated 24 April 1945, reached SOE HQ expressing concerns about 'her justifying herself for her past activities with those with whom she comes into contact'. A message was sent to the Press Attaché in Paris, but whether it affected her employment is not known.

In an interview with the Imperial War Museum, Starr admitted wanting to have her shot. Hewson detailed how she had initiated an investigation into Starr allowing the torture of captured Miliciens to get information out of them. They were put on a salt diet, left in a dark cell and then interrogated under bright lights, given a stool pigeon, someone who encouraged them to talk, and a microphone was installed. There was one case of a prisoner having the bottom part of his leg burned off over a fire. It was found that he was 'never party to, nor did he authorise, approve or condone such ill-treatment or the inflicting of torture'.[10]

The following year, 1946, Anne-Marie published *Moondrop to Gascony*, an account of her experiences. It provides a vivid portrait of Starr and Arnault, with whom she was romantically involved, and won the John Llewellyn Rhys Prize in 1947. The revised edition, published in 2009, sheds more light onto her experiences.

The citation for her MBE stated that: 'She covered the whole region with trips by car, train and bicycle carrying messages for Lt. Col. Starr and his regional organisers. Several days after J-Day she rejoined the Maquis but continued to conduct different liaisons. She never shrank from any effort to accomplish her missions. Her coolness and profound imagination helped her through her adventures.' Major General Gubbins also added that 'she worked courageously for six months in difficult conditions, and her commanding officer has commented on her personal courage and willingness to undergo any danger'.

What Hewson failed to mention was that Anne-Marie was also awarded the *Croix de Guerre* and the *Médaille de la Reconnaissance Française*. After the war she lived in Spain and France and was known under her married name of Anne-Marie Comert as a translator and editor. She died in France on 3 October 1998.

Marguerite Petitjean

Marguerite Petitjean, also known as 'Binette', was recorded by Harrison as parachuting into France on 29/30 January 1944 with Yvon Morandat, René Obadia and Eugenie Déchelette.[11] Not mentioned by Clark, they were four members of the French BCRA, and like Reddé, were part of de

Gaulle's RF Section. Wing Commander Speare of 138 Squadron dropped them from his Halifax on a drop zone, codenamed Ajuster, near St Uze in Drôme, about sixty kilometres south-west of Grenoble. Déchelette broke his ankle on landing so needed assistance in reaching the safe house. Apart from her being a member of the Corps Auxiliaire Féminin, very little detail about her has come to light in SOE literature.

It was her obituary in *The Miami Herald* that provided most detail. 'She was an extremely kind and loving woman,' said her daughter-in-law, Melissa Bassett. 'But at the same time, she was very stern. You really saw the soldier in her.' Marguerite was born in Strasbourg, France, in 1921 and trained as a nurse during her teenage years. In 1939 she volunteered as a Red Cross ambulance driver, but a single act of cruelty persuaded her to become a World War II soldier. She witnessed a Nazi officer shoot a little girl who lived in her town. The incident inspired her to join the French Resistance.

Joining the Free French Forces, she went to England, where she received SOE training. When she returned to France, she worked as a wireless operator for Alexandre Parodi's network and was involved in seventeen missions before and after D-Day. Her assignments supported military actions to disable enemy bridges and power stations. In one escapade, she suffered multiple injuries, including a fractured skull and a broken spine, and her life was often in grave danger. During one sabotage mission, she was captured by two enemy soldiers. She waited until they fell asleep and then tied them up while holding her .32-caliber gun, which she nicknamed 'Josephine' and kept throughout her life.

Her missions were so successful that the Germans placed a 10-million-franc ($500,000) price on her head. To avoid capture, she escaped by crossing the Pyrénées into Spain. In recognition of her work she attained the rank of captain and was awarded the *Legion d'Honneur*, the highest military decoration in France. She was also a five-time recipient of the *Croix de Guerre*, a French award for bravery.

On 23 June 1946, she married Henry Bassett, an American she met during the war, at the Cathedral de Notre Dame in Paris and went to live in Florida. She died in August 1999.

Madeleine Damerment

Clark has detailed how, on 28/29 February 1944, Pilot Officer Caldwell of 161 Squadron took off in his Halifax to complete PHONO 4. Over Ouistreham on the French coast, he flew through a pyrotechnic display of light flak, searchlights and red and orange flares. His navigator pinpointed Angeville, about forty kilometres south-east of Chartres, and the plane descended to 700 feet to make a DR (dropping run). Three agents, J. F.

Antelme, the leader, Lionel Lee, the wireless operator, and twenty-six-year-old Madeleine Damerment, a French captain in the Resistance, were dropped straight into waiting German hands. Unbeknown to the pilot or the agents, the arrangements for their drop had been made by the Germans, who had captured Noor Inayat Khan's wireless set. The flashing code for the circuit was correct but, as the network had been penetrated, Madeleine and her colleagues were caught in a trap. After a brief struggle, they were arrested and taken to Avenue Foch, the Gestapo headquarters in Paris.

According to Foot, she was brave, young, and gentle, and the least conspicuous of all the available couriers. 'Mlle Damerment's *ordre de mission* gives the dropping zone as 3km SE Sainville, 31 km ESE of Chartres', some twelve kilometres north-west of Angeville, from where Caldwell made his dropping run. She had two codenames, 'Solonge' and 'Dancer', and separate identity cards, which showed her as 'Jacqueline Duchateau' and 'Martine Dassautoy'.

Born in Torte Fontain, Pas de Calais on 11 November 1917, she grew up with two sisters in Lille, where her traditional Catholic father was the Postmaster General. After doing well at school, she worked for the telephone service, but following the German occupation, the whole family helped the Resistance. She and her sisters provided food parcels to prisoners of war and Madeleine helped as a courier in Michael Trotobas' FARMER network. She is credited with escorting seventy-five downed Allied aircrew and evaders along the PAT escape line through France and into Spain, Portugal and Gibraltar. Her boyfriend, Roland Lepers, was one of the escorts.

Escott described her as having a cloud of dark curling hair, dark eyes, round cheeks and a generous mouth. She was intelligent, vivacious, gentle and had many friends. It was suggested that through her work, she may have met Andrée Borrel of the PHYSICIAN network in Paris as well as Antelme of the BRICKLAYER network.

After her parents and others were arrested in late 1941, Roland got her away from her house before the police arrived and arrested her family. They went south to Tulles to wait until their escape could be organised, crossing the Pyrénées separately in March 1942. She was interned for months by the Spanish in the Miranda camp and became very ill. Her release was negotiated by the British consulate in Madrid and a passage was arranged to take her to England. After being treated in hospital for a glandular complaint, the nuns at the Convent of the Sacred Heart in Hitchin, Hertfordshire, helped her to recuperate.

When she eventually met Roland, he refused to marry her. However, she made friends with members of the Free French Forces in London and came to the attention of SOE.

In October 1943, after interviews, she volunteered to work for them. Her experiences in France meant that she did not need as much training as the other women. Despite one instructor's report that she was 'lacking in aggressiveness', and another that she was 'quiet and unobtrusive, her courage was proven, and she had seemed a good choice', she was given a commission as ensign in the FANY. Madeleine's mission was to have worked as a courier in Antelme's BRICKLAYER network in Chartres, south-west of Paris.

Antelme and Lee were tortured and eventually executed at Gross Rosen prison. After interrogation at Avenue Foch, where the Germans reportedly just laughed at her when she refused to say anything, she was transferred to Frèsnes prison. On 13 May, Madeleine was sent back to Avenue Foch, where she met seven other captured SOE women, including Andrée Borrel. From there they were sent in cattle trucks to Karlsruhe civil prison, and she was still wearing the same grey skirt and pullover she had been wearing when she arrived.

Kramer interviewed a German woman prisoner with whom she shared a cell and was told that during the heavy RAF raids on Karlsruhe, Madeleine clasped her rosary beads and prayed. Sometimes they sang to keep her spirits up and exchanged stories about their homes and families. Her German cell mate had been imprisoned having been informed on for telling a joke about Hitler in the street.

On 10 September 1944 Madeleine was transferred by train to Munich and then to the Dachau concentration camp with Eliane Plewman, Yolande Beekman and Noor Inayat Khan. Escott detailed how it was a second-class compartment and they enjoyed chatting in the sunshine and looking at the Swabian mountains. 'Madeleine, who was the only one who spoke German, won some small privileges from the guards.' When she arrived at midnight, her clothes now in tatters, she was put in solitary confinement.

At dawn on the 13th all four were taken out for execution. She asked in German for a priest but was told there wasn't one. Holding hands in pairs, they were shot through the back of the neck. Madeleine needed two bullets. All the bodies were then burnt in the crematorium. After the war she was posthumously awarded the KCBC, *Croix Legion d'Honneur*, and the *Medaille de Resistance*.[12]

Eileen 'Didi' Nearne

On 2 March 1944, two days after Jeanne's arrival in France, two Lysanders of 161 Squadron left England with young women on board: twenty-three-year-old Eileen 'Didi' Nearne and twenty-nine-year-old Denise Bloch.

Didi was from an unusual family in that both she and her elder sister Jacqueline and her brother Francis became SOE agents. When Didi was three, her parents moved the family from London to Paris and over the next fifteen years she attended Catholic convents in Boulogne-sur-mer and Nice. When the country was occupied the family moved to Grenoble in the French Alps. Her eldest brother Frederick escaped to join the British army in England and in June 1943 she and her elder sister Jacqueline got out through Spain, Portugal and Gibraltar.

Being bilingual and having experience of living in France, both sisters were recruited by SOE. After interviews they were given commissions in the FANY with Jacqueline being trained as a courier and, disappointed at not being allowed to train to be sent back to France, Didi was sent to train as a wireless operator at Thame Park, SOE's home station, using the codename 'Alice Wood'. After Jacqueline's training, on 23 January 1943 she was parachuted into the Massif central to work with Squadron Leader Maurice Southgate's STATIONER network.

At the beginning of 1944, following widespread arrests in the Paris area, there was an urgent need for replacement wireless operators. Didi was chosen and sent on a 'W/X' training course at the 'Finishing School' in Beaulieu. However, she did not create a good impression. Her assessor commented that:

> She is not very intelligent or practical and is lacking in shrewdness and cunning. She has a bad memory, is inaccurate and scatterbrained. She seems keen but her work was handicapped by lack of the power to concentrate.
>
> In character she is very feminine; and immature; she seems to lack all experience of the world and would probably be easily influenced by others.
>
> She is lively and amusing and has considerable charm and social gifts. She talks a lot and is anxious to draw attention to herself but was generally liked by the other students.
>
> It is doubtful whether this student is suitable for employment in any capacity on account of her lack of experience.[13]

Despite this, she was determined to help in the war effort and Buckmaster overruled her assessor. By the time she had finished the course, Francis Nearne, her other brother, had been Lysandered out of France and was undergoing SOE training in England. Having worked for Jacqueline in south-west France, he had narrowly escaped arrest. In an article Buckmaster wrote after the war he admitted that:

> The way of a radio operator is always hard: when he is being trained to work a Morse set in conditions of absolute secrecy, he requires almost more

than human perseverance and concentration. The instructors at the school will say, 'So-and-so is not feeling well today; his speed is down to 31'. Men and women in training become moody and disgruntled: there was much bickering and bad-tempered gossip, for the strain was intense. In this school hidden away in the heart of the countryside, there were in the winter of 1943 some fifty or sixty students, who were being trained to be dropped by parachute in occupied countries, whence they would send home by Morse those messages which were essential to the carrying out of underground warfare.

In response to messages, aircraft, flying by night from secret bases in England, would take loads of containers slung like bombs, and release them over small fields in the heart of France or Norway, where anxious patriots awaited the distant hum of the aircraft motors before flashing their torches at the western sky. But these parachute operations could not take place without communications, and radio was the essential link. These solemn students, men and women alike, in this country-house, would become the radio operators who would make these parachute operations possible. They had to learn how to install a set, to fix the aerial so that it attracted the minimum of attention, to remedy minor defects, to tap out their messages at speed, to identify, despite jamming, their distant home station. They had to become familiar with the touch on the key of their partner at the home station, and more important still, they had to acquire an individual technique by which they would themselves be infallibly recognised. They, more than any other officers who were to be sent into occupied countries, had to learn how to live unsuspected and unnoticed. The need for self-sufficiency was great; they had to be prepared to live alone without friends, for months at a time if necessary. The preparation was long and severe; it required much patience to go on tapping day after day without apparent progress. Disheartenment was very frequent and any form of mental anxiety was apt to retard progress in the most spectacular way.

Among the group of pupils in December 1943 was Eileen, her fair curls bent low over her set, patiently practising hour after hour, desperately anxious to pass the test which would permit her to be sent to France, where her sister Jacqueline was already working. Eileen was young, and looked even younger than she was. But the determination to succeed was in her, and she showed all the signs of becoming a really first-class operator.

The day I spent down at the school was the occasion on which the instructor was lecturing on radio-detector vans. He explained that the Germans used harmless-looking delivery vans for the purpose of tracking radio transmitters. The principle was as simple as the apparatus was complex. If the equipment in a van picked up a transmission on a wavelength which was not catalogued, the site of the transmitter was stalked by three vans, each moving in the direction in which the signals became stronger and stronger. By this means a 'fix' was obtained which enabled the detectors to locate the transmitter within an area of twenty or thirty yards square. A police cordon was then thrown round the suspected area, and the flats or houses combed until the set was found and its operator arrested. Eileen's face was grim as she listened to this explanation, but her chin was thrust forward as the means for as the means for avoiding detection were examined and explained. She was determined to remember this complicated business. She felt that Jacqueline would be pleased if she could get through the examinations with credit. Besides, her life might depend upon her remembering. But she found the effort a great strain, and when the time came for her to leave the school and prepare for her departure, she showed by certain signs of emotion that she was not as confident as her ready smile would lead one to believe.

She was chosen by Jean Savy, a French lawyer, to be his 'pianist' in WIZARD, a new circuit he was sent to set up in Paris after the PROSPER circuit had been infiltrated and broken up. As he had a withered arm and could not parachute, he and Didi were landed in a field two kilometres north-west of Les Lagnys, about ten kilometres south of Vatan, not far north of the Châteauroux drop zone. Clark's book sheds no light on the drop, only saying 161 Squadron went on seven sorties that night and 138 Squadron on seventeen. One of the reception committee, according to her obituary in the *Daily Telegraph*, was reported as saying: 'Oh, you're a young girl. Go back. It's too dangerous'.[14]

She stayed and made her way to Paris to rendezvous with 'Louise' in the snow beside the statue of King Henri IV on the Pont Neuf bridge. Provided with a room on Boulevard St Michel and given a wireless set, she began her work. Later she transmitted from a deserted house at Bourg-la-Reine. Codenamed 'Rose', she helped Savy in his mission to arrange for the reception and utilisation of the Jedburgh teams. Using his business contacts, he approached French financiers for money that the Resistance needed. To reassure them that the money would be repaid by the British government, they volunteered a phrase which she transmitted to London. It was then passed to the BBC's French Department, who added it in their *messages personelles* after the evening news. When the message was heard, the money was handed over.

Didi's other codenames were 'Petticoat' and 'Pioneer', and her identity cards showed her as 'Marie Tournier' and 'Mlle Jacqueline du Tertre'. The first of her 105 messages containing important economic and military details went out on 26 March. It included explosive information that Savy had obtained – details of the Luftwaffe's secret ammunition dump in caves in the stone quarries at Saint Leu d'Esserent, Picardy. Stored inside were about 2,000 V1 rockets ready for shipment to launch sites on the French coast. Within weeks the RAF went in and bombed the quarry and eighty-five per cent of the town, seriously hampering the Germans.

As Savy was known to the Gestapo, SOE planned a Lysander mission to pick him up and return him to England. Accompanying him would be Mrs Josette Southgate, and Didi's sister, Jacqueline, who had been in France fifteen months.

On 10 April 1944, after four days' wait in the open air close to Galèteries farm buildings, two kilometres south-south-west of Villers-les-Ormes, north-west of Châteauroux, they were understandably pleased to see Flight Lieutenant Robert Taylor's Lysander appear in the night sky. Lise de Baissac, Philippe de Vomécourt and Arnaud de Vogüé got out and Savy and the two women went back to England.

Prior to D-Day, Didi and another wireless operator went to Paris to work for the SPIRITUALIST network, which was planning railway sabotage and had urgent need for communications with London for supplies. Afterwards she handled messages about dropping supplies for the MUSICIAN and FARMER circuits, which were attacking railways carrying German troops to the front line in Normandy. In Lilian Jones's *A Quiet Courage*, Didi recalled one occasion when she was sitting in a train compartment with a radio in her suitcase.

> There was this German soldier who kept looking at me and smiling, so I smiled back. Then I was looking through the window and he said, 'Cigarette, Mademoiselle?' And I said, 'No, thank you, I don't smoke.' And my hands, you see, were stained with nicotine. You could make mistakes like that. He was looking at me and he said 'What is in your suitcase?' So I said, 'Oh – *c'est un phonographe, savez, de la musique,*' and he said, 'Oh, *oui*' and he was looking at me and I thought Oh la, la, I must get out quickly.

In her debrief once back in England after the war, she admitted that it was a lonely life.

> I used to go out a lot and have my meals in restaurants alone. Sometimes I would meet my contact Louise, but all we would do was to pass a note. It was very solitary. I wasn't nervous. In my mind I was never going to be arrested. But of course I was careful. There were Gestapo in plain clothes everywhere. I always looked at my reflection in the shop windows to see if I were being followed.[15]

Buckmaster[16] acknowledged that life in Paris for Eileen was very lonely.

From time to time she had to meet her Organising Officers, the people from whom she received special instructions. These meetings had to take place in streets, trams, trains; a message would be passed and possibly no word spoken, so great was the danger of being observed and discovered. Living in houses from which she had to move constantly, she continued to send and receive messages in code. She knew that discovery meant interrogation by the Gestapo, with possibly torture, the concentration camp, or death.

Her state was made no easier by her inability during her service in France to get in touch with any of her family. How were her father and mother? Her brother? What had happened to her only sister, engaged on such hazardous work? Eileen went for lonely walks, thinking, worrying, passing cafés where the invader lounged at ease. Paris can be lovely in June, but for Eileen the loveliness was encased in nightmare.

And then, one June morning, came disaster.

Other sources state it was on 25 July, two days after Savy was lifted out in a Lysander for the second time, and about four months after landing in France, that Didi had just finished transmitting a message for the SPIRITUALIST circuit when seventeen Gestapo in seven cars arrived. The Germans had radio receivers disguised in bread vans which, within twenty minutes, could detect a transmission and send in a hit squad.

She had just enough time to burn her messages in the oven and hide the radio and revolver in the box-room. However, a thorough search of the house uncovered them and her unused one-time pad. She was arrested and taken to Avenue Foch for interrogation. In her obituary in the *Guardian*, it was described how, despite the incriminating evidence, she maintained, with considerable sang-froid, that she was an innocent shop assistant called Jacqueline du Tetre who had no idea that the messages she was sending for her boss were being sent to England. She claimed she had met him three months earlier in a coffee shop and he had given her the code pad. It did not take long for the Gestapo to discover that his name and address were false.[17]

Although subjected to the *baignoire* treatment, a bath of cold water into which prisoners were held down until their lungs almost burst, she kept to her story. Eventually she 'admitted' to a planned meeting with her boss at Gare St Lazare at 1900 hours that evening. She was taken to the rendezvous and won some more time when an air-raid warning went off at 1915. The next day, to avoid more *baignoire* treatment, she offered to take the Gestapo chief to the addresses she had given them. They did not take her up on her offer and transferred her to Frèsnes Prison.[18]

In an interview in 1950 with James Gleeson, she told him that she had created the impression that she had been imprudent and was unaware of the political implications of her involvement with the Resistance, claiming she was 'a bit of a scatterbrain and a tomboy ... helping the Resistance for fun and excitement'. Her colleagues made a desperate bid to bribe the German guards to release the Nearne sisters, but it backfired. Two prostitutes were handed over instead.

In Foot's *SOE in France*, he noted that Didi 'put on her act of being a sweet little thing who knew nothing she ought not' and that, consequently, she 'brought off a dexterous bluff, and persuaded the Gestapo she was only a foolish little shop girl who had taken up Resistance work because it was exciting'.

Pattinson commented that this gendered strategy was only open to women. Didi had been informed by her training instructors that she was a good liar and found that during interrogations she could improvise plausible explanations and remain calm: 'All sorts of things I pulled from my head. And the more I was lying, the more I wanted to and the more it was easy coming to me'. Her conscious strategy was 'to act confusion and misunderstanding'.

On 15 August, Didi was put in a cattle truck with a batch of suspected English women agents and French girls, who had worked for the Resistance and spent a week with little food, drink or sleep on the journey to Ravensbrück. The typescript of her debrief details her experiences but names of other prisoners have been blanked out.

I arrived there in September and met [blanked out] and [blanked out], two English girls. We stayed there about 15 days and in October we went to Torgau, where we stayed two months. I met [blanked out] at Torgau, where we all worked in the fields. I knew that [blanked out] wanted to escape, but after that I left the camp and arrived at Abteroda (6 km. from Sisnak) in October. [Blanked out] and [blanked out] stayed in the camp (Torgau) and I worked in the factory. At Abteroda the Commandant S.S. from Torgau came and we heard that he was looking for two English girls who had escaped from Torgau and there were rumours that it was [blanked out] and [blanked out]. They were always with a girl called [blanked out] I did not want to work in the factory so they shaved my head and told me that if I did not work in 20 minutes I would be shot. I then decided to work. I left the camp on the 1st December and went to Markleburg (7 km. from Leipzig). There we worked on the roads for 12 hours per day and one day they told us we would be leaving the camp for a place 80 km away (5 April). Two French girls and I decided to escape and while we were passing a forest I spotted a tree and hid there and then joined the French girls in the forest. [Blanked out] We escaped on the night of 5th April. We stayed in a bombed house for two nights and the next morning walked through Markleburg and slept in the woods. We were arrested by the S.S. who asked us for papers. We told them a story and they let us go. We arrived in Leipzig and at a Church a priest helped us and kept us there for three nights and the next morning we saw white flags and the first Americans arriving and when I said that I was English they put us in a camp.[19]

Buckmaster[20] provided more details of her time in Ravensbrück.

Eileen did her best to adopt the technique of the hunted animal and to merge into her background. At length she tricked the camp guards and got herself included in a working party in a factory. But she had no intention whatever of helping the enemy war machine. She made up her mind to do all the sabotage that her instruments and gauges would allow. Day after day she succeeded in falsifying precision instruments and graphs, and the aero-engine parts she turned out were all rejected by the inspection department. To her delight, it was a long time before they traced the faults to her. As a punishment her long golden hair was shaved, and once more she went through the torments of the icy plunge. She was allowed to return to the factory, and although she now had only limited opportunities for sabotage, she contrived with one wild swoop to wreck a vital machine. She was careless of consequences, and would not yield to force.

The camp authorities decided that she must be punished again, and more severely. Meanwhile Eileen had disappeared among the thousands of French prisoners. By the time she had been found again, trace of her misdemeanour had been lost.

While in this camp she caught diphtheria through drinking filthy water. She recovered eventually, and escaping while in a working-party convoy, reached the American lines.

The 5th Corps of the First US Army reported finding her on 15 April 1945 but, doubting her story, put her in a prison camp with captured Nazi women. Their report, dated 2 May and marked 'SECRET', commented that:

Subject creates a very unbalanced impression. She is often unable to answer the simplest questions, as though she were impersonating someone else. Her account of what happened to her after landing near Orleans is held to be invented. It is recommended that Subject be put at the disposal of the British Authorities for further investigation and disposition.[21]

She had to withstand further intense interrogation until she was believed. The Americans were worried that she might have been a German agent.

Eventually, after a month in captivity, she was identified by a British major and taken to safety.

Liane Jones mentioned that one of the English girls Didi met in prison was Violette Szabó.

> Didi warned Violette that she was passing herself off as French. Violette asked her what the Gestapo had done to her and, when Didi told her about the '*baignoire*' in the Rue de Saussaies, she was horrified. She told Didi that neither she nor Lilian nor Denise had been tortured, and she advised Didi to change her story and admit her British nationality. 'She said. "You should have said you were English. English girls are better treated than the French." but I said, "No, I'm sticking to my story."' ... She was wary of being seen with the British women, her alias of Jacqueline du Tetre was important to her as a way of protecting her SOE knowledge and it was as Jacqueline that her fellow prisoners knew her.

Pattinson reported that Maisie McLintock, a FANY coder, had been close friends with Didi during her training, in which she had deliberately disobeyed rules like having baths after hours. When spoken to by her superiors she always 'played the daft lassie' by pretending not to understand.

> She was very clever, I think. It explained a lot when she survived the Germans and that concentration camp using the same method as she had done when she was a FANY. Wide-eyed innocence ... One of the first things she said when she was telling me about her experience, she was taken to the Avenue Foch in Paris, that was where she got her preliminary going over, and she said, 'You see, Mac, I did what you said, I played the daft lassie with them' ... She was still getting through life somehow, looking innocent and not quite sure why she was there.

In an interview after the war, in response to a question on how she kept alive, she said that it was:

> The will to live. Will power. That's the most important. You should never let yourself go. It seemed that the end would never come, but I have always believed in destiny and I had a hope. If you are a person who is drowning you put all your efforts into trying to swim.

On returning to England on 23 May 1945, Didi was met at the airfield by Buckmaster and Atkins, who could hardly recognise her as the smart, charming girl who had left a year earlier. When they took her to meet her sister Jacqueline in London, she walked jauntily over the threshold, embraced her and then collapsed in tears. She was ill for several months, suffering from nervous exhaustion, but must have been uplifted when she learned that she had been awarded the MBE and the *Croix de Guerre* for her 'cool efficiency, perseverance and willingness to undergo any risk in order to carry out her work ... [She] made possible the successful organisation of her group and the delivery of large quantities of arms and equipment'.[22]

In 1997 she agreed to be interviewed for BBC2's *Time Watch*. To protect her identity, she wore a wig, was introduced as Rose and spoke only in French. In fact, she was given the last word in the film: 'When I returned after the war, I, along with lots of others, missed that kind of life. Everything seemed so ordinary'.

Her death in September 2010 provoked such a widespread interest in her wartime exploits and post-war experiences that most British and some foreign newspapers and television companies ran stories on her. *Agent Rose*, a detailed account of her life and wartime experiences is about to be published.

Denise Bloch

The other woman Lysandered out with Didi during the moon period in early March 1944 was Denise Bloch. According to Escott, she was born in Paris on 21 January 1916 to French Jewish parents and thought to have been educated at Louveciennes, where she learned English as a second language. In 1940, she, her parents, and three brothers were living in Lyon, where she worked as secretary to Jean Maxime Aron in the Citroën organisation. Her engagement to one M. Mendelsohn, she claimed, was to help her in her work. According to Nigel Perrin's website, she had joined the Resistance following her parents' arrest during the round-up of French Jews in 1942. She was recruited by Réne Piércy, who was impressed by her English, and was joined by Mendelsohn. She worked as a courier for Philippe de Vomécourt, codenamed Gauthier, who was the Inspector of Railways and had been running the VENTRILOQUIST network since 1941. Aron, her boss, codenamed Joseph, was his second-in-Command.

When Henri Sevenet, codenamed Rodolphe, was parachuted in in August 1942, part of his mission to encourage de Vomécourt to come to England failed. The other part was to revitalise the DETECTIVE network in Lyon, which was overseeing the Tours-Poitiers railway. Denise then became Sevenet's courier and met Brian Stonehouse, an SOE wireless operator for the DETECTIVE and VENTRILOQUIST networks. She had to find safe houses from where he could transmit, and help him out as his French was not good. When he was carrying his wireless set around in a suitcase, Denise carried his sketchbook for him as he was a keen artist.

Sometimes she had to carry the set herself and on one occasion, waiting at a bus stop, she saw the Gestapo doing an inspection on travellers' papers. In Escott's *The Heroines of SOE*, she describes how Denise 'immediately got into a conversation with one of the Germans in the queue, her fractured German making him laugh. Having established friendly relations, she took her opportunity to ask him to watch her case while she went to buy a newspaper. On returning she showed her papers to a civilian inspector, retrieved her case, coolly got on the bus ... and got away with it'.

There were times when she accompanied Francis Suttill of the PROSPER network in the Île de France, pretending to be his sister. When she saw Stonehouse being escorted to Lyon police station on 14 October 1942, closely followed by Blanche Charlet, his wireless operator, she made herself scarce. Her father tried unsuccessfully to bribe the guards.

On 26 October, realising she was in danger, she went south to Marseille. On receiving information about drop zones, she volunteered to return north, but Sevenet felt that he and Aron should accompany her. When they were leaving Lyon station, Aron was arrested but she and Sevenet evaded the blue-coated, brown-shirted, blue-bereted *Miliciens*, the Vichy government's police force, and moved from safe house to safe house in St Laurent de Samouchet, Villefranche-sur-mer and Toulouse, where she heard that Mendelsohn, her 'fiancé', had been arrested on 30 October. There she was introduced to Sergeant Maurice Dupont, the organiser of the DIPLOMAT network.

Denise was described as a tall, sturdy, broad-shouldered blonde, but her SOE photograph shows her as a dark-haired beauty. She dyed it after the police raided her flat in Lyon. Maurice helped her to try to escape over the Pyrénées but, as the snow was too deep, they had to return. She then met George Starr, who put her in touch with Philippe de Vomécourt, who was then working in Agen. When this network was broken in April 1943, she successfully accompanied Dupont over the Pyrénées to Spain. From there they made their way safely to Gibraltar and caught a boat back to England.[23]

Martin Sugarman, the archivist of the British Association of Jewish Ex-Servicemen and Women, researched Denise's life and on the Jewish Virtual Library website he related how, after her debrief in London, she was recruited by the SOE. Under the cover name of Denise Williams, she spent ten months training in Wanborough, Arisaig and Beaulieu, and then on a wireless transmitters' course. One of her instructors commented that she 'was not very fit on arrival and was rather heavy and found the PT and ground training very tiring and also very stiffening'.[24]

Escott mentioned that part of her wireless security course included the dangers of detection. There were staff employed at the Gestapo Headquarters on Avenue Foch who were on shifts keeping a continuous lookout for wireless operator signals.

> Relays of about thirty German clerks gazing at their cathode ray tubes in every available frequency, searched for any new blip to appear on their tube. They would then telephone the Direction Finders at Brest, Augsberg and Nuremberg, giving the reading of the new frequency, and ask for cross bearings. These found, the Detection Finding vans, full of the most sensitive equipment, would take up the hunt, forming a triangle within a triangle, until they were within a mile of their quarry, and moving slowly along the lanes and streets. Finally, men on foot in long raincoats, their earphones hidden by their high turned-up collars and hats, read off the distances by miniature meters, on what looked like large wrist watches. In this way they could pin-point the very house from which the signal came.

With no time for parachute training at Ringway, she was taken to Tempsford on 2 March 1944, from where Flight Officer 'Dinger' Bell flew her and Robert Benoist, this time on his second mission, in one of 161 Squadron's Lysanders to a field one and a half kilometres west of Baudreville, east-south-east of Chartres. Other SOE records state that she landed at Soucelles, ten kilometres south of Vatun, near Nantes. Codenamed 'Ambroise', she met up with Jean-Pierre Wimille, Benoist's former BUGATTI co-driver to join the 2,000-strong CLERGYMAN circuit as a wireless transmitter. Benoist's orders told him that he would 'be accompanied to the field by Ambroise, who is to act as your W/T operator. She will be under your command, but it must be understood that she is the ultimate judge in all questions regarding the technicalities of W/T and W/T security. She will encode the messages herself. They should be as short and clear as possible, since it is of the utmost importance that her time on the air should be reduced to a minimum'.

They stayed at Villa Cécile on Benoist's estate near Rambouillet, south-west of Paris. Their mission was to bring down the high electricity pylons that crossed the river Loire at Île Heron and linked the hydro-electric power stations in the Pyrénées with Brittany, as well as to sabotage the telephone and railway system around Nantes. This would disrupt German communications before D-Day. Over a period of three months she sent thirty-one messages back to London and received fifty-two, using Leo Marks's poem as her code.

Make the most of it

A coast to coast
Toast of it
For what you think
Has been God-sent to you
Has only been lent to you.

An indication as to how extensively she travelled on her missions was the number of aliases she used. Harrison recorded them as 'Micheline Claude de Rabatal', 'Chantal Baron', and 'Katrine Bernard', with the codenames 'Criniline' and 'Line'.[25]

On 18 June, Benoist was arrested when he went to see his dying mother in Paris. News reached Villa Cécile but they didn't expect the Gestapo to pounce so quickly. The following day they caught Denise and Mme Wimille while they were having lunch. Jean-Pierre Wimille escaped. Denise was taken to Avenue Foch for questioning and, when she revealed nothing, was transferred to Frèsnes prison. On 8 August, with the Allies approaching the capital, the Germans transported thirty-seven of their SOE prisoners further east. After various stops, including the concentration camp of Neue-Bremm Saarbrücken, on 24 August she arrived at Ravensbrück prison. From there she was sent to work camps in Targau and Königsberg, where, still in her light summer clothes, she was forced to fell trees and do heavy building work for a new airfield. In the film *Carve Her Name with Pride*, there is a scene where she tells a fellow inmate that she's made face powder using whitewash from the kitchen wall.

Seriously ill with cold and exposure, she was returned to Ravensbrück, and on 27 January 1945 she, Violette Szabó, and Cécile Lefort were taken out to a yard, shot in the back of the head and, after the German doctor checked to see if they had were any gold fillings he could remove, she was put in the crematorium furnace. There is no known grave, but her name is proudly carved on four SOE memorials in Britain, France and Germany. Denise was posthumously awarded the King's Commendation for Brave Conduct, *Chevalier de la Legion d'Honneur*, *Croix de Guerre avec Palme*, and the *Medaille de la Resistance avec Rosette*.

Yvonne Baseden

A fortnight after Denise Bloch's Lysander flight, Flight Lieutenant Downes took off from Tempsford on 18 March and, forty kilometres away from the intended drop zone, picked up the Eureka beacon of WHEELWRIGHT 64. His passenger was twenty-two-year-old Yvonne Baseden, whose story has been told in several publications. She was born in Paris on 20 January 1922 to an English engineer in the Royal Flying Corps, who had crash landed in the grounds of a château, the home of the Comte de Vibraye. She invited him to have dinner and he fell in love with and later married their daughter. Yvonne had lived in Belgium, Holland, Poland, Italy, and Spain before returning to Arachon, where she joined the ice hockey team and enjoyed clay pigeon shooting. In 1937, the family moved to Tottenham in London. Uninterested in convent school education, she left when she was sixteen and worked for a time picking apples in Bedfordshire. In 1939, she moved to Southampton, completed secretarial courses in Pitman and Prevost-Delauny, and worked as bilingual shorthand typist in an engineering firm.

Her attempts to join de Gaulle's Free French were thwarted when they discovered that her father was an English engineer. Instead, aged eighteen, she joined the WAAF as a Craft GD (Aircraft General Duties) at Kenley airfield, near London. Here she met and admired the men who flew and the men who worked on the planes. When the Free French pilots formed their own squadron, she was asked to help them with their technical English. Being bilingual and skilled at shorthand were distinct advantages. A year later, she was commissioned as an Assistant Section Officer in the Intelligence Branch, where she assisted in the interrogation of captured Luftwaffe and U-boat crews. Her special skills eventually got her a position in the Directorate of Allied Air Co-operation.

In an interview after the war with James Gleeson, who researched women agents, she reported being introduced to such issues as the supply of aircraft, personnel training, and co-ordination of plans. She was also in contact with men who had escaped from enemy-occupied territory and told her stories of oppression and brutalities. This work brought her into contact with Pearl Witherington, who was already working there and it was she who mentioned working with the SOE.

A dull official envelope arrived one morning from the Ministry of Pensions, which asked her to attend an interview in Whitehall. Her friends commented that she was lucky to be given a pension when she was only nineteen.

The middle-aged man who interviewed her opened a folder and told her her name and that she had been born in the Rue Violet in 1922. Yvonne thought it was to do with her pension. He went on to tell her about her family and the work she was doing. Acknowledging it was important, he suggested there was other very important work she could be doing and asked her if she would like to return to France and help the Resistance in its fight against the German occupiers. She told Gleeson that the idea came so out of the blue it made her breathless and exhilarated. 'Yes,' she said, 'I would love to.'

Two interviews later she started her SOE training in May 1943, a month before Pearl. Over five months she was trained as a wireless operator at Thame Park mastering Morse, codes, wireless set maintenance and continuous practice in transmitting and receiving. According to Gleeson:

> Speed and accuracy were vital 'in the field' when the success of operations and often lives were dependent on the skill of the W.T. operator.
>
> When she had reached the required standard she was sent with her set to a town in the north of England to carry out a practical exercise. She had never been in the town before, she had to obtain digs, and operate her set from her location avoiding detection from our own security forces who would be searching for her and also from our own wireless detection services. She had certain information to transmit and she knew she must send it so quickly that the wireless detection vans would not have time to get a 'fix' on the location.
>
> Yvonne found a room in a boarding-house and at the appointed hour rigged an aerial from the curtain hooks and safely dispatched the message. She was not detected. She left the wireless school a fully-fledged wireless operator.

Given that she was going to be living into enemy territory, she was also sent on a paramilitary course to Arisaig in Scotland. In an interview after the war, Yvonne commented how

> I had to blow up some railway lines. I was rather fond of explosives and did it effectively. Then there was weapons training. We handled everything from anti-tank guns to Continental automatics. At the end of the course I had developed a great affection and a lot of skill with grenades, the Bren gun, and the Colt .45 revolver. But there was one bad moment for me. The instructor gave me a long, black-handled commando knife. I had to learn how to use it. In a glade among the fir trees were three dummy men, which the instructor manipulated by wires. I had to learn to stab them and kill. 'Stab upwards, stab downwards' was the order repeated over and over again. I hated it. I hated it so much I never did use a knife in France. Then came unarmed combat training with a tough Commando sergeant-major. By the time I returned to London I had learned a lot of ways of killing.[26]

On one of her practice jumps during her parachute training at Ringway she landed on the roof of the canteen and her colleagues had to find a ladder to help her down. On another occasion her colleagues had gone back to the country house where they were accommodated and it was two hours before they realised Yvonne was missing. They went back and found her dangling safely from the branches of a tree in Tatton Park.[27]

There was then a four-week course at Beaulieu in clandestine warfare, with twenty other students.

When she was asked by Pattinson whether she had been prepared to shoot someone in the field, she replied, abruptly and decisively, 'Oh yes. Yes, absolutely. I don't know whether I would be prepared to knife them because we were trained to do that as well. Oh yes. Certainly I would. It was part of the training and a job to be done.' In a diary entry quoted in Jerrard Tickell's *Moon Squadron*, having almost completed her course, she wrote:

> Another wartime Christmas was over, the Christmas of 1943. It had been a blacked-out Christmas, with no turkey, no ham, no crackers, few carols and even fewer soya-bean sausages. But it had been more than a day in the calendar. It was a day on which one had to pause and look both backwards and forwards ... We all knew what the future would hold. There were those among us who wouldn't see another Christmas – or if we did, we would see it through the bars over the window of a cell ... I suppose I thought I would be one of the lucky ones who would get away with it. It's somebody else who is run over by a tram ... But I said my quiet prayers all the same.

Before being flown out of Tempsford or Tangmere, agents had the opportunity to further practise weapons training in underground shooting galleries in London. They had to be fully prepared for their clandestine mission. Tickell narrated Yvonne's first attempt to be dropped into France with her future organiser, Baron Gonzagues de St Geniés, a very patriotic, brave French nobleman, codenamed 'Lucien'.

> Like those who had gone, we made no farewells. We simply faded out. Lucien was wearing an untidy suit of unmistakable French cut. Nobody would look twice at him in a Paris street. I wore a skirt and a blouse, with a loose topcoat and a coloured scarf over my head. I hoped that nobody would look twice at me either.
>
> A car called for us. It was driven by another of those cheerful, healthy F.A.N.Y.s. We went along a winding lane and had to wait a minute or two at some closed railway gates. Beyond it, in the gloom, was a flat expanse of land, with some farm buildings. I asked where we were and realised at once that it was a foolish question. The F.A.N.Y. driver said evasively that it was the place where we took off from. The railway gates opened and we went on. It didn't look like an airfield but now I know it to be Tempsford. We arrived at what I thought vaguely was a cowshed. It turned out to be a Nissen hut and it had been made warm and welcoming with a blazing fire. There we were greeted by an R.A.F. officer who called us by our code names

and helped us once again to check all our clothes and belongings. No British labels on the coat; no betraying, forgotten bus tickets to Baker Street; and what about this handkerchief with an embroidered initial other than that of the new name I had now assumed? The final check was as thorough as it was necessary. Then I turned out my handbag. Lipstick, comb, powder-puff – all unmistakably French; the silver powder-compact given to me by Colonel Buckmaster. No doubt at all about where that had come from – Paris.

Now for the money. The Nissen hut within the cow-shed was suddenly transformed into a sort of surrealist bank. After the search, I struggled into my jumping suit, pulling on the trousers over my top-coat. A bundle of five hundred thousand franc banknotes was slid, as a sort of cushion, into the small of my back by the obliging cashier in R.A.F. uniform. Lucien was given even more and, over and above these large sums, we were each handed some small change for immediate necessities.

I found it almost impossible to move once my parachute harness was strapped on over my suit. My handbag was on my front, hanging from a string round my neck, inside the suit. All this trussing up business gave me a slightly comic sense of unreality. And then, on a small table, I saw my crystals, my loaded Colt revolver – and my lethal tablet. The sight of this last item wiped the smile from my lips. My instinct was not to take it with me, not even to have it in my possession, and that instinct proved to be abundantly right. There were moments to come when I could have been tempted. So I left it where it was. The other things were stowed in their respective pockets, a protective rubber helmet was put on my head and I was ready to go. Lucien had been similarly trussed up and armed and, there we were, cap-a-pie!

On their way to the waiting aircraft they were told to take a few shots with their revolvers, to ensure they were working properly. Several hours later, sitting with her feet dangling out of the Joe hole ready to jump, she didn't see any lights. The reception committee was not there, so the pilot took them back to Tempsford, where they were told to go to London and wait for the next moon period. She and Gonzagues dined around in different restaurants and patronised London shows until the message came through on 18 March 1944 that their flight was arranged.

This time they were dropped successfully in Gabarret, near Auch in the Marmande area of Lot et Garonne, along with fifteen containers and four packages. They were met by a reception committee from Starr's WHEELWRIGHT network and briefly met Yvonne Cormeau and Anne-Marie Walters, his wireless operators, before travelling separately to the Jura mountains. Their mission was to reorganise the old DIRECTOR network. With the identity card of Madame Yvonne Marie Bernier, the codename 'Odette', and using the cover story that she was a shorthand typist and secretary, she worked her wireless set for the SCHOLAR network almost on the Swiss border. Her wireless codename was 'Bursar'. To be as inconspicuous as possible, she dressed like the local women without any make-up. She wore a very casual, plain grey skirt and a blue blouse and did her hair so as not to attract attention in her cover as a shorthand typist. She still had some intense moments, which she revealed in an interview with Juliette Pattinson.

> We had to go from where we were, which was near Auch, which is north of the Pyrénées, to Marseille by bus and take the train from Marseille to Dijon and Dôle where we were going ... Naturally very anxious to get on with things ... I had my crystals on me and my ciphers ... First we went by coach ... That was quite worrying in a way because it was the first time one travelled on public [transport] in occupied France and because it was a coach there was no other way out except the front door. Anyway, there was no trouble. We were stopped once or twice. They just glanced at the papers as we walked out and walked back into the coach ... Marseille was terrible of course because there were several hours to wait there. I think I waited about four hours on a bench and of course I was on my own ... It was very difficult because there were patrols in the station. Anyway, I got on the train and it's quite a long way to Lyon ... I got off at Lyon without much trouble and got into Dôle. It took a day and a half.

Her main task was to locate suitable drop zones and provide a base for air drops to the local Maquis. Using three wireless sets hidden in hedges, haystacks, fields, barns and attics meant a lot of bicycle travelling. When St Geniès investigated the loss of contact with two overlapping networks, he discovered that their organiser had been captured. This meant Yvonne had to carry messages by day and transmit by night. Occasionally she joined in training men in using the guns and explosives dropped to them by the Tempsford Squadrons.

There was also an opportunity to use the new S-Phone, a ground-to-air telephone. In the grey morning of Sunday 26 June 1944, she played a major role in a huge daylight drop to her circuit. Over 400 containers were dropped by thirty-six Flying Fortresses of the American Eighth Air Force in operation CADILLAC. In an interview with Pattinson she recalled that she 'found a sort of culvert where I could be in with my radio, yet open in the field and so I sat there with my radio and established contact with England and to guide the planes in ... It was incredible. I was jumping around, waving madly to them!'

Leaving her wireless set for a student volunteer to carry, she cycled to Les Orphelins – a warehouse with a main hall, cellar and a loft for ripening Graf cheeses. Here the leaders of her network celebrated their success. Unknown, however, was that the student carrying her set had been captured and her destination beaten out of him. She and Lucien were arrested on 28 June. Foot, in his *SOE in France*, describes how:

> Two days after Cadillac, the first mass daylight drop by the USAAF, the inner circle of SCHOLAR dined together at their best safe-house, a cheese factory near Dôle, to celebrate the safe stowing of thirty-six Fortress-loads of arms. A sub-agent in his middle teens was caught nearby carrying a transmitter, and the Germans raided the factory. They found the caretaker's wife, wringing her hands beside a table laid for eight, and an atmosphere of alarm. An NCO, impressing on her that he meant business, fired a random burst of bullets through the ceiling, and so shot through the head of de St Geniès who was hiding in the loft. The bloodstain was at once noticed, and Yvonne Baseden and several companions were found and arrested.

They were bundled into the back of horse-drawn wagons and taken through heavy rains and a thunderstorm to be questioned. Lucien almost certainly swallowed the 'L' pill he had been issued with at Gibraltar Barn. Pattinson says Yvonne was caught having a meal with her friends in the regional Resistance and not with her wireless set, so she was able to keep to her cover story of being a shorthand typist who had unknowingly become involved with them. She said that, 'In all fairness I wasn't put to any form of distress, if you like, till someone who had been arrested said I was a radio operator and probably come from England.' Those captured were taken initially to the military barracks in Dôle, and then to Gestapo HQ in Dijon. There, despite being questioned in English, being shown photographs of HQ staff of various British organisations, having her bare toes stamped on by guards in army boots and a mock execution being staged to try to make her send a transmission to England, she kept to her cover story. At one point, she told Pattinson that she thought she was going to be raped.

> I felt a threat once ... I was in solitary confinement at the time and somehow or other I had a feeling that there was something afoot to possibly try to get me down into the cellars by two or three of the guards. But this is something I vaguely understood through their shouting and things like that. Certainly nothing like that happened. I wasn't raped.

The Germans were unable to prove her to be a British agent, like Denise Bloch, and so Yvonne was kept in an underground cell, beaten, starved and badly treated. In her affidavit in the Imperial War Museum about war crimes and ill treatment of British nationals at Dijon and Ravensbrück, she described being:

> ... placed in a cell which had no light and one tiny window blacked out and which only had two boards to act as beds, one of which was completely covered in blood, and one blanket. I was left in this cell for three days and three nights without any food, water or amenities of any sort other than those mentioned above. I was visited twice during my incarceration in this cell and asked if I was yet prepared to talk and on the morning of the fourth day I was taken from the cell and back to the interrogation room.

While in prison, she met Mary Lindell, an escape-line worker whom she had already met in Dijon and who was also a qualified Red Cross nurse. In late-August 1944, they were put on a train and taken to a concentration camp in Saarbrücken in Germany. Her experiences are recorded in Escott's *Mission Improbable*. On the journey she saw Violette, Denise, and Lilian.

> I thought it's incredible, they've got the whole of SOE. I hesitated about speaking to them and they naturally reacted in the same way until I realised it was safe to speak with Violet and I thought I would love to be with them, if only I could get into their group. But fortunately, as circumstances worked out, it was just as well that I was not able to do this. I saw them just to see that they were OK and they were on their way before us.

In her interview with Pattinson, she said she met up with Violette, Denise and Lilian at Saarbrücken.

> They were all going off on a transport ... in another part of Germany and I thought I must try and get in with them, which was crazy of course and thank goodness I didn't achieve that. They were not particularly keen. They could see both sides of me going with them.

On one occasion a feather from a pillow she was unloading from a truck landed on the uniform of one of her guards. He immediately raised his truncheon to hit her, but one of her fellow inmates pushed her out of the way and received the blow herself on the thigh, an action which she was severely beaten for. Who her anonymous helper was, she never knew.

Later, Yvonne was transferred to Ravensbrück, where she was given a red pleated skirt and sailor boy's shirt, just enough to cover herself. As number 62,947 she worked under armed guard on agricultural work as inconspicuously as she could until she developed tuberculosis in February.

'I was just part of a group of French women, which probably saved me in the end.' Like the others, she was forced to wear a red triangle on her baggy prison dress with a black F in it and the words *Politischer Franzose* in black. If it had been an E for 'Englander', she would have been shot like many of her compatriots.

Her planned transfer to Belsen was thwarted when she was found to have a spot on her lung diagnosed as tuberculosis and transferred to the hospital wing. Stafford reported that, by some miracle, she met Mary Lindell there, who removed her name from the list to be executed. Like Didi Nearne, she kept to her cover story that she was French. It was the timely intervention of the Swedish Red Cross on 28 April 1945 that saved her from the fate of her other colleagues. She was driven north to Denmark and then taken by ship to Malmo in Sweden, where after being cleaned and deloused, she slept on a mattress under the dinosaur skeletons in the Museum of Prehistory. A message was sent to SOE in London telling them that they had a woman calling herself Yvonne Baseden and what did they want doing with her. The Air Ministry arranged for her to be flown to Scotland. When she arrived at Euston Station there was no-one to meet her. Ringing the Air Ministry resulted in Vera Atkins going to pick her up and look after her. After several months in hospital being nursed back to health, she reported back to work. Escott said that Yvonne had been one of the fortunate ones who had done something few had achieved. 'She had been to hell and come back alive.' In recognition of her work, she was awarded the MBE and the *Croix de Guerre*.

In the mid-1950s, she appeared on *This is Your Life* with Eamonn Andrews. She married and moved to what was then Northern Rhodesia, where her husband worked in the Colonial Service. She remarried in 1966, took the name Yvonne Burney, and moved to Portugal, and then in 1999 returned to London. Although for years she did not want to talk about her wartime experiences, she gave a brief interview to Sarah Helm for her biography of Vera Atkins. She also appeared in a French documentary, *Robert et les Ombres*, directed by Jean Marie Barrère, in which, sixty years later, she met two of the reception committee who welcomed her into in the field when she was dropped.

Yvonne Fontaine

On 21 March 1944 Yvonne Fontaine and Virginia Hall, the second American agent, were landed by a gunboat at Beg-an-Fry on the south coast of Brittany. Born in Troyes on 8 August 1913, Yvonne grew up in a busy industrial area which, with its road, rail and canal connections to Paris, became one of the targets at the beginning of the war for Allied air attacks. When Allied aeroplanes were shot down, Yvonne worked with Pierre Mulsant's TINKER network south-east of Paris, a group which organised shelter for downed pilots and air crew. Provided with food, clothing, and money, often in containers dropped by the Special Duties Squadrons, their guides escorted them down an escape line to the Brittany coast or the Swiss or Spanish border.

On 11 April 1943, Ben Cowburn was parachuted south of Blois to revive the network. Accompanying him was Denis Barrett, his wireless operator. They met up with Mulsant, a timber merchant who used his father-in-law's fleet of lorries for picking up containers after the curfew. Through him, they met Yvonne and she agreed to work with them. In Escott's *The Heroines of SOE*, she commented that,

> Quick-witted and trustworthy, Yvonne easily slipped into the role of courier to other networks, as well as TINKER. Now known as Nenette she travelled everywhere – Piney, Romilly, Chartres, Tonnere, the forest of Chatillon and even, but rarely, to the PHYSICIAN network in Paris, carrying not only messages but sometimes sabotage materials.

Amongst her networks successes were sprinkling itching powder on the shirts and vests of German submarine crews when they had been washed at the laundry. This resulted in submarines not being able to operate for long as the crew needed medical treatment to control the itching. On 3/4 July 1943, they destroyed six railway engines and put another six out of action in a locomotive roundhouse in Troyes. In Marcus Binney's *Secret War Heroes*, he mentions her acting as Ben Cowburn's courier in the revived SPIRITUALIST network around the Seine-et-Marne department to the east and south-east of Paris. He described her as

> an ardent patriot, quite fearless and ready for anything. She worked in a laundry, and for her SOE work he paid her 2,000 francs a month. Thanks to Nenette, Cowburn did not feel in need of a woman courier from London ... Nenette had found a 'nice, safe restaurant where they could get meals without tickets, ironically named the Paul l'Allemand, opposite the town theatre'.

She helped organise five drops over two months, which provided her group with a total of sixty containers packed with Sten guns, rifles, grenades and explosives. Following Cowburn's successful sabotage of the rail transport around the important junction town of Troyes, the ensuing clampdown by the Gestapo made her lie low. When a fleet of Flying Fortresses flew over Troyes on their return from bombing Stuttgart, seven of them were shot down. Of the thirty American crew who bailed out, eighteen were rescued by local people, and Yvonne helped make arrangements for them to escape into Switzerland.

The German response to the Resistance activity was to offer rewards for information leading to the arrest and conviction of those involved. Money talks and it is claimed that several leading resisters were caught, who revealed information under interrogation and torture. Sending German agents disguised as evaders who needed getting out of the country allowed them to infiltrate the PHYSICIAN network and arrest hundreds of Resistance members in July 1943.

The SOE ordered Cowburn to return in mid-September 1943, leaving Yvonne working for Mulsant and Barrett. As the Gestapo closed in, Henri Dericourt organised a Hudson pick-up from a field one kilometre south-east of Sourcelles, north-east of Angers. Lieutenant Hodges of 161 Squadron picked up eight passengers including Yvonne, her two comrades, Francois Mitterand, the future President of France, Francis Cammaerts, the head of the JOCKEY circuit, and other Resistance members and allied airmen. Unknown to them, their departure was watched by the Gestapo, who then captured three men who went to see them off.

Arriving in England on 16 November 1943, after being debriefed, Yvonne underwent SOE training to be sent back into the field. Her personnel file suggests she didn't create a good impression on some of her instructors.

> She is egocentric, spoilt, stubborn, impatient, conceited and anxious to draw attention to herself ... hair worn loose in rather unbecoming disarray, liable to frequent alteration no doubt ... very large goggly eyes. She likes a great deal of attention from those whom she is pleased to call les boys![28]

Desperate for more female agents, Buckmaster agreed to send her back. On 25 March 1944, she was landed by motor boat on the north Breton coast. She made her way to Paris and rendezvoused with Mulsant, who had been dropped earlier with Barrett to create the MINISTER network. Using identity papers in the name of Yvonne Fernande Cholet, codenamed 'Mimi' and also using the names 'Yvonne Dumont', 'Yvette Fauge', 'Nenette' and 'Florist', she was briefed for her courier work and taken to a safe house in Melun.

She began by locating safe drop zones for container drops and agent landings and finding men to join reception committees. Using the skills taught at Beaulieu, she showed them where to set up guards, and how to lay out lights to guide the pilot bringing supplies. Often, she led these night-time operations. Between April and May 1944, she organised five receptions and helped collect sixty containers. She also took and received messages from Barrett and Mulsant.

When Mulsant moved his operations to Negis, she had to move. With D-Day approaching, she was busy travelling by train, tram, lorry, bus, and bicycle between Bray-sur-Seine, Nemors, Donnemarie-à-Moutois, Paris, and other towns and villages. On 17 April she welcomed a three-man team of American officers, and another on 10 May. Their mission was to co-ordinate the Resistance for the invasion.

When the local doctor told her that he had been asked to provide details of her private life, being involved with the Resistance, he advised her to keep out of circulation. Disaster struck in late-July 1944 when she accompanied a Resistance group to help a uniformed party of Special Air Service troops trapped in the forest of Fontainebleau. They had just been parachuted in but had run into difficulties and radioed Barrett, asking for assistance. German troops attacked them, and although Yvonne managed to escape, Mulsant, Barrett and other comrades were caught. They later died in Buchenwald.

The MINISTER network continued, despite having no organiser. Yvonne, however, knew what was needed but missed not having radio contact with London. Despite this, underground telephone lines were cut, overhead lines were brought down, trees were felled so that they blocked the road, and tyre bursters were laid to slow down the German troop numbers. Hit and run tactics reduced their numbers. Breaking the lock gates near Bray-sur-Seine, reduced water levels in the canal by twenty inches, causing long delays for the barges carrying vital supplies to the beleaguered German Army.

To reduce such attacks, the Germans set up road blocks and check points so Yvonne's journey became more difficult. Escoot described how,

A wallet full of papers was needed and much time wasted, severely affecting the number of visits, some very urgent, that she could do in a bay. The Germans also increased paid informers, making receptions and sabotage even more hazardous. Supplying food and necessaries to growing numbers of Maquis and FFI [French Forces of the Interior] troops also put more strain on a population already hit by shortages, especially in the larger towns. Nor were the German troops so well disciplined as before, becoming more nervous as the Allies neared.

The Germans taking hostages and shooting them in broad daylight added to the problems. Yvonne had to restrain angry *résistants* from taking revenge, as it would only draw heavier reprisals. She had to focus their attention on lightning-fast strikes and disappearing.

On 25 August, shortly after the Allies landed on the Mediterranean coast and began their push north, the Germans surrendered. Although there were attacks on the retreating troops, Yvonne and several liaison officers, had to count the cost of liberation, arrange funds for those who had helped and those who had lost family members. They had to collect left-over equipment which might be useful for the Allies in other areas and then extract reports from leading Resistance members before helping the local population celebrate.

Once the Allies reached her area, she was flown back to England on 16 September 1944. Once she had written up her report, she met up with two other female agents, Odette Wilen and Anne-Marie Walters. Their night chatting about their experiences caused concern to someone in the SOE.

I saw these ladies this morning. They are all staying at the same hotel and I found them this morning for different reasons in a highly excitable and appeared to me, unsatisfactory, frame of mind.

Mme FUAGE. This agent, I think, has probably performed her duties well. Her present nervous condition is largely due to the fact that she blames the organisation for the arrest of her two friends GUERIN AND STEPHANE. Apparently uniformed party was dropped into the Foret de Fontainbleu, which was already being used for two other receptions organised by GUERIN. The result was a thorough search of the woods in which GUERIN AND STEPHANE were caught. I am not anxious to go into details, but I think it is only right to notify the slightly unsatisfactory frame of mind in which she finds herself at present.

... I was very seriously shocked by the attitude of these three ladies, who had spent the night in exchanging confidences in the hotel. For one thing they were talking freely of the arrests of a great number of our agents, the facts of which they had no reason to be informed. I pointed out particularly that in the case of GARDE, we did not wish the news of his arrest to be spread since his wife had been seriously ill and we had been unable to inform her of this bad piece of news.[29]

Escott added that because Yvonne was registered under her married name of Fauge, Vera Atkins did not recognise her as one of the SOE. Because she worked for the SOE's F Section, the French did not regard her as highly. After the war, de Gaulle awarded her the *Medaille de la Resistance*. She married a Frenchman called Dupont and died in 1996.

Virginia Hall

Virginia Hall was the next woman to go out. Denis Rake, one of SOE's wireless operators, stated after the war in his book *Rake's Progress* that 'Virginia Hall in my opinion – and there are many others who share it

– was one of the greatest women agents of the war'.

Born in 1906 into a wealthy English-Dutch family in Baltimore, she attended the best schools and colleges and then finished her education in France, Germany and Austria, becoming fluent in French, German, and Italian. In the early 1930s she worked in the American embassy in Warsaw in Poland, Tallinn in Estonia, Vienna in Austria, and Izmir in Turkey, but her hopes of a long career in the diplomatic service were dashed when she had to have her lower left leg amputated after a hunting accident. The aluminium leg made for her she called 'Cuthbert'.

Peter Churchill, one of numerous SOE agents who were helped by her, reported in his autobiography, *Of Their Own Choice*, how surprised he was when she showed him a little opening in its heel. She told him that she was able to hide various documents in her 'aluminium puppy'. His response to her was that it was, 'A walking ground-floor letter-box that nobody would ever find. Hermes has nothing on you...'

Although she resigned her job in 1939, it did not deter her. She got a job in the Ambulance Service in Paris but disgusted at Pétain's Armistice with the Germans, she made her way south, crossed the Pyrénées into Spain and made her way to England.

Fluent in French and German, knowledgeable about France and having an American passport, she was reckoned by Vera Atkins to be a potentially valuable agent. An interview with Jepson was arranged, during which she volunteered her services to Baker Street. After specialist training at several SOE schools, they had her sent back to Vichy-controlled France on 23 August 1941. Unable to be parachuted back in, she is thought to have flown from Tangmere to Gibraltar. From there a felucca took her to the south coast. Codenamed 'Philomène' and using the pseudonym 'Marion Monin', she worked under the cover of an accredited Vichy correspondent for the *New York Post*.

She moved to Lyon, the main centre of the Vichy government, to work with those who refused to collaborate. Whilst there, she developed relationships with and collected information from all kinds of people including nuns, a brothel keeper, prostitutes, a gynaecologist, a factory owner, and Police chiefs who, according to Escott, 'turned a blind and sometimes benevolent eye on her activities'. The information she gleaned was regularly passed on to the American Consulate who arranged for it to be sent to the SOE in London.

Apart from Giliana Gerson, who only spent three weeks in France, Virginia was SOE's first permanent agent. In Patrick Howarth's *Undercover*, he mentioned that one of Virginia's services was to find Denis Rake, one of SOE's wireless operators, who was lodging with a prostitute. 'Being an undeviating homosexual, Rake had to explain his predicament to the girl, but it was accepted in good part, and, so far as security was concerned, the arrangement was an excellent one.'

In Dennis Casey's biography of Virginia on the now defunct 64 Baker Street website, he states that:

> She described Vichy as a small town increasingly beset with shortages and deteriorating living conditions including the absence of butter and milk. By early 1942 her reports indicated that people were near starvation which curiously occurred simultaneously with the tightening of German control.[30]

Sometimes she included a personalised shopping list. As well as the usual requests for arms and ammunition from the Resistance, she regularly ordered Elizabeth Arden cosmetics with details of her skin texture, lipstick colour, powder shade, and scent. She even gave them the address of the suppliers for a new stump sock for 'Cuthbert'. Thanks to the Tempsford 'Moon Squadrons', she got them all delivered to her safe house.

From her apartment she helped arrange the return to England of downed American aircrews and escaped prisoners. While doing this she continued to write newspaper stories, but when Germany declared war on the United States in mid-December 1941, she became an enemy alien and had to conduct business clandestinely from restaurants and cafés, constantly vigilant of plain-clothed Vichy and Gestapo officers.

According to James Gleeson, journalist and writer, she kept up a constant flow of information to London through her wireless operators,

> ... and answered all London's queries about conditions, agents and suspected traitors ... She found dropping zones for supplies and landing strips for aircraft, arranged to supply food to men and women in the jails, patched up internal strife; arranged escapes from prisons; stored arms, money and wireless sets, which she distributed as required, and acted as a recruiting agency for SOE and the Resistance forces – in fact, she ran a busy kind of de-centralised H.Q.

Following the Allies' invasion of North Africa, in November 1942, the Germans took over the Free Zone and occupied Lyon. The leader was heard to have said that he would give anything to lay his hands on that Canadian bitch. This prompted her minders to use Victor Gerson's escape line to get her out. A Spanish *passeur* took her, a Belgian army captain, and two Frenchmen over the mountains. In Judith Pearson's 2006 Clement Lecture on Virginia Hall, she told how:

> In the SOE, she learned coding, hand to hand combat, and weaponry ...

Since America had not yet entered the war, Virginia returned to France as a journalist, with the secret mission of setting up networks. Stationed in unoccupied Lyon, every British resistance fighter who came to France in that first year came by Virginia's apartment. By the time the Allies made their advance into Nazi territory in November of 1942, the Nazis were on the lookout for 'the most dangerous Allied spy', a woman with a limp. Virginia was forced to flee over the Pyrénées to Spain, in the dead of winter, on her very painful artificial leg.[31]

Cate Lineberry, writing about 'The Limping Lady' for the *Smithsonian*, added an amusing related snippet:

As her guide led her across the frozen landscape in mid-winter, she transmitted a message to SOE headquarters in London saying she was having trouble with her leg. The reply: 'If Cuthbert is giving you difficulty, have him eliminated'.[32]

Having escaped into Spain, she was captured by the Spanish civil guard and taken to Miranda del Ebro, a notorious prison camp. She needed the help of the SOE, who put pressure on the American consul to negotiate her release. She spent a few months doing SOE work under the cover of being a reporter for the *Chicago Times* in Madrid before returning to England. She taught herself Morse privately and learned how to operate and maintain a wireless set so the SOE would take her on as a wireless operator.

When she arrived back in England in January 1943, she found work as a code clerk for the Military Attaché in the American embassy but was soon transferred to the SOE, who sent her for paramilitary training in Scotland.

In Judith Pearson's *Wolves at the Door*, she described Virginia having to practice on straw dummies during the silent killing exercises.. To show how accurate she was, she was told to smear the blade of her Fairburn and Sykes knife with red lipstick. When she graduated to working on the other recruits, the drill was to sneak up behind one of the others and slit their throat. 'Virginia accomplished the task with no problem. But when the man turned round and Virginia saw the lipstick smear on his throat, reality sank in.' She also underwent wireless training at Thame Park and clandestine training at Beaulieu.

According to Escott, despite having mastered Morse and coding skills, she had to learn how to assemble wireless sets and take them apart. She had to diagnose faults and repair them with makeshift materials if they went wrong. 'When receiving, there were other problems: atmospherics, oscillation, static, skip, dead spots, jamming and other details they had to cure, as well as the mysteries of handling 70-foot-long aerials, disguising and hiding sets and general security.'[33]

During this course, she must have been pleased to learn that her earlier contribution to the war effort was acknowledged by King George VI, when he awarded her the Member of the British Empire in July 1943.

In Pearson's account, she pointed out that:

> Returning from Spain, Virginia was recruited by the new American Office of Strategic Services (OSS), headed by 'Wild' Bill Donovan. Donovan, whose recruits included contortionists and safe crackers, found a way for Virginia to return to France and the Resistance without being recognised. Since the Nazis were still looking for the woman with a limp, Virginia disguised herself as a French peasant, with padded, rustic clothing, grey hair dye, and the shuffling gait of an old woman.

On 21 March 1944, she was landed by motorboat at Beg-an-Fry Cape, three kilometres north of Guimaec, north-east of Morlaix on the Finistère coast.[34] With a new identity as a social worker called Mademoiselle Marcelle Montegrie and codenamed Diane, Virginia made her way to the Haute-Loire, where she set up the SAINT network. Concerned about the lack of discretion and unreliability of the OSS officer attached to her, she chose to leave and slowly made her way to the rural department of Cher, Nièvre, and Creuse in central France. There, using her own wireless set, she chose suitable drop zones for Allied parachute supplies and trained Resistance fighters to blow up railway lines, engines and train depots, and capture supply caravans. Despite the Gestapo knowing of the work of the 'lady with a limp', she successfully evaded detection.

Virginia was also responsible for a great deal of the wireless transmission that would be so valuable in the Allied attack on D-Day. She and her Resistance compatriots continued to provide false information to the retreating Germans and destroyed their lines of communication. One snippet she sent back was that the German General Staff had relocated its headquarters from Lyon to Le Puy. On one occasion, she had to cycle all day to deliver a vital message but got so desperate to go to the toilet that she deliberately wet herself rather than getting off the bike. She said she would never have got on again if she had got off. On another occasion she is said to have thrown a grenade into a restaurant where a group of Gestapo officers were eating. She met Jedburgh's team 'Jeremy' when they dropped from Tempsford into Le Chambon-sur-Lignon on 24 August 1944, and liaised between them and de Gaulle's FFI, the Free French Forces of the Interior.

Lineberry's article provided more detail about Virginia's work.

> By staying on the move, camping out in barns and attics, she was able to avoid the Germans who were desperately trying to track her radio signals.
>
> D-Day loomed. Everyone, including the Germans, knew an Allied landing was imminent, but they didn't know when or where it would take place. Hall armed and trained three battalions of French resistance fighters for sabotage missions against the retreating Germans. As part of the resistance circuit, Hall was ready to put her team into action at any moment. In her final report to headquarters, Hall stated that her team had destroyed four bridges, derailed freight trains, severed a key rail line in multiple places and downed telephone lines. They were also credited with killing some 150 Germans and capturing 500 more.

When she returned to liberated Paris, she met up with Paul Poillot, another OSS agent, who she subsequently married. They went to foment resistance in Austria but the rapid collapse of the Third Reich meant she returned to Paris in 1945. After making reports on those who had helped them, and collecting abandoned equipment, Virginia resigned from the OSS.

After the war she returned to America, where President Truman awarded her the Distinguished Service Cross, the second highest US military award for bravery. Although the French government did not honour her, Jacques Chirac, the French President, claimed that 'Virginia Hall is a true hero of the French Resistance'. She died on 8 July 1982.

Maureen 'Paddy' O'Sullivan

On 22 March 1944, twenty-six-year-old Maureen O'Sullivan, a second officer in the WAAF and known to her friends as 'Paddy', was flown out of Tempsford and dropped at Angoulême, south-west France. Clark was unsure whether the plane was flown by Pilot Officer Smith, of 161 Squadron, on Operation JOHN 72 or by Pilot Officer Pick, of 138 Squadron, on Operation JOHN 59. Both dropped one agent that night.

According to Escott, she was born in Dublin on 3 January 1918, her father the editor of *The Dublin Freeman's Journal*, an Irish national newspaper. Her mother was a Breton, who died of Spanish flu before Maureen was one year old. Wikipedia claims her mother, Johanna Repen, was German, and died when Paddy was fifteen-months-old. After attending St Louis Convent in Dublin, she was brought up by her Belgian aunt Alice in Bruges. There she went to a convent school in Coutrai and then the Athenée Royale in Ostend. She left school fluent in French and English, speaking some Flemish and German and having a wide repertoire of Irish swear words. Escott described her as having ginger hair and matching temper, highly intelligent, a happy and chaotic mass of emotions, strong-willed, and a real tom-boy, popular with men and women.

On returning to England, after a course at a Commercial College, she trained as a nurse at Highgate Hospital in London and in 1941 joined the WAAF as an Aircraft Handler General Duties. Later she was promoted to Section officer. Whilst stationed at RAF Gosforth, she became friendly with Sonya Butt and both were recruited by the SOE. Being bilingual, and described as very attractive and quite fearless, made her an ideal recruit as a wireless operator. Acknowledging her previous experience, her commission in the FANY was as Second Lieutenant. Her training was delayed by pneumonia and chronic chest trouble, which she tried never to let interfere with her work.

She and Sonya had their assessment at Winterfold in December 1943. After training at Inverie House (STS 24) in Scotland and for a time at Beaulieu, she was sent for additional radio training at Thame Park. In her obituary in *The Irish Independent*, it was said that although she seemed popular with the other students, her Commanding Officer's reports were nearly all bad and her instructors were exasperated by her temper. One instructor, annoyed at her back-chat, later described her as 'a tough type of woman, at the moment growing quite a successful moustache'. At one point she went absent without leave. Her wireless instructor commented that she could be a good operator 'if her temperamental difficulties could be overcome'.

SOE was desperate to get another agent into the field, so she was ordered from her course to a meeting in Baker Street and asked if she would be prepared to go into the field on the next moon. Although she hadn't finished the training, she said yes. This so annoyed Percy Mayer, her conducting officer, that he commented that:

> Miss O'Sullivan spent six weeks in Scotland on demolition and weapon training. I suggest that this time could have been more profitably spent at a security and radio school, or simply learning to ride a cycle. The requirements for a radio operator are not that she should be able to shoot straight or even shoot at all, but that she should know how to use a W/T set properly. Her means of defence should be to know how to baffle the Gestapo rather than to know how to shoot them.[35]

Over the next few weeks she had to learn her cover story, study the maps of the region she would be sent to, and learn the codes for her radio transmissions. Paddy was waiting at Gaynes Hall to see when her name would appear on the blackboard. According to Escott, when it did:

Quietly and hardly noticed, she slipped away from the other expectant groups to join the car which whisked her away in the darkness to a hut on Tempsford airfield ... then she joined her aircraft, looming in the dark like a gigantic bird, bade farewell to her escorting officer and the engines began to throb, pulsing along the cold floor where she squatted, senses alert, ready for her journey to France. Soon she was airborne and the heavy aircraft droned its way to a dropping zone in Maurice Southgate's great Stationer circuit in the middle of France. The flares were there and the Morse signal flashed to confirm that the reception was ready.

Paddy leapt out into the night sky, feeling that at long last she was starting on her great adventure, a feeling that soon evaporated when she realised that although she had done all that she had been taught, her parachute cords had become tangled and her parachute would not open properly. This was the great fear of all parachutists, as falling from such a height was almost always fatal. Her descent became swifter and she was almost losing consciousness as she struggled with the lines trailing above her. Now, short of an unexpectedly soft landing, she was doomed before she had begun. Seconds became hours, when suddenly her fall was halted by a great jerk, as her parachute flowered out high above her.

With the ground only a short way below, it had opened just in time. Even so, she made an awkward heavy landing, rolling as the ground met her, suffering a bad shaking and bruising as her parachute dragged her along, working now when she had no need of it.

She landed so heavily she wondered if she had broken her neck. When she recovered consciousness, she felt hot breath on her face – a herd of friendly cows. In an interview with James Gleeson, she told him how her worst fear was of cows. She felt sure the two million French francs (£11,200) strapped to her back cushioned her fall. Twenty containers, two packages of personal belongings and two radios were collected by the waiting reception committee but it was some time before they found her wandering around a kilometre or so from the DZ. After a big meal, she slept for twenty hours.

She awoke to discover the house was near a barracks occupied by German soldiers. To assist her in her work she was given a bicycle but she had to confess that she had never ridden one before. Ordered to master it, she practised on the road near the German soldiers. Annoyed at them making fun of her, she harangued them, saying if they were gentlemen they would help. With their aid she became so proficient she was able to cycle off to a remote farm to begin her work.

In Russell Miller's *Behind the Lines*, he reported an interview he had with Claudia Pulver, one of the seamstresses at SOE's clothes section at the Thatched Barn in Hertfordshire. Here and under the police station in Savile Row, a staff of Jewish tailors and seamstresses produced first-rate copies of French suits, dresses, bodices and knickers.

Claudia recalled dressing a wild Irish girl called Paddy who told her that she carried her radio with her in her bike's saddlebag. When the Germans stopped her and asked her what she had in her bag, she jokingly suggested that it was a radio. She got away with it and survived the war. Claudia also mentioned providing dresses for a pregnant French countess who came to England in a rowing boat, and another girl who had to have the most unusual and very elegant clothes, a riding outfit and an evening dress. Who these women were remains a mystery.

Paddy's new identity was Micheline Marcelle Simonet and her cover story was that she was a '*dame de compagnie*' of a doctor in Paris, where she helped in his surgery and looked after his children. In order to find a missing Belgian parent in the Creuse area, she had taken a month's leave. Her mission was to work as a wireless operator with the Mayer brothers in the FIREMAN network around Angoulême. Edmund Mayer, codenamed 'Barthelemy', was advised that Paddy's smoking might expose her. Pattinson referred to her debriefing file, which said that:

> Informant is a very heavy smoker and most French girls do not smoke, or if they do, they could not afford to keep packets of cigarettes which were a terrible price in France. It would have looked very suspicious if informant had smoked too much in public places and was told not to by Bartelmy [*sic*].

Her other codenames included 'Josette', 'Marie-Claire', 'Stenographer' and 'Stocking'. She was a valuable asset, being able to speak French, English, Dutch, Flemish, and some German, but was also described as hot-tempered. On one occasion, when the hated Milice searched her bag, they missed her coding sheet, which was hidden in a false side. Escott identified her chief difficulties being 'her erratic handling of messages, many of which had her running after them, when they were being blown away in the open. Eventually, by using four envelopes, the contents of which were carefully destroyed within 24 hours, two for un-coded and coded messages IN, and two for coded and un-coded messages OUT, order was restored'.

On one occasion, Escott described Paddy cycling down a country lane with her radio set in her bicycle basket. When she saw two German soldiers at a checkpoint ahead of her, as there were hedges on both sides, she could not avoid them.

Putting on her most sunny and beguiling smile, she rode boldly up to the two men, one of whom, who liked the look of her, advanced some way up the road to meet her. She stopped and leaning on her bike, chatted animatedly with him. Flattered by her friendly attitude, he asked her to meet him for a drink ... the other German awaited her, and while he examined her papers, she laid herself out to be just as delightful to him, consequently so bemusing him also that he completely forgot to examine her case, while excited by the notion of making his own assignation with her for the same evening ... It had been a very close shave, only carried off by consummate acting and the brazen use of her charms.

All the girls would have found it difficult to carry out their missions unless they had been consummate actresses, studying each new person that they were to become and slipping into it like a character on the stage.

The Irish Independent article described her as a real-life Charlotte Gray, one of the fifty female Allied spies dropped into occupied France who used seduction as a weapon of war.

To a lonely, lustful German officer – and frequently to an ally in the French resistance, as well – a woman was rarely an aggressor. Instead, she was a thing to be charmed and, where possible, used as a sexual plaything. Like Cate Blanchett in the recent big-screen Second World War epic, who saves her lover from a German machine gun not by opening fire but with a passionate, lingering kiss, O'Sullivan and her fellow agents knew how to play the part – and the men who underestimated them sometimes paid with their lives. Playing dirty was par for the course, part of what Winston Churchill, who had ordered the Special Operations Executive to 'set Europe ablaze', called total war.

Despite falling off her bike a few times and being bruised and bandaged, Paddy used to cycle sixty kilometres per day, delivering and picking up messages. Her network was quite small, covering the area between Châteauroux, Montluçon, and Limoges, interspersed with hills, lakes, woods and fertile farmland. Over time she had seven wireless sets hidden in convenient but unlikely places. She befriended the Fresselines schoolmaster, the leader of the local Resistance. On their advice, she changed her cover story to being his wife, searching for a missing parent. Her cycle rides took her to Puylandon, Ganoillat and St Dizier, where she transmitted from a grocer's shop. To warn her of approaching Miliciens or the Gestapo, the shop assistant would start singing.

In spite of numerous arrests and extensive searches by the Germans, Paddy managed to evade arrest. There was one incident she told Gleeson where the woman who lived at the safe house told her that a lorry load of Germans had turned down the farm track.

The old grandmother was sitting in her usual chair in the kitchen and there was a pot of meat boiling over the open fire. Swiftly the old lady stood up and the wireless set was placed on the chair, she sat on it and spread out her voluminous skirts to conceal it. Paddy, dressed like a country girl, sat by the simmering pot stirring it and holding the messages she had been transmitting in her hands. Soldiers came into the kitchen so Paddy dropped her messages into the stew and continued her stirring, but they only wanted to know if there were any eggs they could buy. The old lady abused them, Paddy went on silently stirring, the housewife collected some eggs and handed them over. Then the soldiers left.

Heavily overworked in the run-up to D-Day, she sometimes had seven 'skeds' a day. In all she transmitted over 332 messages, almost all in candlelight, which she considered explained why London reported her coding sometimes rather puzzling. Yet, she still managed to train two local wireless operators and act as a courier.

The FIREMAN network played its part in harassing the Das Reich Panzer Division as it attempted to make its way north to Normandy. According to Escott, over 100,000 troops were cornered by guerilla and Maquis action, eventually surrendering to the Allies at Limoges. Her circuit was overrun by the Allies after D-Day and, suffering from ill-health, she was glad to be returned to England on 5 October 1944. The SOE had plans to send her to Germany, but the progress of the war led her to say that 'Monty beat me to it'.

After the war, she was awarded the MBE and the *Croix de Guerre* and received a lot of media attention following a *Daily Mail* article, which noted that '"Paddy the Rebel"... until the invasion, crawled through hedges and ditches watching the movements of German troops'. Following her cover being blown, she was posted to Calcutta as a liaison officer with the French in Force 136. She died on 5 March 1994.

Lucie Aubrac

Lucie Aubrac and her husband Raymond endured trauma during the war. Details of the couple's background were provided in Margaret Collins Weitz's *Sisters in the Resistance*. Lucie was a teacher in Strasbourg in the late 1930s, but the war and falling in love and marrying Raymond Samuel, a Jewish engineer, stopped her from taking up a scholarship in the United States. Shortly after her husband was called up, he was captured. Lucie helped him escape from a POW camp and they settled in Lyon, where they helped set up *Libération-Sud*, a Resistance network. Using 'Catherine' as her codename, she did liaison work and helped publish and distribute

Libération, a clandestine journal. Raymond changed his name to Valmont, then Aubrac, in order to disguise his Jewish identity following anti-Semitic legislation. His cover name was 'Clause Ermelin'. Their first baby was born in 1941 and, to allow them both to continue their fight, they placed their son in a children's home.

In 1943 Lucie joined a hit squad that rescued *résistants* from Vichy and German prisons, but when one of the members was captured, the group was betrayed and nearly thirty were arrested, including Raymond. Lucie went directly to the district prosecutor's home and threatened him with reprisals from London unless he released her husband, the then leader of the Lyon Resistance. It worked. However, less than a month later he was arrested again, this time by the Germans, and was tortured by Klaus Barbie, the chief of the Gestapo in Lyon. Margaret Collins Weitz says how:

> After careful reflection, Lucie decided upon a daring and dangerous plan to get Raymond out of Barbie's clutches by staging an armed attack while he was being transported somewhere. Lucie went to Gestapo headquarters and met a sympathetic German officer particularly appreciative of her gifts – Cognac, Champagne, silks and stockings. Posing as the aristocratic 'Guillaine de Barbentane' seduced by 'Claude Ermelin', Lucie, who was indeed pregnant, begged an SS lieutenant introduced to her by the officer to arrange a marriage before 'Ermelin' (Aubrac) was executed. She claimed not to care for him – all the more so now that he had been 'exposed' as a 'terrorist' – but she was adamant that her unborn child be legal. French law permits marriage in extremis to regularise such situations. She came from a conservative, Catholic, military family, and, she insisted, honour was at stake.

While planning Raymond's escape, Lucie managed to rescue two wounded comrades from St Étienne's hospital, but nearly had a miscarriage. She circulated the wards dressed in a doctor's smock and carried a stethoscope, which allowed her to memorise agents' medical charts and make arrangements to free them. The plan was to inject some sweets with typhus and give them to her husband in prison. Seriously ill, he would have to be transferred to a clinic and be rescued on the way. However, there would be a guard in the back of the armoured car carrying him, so they needed a silencer if he was not to be alerted. To get one she had to cross over the border into Switzerland. Twenty minutes later she was back in France, but the timing of the attack went wrong. Another mission had to be planned. This time, they did get 'married' and on the way back to prison the 'party' was attacked, three German guards were killed, thirteen prisoners were released, but Raymond was wounded.

The Gestapo was now after both of them. They had also learned the whereabouts of their three-year-old son, so a quick escape was vital. The boy was rescued an hour before the Germans arrived. When Lucie, then eight months pregnant, found him in the back of the truck, he was playing with a live grenade. Somehow the agents must have left it. She managed to get him to put down the lethal 'toy' before she fainted. In her memoirs, *Outwitting the Gestapo*, she said that:

> The resistance leaders decided that the three of us had to go to London. We went into hiding in central France to await the low-flying British plane [Lysander from RAF Tempsford] that was to take us to England and safety. All the peasants and the villagers in the area were aware of our situation. They were extraordinary and took us from one home to another. Because of the unfavourable atmospheric conditions, two full moons passed. We were transferred to the Jura area. The farmers – who had little enough themselves – treated us (and a downed British aviator now with us) royally. I think of the peasant woman who cut up her precious blankets to make diapers for the baby I was expecting. We learned then that some of our family – including Raymond's parents – had been betrayed and captured. In preparation for the next landing, we were taken to stay with three elderly sisters – fiercely patriotic. Finally, on the evening of February 8th, 1944, a plane managed to land.

Freddie Clark related how RAF Tempsford had been sent information that the Gestapo in France were about to go in and pick up seven people in the Resistance. Operation BLUDGEON was set up. On the evening of 8 February 1944, Flight Lieutenant Johnnie Affleck piloted his Hudson on yet another mission to France. At 0300 hours the following morning he landed in a small field in Bletterans, France, and turned ready for take-off, but once the seven were safely on board he couldn't get his plane off the ground. The port wheel was stuck in the glutinous mud. The reception committee mustered about 200 local men and women who came to the rescue. With sheer guts and determination and, after fervent cries of *Allez-oop*' and much heaving and pushing, they managed to free the wheel only to discover the tail wheel bogged. Through bitterly cold wind and driving snow, they struggled until some farmers harnessed a team of six horses and twelve oxen. Once ruts were dug for the wheels, the plane was able to make its getaway two and a half tense hours later.

On their arrival at Tempsford at 0640 hours, Lucie was rushed to Queen Charlotte's Hospital in London to have her second child – a daughter. She had told her friends that if her baby was a boy he would have Maquis as one of his names. Catherine Mitraillette was named after a little machine gun. The Tempsford ground crew had the task of cleaning the red mud off the undercarriage of the Hudson. It was said to have looked like a tank. To put the Germans and anyone else off the scent, the disinformation put out was that this French family had been taken by train to Spain concealed beneath a railway carriage. Affleck got his DFC (Distinguished Flying Cross) a few days later and, after liberation, Lucie returned to France, where she was appointed the first French female parliamentarian.

Violette Szabó

Three days after Alix's drop, perhaps the most well-known of female agents flew out of Tempsford. Violette Bushell, the daughter of an English taxi driver and a French mother, spent part of her youth in Paris and part in the Pas de Calais with her Aunt Marguerite. In *Young, Brave and Beautiful*, a biography of her written by her daughter Tania, there is a suggestion that, during the 'phoney war' in 1939 and 1940, Violette had helped her Aunt in clandestine resistance work when she visited her in the summers, sheltering downed Allied aircrew and spiriting them across the Belgium–France border and onto the escape line through France, into Spain and safety.

When in London, she worked as a hairdresser's assistant, then on the perfume counter in the Brixton branch of Bon Marché and later as a sales assistant in various shops, including Woolworths on Oxford Street. She joined the Land Army in 1940 when she was only nineteen, and spent a few pleasant weeks picking strawberries. On Bastille Day that year, her mother sent her to find someone French to invite back home to celebrate. She returned with Etienne Szabó, a thirty-year-old Czech officer in the French Foreign Legion. They fell in love and within a month were married. She joined the Auxiliary Territorial Service and served competently in an anti-aircraft unit in Liverpool until a few days before her twenty-first birthday. She gave birth to a daughter, Tania, who never saw her father. He was fighting with General Koenig's French Force at Bir Hakeim and was killed at El Alamein in October 1942.

George Clement, an SOE agent, reported how he met her in some swanky London clubs, where she had mentioned a willingness to do something useful in France. A check was done on her and she was invited to an interview with Captain Jepson and Vera Atkins, the deputy intelligence officer of SOE, and was reported as saying, 'My husband has been killed by the Germans and I'm going to get my own back.' She took up the offer of clandestine activities in France with great determination, using the cover name 'Vicky Taylor'.

After her assessment course at Winterfold the report stated that she was 'a quiet, physically tough, self-willed girl. Has plenty of confidence in herself and gets on well with the others. Plucky and persistent in her endeavours. Not easily rattled. She could possibly do the work of a courier'. She then underwent paramilitary training at Knoydart, and went to Ringway for parachute training. On one of her jumps, she sprained her ankle and had to spend time convalescing in Bournemouth in a wheelchair. So determined was she to continue that as soon as she was considered fit, she went back. In her personnel file her training instructor commented that:

> ...she still seemed to be as nervous as she was on her first visit, but after making her first descent she gained confidence and carried out the remaining descents with verve. She carried out the ground training in good style, having difficulty only with the landing training. On all three descents, one from aircraft and one from balloon by day and night, her exits were good. On her first landing she parted her feet slightly and on the second she brought her knees up to her chest. These points were brought to her notice and she seemed fully to appreciate their danger, especially if she were to jump into any wind.

She then went down to Beaulieu to continue her training in Blackbridge, one of the country houses on the estate. Revenge was said to have been her prime motivation. Peggy Minchin, her escorting officer, reported Violette as saying that she wanted some Germans to fight and she would be happy to die if she could take some of them with her.

One of her instructors commented in a film about her, *Carve Her Name with Pride*, that 'it takes time to turn a pretty girl into a killer'. Tania reported how Violette and the other trainees, including Nancy Wake and Sonia Butt,

> had all learned survival skills like silent killing, the use of codes and wireless transmitters, parachuting at night or in the day, rowing boats, the use of many kinds of plastic explosives and detonators along with grenades, guns, rifles and pistols. Physical training was important and weeks spent on learning various cover stories and withstanding interrogation under fairly harsh conditions such as sleep deprivation, to break those same stories and intelligence they had been given to learn. Cycling, swimming, and other physical training was given. Violette was exemplary in them all. She annoyed her instructors as amply described in her reports for not taking it all seriously enough. However, she did not fail any of these 'exams', so under her sparkling fun-loving attitudes was a steel-like determination to succeed, plus the inherent abilities to do so.

Her training instructor at Beaulieu did not think very highly of her. His report in her personnel file stated:

> I have come to the conclusion that this student is temperamentally unsuitable for this work. I consider that owing to her too fatalistic outlook in life and particularly in her work [and] the fact that she lacks ruse, stability and the finesse which is required and that she is too easily influenced, when operating in the field she might endanger the lives of others working with her. It is very regrettable to have come to such a decision ... with a student of this type who during the whole course has set an example to the whole party by her cheerfulness and eagerness to please.

Buckmaster disregarded this advice and decided to send her anyway. In his book *Specially Employed*, he devoted a whole chapter to Violette. He considered her really beautiful, 'dark-haired and olive-skinned, with that kind of porcelain clarity of face and purity of bone that one finds occasionally in the women of the south-west of France'. He described her as '*nerveuse*' in the French sense, having a 'wholly admirable tension of the mind and senses which causes people to overcome fear and hardship when there is a tough job to do'. She so impressed Leo Marks, the head of SOE code room, that he gave her the following romantic code:

> The life that I have is all that I have,
> And the life that I have is yours.
> The love that I have,
> Of the life that I have,
> Is yours and yours and yours.
>
> A sleep I shall have,
> A rest I shall have,
> Yet death will be but a pause,
> For the peace of my years
> In the long green grass,
> Will be yours and yours and yours.

He thought her a 'stunning-looking slip of mischief'. Prior to being sent out, she was taken to Station XV, the Thatched Barn, a requisitioned hotel on the A1 at Barnet, to provide her with some French outfits. Claudia Pulver, who worked there, thought she was 'probably the most beautiful girl I'd ever seen. I remember making black underwear for her – God knows why she wanted black underwear – among other things'.

Although strongly discouraged to undertake secret work overseas as she would be leaving her one-year-old daughter behind, Violette insisted, ensuring Tania was cared for by a friend in Mill Hill. She flew on two missions, both said to have been from Tempsford, but there are discrepancies in SOE literature about the date of the first, the plane, the pilot and whether she was landed or jumped by parachute. It is possible some historians conflated the two. According to Clark:

> Cookridge says they [Violette and Philippe Liewer] landed by Lysander on the 15th April but there were no Lysander operations that night. Minney, Violette Szabó's biographer, says the Lysander which took off from Tempsford was spotted by a German fighter (this sounds fictitious) near the landing field between Chartres and Orléans.
>
> F/Lt Taylor and F/Lt Whitaker both flying Lysanders took off from Tempsford (returning to Tangmere) each taking two agents on operation UMPIRE, both landing in a field 1.5km ENE Azay-sur-Cher some 7km ESE Tours. Verity names three of the passengers, the 161 Squadron diary records that Lt Hysing-Dahl took three agents with 4 packages on operation LILAC. Verity says the field was 1.5km W Baudreville some 30km ESE Chartres but does not mention that passengers were taken out. It could be possible that the Norwegian, Hysing-Dahl flew them in, the landing field was certainly between Chartres and Orléans, and a train to Paris could have been caught at nearby Angerville.
>
> M R D Foot says they were parachuted in; it is questionable if they were included in the Tempsford parachute operations that night which were, as it can be seen, way to the south and Szabó and Liewer were going to Rouen. However, Vera Atkins, the intelligence officer who worked closely with the women of 'F' Section, SOE, was recently kind enough to clarify this mystery by saying that she remembered escorting Violette Szabó to an awaiting Carpetbagger B-24 sent to collect her from Tempsford.

Their flight was on Wednesday 5 April 1944 in a converted USAAF Liberator. They parachuted into a field outside Azay-le-Rideau, near Rouen, east of Le Havre. This was in the *zone interdite* – an area heavily guarded by Germans within twenty-five kilometres of the Channel coast. Violette's codename was 'Seamstress' and her cover was as a professional secretary from Le Havre called Corinne Reine Leroy, on holiday with a task of trying to find an uncle missing after an Allied air raid. Her real mission was to find out how much the SALESMAN *réseau* had been broken, distribute money to families who had suffered financially when the breadwinner was arrested, gather information about the German V1 rocket installations, and organise whoever was left to blow up the

Barentin viaduct. To help, she had been given 250,000 francs. According to Tania, Philippe had instructed her

> to have a substantial sum on her at all times, the larger part of it well-concealed in her worn-looking leather shoulder-bag with a cleverly disguised double lining and base. Perhaps some in her jacket. More in her money belt. Once she was on her own, which could be at any moment, she might need the extra cash for travelling (first class) by train, for bribes, buying various clothes, getting and paying for forged ration cards or even new forged identity cards, maybe even buying a car, truck or bike – with or without motor. Everything had to be considered.

Rouen, where German soldiers, the Gestapo, and the Milice had just broken a Resistance group and were watching known contacts, was a very difficult place for Violette to move around. She had to travel alone as Liewer was known to the Gestapo. Using a borrowed bike, she managed to meet a number of women who had been involved and succeeded in completing her mission, even getting close enough to the concrete bases hidden in the woods near Saint-Leu-d'Esserent from where the V1 flying bombs were to be launched. She also pulled from a wall a 'Wanted' poster of Liewer.

In Rouen she successfully re-established contact with the surviving agents of the penetrated *réseau*, despite having several brushes with the Germans. They arrested her twice, once keeping her in a police station for four hours – but she managed to talk herself out of trouble and made her way back to Paris to rendezvous with Philippe. Given the level of German activity in the area, he arranged for her to be brought back to England on the evening of 30 April. He also informed her that the viaduct had been brought down.

Pleased with the success of her mission, she decided to reward herself. A display in the shop window of Molyneux, a top Paris fashion house, caught her attention. According to Tania, the bill for a black *crêpe de chine* evening dress, a crimson and deep-blue plaid dress, a floral silk dress and yellow jersey was for 37,475 leftover counterfeit SOE francs – the equivalent of £21,300 today. A pair of wedged-heel, sling-back, peep-toe sandals bought the next day were perfect with the dresses. Three Maigret novels, red earrings, a silk dress for her daughter, Worth's Je Reviens perfume, silk-lined kid gloves, Bourjois rouge, silk ties, ivory fan, silk scarf, linen handkerchiefs, a Meccano set for her family and an unusual bead brooch for Vera Atkins were additional purchases.

A train journey of a few hours to Issouden, near Châteauroux, and a short car journey took Violette and Philippe to a small farm near the disused Le Fay airfield, at Ségry, near St Aubin. It was a double Lysander pick-up by Flight Lieutenant Bob Large and Flight Officer J. P. Alcock on 30 April 1944. Within minutes of the three agents arriving, Philippe was strapped into one of the Lysanders, Violette in the other with her suitcase and packages containing all her presents.

The flight back to England, according to Large, was not without incident. They were attacked by enemy fighters near Châteaudun airfield. Flak burst all around the plane, holing the propeller, but Large flung his Lysander around the sky to escape the danger zone, knowing there was a female agent in the back whom he had to save. It was a very bumpy landing at Tangmere. The plane tipped over, sliding along on a wing, causing Violette to bang her head. One of the tyres was in shreds, having been punctured by a piece of flak, and Large said it did a 'ground loop'. He got out and went to help out the passenger and was greeted by an angry tirade in rapid French and an assault with an umbrella. He was pleased she did not have a gun. She was said to have been more shaken by the fact that her intercom had become unplugged and she had thought they had landed in enemy territory. It being too dark to recognise the pilot's uniform, she presumed that he was a German who had come to arrest her.

Unable to understand her screaming and shouting, Large tried to placate her by calling for a car to fetch them. When the mix-up was sorted out, a broad smile appeared on her face. *'Vous est le pilot!'* she exclaimed, flung her arms round his neck and kissed him. He felt it was all worth it just for that one kiss.

Dressed in FANY uniform, the common disguise for female agents back home, she spent a few days with her family during the hottest summer of the war, celebrating her promotion to lieutenant and impressing onlookers with her stunning French outfits. Tania reports her spending time with Nancy Wake and Sonia Butt, other female agents with whom she had trained.

On the afternoon of Monday 5 June, Violette and her new team, nineteen-year-old Jean Claude Guiet, twenty-year-old Bob Maloubier, and thirty-two-year-old Philippe Liewer, were driven in a black Humber out of London, up the A1 to Hasells Hall, a few miles south-east of Tempsford. Like Gaynes Hall, it was a handsome red-brick Georgian mansion belonging to the Pym family, situated on the crest of the Greensand Ridge. It was set in beautiful grounds, landscaped by Humphrey Repton, with arbours, paths and follies. Tania described it being used as

sleeping quarters and clubhouse for agents and flyers leaving for France on so many undercover missions. Woods and fine grounds surrounded the house. It was a good and peaceful place to try to relax and keep things in perspective while waiting for the right weather conditions or pilots and aircraft to wing them away to danger.

The RAF had requisitioned this already decaying but lovely house so amenities were sparse but adequate, there was, however, plenty to drink in the way of alcoholic beverages, much brought over from occupied countries. Reasonably good food was on offer. All at the government's expense. There was just enough hot water for showering or shallow baths, the bedrooms were clean and basically comfortable. Unfortunately, perhaps, the wooden floors kept naughty activities to a minimum as they creaked and groaned at the slightest step or ...

A FANY driver arrived at dusk in a blacked-out car to take them the few miles down the hill to the airfield. When their preparations at Gibraltar Farm were complete, Vera Atkins sent them off with the traditional salute, '*Merde!*' As the Halifax was taxiing to the runway, the pilot suddenly brought it to a standstill. One of the ground crew gesticulated with his arms to abort the flight. The operation was cancelled due to stormy weather. There were 66 mph gales reported over the south coast, thunder, lightning, and very heavy rain.

Imagine the tension that had built up prior to their departure and the disappointment and anti-climax when it did not happen. Her team were taken back to Hasells Hall. Nancy Robert, Violette's conducting officer, said she had had to get her ready and

make sure she had everything and say goodbye, and then it didn't happen. And then we just had to wait. I will never forget it. Ever. Where we were, it was beautifully sunny and there was Violette sitting on the lawn with this Polish young man who was going too. They were laughing and chatting and playing a gramophone record over and over and over again. I can still hear it: 'I want to buy a paper doll I can call my own'.

When the flight was postponed, Violette is said to have remained calm and enjoyed the trip to Cambridge the following day, despite the low clouds and strong winds. A punt on the Cam, a pleasant lunch of bangers and mash in an olde worlde pub, and a stroll around the city was lightened by lots of laughing and joking and singing of their team's song, 'I'll Be Around'. When they got back to Hasells, she relaxed in the company of two SAS officers, Lieutenant Richard Crisp and twenty-two-year-old Captain John Tonkin. In a letter Tonkin sent to his mother, quoted in Helm's biography of Vera Atkins, he described Hasells as the:

'last resting place' for all agents to enemy countries. We were very well looked after by the ATS [Auxiliary Territorial Service]. The only operational people there were Richard and I and the Jedburgh team for Operation Bulbasket, two of our officers for Houndsworth, two for Titanic, and four agents, of whom two were surprisingly beautiful girls. We had checked and rechecked everything and packed our enormous rucksacks about fifty times. Finally, there was nothing more to do, so we spent the time very profitably with the girls, doing jigsaw puzzles.

That evening, Violette and her team were driven down to the airfield. Checks were carried out. Equipment was issued. Goodbyes were said and the Halifax took off. They settled down to coffee and sandwiches and prepared for the drop. Three hours later the pilot reported no lights from the reception committee, so the operation was aborted. Playing blackjack in the back, they were unaware on their return to Tempsford of the enormous operation that was going on beneath them in the English Channel off the Normandy coast. It was 6 June – D-Day.

Three hours after getting back to Hasells, Violette woke up her team members with the news of the landings. Annoyed at having been rudely awoken by 'that Bloody woman', Bob went back to sleep. She sat around talking about what would be happening from now on. They were very annoyed not to have been told by the pilot as it would have been a wonderful sight, watching the invasion through the Joe hole.

That day was dominated by games of ping-pong and cards, Violette surprising Vera Atkins by her calm. That night, according to Tania, Captain Nancy Frazer Campbell drove one of two Humbers the 45 miles to Harrington, USAAF 36 Bomber Squadron's base. Mike Fenster's Liberator B-24 was waiting to pick up Violette and the other three agents. Her escort officer commented that 'in a group of heavily armed and equipped men waiting to take off from the same airfield, Violette was smiling and debonair. She wore a flowered frock, white sandals and earrings which she had bought in Paris during her first mission'. She insisted on kissing each member of the crew, the pilot, and the co-pilot.

The day before her baby daughter Tania's second birthday, Violette and her team were dropped by parachute at Saint-Gilles-les-Forêts, hilly farmland near Limoges, central France, at 0149 hours. Twenty-two containers containing machine guns, hand grenades, ammunition, explosives, clothes, food, and medicine were dropped with them. While some of the reception committee disposed of the supplies, she was taken to Sussac and provided with a room over the grocer's shop opposite the church. She was to be known as Madame Villeret, codenamed 'Corinne', and her mission was to take messages from Liewer to various units of the Resistance and bringing their messages back. The 600 Maquis and 200 gendarmes who had joined them following D-Day needed co-ordinating and instructing. Armed saboteurs cut electricity supplies for the submarine base at Rochefort and blew up the railway lines between Limoges and Paris, and between Bordeaux and Toulouse. Maloubier claimed to have blown up seven bridges in one day. The group claimed to have held back the 2nd Panzer Division, which was being rushed from the south of France to Normandy to strengthen the German resistance to the Allied landings. In revenge for an attack in Tulle, just south of Limoges, in which 137 Germans were killed, ninety-seven men were rounded up and hanged from the lampposts.

According to Robin Mackness' research into the massacre at Oradour, German General Lammerding was in charge of getting the 2nd Panzer Division from its base in Montauban up the Rhone valley. Major Kampfe, the head of the 3rd Battalion, had been kidnapped on his way to Tulle and his empty car was found near Oradour-sur-Glane. Added to Lammerding's problems was the fact that he was said to have had secretly amassed 600 kilos of gold, about half a ton, while on operations. As he couldn't leave it in Montauban, he had it crated and labelled as the division's records. His plan was to have it trucked with his papers back to Germany. On the way, however, the convoy was ambushed and the gold taken. The only SS survivor said that it happened near Oradour-sur-Glane, which prompted widespread patrols in the area Violette was sent to.[36]

Three days after landing, Violette met up with Anastasie, a Maquis leader, and another Resistance fighter. They planned to drive her to rendezvous with Jacques Poirier, a Resistance leader who had taken over the AUTHOR and DIGGER networks in the Dordogne area., following the arrest of Harry Peulevé. A plastic-explosive bomb sat between her feet on the floor of their black Citroën and her bicycle was strapped to the front passenger seat door. As they drove towards Salon La Tour, they were intercepted by a party of SS troops. The car was fired on. It stopped and, running for safety through a wheat field, she was shot in the arm, stumbled through rutted furrows, fell and twisted her ankle. The film *Carve Her Name with Pride* shows her telling Anastasie to go on without her and providing him with covering fire as he swam across a river until she ran out of ammunition. Tania tells of her hiding behind an apple tree, firing at the advancing enemy. However, historian Howard Tuck's investigations suggest there was only one Sten gun in the car and she did not use it.

During her training, she is reported to have said that 'I only want to have some Germans to fight and I should die happy if I could take some of them with me'. The film shows her shooting five soldiers before she gets wounded, and another afterwards. A high-ranking officer congratulates her on her performance: 'You put up a good fight Mademoiselle. Cigarette?'

After being captured and imprisoned at Maison D'Arret in Limoges, she was taken daily for interrogation at the nearby Gestapo headquarters on Rue Louvrier de Lajolais. There, she was said to have been tortured. Hugette Desire, a member of the French Resistance, recalled in a BBC programme, *Secret Agent: The True Story of Violette Szabó*, that Violette had told her that an SS man had put his pistol into her neck, said he could kill her tomorrow if he so wished, and then raped her. Bob Maloubier planned a rescue attempt but, hours beforehand, she was transferred to Paris.

On the same day that Violette was captured, the same SS division carried out another savage reprisal, one of the worst atrocities of the war. Troops arrived in Oradour-sur-Glane, a 20-minute drive north-west of Limoges, and instructed all the men, women, and children to gather in the main square. The women and children were locked up in the church while 200 men were herded into barns. The men were gunned down and the barns set alight. Then the women and children were shot and the church set ablaze, by detonating a box of explosives sat upon the altar, along with all remaining buildings in the village. Women from nearby villages who came to pick their children up from school were shot. In Max Hasting's *Das Reich*, he states 642 were killed and 80 escaped. The following morning, soldiers disposed of the bodies to prevent identification.

In Paris, Violette then suffered weeks of interrogation at Avenue Foch, the Gestapo HQ, and then imprisonment at Block Five in Frèsnes Prison along with many other captured SOE agents. She was still wearing the same white blouse and navy skirt she was caught in. It is claimed in Joe Saward's *The Grand Prix Saboteurs* that the details of a safe house in Paris were extricated from her, which led to the arrest and death of several other SOE agents.

Following the instructions given to every captured prisoner to try to escape, she began working loose one of the bars in the roof light of her cell. She had become so thin that one bar forced a few inches to one side would allow her to squeeze through. Before she managed it, though, there were orders to assemble for a mass transfer. The Germans were retreating following the Allies' push towards the city and sent many of their prisoners by train to concentration camps.

The date of her departure has been given by Madame Rosier, an inmate at Ravensbrück, as 8 August, eight weeks after her arrival. Ironically, the cattle truck Violette was in was strafed by the RAF at Compiègne. Unable to escape without being shot by the guards, Violette, still chained to Denise

Bloch, got hold of a tin cup and crawled to the adjoining compartment to give water from the toilet to the men. In Bruce Marshall's *White Rabbit*, he narrates how SOE agent Yeo-Thomas was picked up by a Lysander and returned:

'We all felt deeply ashamed when we saw Violette Szabó, while the raid was still on, come crawling along the corridor towards us with a jug of water which she had filled from the lavatory. She handed it to us through the iron bars. With her, crawling too, came the girl to whose ankle she was chained.

This act of mercy made an unforgettable impression on all. She spoke words of comfort, jested, went back with the jug to fill it again and again.'

'My God that girl had guts,' says Yeo-Thomas. 'I shall never forget that moment,' says Harry Peulevé [an old friend and fellow SOE agent], 'I feel very proud that I knew her. She looked so pretty, despite her shabby clothes and her lack of make-up – and she was full of good cheer. I have never under any circumstances known her to be depressed or moody.'

Buckmaster said that one of the other prisoners who escaped death in the camps told him that Violette gave him half a bottle of wine abandoned by the guards, saying, '*Bon courage. Les alliés sont aux portes de Paris. Rassure-toi.*' She and Denise were hit with rifle butts when the guards returned. On reaching Metz, the prisoners were 'billeted' in stables where she met Harry Peulevé, an old friend and SOE agent who Tania was convinced was in love with her mother. Tania reported it as being extremely crowded:

They were there for about two days with little food but adequate water. So much so that Violette was able to wash out her white blouse and underwear. Other women undoubtedly did likewise. Yvonne Baseden particularly remembers as she told the author on a visit to her flat, seeing Violette washing her blouse in a bowl on what seemed to be a stack of crates ... Harry had this to say:

'Violette and I talked all through the night. Her voice, as always, was so sweet and soothing, one could listen to it for hours. We spoke of old times and we told each other our experiences in France. Bit by bit everything was unfolded – her life in Frèsnes, her interviews at Avenue Foch. But either through modesty or a sense of delicacy, since some of the tortures were too intimate in their application, or perhaps because she did not wish to live again through the pain of it, she spoke hardly at all about the tortures she had been made to suffer. She was in a cheerful mood. Her spirits were high. She was confident of victory and was resolved on escaping no matter where they took her.'

In Foot's *SOE in France*, he claims to have found no evidence that Violette was tortured, suggesting the accounts were 'completely fictitious'. After being separated from the men, the women were taken first to the Gestapo headquarters in Strasbourg and then to Saarbrücken, a transit camp and finally Ravensbrück concentration camp in the third week of August. 'Rolande', one of the captured SOE agents on the train, noted that the women were taken to the bathhouse and when they were naked, chained and handcuffed, *les souris*, the grey-uniformed women guards, forced them to squat and defecate under the leering gaze of male guards.[37]

In Nigel Perrin's *Spirit of Resistance*, he mentions that Harry Peulevé, in his unpublished memoirs, admits to having fallen in love with Violette while in London and that, having managed to escape from concentration with Yeo-Thomas's help, he captured two SS guards. On them he found photographs of nude female prisoners, Violette among them. Perrin doubted the veracity of Harry's memory. Tania writes:

> Violette's world and that of her companions had reduced to endless grey railway tracks and sidings, grey stations, grey platforms and the noise of grey guards and grey dogs. Even a few of the young women turned grey while screaming in pain or fear. Everything became grey – grey uniforms, grey bread, grey faces, grey world.

Escott details how, on 3 September 1944, Violette and six other women, including Lilian Rolfe, Denise Bloch, and Eileen Nearne, were taken to Torgau, another manufacturing slave labour camp like Siemens. Here they were forced to make ammunition but they made a stand, refusing to make bullets and shells that would be used to kill their brothers and fathers. Suffering bad whippings and faced with being shot, they gave in, but did as much as they could to sabotage the work, slow down production, as well as plan an escape. On 5 October they were returned to Ravensbrück before they could act on their plans. Violette seemed to be under suspicion, probably about the escape attempt, and was beaten and sent to the punishment block. Odette Sansom reported hearing her in the next door cell berating her jailer.

On 19 October, still in their tattered, thin clothes, they were sent to Königsberg, 480 kilometres to the north. They were forced to clear a swamp for an airfield. Working up to their knees in freezing cold, muddy water or deep snow with very basic food rations, disease was widespread. Although it dampened Violette's spirit, she managed to cheer up her friends.

Although undocumented in other SOE histories, Tania Szabó states,

'Violette and other women having been cleaned up, were forced to make a number of appallingly degrading visits to the Sachsenhausen camp bordels and sub camps where a group of SS guards and officers took photographs of the sexual acts committed on Violette and other women.'

Eventually, on the direct order of Heinrich Himmler, they were returned to Ravensbrück. Violette was sent to the infection block for a few days as her legs were covered in ulcers. On the evening of 27 January 1945, she was taken out with Denise Bloch and Cécile Lefort to the yard beside the camp commandant's quarters. Their clothes were in rags and their faces and hair were dirty. After being forced to kneel, the formal order of their execution was read out and they were all shot in the back of the head. Their bodies were then disposed of in the crematorium.

Although the camp overseer testified that they were shot, Escott suggested that there was doubt about it as hanging was commonly used. The Gestapo didn't want anyone providing evidence against them about their radio games and wanted to ensure SOE and SIS agents were disposed of. Of Violette, Odette Sansom simply said, 'She was the bravest of us all.' There was the point made by Escott that at least Violette and her friends knew that they had given their lives for the liberation of France and that very soon the Nazi regime would come to an end.

After the war, in recognition of her bravery, Violette was posthumously awarded the George Cross – the first woman ever to receive it. The *London Gazette* of 17 December 1946 included a slightly inaccurate citation.

Madame Szabó volunteered to undertake a particularly dangerous mission in France. She was parachuted into France in 1944, and undertook the task with enthusiasm. In her execution of the delicate researches entailed she showed great presence of mind and astuteness. She was twice arrested by the German security authorities, but each time managed to get away. Eventually, however, with other members of her group, she was surrounded by the Gestapo in a house in the south-west of France.

Resistance appeared hopeless, but Mme Szabó, seizing a Sten gun and as much ammunition as she could carry, barricaded herself in part of the house and, exchanging shot for shot with the enemy, killed or wounded several of them. By constant movement she avoided being cornered and fought until she dropped exhausted. She was arrested and had to undergo solitary confinement. She was then continuously and atrociously tortured, but never by word or deed gave away any of her acquaintances or told the enemy anything of any value. She was ultimately executed. Mme Szabó gave a magnificent example of courage and steadfastness.

The French gave her and her husband the *Croix de Guerre* with clasps, and later the *Medaille de Resistance*. She is also listed on the 'Roll of Honour' at the Valençay Memorial. Thanks to the efforts of Rosemary Rigby MBE, a museum was opened in Violette's memory by her daughter Tania, at Wormelow in Herefordshire in 2000. Annual reunions are held on the nearest weekend to Violette's birthday, 20 June, which attract many people who were involved directly and indirectly.[38]

Although Violette was the last woman agent mentioned by Clark as having been flown out of Tempsford, SOE records show that numerous other women were sent into occupied Europe after D-Day.

Lilian Rolfe

Almost three weeks after Lilian Rolfe's thirtieth birthday, she became the next female agent flown into France by 161 Squadron. She was a passenger in one of two Lysanders from Tangmere on 5/6 April and landed one and a half kilometres east-north-east of Azay-sur-Cher, the same landing site that Julienne Aisner and Vera Leigh used. In fact, Julienne returned to England on the same plane. According to Verity, accompanying Lilian on the outward journey were Marie-Christine and André Studler, who Verity indicated were OSS agents. André was the head of the HISTORIAN and later the SQUATTER networks, and needed lifting out to evade arrest. Whether Marie-Christine was his wife, girlfriend, or worked in the Resistance is unknown.

Lilian and her twin sister Helen were born in Paris on 26 April 1914. Their father was a British chartered accountant and their mother was Russian. Although she grew up in Paris, she often visited her grandparents who lived in London. To improve her English, her parents sent her on holiday, possibly to Woking, but a rheumatic fever cut short her stay. When she was nineteen, the family moved to Rio de Janeiro, where she worked in the Press Department at the British Embassy.

In February 1943, wanting to help the war effort in some way, took a ship back to England and joined the WAAF as an assistant second officer on 16 May 1943. Described by Escott as a tall, dark-haired girl, with steady dark eyes and a mouth made for smiling, she proudly wore the Brazilian flash on her uniform. Being fluent in several languages, intelligent, mature, and very patriotic, she was accepted for training in the SOE on 24 November 1943. They wanted her to return to France as a wireless operator. Bob Lyndall, her instructor, said that she completed it in six weeks. In Escott's *The Heroines of SOE*, she mentioned that a training report in the following March commented that she was 'good at coding and steady with Morse, although not as good at "handling" wireless equipment, but would improve with practice. Friends training with her at that time commented that she was very unhappy, recovering from a failed love affair, but this did not seem to affect her work'.

Audrey Ririe, who knew Lilian when she was in WAAF, made a comment, quoted in Escott's *The Heroines of SOE* that she was

> a small, dark, pretty little woman, earnest and serious ... Later we girls thought of her with awe at the enormity of the task she had taken on ... I always shudder when I think of those vast empty fields of France and how they must have looked to a young woman dropped into enemy territory.

She went to work as a wireless operator in George Wilkinson's HISTORIAN network in Montagris, near Orléans using identity papers in the name of Madame Claudie Rodier, codenamed 'Nadine' and also known as 'Recluse'. It was a difficult time as she was working in the towns of Montagris, Orléans and Nangis, formerly in the 'burnt' PROSPER network. Rebuilding it was Wilkinson's mission and Lilian had to arrange parachute drops to supply the growing number of men who were expecting an Allied invasion. The neighbouring networks of VENTRILOQUIST and HEADMASTER were also being rebuilt, as well as Pearl Witherington's WRESTLER network. Escott narrates how:

> When she arrived she carried a tiny transmitter and receiver strapped to her body. It was more fragile than the sturdier B2, one reason why she didn't parachute in ... She had little cause to use, however, as she was separated from her organiser for several weeks, as he travelled around his circuit. She was able therefore to settle in the area, establish her cover story, met and get over the shock of her first Germans, get to know the routes she would have to use with her bike and make some useful contacts of her own, including the leaders of the local Maquis. Apart from a few messages she used her wireless very little until George, having got his circuit organised, came back to find her. Then she started work in earnest.

Although her mission was to report on German troop movements, organise arms and supply drops, she also took part in sabotage missions, including taking part in a gun battle in the small town of Olivet, just south of Orléans.

Shortly after the D-Day landings, Wilkinson, her organiser, was arrested but she kept on transmitting until she too was caught in Nangis on 31 July. Apparently, the house she was staying in was raided while the Germans were looking for someone else. They found her in bed asleep and queried her identity papers. Despite the difficult conditions she had to operate under, she had managed to transmit sixty-seven messages in just under four months.

After being arrested, Lilian was handcuffed and taken to their headquarters in Orléans. Whilst searching the house, they found her wireless set and realised that they had caught an important member of the Resistance, Wilkinson's wireless operator. This resulted in her being transported to Avenue Foch in Paris for rough, intensive interrogation and brutal torture by the Gestapo. As she revealed little that helped them, she was transferred to Frèsnes Prison but she did not stay long. Aware that the American forces were close at hand, on 8 August 1944 she and thirty-seven SOE men and women prisoners were taken by train to Germany. Lilian and the other women were sent to Ravensbrück.

On the hot train journey, chained at the ankles to Violette Szabó, they were attacked by RAF planes. Escott narrated how the attack halted the train so that the prisoners had to wait for alternative transport 'that turned out to be cattle trucks, which stopped occasionally at a few places, a stables, a Gestapo headquarters and the Neue-Saarbrücken concentration camp, where they stayed a few days before continuing their journey.'

They were thought to have arrived at Ravensbrück on 22 August, where she shared a top bunk in an accommodation block with Violette and Denise Bloch. Treated badly, they were expected to work on starvation rations.

Three weeks later, along with Eileen Nearne, she and two other women were sent to Torgau, another camp, where they planned their escape. The details are found in Violette's account. The problem, according to Escott, was that,

> although they should have been classed as prisoners of war, the Germans had ignored this fact and were treating them as civilian malcontents or political prisoners, and apart from not sending them to a prisoner of war camp – often a death sentence although they did not know it – they had never been brought to trial. In fact, none of the SOE girls was tried so their imprisonment was breaking all the rules of war drawn up in the Geneva Convention to which Germany had subscribed. But this was a small matter in comparison with the terrible crimes of which the Germans were later found guilty.

They were sent back to Ravensbrück before their plans could be materialised and, because they were relatively fit, were then sent to Königsberg to help clear land for the construction of a new airfield. The extreme conditions Lilian had to endure were described by Escott:

> It was now winter, freezing cold, with ice and snow. They were thinly clothed for the conditions, the food was bad and there was very little of it. They had

to lift and carry heavy weights, to dig in deep frozen water for hours on end, to fill swamps with sand, to cut and lay slabs of turf, to hew and haul trees and tree stumps, to drag boulders and equipment, all in the open, without covering or shelter. There was no medical treatment and many died from pneumonia, dysentery, cholera and tuberculosis, if they did not break down from sheer exhaustion, malnutrition or cruel treatment by the guards, who thought nothing of beating women staggering with heavy loads or almost dying on their feet. Indeed when the German Air Force came to occupy the camp, so painstakingly created, even they were horrified by what they saw. Under these conditions, Lilian no longer spoke of escape. It was all she could do to survive. She was already sick with a spot on her lung and her breathing becoming hard and laboured. All her former cheerfulness failed her and she found it hard not to sink into the torpor which usually preceded a loss of will to live, and then death.

In January 1945 the three of them were transferred back to the main camp and put, not in the huts with the other women, but in the punishment block. From there she was put in an isolation cell close to the crematorium and, according to the testimony of the camp commander and guards after the war, had to be stretchered into the yard on or about 5 January. She had to watch the two other women sentenced to death being shot in the back of the neck before she too was executed. The bodies were then disposed of in the crematorium. Other sources state she was dragged out and executed on 27 January 1945.

Escott reported that Mary Lindell, who (like Yvonne Baseden) survived imprisonment at Ravensbrück, said after the war that she thought the three women had been told that they were to be sent to a POW camp near Lake Constance, but that there is no evidence that any women were ever sent there. Mary felt that their deaths were a direct result of this; she added that the normal method of execution was hanging and she had been reliably informed that the women's clothing had been returned to the store unsoiled. In honour of her brave venture, Lilian was awarded an MBE, 'Mentioned in Dispatches' and awarded the *Medaille de la Resistance* and the *Croix de Guerre*.

Muriel Byck

After four nail-biting attempts were cancelled because of poor weather conditions, eventually on 9 April 1944 petite, dark-haired, twenty-three-year-old Muriel Byck, codenamed 'Violette', was flown out of Tempsford along with three other men to work as a wireless transmitter with Philippe de Vomécourt's VENTRILOQUIST network in the Orléans–Blois area.

Martin Sugarman, on the Jewish Virtual Library website, and Squadron

Leader Beryl Escott, reported how Muriel was born on 4 June 1918 in Ealing, London. Her parents, Jacques Byck and Luba Besia (née Golinska), were Russian Jews who had settled first in France and then in Britain, where they became naturalised British. Her SOE personnel file showed that between 1923 and 24 she studied in Weisbaden in Germany, and in 1926 she was at the Lycée de Jeunes Filles, in St German, before moving to London in 1930, where she attended the Lycée Français in Kensington. After completing her baccalaureate in 1935, she studied at the University of Lille in France. She returned to London and from 1936 worked as a secretary, then as an assistant stage manager at the Gate Theatre. Following the break out of war 1939, she joined the Red Cross as a volunteer worker. In 1941, when her parents divorced, she moved with her mother to Torquay in Devon and found work as a National Registration clerk as well as an air-raid warden.

She joined the WAAF in December 1942 as a General Duties clerk and worked in their Records Office, where her fluent French drew her to the attention of the SOE, which she joined in July 1943. After an assessment at Winterfold and paramilitary training at Moeble, Inverness, in October she underwent wireless training at Thame Park, Oxfordshire. According to her instructors' records, she was given a high intelligence rating with a high grade for Morse and Mechanical Aptitude. Her observers described her as

> a quiet, bright, attractive girl, keen, enthusiastic and intelligent. Alert but not very practical and as yet lacks foresight and thoroughness. She is, however, self-possessed, independent and persistent, and warm in her feelings for others ... a girl of considerable promise who will require much training to help her overcome her lack of experience, her complete ignorance of what the work really involves and her general guilelessness. Her temperament would appear to be suitable for work as a courier, or possibly propaganda.[39]

However, Vera Atkins, the woman in charge of all the 'F' Section women in SOE, thought Muriel to be very self-assured and committed to go into the hazardous work to defeat Nazism and all it stood for.

Escott commented that Muriel's 'pretty, chubby, tiny and almost childlike appearance masked the maturity and resilience of a 25-year-old woman'. De Vomécourt, who had not had good experiences working with SOE agents, said: 'she looked so young, but I had seen enough of France to know that courage knew no barriers of age'. In fact, Muriel's youthful looks meant that she was given special training to make her look older by using a pencil under her eyes.

She got engaged to a French agent working for the OSS, who she met on her training course. As a memento, he gave her a leather-covered powder compact, but when Muriel arrived at RAF Tempsford for the flight, de Vomécourt insisted that she was not allowed to take the compact unless she agreed to make it look old. Nothing like it could be bought in France, so she agreed that it could be rubbed with ammonia.

Promoted to second officer before her trip, she parachuted into Issoudun where, because it was Easter, one of the reception committee pressed a small gold cross and chain into her hands – said by Escott to have been 'a kind of talisman against evil from which she was never to be parted'.

As de Vomécourt had twisted an ankle, his flight was delayed, so Muriel had been instructed to work with Christopher Hudson, one of her fellow passengers. He and de Vomécourt had escaped from Eysses prison in January that year and he was on his way to take over the HEADMASTER network in the Le Mans area.

On her first day in Salbris, she was given a baptism of fire. Antoine Vincent, the owner of the garage where she first stayed, took her out for a meal in a little restaurant on the outskirts of town where she was to meet up with de Vomécourt. It was normally used exclusively by the Germans, and that day it was full of them. She was terrified and asked to leave but in his wartime memoirs, *An Army of Amateurs*, Philippe told her not to worry. 'We brought you here on purpose. You must get used to the sight of the *Boches* and realise there's nothing different about them. Once you're used to seeing them, you won't worry about them anymore.'

When she was taken to her hosts' house, they were shown papers indicating that she was a secretary from Paris who had been given orders by the doctor to take a rest in the country. They specified that she had to ensure that her medicines were taken at specified times every day and night. This was to provide an excuse if they heard her alarm clock ringing at odd hours so she could make her scheduled wireless calls. The doctor also told them not to be surprised if she had the occasional visit from her 'uncle' who might pop down to see how she was.

With identity papers in the name of Madame Michele Bernier, codenamed 'Michelle', she was also known as 'Benefactress'. In *An Army of Amateurs*, de Vomécourt wrote that:

> Muriel was provided with three different photographs of herself for identity papers, each of them projecting an entirely separate person, by the adoption of a changed hairstyle. By drawing back her hair from her forehead, or by fluffing it out, untidily, she could assume different identities in an emergency. And she would have the identity papers, bearing the appropriate photograph of herself, to aid the transformation.

Part of her mission was to train local recruits in wireless transmission for the VENTRILOQUIST network. To assist her she had four of the smaller A Mark III variety wireless sets hidden within a sixteen-kilometre radius of the garage. One was discovered in a barn that was being demolished in 1999. The others were in an attic in a village house, a shack in a wood, and the other in a scrapyard shed near the garage. She ensured her operators never used the same set at the same time each day, and whenever reports arrived of Germans in the vicinity, the set was moved to another spot. According to the Jewish Virtual Library website:

> Her circuit had four transmitters in different locations covering a wide area within a ten-mile radius of Vincent's house, and – in accordance with her orders – were constantly moved about to avoid detection by the Germans, with transmissions being as brief as possible Her first transmission was on 7 May 1944 and she subsequently sent twenty-seven messages and received sixteen. She never used the same set consecutively or at the same hour on any day. She was thus continually cycling from one to the other, and although many a man's health and nerves degenerated under the stress, Muriel remained cheerful and buoyant despite her frail and youthful looks. Rushing from location to location, she would encode, send, receive and decode messages, always on schedule, and on her own initiative often do this for other circuits as well, so messages would not ever be delayed. She also acted as a courier, alerting sabotage teams over a wide area.
>
> Her base was in Vincent's junk yard, twenty-five yards from his garage which was used as a repair shop by the Germans. Her station consisted of a rickety hut with a rusted corrugated iron roof, with light filtering through cracks in the wall. She was surrounded by old tyres and car parts and the reek of oil and petrol. She had a box and table to work at. Whilst transmitting, a guard was posted at the yard gate to give her warning if need be.
>
> One day in late April, ... whilst transmitting to London, she noticed an eye looking through a hole in the shed wall. Her stomach lurched but she quickly switched to plain language to tell London she was being watched. Continuing to send, she picked up the set and approached the hole, in time to see a German soldier leaving the yard. Full of fear, and not understanding where her lookout was, she packed her equipment, threw dust over her box and table to disguise the fact that anyone had been in the hut, and slipped into Vincent's house and told him what had happened.
>
> He decided at once to get her away in a car after consulting de Vomécourt, who came to collect her. When the Germans arrived – forty of them – they were already sceptical that their soldier had actually seen a pretty woman with a transmitter in a junk yard shed! They searched and found nothing

and the soldier was given ten days detention for wasting his officer's time.

Securely relocated in a new safe house (with the help of the Resistance doctor Andrieux) Muriel returned to work; her story was that she was recovering from an illness and had come from Paris to recuperate. She had to take medicine during the night and her hosts should not be worried by her alarm going off at strange hours (this was, of course, to cover her wireless operations) or visits from her 'uncle', de Vomécourt.[40]

Following SOE analysis of her transmissions, in which she reported that the Germans were running trains into the military camp at Michenon and loading them with arms and ammunition, it was decided that the RAF would act on VENTRILOQUIST's plans and bomb the camp. She heard at 1400 hours on 7 May that there would be an attack the following evening. A consignment was due to be sent to Normandy to help soldiers defending the Atlantik Wall. That was time enough for the Resistance to blow up the railway lines outside the camp to stop any trains from leaving, and to inform those civilians living or working near the camp to evacuate. Things didn't go according to plan, however. The attack came at 2330 hours that night. Muriel heard the air-raid sirens and saw the incendiaries dropped by the pathfinder aircraft. Great explosions scorched the night sky. Tracer bullets streaked after the RAF bombers. Five plummeted in flames, smashing into the earth. The trains erupted like volcanic explosions of twisted and burning metal. Buildings rocked up to twenty kilometres away. Searchlights picked out the parachutes of pilots and crews who managed to bail out. Two separate search parties went out to find them, the Germans and the Maquis. Those found by the Maquis were then shepherded down the escape lines to Spain.

Muriel was badly shaken by the huge explosions. Philippe was so concerned by her exhaustion and listlessness that he had her moved into alternative accommodation with a blacksmith in Vernou, nearly fifty kilometres away. As there was a plane leaving shortly for Tempsford, he said he would arrange for any letters to be delivered to her parents. Shortly after he drove away, he had a premonition she had taken a turn for the worse. He returned to discover that she had fainted. The third doctor he rang turned up, diagnosed meningitis, and had her hospitalised at Romorantin, Loire et Cher.

The nuns did all they could, but she died in Philippe's arms at seven o'clock in the morning on 23 May 1944. To prevent the disclosure of her real identity, he arranged a quick funeral, gave her a false name, and had her body put in a zinc coffin and placed in a temporary vault. Worried that the Germans might be able to arrest many of his network in one swoop, he stopped her friends from attending the ceremony. In fact, he alone followed the hearse through the town to the cemetery, and during the priest's committal to the grave of the body, with its gold cross and chain, he heard one then another car arrive. With unusual sensitivity, the Gestapo waited until the service was over, by which time Philippe had taken cover behind the priest and altar boys and climbed over the wall where, by arrangement, his friends were waiting in a car.

His letter to her father was a moving tribute to Muriel, full of praise for her wonderful personality and beauty, her sense of duty and hard work, her laughter and gaiety, and it described her as a unique person who died as a soldier, giving her life for right and justice. She was 'Mentioned in Dispatches' and a memorial was built for her at Romorantin, visited by Resistance members. Her name is on the memorials at Valençay and the Lycée Français in Kensington. Later, her body was exhumed and buried at the Commonwealth War Graves Commission cemetery at Pornic, in Brittany.

Odette Wilen

The next woman flown out was Odette Wilen. Born Odette Victoria Sar on 25 April 1919 in London, her father was from Czechoslovakia and her mother was from France. Her father became a naturalised British citizen around 1931 and joined the RAF. Little is known of Odette's early life but, from her SOE personnel file, we know that she was recruited from the FANY in early 1944 as Odette Wilen. According to the 'psywar' website, she helped train SOE agents so it is possible she was involved as a conducting officer, escorting agents from their 'holding station' to RAF Tempsford. One imagines that she had spent time in France as she was identified as being fluent in French. Escott suggested that her motivation for joining SOE was the death of her husband, a Finnish RAF pilot instructor, in a flying accident. Given the urgent need for more wireless operators in the run-up to D-Day, she was sent on the assessment course at Winterfold. During her training course she met Pearl Witherington, who commented that Odette

> was very, very, very feminine. Of course there she didn't know what she was letting herself in for because one fine day we'd been blowing things up right, left and centre and she said, 'Pearl, I must ask you for some advice.' She said, 'What are we supposed to be doing?' I was so surprised and said, 'Don't you know?' 'Well,' she said, 'no, I thought I was coming into this because I was recruited as a bilingual secretary...' So I said, 'Well, you'd better go and talk to Major Watt about this because that's not what we're doing.'[41]

Communication on the Special Operations Executive user group on

Yahoo.com reported her being belatedly awarded her parachuting wings in 2007. Given the urgency of the situation, she only completed four of five parachute jumps including 'a particularly hairy one from a balloon' and therefore failed to qualify for her wings. According to Escott, she was dropped with René Mathieu, and landed at Dun-le-Poilier, about twenty kilometres west of Verzon and forty kilometres north-west of Issouden on 12 April 1944.

However, Pierre Tillet's list of infiltrations into France indicates they jumped separately on the 11 April. She landed at Issouden and he landed at Pehaurie, four kilometres west of Ayzieu and fourteen kilometres west of Eauze in the Gers department.

Codenamed 'Sophie', Odette was originally sent to act as a wireless operator for Maurice Southgate's STATIONER network near Châteauroux. When she met him at a safe house, he drove her by car to Châteauroux and then took her by train to Montluçon, where he wanted her to work in his LABOURER network. She was introduced to Amédée Maingard, his wireless operator, who was waiting for a replacement so that he could take over as second-in-command. Before she had time to rest, she was given a test on her wireless expertise. Maingard was not impressed and Southgate complained to London that he'd been sent someone only partly trained. Instead he sent for Mathieu who took over Maingard's role and arranged for Odette to be returned to England.

Pearl Witherington, Southgate's courier, in an interview with Kate Vigurs, told her that she had trained with Odette and was shocked that she did not know her codes. She told Southgate that she would take her by train to Le Blanc, where she was to wait in one of Henri Cornioley's safe houses. Southgate met up with Virginia Hall, who had arrived on a second mission, this time for the OSS in Creuse. As they had met each other before in Paris and Virginia had had experience of dealing with agents in difficulty, she agreed to see Odette. It was agreed that she would be used as a courier to Élisée Allard, Marcel Leccia, and Pierre Geelen in Tours, in the Indre-et-Loire department. They had been dropped on 6 April a kilometre east of Néret, near Acre, to form the LABOURER network. What name was on Odette's identity papers is not known but her new codename was 'Waitress'.

According to Escott, they had left a large sum of money destined for Southgate in a country café, which he picked up before he met Odette. Their base was a house in La Châtre, close to where they had been dropped. Leccia had friends and relations in Paris and Tours who Odette was to make contact with and Geelen, their wireless operator, had been one of Francis Suttil's great friends in Paris until his PROSPER network had been broken. This meant that there was a danger the Gestapo knew about him. Unknown to the group, there was a Nazi sympathiser amongst their friends.

While in the field, Odette developed a relationship with Allard and, within weeks, got engaged. Escott suggests they met during their training course. According to Wikipedia, he escaped from a Pomeranian prison camp in 1940, met up with Leccia who had also escaped, and they made their way to Spain, where they were captured and imprisoned. With the help of the British Consulate, they got out and were sent to England, where, after a fortnight being debriefed, they were recruited and trained by SOE. They met Geelen on the course.

On 26 April, Virginia, who was then working in Maidons, was brought a Huntley and Palmers biscuit tin by Allard and Geelen. Inside was a tiny American-made receiver. Weighing only two pounds, its batteries lasted about thirty hours, making it the smallest set in the field at the time. They told her that Leccia and his doctor cousins had taken some wireless equipment to Tours and discovered, to their horror, that the town was full of Germans and the wireless operator they were going to see had been arrested. Why Odette had not taken the parts is not known.

The three men then went to Paris, where a double agent was waiting for them. They were all arrested, along with their wireless equipment, and taken to the Cherche Midi prison. Odette was lucky not to have been caught with them as she had been left behind at la Châtre.

When Southgate was captured in Montluçon on 1 May it transpired that Pearl Witherington and Maingard had only escaped by the skin of their teeth. Before going back to Les Souches, Pearl called on Odette to tell her to stay where she was. Later Virginia met her and, with the assistance of a prison escape expert from Marseille, they planned to rescue Allard, Geelen, and Leccia. Escott detailed how a message was delivered to the men in prison but their response, 'We are not three but eight', dismayed him. It was impossible to get that many out. The three men were later sent to Buchenwald where they were executed by hanging on 10 September 1944.

Virginia had to continue her OSS work in the Haute-Loire, so Odette went to Tours to try and find a wireless operator and contact London to see what she could do. Increased German activity after D-Day made things difficult, but the French she contacted were unwilling to take instructions from a woman. In July, Odette had no alternative and accepted the advice to leave. This involved a well-organised but nonetheless dangerous escape route, which included a memorable bicycle ride down the Champs-Élysées in Paris, escorted by the thirteen-year-old son of a friend of her fiancé. Odette eventually crossed the Pyrénées into neutral Spain before being repatriated to England via Gibraltar. For the rest of the war, she acted as a conducting officer in 'F' Section.

It was during her escape that she met Santiago Strugo Garay, the head of the Spanish escape network. Despite having only known her for three days, he travelled to London when the war ended, found Odette and married her.

In Anne-Marie Walter's personnel file in the National Archives, there is a note, dated 14 September 1944, expressing SOE's concern about Odette:

> We know most details of this lady's excursion into France. She struck me as suffering a little from a guilty conscience, but is in a very defiant mood. She states that she is anxious to make up for time wasted and not to be kept without useful employment for an indefinite period of time. I personally think it is unfortunate still that she should have arrived at a time when her fiancé had been arrested, and what is most regrettable is that she quite obviously placed her private affairs above any other consideration.[42]

Odette, Walters, and Yvonne Fontaine were reported as having spent the night exchanging confidences in a London hotel, talking freely of the arrests of a great number of agents. The writer of the note expressed a wish that Miss Wilen and Miss Walters be requested to write their reports as soon as possible 'and be suitably disposed of'.

She moved to Argentina after the war, where, at the British Embassy in Buenos Aires in August 2007, the RAF eventually gave her her parachute wings.

Nancy Wake

At the end of April 1944, almost three weeks after Odette Wilen left Tempsford, Nancy Wake was flown out. According to Escott, she was born in Wellington, New Zealand, on 29 August 1912, the youngest of six children. When she was two, the family moved to Sydney, Australia, She ran away from home when she was sixteen and became first a journalist in Sydney and then a nurse in a mental hospital. Inheriting £200 from an aunt, she sailed to Vancouver and made her way first to New York and then to London. 'There, in between pub crawls and mixing with all kinds of people from intellectuals, artists, Communists and *bonviveurs*, she took a college course in journalism followed by a job in Paris as a reporter for the *Chicago Tribune*.' She reported on the rise of Adolf Hitler in Germany. Her obituary in the *Independent* told of a trip to Vienna in 1933 to interview Hitler, which led her to become committed to bringing down the Nazis. Seeing Jews being tied to a kind of Catherine wheel and being whipped and pelted by Germans and Austrians, their property stolen or burnt, she commented afterwards that it was quite revolting: 'I thought ... what had they done, poor bastards? Nothing. So I said, "God almighty, it's a bit much and I've got to do something about it."'

When her warnings were ignored, she continued what Escott described as her 'rumbustious lifestyle', as often in the south of France as in Paris, a favourite holiday resort being Juan-les-Pins. In 1939 she upset her parents by marrying Henri Fiocca, a wealthy steel industrialist, playboy, and expert tango dancer in Marseille. Their taste for champagne and caviar in the morning and love in the afternoon came to an abrupt end when the Germans invaded France in June 1940. She drove ambulances and, funded by her husband, helped fleeing refugees, providing them with food, clothes and shelter.

She recalled in her autobiography how French women's *chic* was imitated by the Germans' wives and girlfriends, who joined the occupying forces when they took over the south of France. As French women didn't wear hats, the German women didn't, so the French ladies started wearing them again. This time they wore green feathers in them, which symbolised the green bean, *les haricots verts*, the nickname used for the Germans as they wore green uniform. Any woman wearing a hat with a green feather was overtly insulting the enemy. When the newcomers started wearing expensive stockings, the French women stopped wearing them and used knitted stockings instead and still managed to look *chic*.

On one occasion she was sitting in the Hotel du Louvre when she noticed a youngish man reading an English book. Uncertain whether he was English or one of the Gestapo, she asked her husband to have a chat with him. It turned out that he was one of several hundred British officers who had been captured and imprisoned. Granted parole, he had gone out for a drink. Nancy and her husband undertook to provide him, and later his fellow officers – in turns – hot meals in their home. One of them was Captain Ian Garrow, an SOE officer who managed to escape and establish what became known as the Pat O'Leary's escape line, with Nancy acting as his courier. With the cover name of Mademoiselle Lucienne Carlier, a doctor's secretary, she delivered subversive anti-German propaganda, wireless sets and messages, as well as escorting British servicemen to the Pyrénées.

The SIS used to provide them with rolls of French francs carefully hidden in toothpaste tubes brought in from Switzerland. Loans from French businessmen were guaranteed by London and confirmed when a phrase of their choice was heard among the *messages personelles* after the 1900 hours news on the BBC's French Service.

Gleeson reported her telling him about an incident with a bottle of George IV Scotch whisky. She had hidden it, waiting for a special occasion to celebrate with her husband but one evening found him drinking it with a suspicious character. On asking him where he had found it, it transpired his visitor had searched the house for alcohol and unearthed it. Furious, she booted him unceremoniously down the stairs.

In an interview after the war, Nancy asserted, 'I hate wars and violence but if they come then I don't see why we women should just wave our men a proud goodbye and then knit them balaclavas.' On one occasion, she was stopped by a roving police control and questioned as to why, as a secretary, she travelled so far in first-class compartments, wearing such good clothes. Blushing demurely, she said that she was a very *private* kind of secretary. The gendarme understood and let her go. Her obituary in *The Australian* detailed her experiences:

> It was perilous work despite her cover as the wife of a respectable businessman. She lived on her sharp wits.
>
> 'I'd see a German officer on the train or somewhere, sometimes dressed in civvies, but you could pick 'em. So, instead of raising suspicions I'd flirt with them, ask for a light and say my lighter was out of fuel,' she recalled.
>
> She told how she would get beautifully dressed and hang around making dates with Germans to get information.
>
> 'A little powder and a little drink on the way, and I'd pass their posts and wink and say, "Do you want to search me?" God, what a flirtatious little bastard I was.'

Working for the Resistance, she travelled all over southern France from Nice to Nîmes to Perpignan, with clothing, money and false documents. In Peter Fitzsimons's biography, she is quoted as saying:

> I played the part of a giddy Frenchwoman who didn't give a bugger what happened in the war. I was a good-time girl. I used to give Germans a date sometimes, sometimes three or four times if I was away on a long trip and give them a little bit of hope. I played the part – I should have been an actress.

Despite having her phone tapped and her mail opened by the Gestapo, Nancy managed to evade capture so well that they nicknamed her *la Souris Blanche*, the White Mouse. Every time they had her cornered, she managed to get away. She was arrested twice for questioning, but managed to talk herself out of trouble.

So determined were the Germans to stop her, they put out a five million franc reward for her capture. According to Fitzsimons, she helped 1,037 downed Allied pilots and crew to escape over the Pyrénées into Spain, although this number is disputed by Keith Janes of escapelines.com.

After the network was betrayed, she feared for her life so had to follow the same escape routes as those she had helped. In Russell Braddon's *Nancy Wake: SOE's Greatest Heroine*, he details how, after she was betrayed, the escape organisation was compromised and her husband persuaded her to flee. She made six attempts and on one occasion she had to jump out of a moving train window and dodge bullets as she ran through a vineyard to evade capture, leaving her handbag with all her money and jewellery behind. She had to sleep in pigsties for five days, starved, got frozen, and caught scabies.

When she was questioned at a checkpoint with 200 pounds of pork in a suitcase, she ended up being interrogated for four days, suspected of being involved in a Resistance attack on a cinema. She denied it and was locked in a stinking toilet overnight and only freed when Pat O'Leary marched in to see the Police Commissioner, pretended to be a close friend of Pierre Laval, the premier of the Vichy government, and demanded that his mistress be released.

Hidden under a pile of coal with two Americans and a New Zealander, she eventually succeeded in crossing the Pyrénées in espadrilles, soft sandals, to reduce the possibility of the German guards' Alsatian guard dogs hearing them. It took seventy-two hours with ten minute rests every two hours. Most of the time it was in blizzard conditions. With the sponsorship of the British authorities in Madrid, they made their way south to Gibraltar, where she spent the time waiting for a convoy to take her back to England doing two things: 'I went up to a hotel on the top of the Rock and got pissed every day, and I also read lots of newspapers catching up on what had happened in the war'.

Before Nancy's train pulled into London on 17 June 1943, Ian Garrow organised for the train to be stopped and a car whisked her off to St James's Hotel, where she was very warmly welcomed and suitably entertained by many of those pilots and aircrews she had rescued. But she was never to see her husband again. He was captured, tortured, and killed while she was out of the country, but he didn't reveal her whereabouts.

Her attempts to join de Gaulle's Free French Forces and be returned to France to fight the Germans were thwarted. Colonel Passy, the recruiting officer, refused her application. She thought he thought that she was a British spy. In fact, the following day she was approached by a representative of the SOE keen to know why she had been to see the Free French. She denied it, but when he proceeded to give her the time she went in and came out, what she was wearing and where she went to next, she realised they were the sort of organisation she wanted to work for. They quickly gave her a commission in the FANY as an ensign and sent her to the first training school at Winterfold, near Cranleigh in Surrey.

According to Juliette Pattinson, the author of *Behind Enemy Lines*, Nancy almost failed at the first hurdle. She was sacked from her course for drinking too much. Selwyn Jepson is reported as saying, 'We don't like our girls to drink.' Her report mentioned her being charged with being drunk and disorderly in the village outside the training camp. Buckmaster must have recognised her potential as he overruled Jepson, saying, 'It sometimes happens, I think, that this woman's high spirits, are sometimes mistaken for drunkenness ... she was a real Australian bombshell. Tremendous vitality, flashing eyes. Everything she did, she did well. With all her gay laughter, she had a serious and sensitive streak.' Jepson's comment underneath was the reverse.

More light on the circumstances was shed in Fitzsimon's biography. Nancy had been in the room when there had been a great argument between a Frenchwoman on the course and Denis Rake, an openly homosexual weapons training instructor who later became an agent himself. Nancy ignored it but, after Rake had stormed out and slammed the door, the Frenchwoman asked her to witness what he had said to her, wanting to get him sacked. When she refused, the Frenchwoman,

> sensing that Nancy might have been slightly tipsy after the lunch she had just returned from, accused her of being drunk, and quickly reported this 'fact' to one of SOE's more punctiliously proper officers, Selwyn Jepson, together with the fact that Ensign Wake was refusing to acknowledge what she had heard Rake saying to her. Jepson called for Nancy and upbraided her. She promptly told him, in highly specific terms, where he could stick his upbraiding. He, white-faced with fury, ordered her to leave the premises and return to her flat in London.

She is reported to have told Jepson that he could have her FANY uniform back if he came to pick it up himself. Garrow pleaded her case, arguing that she was volatile, passionate and fearless – exactly what was required of an agent in the field. Buckmaster agreed and she was invited to rejoin the course. He must also have recognised how pro-British she was. In fact, Rake had previously been caught with his radio, imprisoned, and had a number of bones in his foot broken during interrogation. After managing to escape, he crossed the Pyrénées and returned to London, where Buckmaster gave him a job as Nancy's conducting officer. They were to develop a remarkable operational relationship. On the train to her next course in Scotland, Nancy explained that

> when I looked out of the carriage window ... I was looking into the backyards

and tiny gardens of all these houses that backed onto the railway line, and what do you think? They were all growing vegetables. All of them had these great vegetable patches going wherever there was a spare patch of dirt. They were magnificent! England, and the people of England, were growing everything themselves, never mind what the war had to say about it. And they could feed everybody, I've never forgotten it. I don't give a bugger what anyone says – we owe a lot to Britain. I loved Great Britain – and I will die loving it...

She was thirty-one when she was sent for paramilitary training in Achnacarry, Scotland, and admitted evading physical exercise by saying she had a period or had a cold. She cheated on cross-country courses and took shortcuts whenever she could.

We also had a lot of fun, and a lot of laughter. As a relief from the seriousness of everything else, there was a lot of skylarking and pranks, and that sort of thing, and being a bit of a skylarker myself I absolutely loved it.

In her book *The Autobiography of the Woman the Gestapo called the White Mouse*, she described loathing the English overarm throw when using a hand grenade. There was one drill where the students had to sit in a trench. One of the students got out, pulled the pin out of their grenade, threw it in the opposite direction and leapt back into the trench before it blew up. When it was her turn, she asked her instructor what she should do. He replied sarcastically that she should 'pull the pin, throw the grenade into the trench and run ... with a dead pan face Nancy pretended to believe him. The class in the trench – including the sergeant instructor were last seen fleeing for cover'.

She also recalled an incident at Ringway.

All our meals were served in a huge dining hall. The commanding officer and his staff sat at a long table running the full width of the room, with their backs to the wall and facing the students. The students were seated at both sides of several long tables running lengthwise, from the top table to the other end of the room. Thus the staff were in a position to observe everything that occurred in the dining hall.

One morning at the breakfast table an American sergeant sitting opposite me passed me a small packet, saying that it was a present. Although Raymond Batchelor sitting on my right whispered in French not to accept it, I did so, thinking it was chewing gum or chocolate. I knew what a French letter meant in English, just as I knew the French name for it, but I did not know what a condom was until I opened the packet and saw three of them lying there together with the instructions.

I don't know what reaction the American expected, especially at a breakfast table. There was silence all round me. Then I proceeded to read out the instructions, much to the amusement of everyone at our table except the American, who, red in the face, left the table. I put them in the pocket of my battle dress and continued eating my breakfast. As we left the dining hall the CO called me to one side, apologised for the behaviour of the American and offered to disembarrass me of the unmentionables. He was surprised when I declined his offer, adding that they might come in handy later on. We never saw the American again. He vanished. I feel sure he was reprimanded.

She admitted being terrified: 'this is awful, I'll be killed you know. I'll never do it again'. Having survived the parachute training at Ringway, she went to Beaulieu, where she found occasions to use her present later on, surreptitiously attaching them to various instructors' clothing, much to the amusement of her fellow trainees. According to Escott, the men found her exuberant and boisterous character 'good for morale'. One day, hearing that the top brass were about to make an inspection, she used the skills she had been taught to snatch the keys of the filing cabinet where the agents' assessment files were kept, press it into a lump of plasticine she had brought specially for the task, put the key back, then went to the workshop the following day and poured some molten brass into the mould. That evening, while her friend Raymond was on guard, she slipped into the office and sneaked both their files. Hers was very good. She recalled it saying, 'Her morale and sense of humour encouraged everyone.' This was clearly demonstrated in her choice of code poem:

> She stood right there,
> In the moonlight fair,
> And the moon shone,
> Through her nightie,
> It lit right on,
> The nipple of her tit,
> Oh Jesus Christ Almighty!

Much to the amusement of the others, one day she and Violette Szabó managed to pin down one of the instructors, pull his pants off and tie them to a flagpole. When the camp commander didn't invite them to a party, they broke into his room, removed all the furniture and then barricaded themselves into their own room for the night.

Her training reports record that she was 'a very good and fast shot' and had a good eye for fieldcraft. On several occasions, she 'put the men to shame by her cheerful spirit and strength of character'.

Her mission was to act as a liaison officer for STATIONER, the codename for the Maquis group in the Auvergne, the mountainous region of central France. As there was no moon visible on 28 April 1944, her flight back from RAF Tempsford into occupied France had to be postponed. This gave her the chance to visit Cambridge and see the sights.

The next night was less cloudy and Nancy, codenamed 'Hélène' and known as 'Madame Andrée Joubert', was seen off personally by Colonel Buckmaster, who gave her a silver compact make-up case. In the late evening of 29/30 April, she was handed up into the belly of a black Liberator B-24. According to Braddon, her codename for the journey was 'Witch'. 'The dispatcher, a lean, good-natured Texan, sidled up to her and asked, "Are you really a witch?" "I am. And don't get your letters mixed." "Gee," he muttered, "a woman! We ain't never dropped a woman before."'

She was parachuted into a field near Cosne d'Allier, on the outskirts of Montluçon with Major John Farmer, an SOE agent codenamed 'Hubert'. Suffering from a double hangover and half-frozen, she had her parachute caught in a tree, and Henri Tardivat, the French agent who helped her down, told her that he wished all trees could bear such beautiful fruit. As a typically straight-talking Australian, she was unimpressed by his Gallic charm and told him, revolver in hand, not to give her 'that French s**t'. Fitzsimons tells us that:

She was dressed, oddly enough, as a very lumpy version of her normal self. For the jump she had on her favourite camel-hair coat atop regulation army overalls, but beneath this army issue she wore silk stockings and stylish shoes beneath heavily bandaged ankles to protect her bones and tendons against the impact of landing. In the pockets of these clothes were two revolvers. On her head, a tin hat. In her small backpack, she had several changes of clothes, and among other things, a red satin cushion that she simply adored and two hand-embroidered nightdresses she'd insisted on bringing. On her arm, topping the whole thing off, her handbag stuffed full of over one million French francs with which she hoped to help finance the Maquis, plus her favourite red Chanel lipstick and tightly packed articles of feminine hygiene, while securely memorised in her head she had a list of targets for demolition – railway junctions, bridges, underground cables and factories that had to be attacked and destroyed the moment D-Day arrived. In the same spot, securely stored away, she also had the addresses of various safe houses in the area, together with the names of their residents and the passwords by which she would be recognised. Finally, secreted in the second button of the cuff on her left sleeve was a cyanide pill which guaranteed an all-but-instant death should she ever find herself in a situation where that was clearly preferable to what lay before her.

Captain Dennis Rake was dropped separately. He had convinced Buckmaster that he was fit enough to return as Nancy's wireless operator. As well as making arrangements to provide the Resistance with funds, their mission was to help the French establish ammunition and arms caches, and to arrange wireless communication to England in preparation for the D-Day landings. She lived in the forested hills, criss-crossed with tracks, with about 7,000 male *résistants* and wore army boots, khaki trousers, shirt, tie and beret.

Howarth mentioned that shortly after her arrival, Nancy overheard one of the Maquis suggest to another that he should seduce her, murder her and then take her money. This influenced her judgement as to which group she would arrange arms for. This involved sending messages to London for weapons, ammunition, food, clothes, money and Elizabeth Arden face cream.

On the first morning, when she went out to urinate, she noticed that all the bushes around her were shaking. Although she understood, she insisted that, once they had seen her it was to be the last time. When ten men in her camp refused to do the water-carrying duties, she persuaded them by emptying a bucket of water over each. During the day she would join them in physical training, go on reconnaissance with them and provide them with weapons training. In the evening, she would sit around the camp fire swigging whisky and having drinking competitions, which she claimed she always won. She played cards, swore blindly and joined in with raucous singing. When she went to bed, she reasserted her femininity by putting on a silk nightdress and applying her face cream.

During her time in France, she developed two great passions: a taste for '*Baba a Rhum*' (sponge ring doughnuts steeped in rum, and served smothered in whipped cream with a glacé cherry on top), and *Pastis* (a French anise-flavoured liqueur and *apéritif*). Anecdotally, it is said that, after a Pastis session with her Maquis colleagues, she became maudlin and 'fell' for a 'lonely' horse in a nearby field and transported it to the ramshackle bathroom made of corrugated iron that the Maquis had built for her. During the night there was a torrential thunderstorm, and the heavy rain on the iron roof spooked the horse, which kicked the place to pieces and bolted into the night.

Her Maquis colleagues, when asked for a code phrase to report safe delivery of their supplies, came up with 'Madam Andrée has a horse in the bathroom!' 'Madam Andrée' was the nickname the Maquis gave her.

According to her obituary in the *Guardian*:[43]

> Circumstances gave her considerable freedom of action. The circuit's orders
> were to help organise and arm the local Maquis, and soon Wake was fighting
> alongside them in pitched battles with the Germans. 'I liked that kind of
> thing,' she said, although she had to prove herself first as an honorary man,
> a feat easily accomplished by regularly drinking her French comrades under
> the table. 'I had never seen anyone drink like that,' confessed Farmer, 'and
> I don't think the Maquis had either. We just couldn't work out where it all
> went.'

On the night of 15/16 September 1943, a bombing raid of 389 RAF planes
halted production of the Dunlop rubber factory in Montluçon. The
following year, when it was back in production, it only took two pounds
of plastic explosive planted by Nancy's team to bring it to its knees. She
played a prominent role in blowing up the bridge over the Allier River.
She and four men, with explosives strapped to their bodies, climbed
down the struts of the bridge to lay the charges. Fitzsimons reported
her ambushing German convoys using home-made bombs, which would
result in the deaths of twenty to thirty soldiers. She shot dead four
German officers at point-blank range, fought her way out of roadblocks
and went into battle with German troops on numerous occasions when
the camps were attacked. She led a raid on the Gestapo headquarters in
Montluçon, throwing a grenade into the room before retreating. 'Several
dozen Germans did not lunch that day, nor any other days for that matter.'
When she found out that a group of her men were torturing and sexually
abusing three women who had been collaborating with the Germans, she
interviewed the women, released two and ordered the third shot, even
offering to execute the woman herself since the Maquisards' sense of
honour permitted her rape but not her killing. 'It didn't put me off my
breakfast,' she said. 'After all, she had an easy death. She didn't suffer.'

On another occasion, Fitzsimons tells us, a disaffected and drunken
communist Maquisard was threatening to shoot Madame Andrée for
not providing him with weapons. She hadn't because of his slovenly,
disorganised organisation. When he came out of the bar to throw the
grenade at her car, he took the pin out but didn't throw it in time. 'All I
knew was sitting in the car and bits of flesh were going all over the place,
landing on the bonnet and the windscreen.'

In an interview with Pattinson, Nancy explained why she had become
so aggressive and desensitised to the violence of war. It was witnessing
anti-Semitic actions in Vienna, observing a seven-month-pregnant
Frenchwoman being bayoneted in the stomach and hearing about a male

colleague who had been beheaded. Asked about the source of her courage, she replied, 'Freedom is the only thing worth living for. While I was doing that work, I used to think it didn't matter if I died, because without freedom there was no point in living.'

Fitzsimons reports her saying that she pro-actively sought to kill as many Germans as she could as she 'longed to break their fucking necks'. After being cut in the arm by a sentry's bayonet during an attack on an armaments factory in Mont Mouchet, she killed the man with a karate-like chop to the back of the neck to keep him from alerting the guards. 'They'd taught this judo-chop stuff with the flat of the hand at SOE, and I practised away at it. But this was the only time I used it – whack – and it killed him all right. I was really surprised.' Fighting, she believed, was part of war. The idea of women having a homely, peace-loving, compassionate, caring nature was not found in Nancy during her war years. In her interview with Juliette Pattinson, she commented on her position among so many men:

> If I had accommodated one man, word would have been spread around. They would have been coming over from the next mountain! [laughs!] I would have had a very sore arse! [raucous laughter] The pine needles! And when would I have done the work that I had done and would those men have had respect for me? They wouldn't have. They wouldn't have.

There was one occasion when Nancy had to adopt the disguise of a middle-aged peasant to avoid detection. According to her autobiography,

> I borrowed a long white piqué dress which must have been fashionable before World War I ... I was ... looking like a real country bumpkin, wet hair pulled back tight, no make-up, an old fashioned dress, and wearing a pair of the farmer's old boots ... Our cart and the produce were inspected several times by the Germans as we entered Aurillac; they did not give me a second look, even their first glance was rather disdainful. I did not blame them. I did not look very fetching.

In Russell Brandon's biography of Nancy, he said that the dress dated from 1890 and had been borrowed from an elderly lady. 'The Germans questioned him [the farmer] and searched the vegetables, but they showed no interest at all in his revolting-looking daughter.'

Having lost her radio and codes during a skirmish with German troops, she was unable to make contact with her controllers in London. Without a radio she could not receive, order or arrange air drops of weapons, ammunition and food. Accordingly, she volunteered to cycle more than

400 kilometres over rough terrain with no identity papers to deliver a vital message. It took her three days. So as not to look unkempt she took her dress off at night when she slept in deserted barns. One time, desperate to go to the toilet, she knew that she would never be able to get back onto the bike if she got off. So, she hitched her dress up, moved her underwear to one side and urinated onto the ground. She commented in her autobiography that she was fortunate that she didn't have to do the other. 'I was just a normal young woman ... I cycled to the local markets and filled my string bag with all the fruit and vegetables I could buy without food coupons hoping that I would pass for a housewife out shopping.' When she was stopped, she said she only had to 'look over to the officer, flutter my eyelashes and say "Do you want to search *moi*?" And they would laugh flirtatiously, "No, Mademoiselle, you carry on."' On her return, she was asked how she was. She cried. 'I couldn't stand up, I couldn't sit down. I couldn't do anything. I just cried.'

After the Normandy landings, her circuit was getting up to four drops a week, with fifteen containers of supplies, including army trousers and black boots and fifteen million francs (£85,000) a month to pay the wages and pensions of her 7,000-strong force. Rake commented that 'it was no exaggeration to say that Nancy Wake armed and supplied the vast majority of them'. They were attacked on the plateau of Chuade-Aignes by 12,000 SS troops in June with aerial bombing, artillery, mortars and machine guns. Working with two American officers when the Germans launched an attack, she took command of a section whose leader had been killed, and with exceptional coolness directed the covering fire while the group withdrew with no further loss of life.

During the battle she drove a van-load of ammunition to supply the rearguard and, when it was attacked, she only just managed to jump clear before it exploded in flames. Although Nancy managed to escape, a hundred of her colleagues were killed and 1,400 German troops lay dead on the plateau. Speaking about a film she made after the war, she denied feeling any anxiety.

> I never had any time to worry and I must admit some people don't believe me. I never was afraid and sometimes I think that people probably think I'm mad or that I'm telling lies. But I can honestly say I was never afraid. I was too busy to be afraid.

On 25 August 1944, the day Paris was finally liberated, she led her celebrating troops into Vichy. Her exuberance was only halted when she was told that Henri, her husband, was dead. He had been arrested and interrogated to reveal her whereabouts. When he refused to do so, he was tortured and finally shot. She blamed herself. If it had not been for her, he would have survived the war. Farmer ordered her to work with an SOE network whose headquarters had moved to Paris.

During a celebratory party at which British and American agents were toasted, they were expected to reciprocate and sing their respective national anthems. Nancy knew enough verses of 'God save the King' but her American colleagues needed help with theirs. Although they knew the 'The Star Spangled Banner', she taught them another ditty to be sung to the tune of 'Hark! The Herald Angels Sing' and told the French it was a new anthem to honour the *Entente Cordiale*:

> Uncle George and Auntie Mabel
> Fainted at the breakfast table
> Wasn't that sufficient warning not to do it in the morning?
> But Ovaltine has put them right
> Now they do it morn and night
> Uncle George is hoping soon
> To do it in the afternoon.

Her comment afterwards was that, 'We just laughed all the way through the war. What else could we do?' Probably owing to the stress of the preceding summer, she fell ill and did not report back after sick leave. She subsequently wrote to SOE headquarters in London, requesting to be 'sworn out' of the organisation.

In her interview with Pattinson, she claimed that Tardivat, the French Resistance leader, said that:

> 'She is the most feminine woman I have ever met in my life, but in battle she's worth ten men!' So I changed. I was feminine but fighting. All I wanted to do was kill Germans. I didn't give a bugger about them, to kill Germans. Didn't care about it. I hated, I loathed the Germans. I loathed them. As far as I was concerned, the only good one was a dead one and I don't care what anyone thinks of me. A dead German!

After the war, her bravery and leadership were recognised and she was awarded the George Medal, *Croix de Guerre* with two palms and Silver Star, *Chevalier de la Legion d'Honneur*, French Resistance Medal, and the United States Freedom Medal. It was said that she used to threaten that if the Australian government ever got round to giving her a medal, she would tell them 'to stick it where the sun don't shine'. In 2001 they eventually awarded her the Companion of the Order. In fact, Nancy was the most highly decorated servicewoman in the Second World War.

Wake continued working for British intelligence in Europe after the war until 1957, when she moved back to Australia and married British RAF fighter pilot John Forward. When an Australian television drama was made about her wartime experiences, she commented, 'For goodness sake, did the Allies parachute me into France to fry eggs and bacon for the men? There wasn't an egg to be had for love nor money, and even if there had been why would I be frying it when I had men to do that sort of thing?'

She moved back to Britain in 2001, four years after Forward's death, and is said to have inspired Australian actor Cate Blanchett's role in the film *Charlotte Gray*. She never had children and died on 7 August 2011. According to her wishes, her ashes were scattered in Montluçon, where she fought a heroic battle in 1944 at the Gestapo headquarters.

In September 2010, the former Olympic gymnast Suzanne Dando led a group of young women on a charity trek, *Le Chemin de la Liberté*, across the Pyrénées on behalf of the Royal British Legion. They followed in the footsteps of Nancy Wake and thousands of civilians and servicemen who escaped from France during the war.

Phyllis 'Pippa' Latour

On 1 May 1944, Carpetbagger Crance's mission parachuted twenty-two-year-old South African Phyllis Latour, another second officer in the WAAF, into Mayenne, near Hardanges. Using three codenames, 'Geneviève', 'Plus Fours' and 'Lampooner', she worked as a wireless operator in the revived SCIENTIST network in south Normandy under the command of Lise de Baissac.

In Judith Martin's interview with her for New Zealand's *Army News*, she described how she was born on a Belgian ship tied up in Durban, South Africa, in March 1921 to a French doctor and a British mother. Escott gives the date as 8 April. Her father was killed in fighting in the Congo when she was three months old. Her mother remarried when she was three and Phyllis went to live with her stepfather and his sons in the Congo.

'My stepfather was well off, and a racing driver. The men would do circuits and they would often let their wives race against each other. When my mother drove the choke stuck and she couldn't control the car. She hit a barrier, the car burst into flames, and she died.'

Her father's cousin became her guardian, and she went to live with him, his wife and his sons in the Congo. 'They were really the only parents I knew. When I was seven my "new" mother went riding as she always did. The horse came back without her, and a lot of time elapsed before they found her as they did not know where she had been riding. Apparently the horse had stepped on a puff adder. She was thrown, and then bitten in the face by the adder. When they found her she was dead.'[44]

Known by her family and friends as Pippa, she grew up with her 'brothers', who taught her how to shoot. In her interview she claimed to have been motivated by revenge. Her godmother's father had been killed by the Germans and her godmother committed suicide after being imprisoned by the enemy.

When she arrived in Britain is uncertain but, fluent in French, she joined the WAAF in November 1941 as a flight mechanic. She had visions of working on an airfield and interviewing French air crews returning from sorties. Two years later, her fluency in French brought her to the attention of the SOE. After a successful interview, she was commissioned as an Honorary Section Officer and trained at Thame Park as a wireless operator.

'They took a group of about 20 of us away for training. It was unusual training – not what I expected, and very hard. It wasn't until after my first round of training that they told me they wanted me to become a member of the SOE. They said I could have three days to think about it. I told them I didn't need three days to make a decision; I'd take the job now.'

The training members of the SOE were given was tough, and women were given no quarter, says Pippa. The men who had been sent in before me were caught and executed. I was told I was chosen for that area (of France) because I would arouse less suspicion.

As well as extensive physical fitness training, the operatives were given other training to suit their work. 'We climbed ropes, and learned to climb trees and up the side of buildings. Our instructor was a cat burglar who had been taken out of prison to train us. We learned how to get in a high window, and down drain pipes, how to climb over roofs without being caught.'

'... I was scared. I didn't like jumping, no matter what part of the aircraft it was from.'

Her arrival in France came at a time of great upheaval in the de Baissacs' networks following hundreds of arrests in and around Paris. Escott narrates how the area around Mayonne, where she landed, was thick with German troops and German patrols. They flashed false signals to the incoming plane and the reception committee had to douse the lights three times for fear of attracting their attention. When she finally jumped, she landed three fields away from where she was expected and the reception committee took an hour to find her. She had to be helped to be disentangled from the only apple tree in the area.

Once she had buried her parachute, she was taken to a safe house belonging to a local doctor. She made her first transmission to London from there two later. When told that the house was being watched, she moved to Lise de Baissac's isolated farmhouse, where she told her that she was unhappy with the cover story that she had been given. Lise acquired some forged documents showing that she had left Paris to study painting. Later she obtained real papers from the *Mairie* in Caen saying she was an art student there.

In Escott's *Heroines of the SOE*, she detailed how a week later, Lise went to Paris to meet some *résistants* in the Fire Brigade.

> Phyllis went to the Caen and Vire area with Dandicolle, a very pleasant young man, making contacts for his intended stay there. It was in late-May when they were returning to de Baissac's headquarters that they heard that there had been a spy, (a grocer) at her reception, and the Germans had found her parachute. Fear of German reprisals had kept locals from helping at receptions, except when offered money, which was why de Baissac usually only used a few local policemen, recruited and well paid by the doctor.

She and Dandicolle took their belongings from the farmhouse and moved into an half-derelict old barn, which they had to make habitable. On the first floor they sat on wooden benches, slept on piles of straw, and foraged the local countryside for food and water. They warned Lise not to return. Then Phyllis cycled around the surrounding countryside, locating safe places for her seventeen wireless sets; some were in buildings, but others were hidden in tin boxes in the surrounding countryside. They spent hours coding and decoding the messages she sent to and got back from London and then passed the instructions to various members of the network. Escott says she sent 135 messages while in France. Her work as a wireless operator was so vital for the network that she was not allowed to be involved in any sabotage mission or to take part in any reception committee.

In Ross Dix-Peek's article, 'A South African Girl in the Special Operations Executive', he commented that her codename was intriguing,

> as 'Genevieve' was the name of the patron saint of Paris, a shepherd's daughter who lived in the 5th century, and who encouraged the citizens when threatened by Attila and the Huns, and also brought them aid when Childeric attacked the city. And, 1500 years later, yet another 'Genevieve', this time in the form of a young lass from South Africa, was again helping France to resist the invader. Latour operated bravely and stoically, sending a plethora of coded messages back to London, all the while evading the

enemy.[45]

When Dandicolle was sent to set up the VERGER network in the Calvados coastal area, near where the Allied landings were to take place, Claude de Baissac used Phyllis as his main contact with London. Following the invasion, in recognition of her importance, he provided her with armed guards to ensure her messages went through. She experienced considerable interference whilst transmitting as there was 'knocking', caused by the number of military sets in the area. 'In the fields her long aerial sometimes could not make good contacts, though her home station was always helpful and clear.'

She arranged the arrival and accommodation of the VERGER Jedburgh team, who undertook useful sabotage missions until they were caught and shot. However, she admitted after the war, 'I hated what I was doing. At first I was proud of myself because I was doing something for the war effort. But when you see what the bombers do...'

The rebuilding of a more secure network took time and Pippa had to keep tight security, transmitting at different times from different houses using the three sets that had been dropped with her. To assist her getting about, she had six bicycles hidden around the countryside and dressed like a fourteen-year-old schoolgirl living with her extended family to avoid the bombing.

With just one blue cotton dress to her name she pedalled across the countryside selling soap to mostly German soldiers, crossing fields on foot to where she had hidden another bicycle.

The Gestapo and SS were everywhere. And to add to the confusion and danger a double agent was working in the area. The SOE operative was friendly and talkative whenever she met German soldiers – 'I'd talk so much about anything and everything, trying to be "helpful" and they'd get sick of me' – and was constantly moving through the countryside where she was transmitting the information urgently needed by the Allied Command.

It was crucial the information she transmitted was accurate – the lives of thousands of Allied soldiers depended on it.

'I always carried knitting needles because my codes were on a piece of silk – I had about 2000 I could use. When I used a code I would just pinprick it to indicate it had gone. I wrapped the piece of silk around a knitting needle and put it in a flat shoe lace which I used to tie my hair up.'

Once she was loaded into a truck along with other locals and taken to the police station for questioning. 'I can remember being taken to the station and a female soldier made us take our clothes off to see if we were hiding anything. She was looking suspiciously at my hair so I just pulled my lace off and shook my head. That seemed to satisfy her. I tied my hair back up with the lace – it was a very nerve racking moment.'

Pippa had no real base, sleeping rough in the countryside and in the forest. She had a courier, and a local married couple who she could contact should things go horribly wrong.

She was constantly hungry. 'One family I stayed with told me we were eating squirrel. I found out later it was rat. I was half starved so I didn't care.'

While she had a Sten gun and a 7mm pistol with a silencer, she couldn't carry a weapon routinely as it would give her ruse away should she be stopped. She used the training she had been given but lived largely by her wits.

'Germany was far more advanced with their DF [direction finding or radio detecting apparatus] than the Allies. They were about half an hour behind me each time I transmitted. Each message might take me about half an hour so I didn't have much time. It was an awful problem for me as I had to ask for one of the three DF near me to be taken out. They threw a grenade at it. A German woman and two small children died. Then I heard I was responsible for their deaths. It was a horrible feeling. I later attended the funeral of a grandmother, her daughter and her two grandchildren, knowing I had indirectly caused their deaths.

'I can imagine the bomber pilots patting each other on the back and offering congratulations after a strike. But they never saw the carnage that was left. I always saw it, and I don't think I will ever forget it.'[46]

Following the invasion, almost every foot of soil in her area was being fought over. Another Jedburgh team was welcomed and put into action while the men harried the arriving German reinforcements in order to allow the Allies to move further east towards Paris. According to Escott:

During this period Pippa had many narrow escapes, flitting to and fro over Orne from one hidden radio set to another, or following after Lise who frequently carried her wirelesses ahead of Pippa. One day during the German retreat, she was on her way to a distant farmhouse from where her next transmission was expected to go out. As the area was filled with Germans, Claude, having no one else to spare and knowing that it was not safe to let her go alone, sent his sister Lise to accompany her. The Allied victories which Pippa constantly heard on the BBC had sometimes made her less careful of her safety and less conscious of the danger surrounding her. This worried Claude, as his pianists were too valuable to lose, and Pippa was both too young and bold for her own safety, only measuring the demoralisation of the mass of soldiery by those units she saw in flight, rather than the individual soldier, who might be driven to revenge if he suspected her mission. They were both on their bicycles and Lise was carrying some spare parts for the set, hidden in the belt around the waist of her dress, believing that what was in full view was less likely to be searched.

As they came to a bend in the country road they had taken, believing it clear of Germans, they saw a soldier at the side examining all those passing by. There was no way of avoiding him. So they rode casually up to him and getting down from their bicycles produced their papers for his inspection. But more followed. He wanted to search them for arms or sabotage materials. The resistance had been quite active over the past week in this area, and the Germans knew that they were being helped by many in the locality who, with the Germans in retreat, were becoming more open in their hostility. A thorough search might mean removing clothes and examining different parts of the body and was usually carried out at the police headquarters, but a wayside search usually meant passing the hands over the body, clothes and all, to detect any unusual lumps or bumps on the person. Pippa was all right, but would the German find the parts in Lise's belt? Quietly Pippa submitted to the search. Then it was Lise's turn. What would they do if he discovered the spares? A minute lasted like an hour, and then Pippa felt like laughing, the German did not bother with the belt, not even noticing that it was rather an odd shape. He merely grunted, and stood back motioning them to go.

The search was satisfactory. They mounted their bikes, overwhelmed with relief, when suddenly there was a clatter on the road at their feet. One of the spare parts had fallen out of Lise's belt. Surely this was the end? To Pippa's astonishment the German hardly seemed to notice, being already busy with another couple riding behind them. Quickly Lise bent down to retrieve the part and then they were off cycling like the wind, in case the German had second thoughts. But he didn't and they got away without further mishap. Nevertheless they had both had a great fright.

Other close scrapes she experienced included being interrupted whilst she was transmitting by two German soldiers looking for supplies. She pretended that she had scarlet fever and was packing to go away. On another occasion, she was transmitting from a farm and a German officer walked in. Luckily it was so dark that he did not see her and the farmer's daughter distracted him by offering him a glass of cider. Then there was the time when she was working in the Foret de Pail and was told that she could continue transmitting as local patriots had destroyed the Direction Finders' car and killed its occupants.[47]

When the American forces drove into the village where she was staying in early August, she lined up with the other residents, waving, shouting and laughing. There was clapping and cheering, attempts to catch hold of the soldiers as they passed in their cavalcade, and the throwing of flowers and blowing of kisses to the men. When she introduced herself to them, they held her prisoner for five hours, suspecting she might be a German agent. The description they had of her did not correspond with her appearance. As luck would have it, a guide recognised her so that they released her. As Escott put it, 'No one particularly noticed the girl from SOE, in her faded summer dress, and yet she as much as any of them had paved the way for their victory. She had sent over 135 messages to London and carried out her mission safely and successfully.' Shortly after she returned to England, in appreciation of the contribution she made in helping the French shed the yoke of tyranny, she was awarded the MBE and the *Croix de Guerre*. A South African newspaper commented after the war that:

> It was lonely work in a land of strangers, and anxiety was an ever-present emotion – anxiety as to what was happening to family and friends, with whom she could not communicate; anxiety about making contact with certain persons at specific times, and the endless anxiety as to how long the deception could be kept up. All this on the shoulders of a girl but twenty-three years-of-age, but triumph she did.[48]

After the war she married an engineer, and went to live in South Africa under the name of Phyllis Boyle.

Marcelle Somers

On 3 May 1944, the moon period before D-Day, Flying Officer Harold Ibbott took eight passengers in his Hudson to a field three kilometres north-north-west of Manziat, north-north-east of Mâcon. Marcelle Somers, codename 'Albanais', was accompanied by seven other passengers, including Commandant Maurice Barthélémy, codenamed 'Barrat', Colonel Paul Hanneton, codenamed 'Ligne', and Jacques Davout d'Auerstaerdt, codenamed 'Ovale'. Exactly what Marcelle's role was has not come to light, but in Gibb McCall's *Flight Most Secret* he says that she worked with the CONE network, and arranged her daughter's parachute reception two months later. Her daughter, Josianne, was parachuted in on D-Day, one of eleven RF agents sent into France by de Gaulle. Their stories are told in *Women of RAF Tempsford: Churchill's Agents of Wartime Resistance*. After the war, Marcelle was awarded the MBE and the *Croix de Guerre* but the full details of her work are yet to come to light.

Eight other passengers were returned in the Hudson, including Mme Fleury and her baby daughter, who celebrated her first birthday in the Royal Patriotic School in Wandsworth. Mme Fleury had only recently been released by the Gestapo after four months' imprisonment for questioning over her husband's clandestine radio operations. A stool pigeon, someone planted to win her confidence in order to make her talk, had been in her cell with her but she didn't provide any information. Her husband told Verity:

> This is why the British and the French decided to bring her and the baby out of France. This is how one was able to see a strange sight on their arrival in England: a tall pilot in operational uniform getting out of the aeroplane and, confronted with a tiny baby, asking her: 'are you a terrorist?' But the reply would have been too long to give him.

Marguerite Knight

Twenty-four-year-old Lieutenant Marguerite 'Peggy' Knight was born in Paris on 19 April 1920, the daughter of a Polish mother and British Army captain who stayed in France after the First World War. When she was sixteen, she moved to England to attend school in Canterbury. Following the start of the war, she moved from working as a shorthand typist for Asea Electric in Walthamstow to a position in the WAAF. After being discharged as being medically unfit in May the following year due to recurring bouts of pneumonia, she found a typing job in an engineering firm which had offices in the City of London. Escott narrates how one day she was present at a party given in the lounge of a London hotel. While the social chatter went on, her attention was caught by a man, whose book seemed to have slipped from under his arm without his noticing it. When she retrieved it he had moved away, giving her time to glance at the cover, the title of which appeared to be in French. Probably its owner could also speak it. Unobtrusively she found her quarry and almost apologetically handed his book back, adding a few courteous and appropriate words in French. The man raised his eyebrows and complimented her on her good accent. Then switching the conversation to French he soon found out how fluent she was. Before the party broke up she found herself the possessor of a name and telephone number, which she was to ring up if she wanted to change her job. This was her entry into SOE, and in April 1944 she joined the FANY.

After successful interviews, she started the SOE's 'Students' Assessment Course' at Wanborough on 11 April 1944. Described as well educated, well above average intelligence, thoughtful, practical, and quick, she was considered by her instructors as an ideal candidate to be a courier. But with time pressing, her call to arms came despite one instructor feeling that she needed more training: 'I could accept no responsibility for passing her out as fit for the field'.

Gleeson described her as 'five feet tall, very slim but a bundle of energy, vivacious ready to smile and always a very popular girl but, nevertheless, unassuming and modest.'

There must have been a degree of urgency with D-Day approaching as she only did one parachute drop at Ringway. After further radio training at Thame Park and clandestine training at Saltmarsh at Beaulieu, she returned to London. Instead of the usual four months, Marguerite only got a fortnight's training. It was a Saturday, she recalled, when she was briefed for her mission and then told to enjoy the rest of the weekend. Imagine her surprise when she was rung up the same afternoon and told a flight had been arranged for her that night.

Driving up to Tempsford, she was introduced to Henri Bouchard, the wireless operator codenamed 'Noel', given her identity papers in the name of Marguerite Chauvin, codename 'Nicole', as well as provided with a cover story that she was a short-hand typist. Once they were checked over at the barn, she was given a pack of Benzedrine tablets to keep her awake, an 'L' pill, and a revolver; she suddenly realised the dangers of her mission.

In the early hours of the morning of 6 May 1944, they boarded one of the USAAF Carpetbagger's Liberators. Codenamed FENSTER, this was the first American mission to drop British agents into France. Her report said that she showed no sign of nervousness in the aircraft.

In an interview with Cameron Ramos, she told how the plane descended towards Marcenay on the Cote d'Or. She jumped from 200 feet, when the plane was doing 150 mph, onto a drop zone lit up with torches in the shape of a letter 'T'. Despite it being only her second jump, she landed slightly off-course in some bramble bushes. Bouchard had to be helped down from a tree he landed in.

They were met by a 'very bad' reception committee under the command of Casse-Cou, which forced them to hang around the field for more than an hour as they were asked questions and had their cigarettes, chewing gum, and even their parachutes and wireless set taken from them before the threat of discovery forced them to the nearest village.

Gleeson reported how the reception committee had not expected any 'bods' to be dropped that night, only containers and certainly no small young woman. They therefore had to find them safe accommodation in a nearby farmhouse and the next day a pilgrimage of curious visitors arrived to see the new arrivals. Concerned about the lack of security, they were moved the following night to an isolated shed, where they were told to remain in hiding until a safer house was found. Peggy told Gleeson that living in a farm outhouse was not much fun, especially when she began to itch all over. However, it served as an introduction to the work she had to do. With the Germans expected to advance through their area, she had to stay and arrange drops of supplies to her network.

Her mission was to work as a courier in Henri Frager's DONKEYMAN network in Yonne and the Cote d'Azur. According to Foot[49], 'She was naïve, modest, efficient, and self-effacing; her French was good; everyone liked her and no one noticed her. She was quite out of her depth in the personal and political intrigues that riddled DONKEYMAN.'

They were 'rescued' from the reception committee's 'unsafe' shed by Roger Bardet and his colleague, Marcel, and taken a few days later to the DONKEYMAN headquarters in Aillant-sur-Tholon in the Yonne. What she did not know, Escott explained, was that Bardet and J. L. Kieffer, another member of the network, were double agents. Bardet had been 'turned' by Henri Bleicher, an Abwehr officer who had already trapped Odette Sansom and Peter Churchill.

She spent most of her days cycling throughout the area, ostensibly looking for a job, but in reality conveying messages to and from Frager and his members further away. Gleeson reported how

> One morning shortly after her arrival and when she had been working all night on an arms drop she was told to go to Paris to pick up a wireless transmitting set. As she sat in the corner of a crowded compartment in a train, which was forced to stop frequently through bomb damage and sabotage, she dozed off and suddenly woke with a start to find all eyes in the compartment fixed on her. She had been dreaming about England and had been talking in her sleep – in English! It was a very worried Mademoiselle Chauvin who waited for the strain to stop at the Paris terminus. Then she nipped smartly out before the train stopped and quickly lost herself in the crowds.

Once she arrived at the rendezvous, the woman who answered the door was extremely worried. A Gestapo swoop was imminent. Although she had another rendezvous planned, she was so exhausted, she was allowed to sleep there. The following morning, as there had been no knock on the door, she decided to visit an old school friend. Although delighted to see Peggy, she was shocked to find her in France and was extremely worried that the Gestapo might have followed her there. She was hidden in the attic and left the next day, shocked to discover that the house next door was the Gestapo HQ.

Her rendezvous was at a seat in the Jardin de Tuilleries, where she would be met by someone with a suitcase. Whilst waiting, a German officer walked past but then retraced his steps and tried to chat her up. Worried that her contact might arrive at any moment, she was in a quandary. Luckily, there was an air raid warning but the officer invited her to his hotel. Unable to consider an alternative, she went with him, where he spent a long time telling her about his magnificent Luger and that his leave was about to end. When the 'All clear' was sounded, she accompanied him to the station, waved him off with her handkerchief before hurrying back to the park. Luckily, the assignment was made and she returned to her sector.

When she arrived, the whole group was said to have been seething with dissatisfaction and suspicion. The local leader of the Maquis had been executed by his own men and she was in danger of being killed. A double-agent had infiltrated the group but, she managed to talk herself out of trouble. Ramos told his readers in the *Harrow Times* how

her time there was marked by constant feuding. Three of her colleagues were shot as traitors, another survived a bungled assassination attempt by two comrades and her circuit organiser was betrayed.

In this atmosphere Peggy had to use all her instincts to survive and managed to remain undiscovered for six months while sending vital information to the Allies.

Colonel Maurice Buckmaster said of her in June 1945: 'A young girl of an altogether exceptional courage and good sense and very marked intelligence.

'She has rendered services of a remarkable nature without regard to the risks she ran.

'Courageous in front of the enemy, she has shown a completely unexpected military sense and has been an inspiration to her comrades.'

When the Gestapo arrived at the farm, she and her friends jumped out of a back window and waded through a deep river to escape, laying undercover all day in sodden clothes. When it got dark, they walked sixteen kilometres to another safe house to be told that it was D-Day. She joined the Maquis in the woods and taught them how to use the weapons that had been dropped. Every night she joined sabotage teams carrying *plastique* to blow up the Marseille to Paris railway, which passed through her area bringing German reinforcements. By-passing farms with noisy guard dogs; throwing herself into a ditch when a German lorry approached; worming her way through a field to avoid check points on the road, and crawling down railway embankments, she then attached a little packet and time pencil to the line. Once she had crept back up the embankment, she would retreat for a safe distance, wait and count how many explosions there were. If there were duds, another visit was paid. As well as attacking railways, Peggy's network was also involved in attacking airfields and oil storage depots.

On 5 June 1944, she, Bardet, Frager, and a few *résistants* had to escape from the farmhouse where they were staying. They walked through undergrowth, wet and nettle-stung to Villers, a journey of thirty kilometres during the night. The next day, she made the same journey there and back on a bicycle. At this new headquarters, they received the D-Day messages to attack the railway lines at Cézy.

On another occasion in late June, she was joined by Captain Thompson, a British officer who had escaped from a prisoner of war camp. He helped in the training of the Maquis and took his turn on sentry duty. One night when they were walking around the farm, she heard a shot in the distance. Going to investigate they found about seven hundred Germans approaching. Rushing back, they informed the inhabitants, gathered up as much arms and ammunition as they could and headed into the thickest part of the nearest woods. Throughout the night and following day they heard explosions and gun shots but they lay low.

Although by day she was an innocent French mademoiselle, at night she became a determined, courageous soldier. She told Gleeson how one night she had to dig up a grave as the dead body buried the previous week was thought to have important papers on it. There was another occasion when her team was sent to execute a chemist who was working as a double agent. Peggy and her companions drove to the chemist's, but, aware that he was in danger, the chemist fired on his visitors, seriously wounding one of her companions. She rushed inside with her Sten gun but the chemist escaped. Her companion died on his way back to the car and the group narrowly escaped a hail of bullets from German soldiers awoken by the commotion.

Escott described how she complained bitterly at the way she was treated by Marcel and his companions. There was no organisation, she claimed, poor discipline and security measures. She wasn't able to get to her wireless set on occasions and they stopped her from going to Paris and, it is thought, sexually harassed her. Bardet 'accidentally' wounded Frager's courier so, when Frager and Bardet arrived to investigate, Marcel and his companions were executed as traitors and Bardet decided to change sides and became a hero of the Resistance.

Waiting for the Allied forces to arrive, Peggy had nothing to do except peel potatoes and prepare vegetables for her group's soup. When they did, Gleeson tells of Peggy having to cross and re-cross German lines on her bicycle to keep in contact with her group and the Allies. Pretending she had a raging toothache and was desperate to find a dentist worked. Her courier work was gruelling but on one occasion she was driven at night without headlights. Once they delivered the information to the HQ of the American 1st Army, they returned to find a German convoy almost blocking the road. The driver decided to make a dash through. Peggy got three hand grenades and threw them at the soldiers as they tried to stop them. They got back without further incident.

Once the Allies were in control, she hitch-hiked to Paris from where a flight was arranged to bring her safely back to England on 13 September 1944. She resigned her FANY commission when she got married in November 1944 and was subsequently awarded the MBE, the *Croix de Guerre* and the *Médaille de la Résistance*.

Ramos related how Peggy's story was brought to the public attention in 1947 by a reporter from the *Sunday Express* who wrote an article titled 'Mrs Smith: Train-wrecker, spy and Nazi-killer'.

> You would not expect that the prim little woman who comes out of the newly built house, 61 Eastfield Road, Waltham Cross, Essex (sic), wheeling her 16-month-old and four-month-old in a second-hand pram ... with shopping basket on the handrail, is our trusted and well-beloved Marguerite Diana Frances Smith who once blazed away with a Sten gun at Germans hunting her down as a secret agent in France.[50]

The caption underneath the photograph showing her playing with her two children in front of the fire read: 'I like a good fight, whether it's with a gun in your hand or whether it's just against circumstances, but I honestly think my present job as a housewife is more exacting'.

Madeleine Lavigne

The next woman sent into France was thirty-two year-old Madeleine Lavigne. Born Madeleine Rejeuny on 6 February 1912 to French parents, she grew up in Lyon, where her father worked as a dress designer. After completing her school education, she married Marcel Lavigne and had two children, Guy when she was twenty, and Noel when she was 24. Escott described her as being buxom, serious, and conscientious, fond of dressmaking, music, boating and tennis.

When war started, her husband joined the army but was captured and made a prisoner of war. Having to survive without him was difficult. To pay for the needs of her family, she sent her sons to live with her mother in another part of the city and she found work at the *Mairie* as a clerk. When her husband was released in November 1943, the relationship did not work and they divorced, never to see each other again. Having developed a hatred of the German occupiers and being very patriotic, she wanted to help the French Resistance.

She was approached by Robert Boiteux, an SOE agent dropped in Ance in the south-west Pyrénées on 1 June 1942. He was a hairdresser on Bond Street before the war, had been a gold digger and was a boxing champion. His mission was working with George Duboudin to build up the SPRUCE network of contacts in around Lyon, but when the wireless operator sent with him parachuted onto the roof of a house near the police station, he was arrested. When Duboudin's wireless operator, Pierre le Chêne, Marie Thérèse's brother-in-law, was also arrested, Boiteux moved into the safer woods, waterways, and vineyards of the countryside and the nearby mountains. His mission had to change from being a propaganda enterprise to one of sabotage and building up stockpiles of arms and ammunition. To help in this work it was essential that he obtained official papers, identity papers, and appropriate official stamps so that his men could pass German and French police checks and controls. Despite the dire consequences of being found out, Madeline agreed to supply him with them.

In time, according to Escott, Boiteux recognised that Madeleine's unexceptional appearance, untapped intelligence, and careful following of instructions made her a potential courier. Travelling on various missions for him under the name of Marianne Latour, presumably with cleverly forged papers, she helped her organiser. In fact, she even loaned him money when he was in need of cash.

It was working in this capacity that she came to the attention of Henri Borosh, who had been a wireless operator of the 'Vic' escape line in the Burgundy area. They too were desperate for large quantities of false papers for the men they were helping to get out of France. Having to wait for SOE's forgery section to obtain copies and then produce fake ones often took months. She agreed to help and was given the codename Leveller.

Boiteux received few arms drops and was unable to attract new members to his network without guns and ammunition. Also, the failure of the British to invade had meant many men were disillusioned with the British. Deciding to wind down his network, he advised his men to lie low and got Déricourt to arrange a Hudson pick-up for him, Madame le Chêne and Victor Gerson.

After they were picked up from a hilltop near Angers on 19 August 1943, Madeleine and Borosh stayed in Lyon. She allowed him to keep his wireless set and other equipment in her house. If the Germans had found out, it was likely she would have been sent to a concentration camp. As the 'Vic' line had been funded by the SIS, Borosh was keen to create another funded by the SOE's F Section. Travelling around with him, Madeline helped locate contacts who might help.

When Gerson returned in November, the plan was explained and it was agreed that Borosh moved north. However, in January 1944, when Madeleine was warned that the police were on the look-out for them, Borosh contacted Déricourt to request a pick-up.

According to Hugh Verity, she was brought to England in a Hudson flown by Squadron Leader Ratcliff on 4/5 February 1944 from a field a kilometre south-east of Soucelles, north-east of Angers. The other eight passengers included Borosh, Robert Benoist, Philippe Liewer, Bob Maloubier, Colonel Limousin, 'Le Berbu', the innkeeper at Tiercé, her husband, and Madame Gouin, the wife of a French politician. In Ratcliff's memoirs, he told how he had been ordered to bring Déricourt back, but he refused. Whether they landed at Tempsford is unknown.

She had just escaped in time. According to Escott, the Lyon police were planning to arrest her. Tried in her absence, she was sentenced to hard labour for life, though the sentence would be reviewed annually.

Having been debriefed, the SOE considered her experiences highly suitable to be trained and returned to France. Borosh was keen that she went with him. She was given a commission in the FANY in February 1944 under her former cover as Marianne Latour, which she kept throughout her SOE training. It was to be a source of confusion for years as it appeared on her citation for an award as well as on her gravestone. In Escott's *Heroines of the SOE*, she stated that:

> ... her training was speeded up in view of her previous experience and the present emergency. It proved quite satisfactory. Since training was all in French, it caused her little difficulty, as it was her only language. Later Borosh excused her only other peculiarity, 'if in English eyes her appearance was rather against her', it was quite acceptable in France. She made a cheerful but nervous student, working hard and being keen to do well. She only did two weeks of a wireless course, it not being considered necessary, as she would be working with Borosh, a fully trained operator, who could complete her training as they worked together so that she would be able to act as his wireless operator. Her ground training was good, but weapons rather frightened her, as did parachute jumping. After watching her two descents, her trainer ominously suggested that 'on operations, the dispatcher may have to *assist* her to make an exit'.

Madeleine was taken to Tempsford on 24 May 1944 and Geoff Rothwell of 138 Squadron reported dropping her at Soane-et-Loire, near Reims in the Ardennes. She was described by Wilf Burnett, 138 Flight Commander, as a VIP agent. Geoff was impressed by her height, good looks, and perfume. When he asked Bob Willmott, one of his crew, if he had noticed her heavy make-up, the response was: 'All these women Froggies make the 'ole bloody aircraft smell like a bleedin' whore's boudoir!'

Major Charles Tice, the Liaison Officer, had told Geoff that she was going back 'into the field' for the second time. She had been captured on her first trip working for the SILVERSMITH network, and the Gestapo stubbed out lit cigarettes on her face to try to get information out of her. The make-up was to hide the scars. After a daring escape from her jailers, she was picked up, returned safely to Britain and prepared for her second trip. This appears to be a different woman as one would have expected Escott to have mentioned it.

Madeleine worked as Borosh's courier and trainee wireless operator in the new SILVERSMITH network, with identity papers as Marianne Henriette Delormes, codenamed 'Isabelle'. One section was to work in the Reims and Épernay area, the other in the lower Saône valley. The latter would work alongside the ACOLYTE network and both were to attack the German troops expected to drive north up the Rhône valley after D-Day.

One of Madeleine's first tasks was to locate and rent suitable premises from where she and Borosh could transmit. As she got to know Reims, she met Madame and Monsieur Benazat, who owned a restaurant and several properties. Becoming their regular customer, she eventually won their confidence and they agreed that she rent their apartments in Épernay and, as a reserve, at Ay.

Once Borosh moved to Épernay, her work began in earnest. Over the following few months, during the time of the invasion, she travelled north and south carrying messages, arranging with London for arms drops and passing on instructions to sabotage the communications network. On occasions she had to rendezvous with *résistants* in other networks, encourage people to join Borosh's group, and deliver instructions to a small group in Paris. Escott describes how,

> Once the northern landings had taken place, Madeleine had also to be even more careful of security, as the Germans were everywhere and more alert and dangerous than the French authorities in watching for saboteurs or spies. She did her work unquestionably well and was of the greatest possible assistance to Borosh. Inevitably, she was sometimes caught up in engagements with the movement of German troops, and often had to pass through areas under fire, showing great courage and common sense.

When the Germans successfully penetrated her network, she went on the run, staying in one of Henri Déricourt's safe houses not far from the DZ. On 13 August 1944 the Allies and the Free French Forces landed on the Mediterranean coast and started a push north up the Rhône valley, forcing the Germans to retreat. The southern group now joined in the action, destroying the rail and telephone links, forcing the Germans to use the roads. Hit and run tactics harassed, slowed down and delayed the Germans from getting to Normandy for weeks.

With the liberation of Paris, the feeling of success spread amongst the French population. The Americans reached Reims on 29 August and Lyon a few days later. In September Madeleine continued her courier work, unable to return to Lyon until the court repealed her life sentence to hard labour. She was eventually reunited with her two boys for whom, before she left England, she had written a note at Vera Atkins' suggestion: 'In case of accident, the circumstances of my two children be enquired into, with a view to helping them with a pension if necessary'.

Completely unexpected, she died of an embolism in Paris on Saturday 24 February 1945. She was only thirty-three. Buckmaster, the head of F Section, wrote, 'We deeply grieve the untimely death of this French woman, who deserved so much from her country.' In November 1946, she was awarded the King's Medal for Brave Conduct and the King's Commendation for Brave Conduct.

Sonya Butt

Four days after Madeleine Lavigne arrived in France, Sonya Butt was flown out of Tempsford on Carpetbagger CHOPPER mission and parachuted into La Cropte, a small community west of Le Mans. It was a fortnight after her twentieth birthday. Codenamed 'Blanche' and with the cover name 'Suzanne Bonvie', she had important courier work to do. According to the now defunct 64 Baker Street website, she was born Sonya Esmée Florence Butt in Eastchurch, Kent on 14 May 1924. Her father, an RAF Group Captain, separated from her mother, who took Sonya and her brother to live in the south of France. Although she attended a private school, Escott describes her as running wild with her brother, probably during the holidays.

Following the German invasion of France, fifteen-year-old Sonya returned to Britain and lived in Woking. As her father was in the RAF, she was keen to join the WAAF, but had to wait until she was seventeen and a half. So, on 14 November 1941 she joined their administrative branch, which she found very tedious. In time, she got to hear of people joining de Gaulle's Free French Squadron and felt that she could do more interesting work by exploiting her fluent French. She requested a job as a translator, but, once Colonel Passy discovered her English background, she was refused. Shortly afterwards, she was taken on and trained by the SOE.

During her training, she got to know Nancy Wake and Violette Szabó and they had many good times together before their missions. Not having a mathematical or logical brain or being good at map reading, she did not think she was suitable material for coding or signals work. The part of the course she enjoyed most was weapons training. Students had to learn everything there was to know about every type and make of weapon that they might encounter, whether they were British, American, German or other foreign makes. They also had to be able to take them apart and reassemble them in the dark and use them accurately. However, her speciality was working with explosives. Escott claims that she had 'a natural gift in mixing explosives, memorising the ingredients and tricky quantities as though she were baking a cake.

Her instructor introduced her to Guy D'Artois, a glamorous older Canadian soldier who was also training as an agent. He had previously trained at Camp X, Whitby, Ontario, the Canadian equivalent to Beaulieu, and was quite happy to help her with her map work and orienteering. According to Escott, romance blossomed at Ringway. He decided to marry her when she winked at him before their second descent. Maybe she was distracted as she hurt her spine on landing. However, they decided to specialise in explosives and ask Buckmaster whether they could be sent into the field together.

Even though she had only known him three months, they got married in London on the day before they were due to leave. Buckmaster was said to not have been very amused by the wedding, because he would not be able to send both into the field as a married couple. They had therefore to be sent separately on different missions. Following Guy's departure to Taizé on 23 May 1944 to arm, train and work with Free French units, Buckmaster realised how upset Sonya was and could not refuse her request to be sent on a separate mission.

Five days later, on 28 May, Sonya was flown out of Tempsford wearing a baggy jump suit over a divided skirt in an American Carpetbagger operation. In the early hours of the morning she was parachuted into a field one kilometre south of La Cropte, thirty-two kilometres south of Laval. Accompanying her were Francis Bec and Raymond Glaesner, whose mission was to help Sydney Hudson's HEADMASTER network in the Le Mans area. The jump did not go smoothly. She landed badly in a ditch and damaged her spine again, which later needed two operations, but the container carrying her clothes and other belongings landed on a nearby road and was almost immediately picked up by a German patrol. It was said that she was more annoyed that she had lost her designer clothes than that the Germans now knew that there was a new female agent operating in the area.

Thinking that they would expect her to lie low and do nothing for a while, she decided to do the opposite. Using identity papers in the name of Madame Suzanne Bonvie, codenamed 'Blanche', Sonya's cover story was that she was an employee of a fashion house in Paris, but, suffering from bronchitis, she had been sent to the country to recuperate in a château. According to Escott, she went to black market restaurants, 'appealing to the nicer kind of German officer, sharing his table, laughing with him and being friendly'. Being five foot seven inches tall, only nineteen, good-looking with dark hair, dark eyes, a gentle mouth but with a determined mouth and chin, she must have been a German soldier's dream French girl.

Over the next few months she was constantly on the move, only staying in someone's home or hideout for a maximum of two nights. By day she and her colleagues were recruiting new *résistants* and training them in weapons and explosives techniques. By night she helped pick up 138 Squadron's drops of weapons and explosives. Her team then used them to attack railway lines, roads and bridges. When the network's weapons trainer was shot, she took over the role. However, officially she was Hudson's courier. Occasionally, she took buses but these were unreliable and were often stopped and their passengers checked. Instead she delivered and brought back messages and distributed money, food and explosives on her bicycle. When she returned to England, she had lost about forty pounds (18.4 kilogrammes).

Just before D-Day, she and Hudson successfully blew up Le Mans telegraph office, forcing the Germans to transmit wireless messages which were intercepted by Allied code breakers.

In Hudson's memoirs, *Undercover Operator*, he recalled that on the morning of D-Day, they were staying at No. 8 rue Mangeard in Le Mans. Presumably to protect Sonya's identity, he changed her name.

> Madeleine was sleeping upstairs and I was installed on the sofa on the ground floor. We were awakened by the sound of bombs falling nearby. Allied bombers were targeting the railway station; in fact it had already been destroyed. Thinking that Madeleine might be frightened I dashed upstairs to her room. I need not have bothered; she was completely unperturbed. The bombardment did not last long and soon all appeared normal on the streets of the town.

The area where she was working was full of Germans, but, rather than hide from them, she was said to have blatantly and brazenly mixed with them. An attractive blonde, she knew she would be noticed, but Sonya was confident with her cover and false papers. On one occasion, she was cycling to a house to tell a group of *résistants* about their next meeting when a sixth sense told her to stop and wait. Just then, a group of German soldiers swooped on the house and arrested the people she was going to meet. On another occasion, she was in a café sitting close to several German soldiers when she accidentally dropped her handbag containing her .32-calibre handgun, When one of the officers reached down to pick it up for her, she managed to beat him to it. The weight of it would very probably have given her away.

After the D-Day landing the fighting by the *résistants* was far more open and Sonya was involved in major attacks involving groups of between twenty and thirty fighters. Trains were stopped and German soldiers captured. In order to avoid capture, she moved constantly, sleeping in safe houses, barns, tents and sometimes, in the hot summer, in fields with only river water to wash in. Escott mentioned that her network had been infiltrated by a recruit in the pay of the Germans. She was invited to a meeting, but suspicious, decided not to go. Several of those who did were captured and shot.

As the Americans troops moved south, they liberated Le Mans on 8 August. Groups of men started rounding up suspected collaborators and, after a brief trial, dealt out justice. Sonya was caught, accused of socialising with German officers in black market restaurants. What were called 'horizontal collaborators' had their heads shaved in a public humiliation ceremony and tied to lampposts in the streets. Protesting that it was part of her cover story, she was only released when some members of the Maquis spoke up for her.

When she was told that she could return to London via Paris, Hudson refused. The Americans needed people who knew the local area and were prepared to identify German troop positions and strengths by travelling back and forth over the front line.

On one incursion, her group was conscious that a German patrol was close by. To avoid being caught with their Sten guns, they buried them in the woods. Although they were caught and interrogated, the Germans didn't know what to do with them and so they let them go. Escott described another lucky escape in *The Heroines of the SOE*:

> One day in late June near Bur-sur-Seine, after the landings, the German soldiers, instead of waving her through a road block, escorted her to their headquarters. They were not satisfied with her papers, which she knew were forgeries. In a small room, another man examined her papers very carefully and began questioning her. As an innocent member of the public, she protested volubly, and was sent to a small cell. Late that afternoon she was taken down a long corridor into a large office busy with German clerks. At one table she was asked her name. Then to her relief and surprise the man handed back her papers, and told her she could go. She was free.

On another occasion she and Hudson walked into a German-held town, only to find it empty and deathly silent. All the men had been rounded up and were under armed guard in the market square, while the women had gone into hiding. It turned out that the Germans were hoping to bargain for their own safety by using the men as hostages. Although Hudson was arrested, Sonya was allowed to leave and went in search of safety. Eventually, the Germans surrendered and their prisoners were released.

Sonya returned to the American lines and continued working for them until she went to Paris. Once de Gaulle took control of France, he ordered all the SOE agents to leave. He distrusted the political motives of the SOE and told them that their place was no longer in France. Sonya and Hudson were allowed to stay as they were working for the Americans. Escott narrated how one day they were driving in an American car with American flags and were shot at by a group of retreating German soldiers. Unhurt, Hudson accelerated away and Sonya later found bullet holes in the shoulder of her jacket that had been hanging on the back of her seat.

After several weeks of celebrations, she was joined by her husband, who, after completing his own SOE work, had been searching for her in other parts of France. They returned to England in October 1944, where, aged twenty, she became pregnant with the first of their six children. After a period in England, they went to live in Quebec in Canada.

Sonya was awarded the MBE and 'Mentioned in Dispatches'. She died in March 1999.

5
Operations to Support D-Day,
6 June 1944 to March 1945

Once the Allies landed in Normandy on 6 June 1944 and the Americans and French landed on the Mediterranean coast in August, a two-pronged attack on the German forces began, in the planned liberation of France. Necessarily, there were also plans to liberate the Low Countries. Although more women were sent into France to replace lost wireless operators and couriers, there were rather different missions for the women trained to be sent into Belgium and Holland. There was a plan to rescue Prince Charles, King Leopold's brother, and bring him back to England and propaganda missions to undermine German morale. One woman was sent into Yugoslavia to work with SOE agents already in place helping General Tito.

Ginette Jullian

Lieutenant Ginette Jullian, codenamed 'Adèle', was dropped from a Carpetbagger Liberator in the early hours of the morning on 7 June 1944, the day after D-Day. She and three other SOE agents landed in a field six kilometres north-east of Saint-Viatre-les-Tannieres in the Loir and Cher department. Her companions were Gérard Dedieu, her organiser, Yvan Galliard, and Henri Fucs.

Born in Montpellier on 3 December 1917 to French parents, nothing has come to light about her early life. Maybe she was the Ginette referred to as the courier helping on the Marie-Claire escape line. It is possible that she escorted escaped prisoners and other evaders over the Pyrénées and came to Britain with them. According to Escott, she was the last woman to be recruited by the SOE. Given a commission in the FANY, she underwent parachute training at Ringway and, one imagines, training in clandestine warfare at Beaulieu. As she was sent as a wireless operator, she probably spent time at Thame Park. She was perhaps the luckiest of the wireless operators as she was sent with the latest model – a Mark III transceiver which weighed less than nine pounds in its suitcase. Her mission was to assist Dedieu in setting up the PERMIT network in the area of the Somme with a base at Amiens. Unusually, they were the only French-speaking team sent into France. Dedieu had been a schoolmaster and a member of the Resistance who had been arrested and imprisoned at Eysses. When he and twenty other prisoners escaped in January 1944, he and other escapees were escorted over the Pyrénées, arriving in Britain in March 1944.

On their return, the situation was highly dangerous. Many SOE networks had been infiltrated by the Gestapo and new ones were needed. Much of northern France was in chaos with Allied and German troops in conflict and people fleeing the combat zones.

When they landed, Ginette's transceiver was confiscated by the reception committee organised by Hutton, codenamed 'Antoine'. He suggested that such a small suitcase would cause suspicion if she carried it around with her in Paris. However, she was allowed to keep her crystals but this meant she had to find another set if she was to be able to transmit.

Arriving in Paris, they found that all their contacts had moved, leaving no forwarding addresses. They had fled following mass arrests. With no alternative, they hitch-hiked to Beaumont, where they acquired bicycles and then went to Beauvais. Their contact there had disappeared as the town had been requisitioned by the Germans. Too dangerous to stay there, they took the train for Paris and decided to separate. Dedieu went to Asnières to see if his father-in-law might help him locate leaders of the different Resistance groups around Paris. Whilst he managed to contact them, they had too many political differences to agree to work together.

Ginette went to find Hutton to locate a wireless set and see if he could get her some forged papers. On the way, she discovered that several hundred German troops had attacked his Maquis and he had disappeared. Searching for another organiser who might be able to tell her where he was, she was put in touch with one of de Gaulle's groups. It was suggested that she went to work with a group desperately in need of a wireless operator in the Eure-et-Loir department. Eventually, according to Escott, after much difficulty, she met an American group in the Seine-et-Marne department who let her use their set.

London then gave her a new mission, not in Amiens but in the Eure-et-Loir department, the northern part of the Loir-et-Cher, and the Orne department. Their new headquarters was a safe house in the cathedral town of Chartres. At the end of June she rendezvoused with Dedieu and received a new set. Whether it was the new, lightweight Mark III was not specified but its reception, Escott said, was very good. 'Any lost skeds were due to the current being cut off when the Germans, trying to track her down, came too near. Indeed there were some lively alerts'.

As the Allied advance progressed, Ginette was busy transmitting Dedieu's plans and requests for arms and ammunition to London. With access to supplies, he was able to win the support of the military delegate of the French Forces of the Interior and through him sixteen groups of *résistants*. Once she had located suitable drop zones, 450 containers were dropped each month, enabling 2,000 Maquis to attack railways, convoys, and other German targets, including blowing up the viaduct at Chérisy, which the RAF had failed to destroy in twenty attempts.

The circumstances of Dedieu's arrest on 8 August are unknown but according to the Special Forces Roll of Honour, he escaped again on 21 August. While he was incarcerated, the slow advance of the Allied forces in Normandy was given a boost when the American and French forces landed on the Mediterranean coast. Helped by information supplied by Ginette, the RAF was able to bomb German garrisons, which helped the Maquis to liberate Bonneval, Dreux, Châteaudun and Nogent. When the Americans met up with Ginette, they helped the Maquis liberate Chartres on 15 August.

Once out of prison, Dedieu found that the military delegate refused to allow him to attend the funerals of those men killed during the capture of Chartres. He was further annoyed when he was not invited to de Gaulle's official visit to the town. Whether Ginette attended is unknown, but de Gaulle was known to have ordered all SOE agents to leave France.

Following the landing of an SAS team, the American Major Rolf availed himself of Ginette's wireless skills and London instructed her to accompany them in the Allied push towards Dijon. When they arrived in September, they divided into two teams of two. The first team located German targets for air strikes and the second team, with a USAAF officer using the first's information, got Ginette to use an S-phone to speak directly to the radio operator on board an overflying bomber, who then directed the bomb-aimer to the targets. Escott described her work as being 'intense and dangerous, as they were all on the front line and occasionally ahead of it.

The rapid advance of the Allies from Normandy met the advance force of the American and French forces from the south at Dijon on 11 September. On 22 September she, and presumably Dedieu, were flown back to England to be debriefed. What happened after the war is not documented in her personnel file or in Escott's books.

Krystyna Skarbek (Christine Granville)

Twenty-two-year-old Krystyna Skarbek, the slim, olive-skinned, raven-haired daughter of a Polish count, was the next agent to be flown into France. She was the only SOE agent not to have been infiltrated from England. It was an SOE-inspired mission from Massingham, their forward base in Algiers.

Born on 1 May 1915 in Warsaw, Poland to Count Skarbek and his Jewish wife, Maria Krystyna, she was brought up a Catholic by her father and described by Hugh Davies, an SOE enthusiast, as 'the sort of woman our mothers warned us about'. When her father's estate was confiscated by the Germans, it led to her developing a deep hatred of them. In Escott's *Heroines of the SOE*, she described her as 'radiantly beautiful ... graceful, deceptively fragile and with brown eyes and a cloud of dark hair. Highly intelligent, she soaked up languages'. When her father died almost penniless, she worked first in an agency for Fiat cars and then as a journalist in Paris, she spent her holidays skiing in the Polish resort of Zakopane, making extra money by smuggling. There she got to know some of the mountain people who would be of help later in the war.

She married in 1938 and was in Addis Ababa with her Ukrainian husband, Jerzy Giycki, when the Germans invaded Poland on 1 September the following year. The gold ring she wore on her middle finger had a band of steel in the middle, which she claimed was in memory of the heroic times in the fifteenth century when her ancestors drove the Teutonic knights out of Poland. She was reported as saying that when Jan Skarbeck was told by the Emperor, Henry II, that resistance was futile and he had coffers full of gold to pay his soldiers, he took his gold ring off and threw it in with the coins, saying, 'Let gold return to gold; we Poles prefer steel.'

Despite Krystyna's attempts to get her mother, the daughter of a Jewish banker, to go into hiding, she refused and was deported from Warsaw. Krystyna and Jerzy managed to get to London, where she successfully applied for British naturalisation. Her new name was Christine Granville. Her husband was determined to make his way to Finland to fight against the Red Army, but Christine had other plans. Wanting to help the Polish resistance, she contacted the SIS in December 1939, who employed her in D Section. She joined the WAAF and underwent training and a flight was arranged for her to get to Budapest with the codename Madame Marchand.

George Taylor, one of SOE's early officers, had a rapport with Christine and arranged her cover story as a journalist with a mission she largely created herself.

Once established in Hungary, her intention was to make her way into Poland with propaganda material which, she hoped, would convince her compatriots that, contrary to nearly all the evidence, Britain had not abandoned Poland and would continue to prosecute the war vigorously.[1]

Escott detailed her mission as organising a two-way system of sending supplies for the Polish resistance, and organising an escape line to bring British prisoners of war and intelligence information out of Poland. In Madeleine Masson's biography, *A Search for Christine Granville*, she details how in Budapest, Christine, codenamed 'Granville', met up with Andrezej Kowerski, an old friend and hero in the Polish army, and engaged in espionage, sabotage, and a *ménage à trois* with another Polish agent. Vera Atkins said of her that 'she was no plaster saint. She was a vital, healthy, beautiful animal with a great appetite for love and laughter'.

Having rescued members of the Polish army from internment camps, she used her skiing skills to escort them over the snow-covered mountains into Yugoslavia. When Italy joined the Axis forces, she was not allowed a visa. Despite being arrested twice in Hungary and once on the Czechoslovakian border, she managed to escape, convincing her guard that she had tuberculosis. She was able to provide the Allies with a microfilm showing plans of new German U-boats and gases, as well as German forces preparing to invade the Soviet Union in June 1941. When Stalin was informed, he is reported to have dismissed it as British disinformation. Her idea of the BBC having a clandestine news broadcasting station for Poland caught some people's attention.

Sir Owen O'Malley, the British ambassador in Budapest, who knew her well and issued her with a British passport, said, 'She is the bravest person I ever knew, the only woman who had a positive nostalgia for danger. She could do anything with dynamite except eat it.'

She and Andrezej escaped over the Yugoslavian border in the boot of a car and made their way through Turkey, Syria, and Palestine to Cairo, where, virtually penniless, she was recruited into SOE using the name Christine Granville. In a lecture at Bletchley Park in January 2010, Dr Mark Baldwin, an SOE historian, added that, on her way through Syria, she made a detailed study of all the bridges – invaluable information for the SOE, who were instructed to protect the Syrian oilfields in case of a Nazi attempt to capture them. Escott stated how, 'everywhere she went, she seemed to know many of the most important people and made useful friends'. However, as there were suspicions that she was a double agent, she was put on numerous training courses in Egypt until 1944.

Said to have been the most highly trained of all the SOE's female agents, her instructor said of her that she was as brave as a lion and as SOE-minded as any of the Poles. Following a commission as a flight officer in the WAAF, she was said to have been the first agent to be flown out of Algiers. Despite a terrible gale, the pilot managed to drop her on the Vercors plateau on the night of 7/8 July. She landed badly, several kilometres off target. The butt of her revolver was smashed, but she hobbled on with a badly bruised hip. Dressed as a peasant girl, rather than wander off in the dark, she waited until it was light, when she was met by the reception committee. The more conventional among them were said to have been shocked by her language.

Codenamed 'Pauline' and also known as 'Jacqueline Armand', she replaced Cécile Lefort as Francis Cammaerts' courier in the JOCKEY network. They managed to leave the wooded Vercors plateau before the German attack on 17 July. Travelling by car, they took the back roads and trails to Seynes-les-Alpes in the Basses Alpes. Her mission then changed.

She was to contact Italian partisans on the border and win their active co-operation with the Allies. This mission successfully completed, not without danger, she was next sent off to win over the Russians serving with the Oriental Legion of the German 19th Army. Her gift for languages and her ability to inspire affection made her welcome and again she succeeded in her object. Once on the journey, while hiding from a German patrol, she was scented by one of the Alsatian tracker dogs which, coming under her strange charm, lay down beside her, instantly changing its loyalties, and never afterwards leaving her side.

> Being thoroughly feminine, she was certainly conscious of her appearance, though she frequently dressed in a manner which attracted little or no attention. This I believe, derived from a certain chameleon quality which helped her to be so supremely successful as a secret agent ...
>
> In reality she was a peculiarly gentle being who disliked noise in general and firearms in particular. When she was being taught how to use a pistol she shut her eyes every time she fired and announced that she could never bring herself to shoot anyone. Nor did she. In emergencies she employed other weapons, including her formidable power of persuasion. This derived partly from feminine charm, partly from a controlled indignation which, it was easy to believe, might suddenly erupt into fury, and partly from an ability to persuade any man on whom she was working that he was unusual in being perceptive enough, not only to understand the arguments she was advancing, but to agree with them.[2]

On one occasion, when faced with a German patrol, she calmly took out of her bag the SOE escape map, which was printed on silk, and used it as a headscarf. Part of her mission was to encourage a group of Polish nationals who had been forcibly enrolled in the German army to desert.

> She managed to contact some who ran a clandestine organisation centred at
> Mont-Dauphin. A more difficult assignment was to make her way to a fort in
> the Col de Larche on the Italian border south of Meyronnes, where 150 Poles
> were manning the garrison. A French patriot took her by motorcycle to the
> house of a guide, who led her up the 1,994 feet of precipitous mountain,
> mainly through woods of larches. She achieved a meeting with her contacts
> and many Poles defected as a result, with their arms. Before doing so, fifty
> of them removed the breech blocks from the heavy guns and brought with
> them mortars and machine guns to join the Maquis.[3]

According to Pawley, when Cammaerts and two other leaders of the JOCKEY network were arrested at a roadblock on 13 August, they were taken to a prison in Digne. The driver, Claude Renoir, the son of the famous painter, was allowed to get away and he told Christine. She then bicycled the forty kilometres to Digne and, pretending to be Cammaert's wife, succeeded in entering the prison.

In Foot's *SOE in France* he said how, three hours before the men were due to be shot, Christine used a combination of steady nerve, disguise, feminine cunning and sheer brass to secure their release. She told Albert Shenck, the liaison officer between the French prefecture and the Germans, that she was Cammaerts' wife, the niece of General Montgomery and a British agent, and that she would arrange to have him killed by the Maquis within days once the American forces arrived. She offered to bribe Max Waem, the Belgian Gestapo officer who acted as an interpreter for the German secret police, with two million francs. Her plan worked. The money was dropped by parachute on 17 August after her urgent request to Massingham, the Allied headquarters in Algiers.

The *message personelle* on the BBC included the words '*Roger est libre; félicitations á Pauline*'. She then accompanied the two men over the Pyrénées into Spain and then back to England, from where, after a brief respite, the SOE sent her to Cairo for her next mission. The plan had been to infiltrate her into Poland, but the speed of the Russian advance towards Germany thwarted the mission.

Following the German surrender and demobilisation, Christine returned to England, where she was awarded the George Cross and the OBE. The War Office had initially been reluctant to recommend the awards as she was from Poland, but many recognised that her bravery deserved recognition. De Gaulle awarded her the *Croix de Guerre*.

She found work as a telephonist in India House in London, then as a salesgirl in Harrods department store before getting a job as a stewardess on the SS *Rauhine*, a liner plying between Southampton and Australia. Dr Baldwin reported how the captain suggested one evening that everyone should wear their war medals. There was amazement when Krystyna wore her three. It was on this ship that she met George Muldowney, an Irish steward, who became obsessed with her. Although his romantic propositions were rejected, he found her lodgings in London and, in June 1952, he stabbed her in the heart outside the Shelbourne Hotel in Kensington when she still rejected his advances. Muldowney was hanged for her murder on 30 September 1952. The Wordiq website states that:

> Since her death, it has been speculated by some that because author Ian Fleming used the beautiful Krystyna as the basis for the double agent, 'Vesper Lynd' in his first James Bond, that Krystyna herself may have actually been a double agent. However, no such claim has ever been suggested by any legitimate authority and SOE's Vera Atkins, who had access to all files and knew her well, stated that Krystyna Skarbek was 'utterly loyal and dedicated to the Allies, and nothing would have made her betray her trust'.[4]

More details of her daring escapades can be read in Escott's *Mission Improbable* and *Heroines of the SOE*, and a film about her exploits, entitled *Christine: War My Love*, is in the making.

Marie-Madeleine Fourcade

Following four women belonging to de Gaulle's Free French Forces being parachuted into France, the next woman flown out was Marie-Madeleine Fourcade. Her autobiography, *Noah's Ark*, details how she was born Marie-Madeleine Bridou, the daughter of the executive of a steamship company, in Marseille in 1909. She married Monsieur Fourcade in 1929 but they separated, leaving her with two children.

Until war broke out she worked for a publishing company in Paris, and when Pétain signed the armistice in June 1940, she joined the Resistance. Working with Georges Loustaunau-Lacau in the ALLIANCE network, she took advantage of her contacts in business, politics, and the military to provide the Allies valuable and continuous information about German troop movements, their supplies, submarines, and ships. It was sent to England along with their political plans, scale drawings of U-boat bases, the launch sites of 'secret weapons', and anything potentially useful to the Allies. When her organiser was arrested in May 1941, she took command. The British military authorities were so impressed with the quality of this information that they sent her a wireless operator in August. Unfortunately, he was a double agent who betrayed many members of her network to the Gestapo. She was arrested but managed to escape and got into Spain inside a post bag in the back of a diplomatic car.

Fearing German reprisals, she was infiltrated back into France where, once she had her children taken into neutral Switzerland, she restarted her resistance work, helping to get downed Allied airmen back to Britain.

In Keith Jeffrey's history of MI6, there was an account of how, in 1942,

> reliable information was received that an agent known as Bla, a former French farm manager, had been captured by the Germans and was now working for them. He was caught in France by agents of Alliance, a network of French spies reporting to SIS. Bla was taken to an Alliance safe house where he was interrogated by the French agent Marie-Madeleine Fourcade (among others) and confessed to 'having given to the Boches all details known to him about us'. They first tried to kill him 'without him knowing it', by putting lethal drugs in his food, but this failed and merely alerted the unfortunate man to 'the attempt we were making'. When he was killed (he was shot) he faced his fate with what Fourcade reported as 'extraordinary moral courage' and 'astounded us by his calm attitude in facing punishment'.
>
> 'The way he died,' she wrote, 'did something to mitigate his past record.' Although in her memoirs Fourcade relates that an 'execution order' was received from London, nothing so explicit survives in the relevant files, and her contemporaneous report asserted that over the weekend when Bla was in Alliance hands no contact was established with London.
>
> A subsequent minute, nevertheless, by the Free French Section in Broadway (SIS headquarters) recorded that because the leading Alliance figures were 'known personally to [blanked out], the danger was such that eventually we instructed them to do away with him should the opportunity occur'.
>
> When his widow made inquiries about him towards the end of 1944 she was simply told that the authorities had had no information of his whereabouts 'since 1942'. As one SIS officer minuted, 'if any sleeping dogs should be let lie I think this is one'.

Following more arrests, MI6 thought it was too dangerous for Marie-Madeleine to stay in France, so they arranged for her to be brought to Britain. The Germans called her network 'Noah's Ark' as all her agents' cover names were animals. Hers was 'Hedgehog'. On 5 July 1943, Johnnie Affleck was said to have flown his Hudson to pick her up, along with her latest batch of airmen. Whether he did or not is uncertain as Hugh Verity says she was returned in a Lysander from a newly cut cornfield at Bouillancy, near Meaux on 17/18 July by Flight Lieutenant Peter Vaughan Fowler, who was able to add a *fleur-de-lis* on his cockpit for another successful mission. Once she was safe in England, the BCRA provided Marie-Madeleine with accommodation in Chelsea, from where she continued supervising her network and arranging pick-ups.

Aware of the Allied plans to invade Europe, she browbeat her minders into allowing her to return to France. Yvonne Fontaine and Pierre Mulsant arranged her landing the day after D-Day. In her memoirs, *Noah's Ark*, she said that she was given two hours' notice of her departure and had to pack into the false bottom of a large, soft holdall the crystals for her wireless set, replacement codes, money, and a set of dentures that transformed her into a French housewife. Her clothes were in a light fibre suitcase and in her handbag she carried a forged identity card and her 'L' pills.

> I gazed at Alliance House for the last time, at the large-flowered cretonnes, the camp-bed with its tearful night-time memories and the telephone that had so often been the bearer of appalling news.

She, Pierre Giraud and Raymond Pezet, her 'husband' for the return visit, were driven out of London in a long, black car. From her description, it is not clear whether she went to The Hasells or Gaynes Hall. Her account of her visit is worth including for the light it sheds on the agents' preparations for the trip.

> We drew up at dusk before the steps of a country house and were immediately taken to a huge dining room that had been converted into a mess, where waiters in white jackets above their service trousers were bustling about.
>
> 'So it's to be tonight?' Teutatès asked Ham, who had come back from the phone box.
>
> 'No, it's postponed until tomorrow.' My heart sank. After dinner I invited Ham to drink a last whisky with me.
>
> 'You're frightened about going back, Poz?' he asked.
>
> 'Yes, I'm frightened; I'm really in a blue flunk. I'm going to be arrested and yet I've got the feeling I shall get away with it.'
>
> We talked until dawn, going over all the ups and downs we had experienced together... His kindness and his tact were a great comfort.
>
> I woke up very late, certainly not before the afternoon. The huge place felt like a haunted house. One sensed the presence of a lot of people lurking behind the partitions, but ... no one ever met anyone else. Kenneth Cohen appeared.
>
> 'It won't be long now, dear Poz,' he said, greatly moved. 'Mary asked me to give you her best love and we'd like you to have this little memento. It's an heirloom.' He handed me a charming ring with a heart-shaped stone. 'Take it with you. It'll bring you luck,' he said when I protested. 'That's why we're

giving it to you. And here's a luminous watch from British Intelligence. It's Swiss and it keeps perfect time...

The airfield presented an extraordinary sight with aircraft lined up wing to wing as far as the eye could see, and in the middle a crowd of agile and athletic-looking RAF men moving about. 'You're not going to tell me that all these are off on secret missions?'

Kenneth Cohen laughed. 'No. They're bombers and will be taking off in waves from dusk to dawn. You're going in just behind them, so that the enemy radar won't be able to pick you out. They'll think you're one of the raiders.'

On arriving at the mess I saw my travelling companions sitting apart with Ham and, in another corner, half a dozen men of all ages and ranks. 'Those are the other passengers,' Kenneth said, going over to greet them, 'but I'm not making any introductions. Take no notice.'

'But we shall meet on the plane. Do you really imagine we will cold shoulder one another in these circumstances?'

The sun began to go down and waves of aircraft headed eastwards, disappearing into the oncoming darkness. An officer asked us to follow him. Another, with a poet's face, came over to us with a pile of little cages, each containing a white pigeon. I received one like the rest.

'You'll slip a message into the ring on its leg as soon as you land,' Kenneth told me.

'This seems very strange on the day of the V. I.'

'No, we do it for people who haven't any transmitters. That's not the case with you, but as you're with a lot of other people you're getting one of your own, so that nobody's jealous.'

We were driven to the tarmac, where I could see the burly outline of a Hudson, its paintwork chipped by machine-gun fire. I fell for it at once. I had the honour of being the first up the ladder into the fuselage, where I bumped into all kinds of containers piled up by the entrance, and went sprawling.

Our party came in one by one and crouched down in any available corner, the sergeant making sure that the weight was equally distributed; then our luggage and the pigeon cases were passed to us and the door shut with a loud bang. I stood up to try to catch through the window a last glimpse of Kenneth Cohen's tall figure in naval uniform and Ham's familiar cap. I felt a terrible urge to cry.

When they arrived, there was no sign of a reception committee. The pilot had to abort the mission and return to Tempsford. Marie-Madeleine got back when the other planes were returning from Germany in the early hours of the morning. With the Liberation of France imminent, many more missions were diverted eastwards. Marie-Madeleine awoke the next afternoon and relieved the tension by playing a piano, but she admitted that her fingers had lost all their agility and she couldn't remember her favourite piece.

She said that, after a day's wait, she was eventually landed in a field at Maisons-Rouges, near Nangis in the forest of Fontainebleu. Verity claims she was taken out with seven other passengers on 5/6 July in a Hudson piloted by Flight Lieutenant Affleck. In just under three hours they landed two and a half kilometres north of Égligny, south-west of Provins. Eight others replaced them for the return journey.

Her first words of welcome were 'Hello, Marie-Madeleine'. After a hearty meal in a nearby farmhouse, she and Pezet hitched a lift in a peasant's cart with squeaky axles to the station and managed after three days to get to Marseille. Within a fortnight she had arranged a drop of six tons of supplies and four million francs. A few days later she was caught and imprisoned by the Gestapo in Miollis barracks. Aware of what would be in store for her, she managed to escape by removing her clothes so that she could squeeze through the bars of a window in her cell room, her slender body lubricated by the sweat of fear. Picking up her batik cotton dress that she had dropped outside, she managed to find safety with the American troops who had just landed on the Mediterranean coast in August. She later found out that 438 out of an estimated 3,000 members of her network had been executed.

After the war she was awarded the Commander of the *Legion d'Honneur*. She died on 20 July 1989.

Francoise Dissart

McCall[5] noted that in late July 1944, Wing Commander Boxer and Flight Lieutenant Helfer flew their Hudson to the disused Le Blanc airfield between Châteauroux and Poitiers. The reception committee had repaired it a few days after the retreating Germans had criss-crossed it with a plough. Tempsford's Station Commander had been invited by the local mayor to a splendid luncheon that was laid on in honour of Francoise Dissart, a rather special woman who they had to take back.

She was described as a white-haired, chain-smoking woman in her sixties who had worked on the PAT escape line for much of the war. Her safe house was not far from the Gestapo HQ in Toulouse. Many of the young evaders who were helped to return to England thought she looked like a witch, always dressed in black, chain-smoking with a black cigarette holder and stroking Milouf, her cat. As the network was collapsing around her, she managed to avoid arrest, secure in her cover as a crotchety old woman who wanted nothing to do with the war. She told Boxer that she was going back to Tempsford with him on the instructions of MI9 to receive a decoration from the King at Buckingham Palace.

Elaine Madden

Online searches for information on female agents sent into occupied Belgium unearths data for just two: Elaine Madden and Olga Jackson. The 'cometeline' website, which focuses on the escape route from Belgium through France to Switzerland or Spain, mentioned that Elaine, codenamed 'Alice', was the only female Belgian agent sent in. Operation MANDAMUS on 3/4 August 1944 involved dropping her, André Wendelen, and Jacques van der Spiegle near Beauraing, a small town south-west of Liège. She was to act as their courier. It appears that André was a clever young Brussels lawyer who had joined SOE in 1940, went down the Comète line himself, and this was his third drop into Belgium. Jacques was the wireless operator. In Michael Foot's *SOE in the Low Countries*, he said that their mission was to locate Prince Charles, King Leopold's brother, and bring him back to England.

However, Elaine's personnel file in the National Archives tells a very different story. Lieven Saerens of the CEGES/SOMA website told me that, according to her extensive dossier on the Belgian State Security, Elaine was born in Poperingen on 7 May 1923 to an English father, Harold Madden, and a Belgian mother, Caroline Duponselle. After attending the British Memorial School in Ypres, and following the invasion of Belgium on 10 May 1940, she dressed up as a soldier and was evacuated to England at Dunkirk. Arriving on 1 June 1940, she continued her studies at St Ellen's College, London, taking up a profession as a 'comptable steno-dactylo'. By March 1944, she was working for the Belgian State Security and had been recruited by the SOE.

Her personnel file in the National Archives sheds no light on her background. It is a report on her mission, codenamed IMOGEN. There was no mention of Elaine Madden, either. The name on the earliest forms, dated 8 May 1944, almost three months before she was dropped, was E. Meuus. This was probably Elaine Meuus, a codename used while she underwent SOE training. The name on the identity card she was to use in Belgium was Hélène Marie Maes, supposedly issued by the Belgian office in Nice. There were salary receipts and a residence permit for an apartment in Paris owned by a Mme Dervaux. Her papers told her that, before she left, she would be given a 'Gestapo-style' interrogation to discover whether her cover story had any weaknesses. Part of it was provided, which she had to learn off by heart:

At about noon on the 17th May 1940 after the first air-raid on Paperinghe [*sic*]

I walked down the Rue de l'Hopital with my aunt named Simone. There was considerable damage everywhere and the services responsible had not yet had time to clear away bodies that were scattered about in the streets. We hadn't walked 100 yards when we saw the head of a man lying in the gutter. Although gruesome it was a fascinating sight and one that neither of us will ever forget. We stopped for quite a few minutes and stared not being able to believe our eyes and then walked away feeling slightly sick and dazed. From there we went on up the Rue de l'Hopital and turned right down the road to the house another Aunt named Antoinette occupied. We stayed there until about 6 p.m. and made our way back home. The streets had been cleared by this time and there were no further incidents.[6]

She was told she would be provided with appropriate clothing and toiletries for the three months she would be in Belgium, and given whatever 'equipment' she thought suitable for her parachute jump and landing. Agents were normally offered a knife, revolver and a variety of pills, one being the 'L' pill. Details were provided for her return trip to England once her mission had been completed, and there were pages of coding that she had to master with the help of Captain Whittaker.

Annexe 'K' in her personnel file provided fascinating details of the coding system being used in the run-up to D-Day. On 31 May 1944, while she was at STS 35 (SOE code for one of their Special Training Schools in the grounds of Beaulieu, near Bournemouth), she met with a Captain Whittaker. He went through the codes she had to use when communicating with HQ from the field.

The cipher being used was Playfair Rimmer, with the keyword BAYSWATER. See if you're as bright as she was. The special arrangements included suppressing the letter 'Z', K = CH, X = EX, Y = IN and Z = EZ. Numbers one to ten were their equivalent letters in the alphabet. The 'dud' letter used for null was X. The security check in case she was compromised was to have twenty-one words in the first sentence. The code was to start at the first word in the third sentence. The interval between pregnant words had to be every fifth, and the code was to end at the last exclamation mark. Courtesy forms at the beginning and end were to be ignored, apostrophes and hyphens were both 1 and the specimen cage of a square was:

BAYSW
TERCD
FGHIJ
KLMNO
PQUVX

Having mastered that, in a document dated 27 July 1944, a week before her flight, she was provided with her codes. See whether you can get your head round them. She was informed that the prefix for all her incoming messages was 578 and, for her outgoing ones, 195. The T.15 check was that 1 and 2 were to be added on the 3rd and 4th and that 'E' would be used for dead letters. Annexe 'J' included her 'MENTAL ONE-TIME PAD PLUS MENTAL INDICATOR', with the remark that the substitution square letter was 'Y'.

A	SEQUESTERED	N	SAVETHE
B	FROM	O	SACRED
C	THIS	P	MONUMENTS
D	NOISY	Q	OVER
E	WORLD	R	WHICH
F	COULDI	S	THE
G	WEAR	T	WINGS
H	OUT	U	OF
I	THIS	V	CENTURIES
J	TRANSITORY	W	HAVE
K	BEINGIN	X	SILENTLY
L	PEACEFUL	Y	PASSED
M	CONTEMPLATION	Z	BY

A	CONTINUOUS	N	OTHER
B	POUNDING	O	ALLIED
C	OFENEMY	P	AIRCRAFT
D	TARGETS	Q	HAS
E	BY	R	SOFAR
F	LIBERATORS	S	PROVED
G	FORTRESSES	T	VERY
H	MOSQUITOES	U	SUCCESSFUL
I	MARAUDERS	V	MANY
J	THUNDERBOLTS	W	FACTORIES
K	MUSTANGS	X	HAVE
L	LIGHTNINGS	Y	BEEN
M	AND	Z	DESTROYED

POEM FOR MENTAL INDICATOR

A	RESISTANCE	N	SETBY
B	CONTINUES	O	THEIR
C	MEN	P	BRILLIANT

D	WORK	Q	AND
E	INDEPENDENTLY	R	COURAGEOUS
F	ORWITH	S	LEADERS
G	ORGANIZATIONS	T	PROPITIOUS
H	FOLLOWING	U	HEAVEN
I	THE	V	MUST
J	GREAT	W	SURELY
K	AND	X	SAVE
L	INSPIRING	Y	THESE
M	EXAMPLES	Z	HEROES

The code word she had to use with the above poem was WORLD. Her true check in every message was the fifth letter indicator chosen by the Mental Indicator System. Just in case she was transmitting under duress, she was given a bluff check which was, '7th letter of message increased by alphabetical equivalent of number of message gives 1st letter of 7th word'. The Mental Indicators were prefixed with the keyword WORLD.

NTRGP	IKFEO	ENTRE	HGRUE	FERCL
FOTSA	PHLMN	CDAPB	TASGI	TLSHD
SZUYC	FEWIR	TMIGN	DINPO	AFTVE
SOJIR	IENAG	HOTER	EABLS	XTSOU
LDFEN	SRTLO	PEOIN	IEODP	
WOLMU				
HILWN	ATONS	RENAS	POEQN	VIESU
IEHNR	FYIAE	UTRDS	UIEVT	BSTVA

Do you understand that? Good. The SOE advisers showed advanced planning and foresight. She was given an address in Basle for any 'innocent' letters she might want to write. In them she had refer to herself as Marie Antoinette, use one if 'the address was her safe house', two if 'the first has been cancelled, here is my new one', three for 'I am in my safe house, come and find me', and four for 'I am going to Nancy'. The signature she was to use was 'Barnabe'.

Letters concerning her return to England had to be sent to either an address in Seville or one in Lisbon. These had to be learned off by heart. Her password in Nancy was '*Je cherche le bougniat*', and the reply would be '*Vous voulez dire le marchaud de charbon*'. Once in Spain her name would be Miss Mary Townsend and, if she got out via Switzerland, she had to ask for Mr Bateman at the British embassy.

To be sure she understood the danger of her mission, she was informed that she would be paid as a third-class agent and, in the case of her death, her salary would continue being paid into her account for the next six months.

She was provided with 5,000 Belgian francs to carry on her person, but hidden in a box of talcum powder were a further 50,000 Belgian francs for her mission and 10,000 French francs for her return. The One-Time-Pad was hidden in her wallet, along with microfilms of questionnaires she had to encourage Belgian sympathisers to fill in. Six identity photographs were hidden in a secret pocket. Her valise and the wireless set to be used by 'Donalbain' (Jacques Van de Siegle), the wireless operator who would accompany her, were to be dropped with them when they parachuted in.

The date of her flight, presumably from Tempsford, was not specified in her file but she was told it would be one night during the moon period between 30 July and 12 August 1944. Records suggest it was on the night of 3/4 August. Documents in her file, dated 22 November 1944, six weeks after the Allies invaded Belgium, showed that she made a perfect landing at 0130 hours, seven and a half kilometres south-south-east of d'Houyet, and three and a half kilometres north-east of Pondrome, and rendezvoused as instructed at 'Ferme du Fisique' without any mishap. It was situated on the crossroads of two farm tracks on the edge of Chy Wood. The password she had to use was, '*Je viens chercher le kilo de Café emballé dans la serviette et apporter de quoi faire use nouvelle bride pour l'etalon*'. She was told that 'Tybalt' (one of André's codenames) had already left the coffee with the farmer, and warned that she didn't have to take the train to Martouz-in-Neuville: '*Le chef de gare est Rexiste et dangereux.*'

'Donalbain was to be known in Belgium as 'Foxtrot'. Elaine's codename in Belgium was to be 'Alice', and her 'Chef de Mission' was codenamed 'Brabantio' (André), but known in Belgium as 'Odette'. The password she had to use with him was '*Je viens chercher Mlle Olive Chartres*' and the response had to be '*Vous voulez dire la cousine de Georges*'. In case additional proof of her identity was needed, she was told that a personal message, '*Nous irons cueillir les murons*', would be broadcast at 1915 hours on Radio Belgium for the first three days after her arrival and repeated on the twelfth.

'Odette' was to put her in contact with 'Huguette', another SOE agent who had been parachuted into Belgium in May 1944, to co-ordinate sabotage of the railway network. Philippe Connart told me that 'Huguette' was twenty-nine-year-old Baron Jules Rolin, an artillery reserve officer also known as 'Messala' and 'Ridder'.

Following the D-Day landings in Normandy in June, the next targets for the Allies were the capture of Paris and the liberation of Belgium.

This gave Elaine's mission a particular importance but also imposed strict limits on it. What she was warned about was the need for strict discipline. Her briefing notes told her:

1. You are going to find yourself amongst people who have resisted magnificently an unprecedented oppression. This will make you ask yourself some questions, to suggest potential contacts, to offer you some actions that haven't been foreseen in your mission. It is an exceptionally dangerous situation, one in which you must not put yourself at any risk. The essential condition amongst all these operations is security and everyone must accomplish their tasks to the best of their ability.

2. You have to avoid engaging the Belgian government or the British authorities in the field of politics. Every initiative in this mission has the possibility of creating a dangerous confusion in the actions and plans of the War Cabinet.

3. The duty of ambassadors like you is to be especially focussed on quiet reserve and to use the utmost discretion as an observer, concerned with your own mission and its planning. Knowledge of both the British and Belgian points of view needs to be at its heart.

Her plan of action, included in Annexe I of her personnel file, was to follow SHAEF's (Supreme Headquarters Allied Expeditionary Force) aims and objectives. The first was to slow down the arrival of enemy troops before they could engage the invasion forces, in particular their artillery units, tanks and armoured cars. The second was to slow down the placement of reinforcements in areas near the Allies' bridgeheads. The third was to hinder German aerial attacks on Allied troops. The fourth was to hinder river transport, and the last was to transmit back to London all information about military matters, no matter how great or small.

She was instructed to inform Huguette, SOE's main organiser, who would execute SHAEF's orders. As his courier, she would be the go-between for him, SHAEF, and the different Resistance groups. To pass on messages, she had to use Huguette's existing contacts. Any personal contact she might have with the chiefs of the Resistance groups had to be kept to an absolute minimum. Her security was not to be put in danger. The individuality of the Resistance groups had to be respected and, where possible, they were to be given autonomy in carrying out appropriate action.

The principal groups Elaine was told she would be working with were the *Front de l'Indépendance*, Group G, Group Nola, and the *Mouvement National Belge*. In the section headed GENERAL NOTES, she was told that the group targeting the railways had to immobilise rail transport. Another had to cut all telephone communications by bringing down pylons, cutting telephone cables, and attacking Brussels' central telephone exchange.

She had to insist that none of the groups had overall control of discipline. Their orders had to come through SHAEF, which included targets for sabotage.

The Allied Command wishes concentrated coordinated attacks to be made on the following types of target when special Action Signals are given:

Railways: Action against the railways will consist of:

a) The elimination of key enemy personnel brought from Germany to control military transport by rail.

b) The destruction of railway lines by the use of explosives or, if sufficient time and personnel are available, by the removal of lengths of rail.

c) The destruction of breakdown trains.

d) The interruption and disorganisation of railway telephone and signals systems by the cutting of lines, destruction of cabins, etc.

e) Destruction of railway turntables.

f) Light destruction of the railway watering system, e.g. by cutting of mains.

General Note: Complicated or heavy installations which would require more than a week to repair should not be destroyed, but should be sabotaged by having their essential parts removed. These parts should be kept carefully and placed at the disposal of the Allied Forces on their arrival. It should be born in mind that as a general rule the continuity of railway dislocation must depend on the repetition of the derailments and light sabotage, rather than on massive destruction.

1. Enemy Road Movements. It is certain that the enemy will use the roads for the massive transport of troops and equipment when invasion takes place. Every effort should be made to sabotage such movements, e.g. by improvised road blocks; displacement of traffic signs; setting of booby traps; placing of small mines. Such action should be entirely clandestine, and no risk should be taken of being involved in pitched battles with enemy effectives.

2. Telecommunications. The cutting of telephone and telegraph lines and cables (preferably undetectably) and the removal and safe-keeping of essential parts of such installations. Installations of this kind, even in cases whether have been requisitioned by the enemy, are not to be destroyed but only lightly sabotaged.

3. Waterways. Dislocation of communications by inland waterways, e.g. by the destruction of lock gates; and by the sabotage of enemy munitions shipments.

4. Air Targets. Sabotage of enemy aircraft; airfield installations; light repair plant and aviation fuel dumps, particularly in the area between Courtrai/Ghent and the coast. Enemy flying personnel should be sniped where occasion presents itself, without the risk of becoming engaged in a stand-up fight with the enemy.

Note: The procedure regarding action signals is known to NELLY and

HUGUETTE.

Action signals were the coded instructions to the Resistance to commence their planned activities. They were to be broadcast by the BBC in their *messages personelles* after the 1900 hours Belgian news. All the information she collected had to be forwarded to London, taking into account the fact that the expression 'large bodies of troops' meant units of approximately 500 men or more, and included concentrations which couldn't easily be seen from the air, e.g. bivouacs in woods. Exact grid references would be essential. Field post numbers or the divisional signs on vehicles had to be provided. Wireless aerials and despatch rider activity often indicated the presence of a headquarters, which could then be identified by its pennants or painted signs. Any information about petrol and ammunition dumps would be particularly important, as would any information about rockets, flying bombs and other secret weapons. It was urged that her reports had always to include:

a) The date and time of observation, as opposed to the time at which the source may have originated the telegram. It must be clear whether zone time (G.M.T.) or local time is being used.

b) A description of the place in sufficient detail to enable it to be pinpointed, in the case of static targets, with a six-figure map reference if possible.

In addition, reports should show whether the originator is himself the source; if the report has been received from a third party, the latter's identity or reliability should be stated.

These instructions do not affect the original proviso that there is no onus on any agent to send information and that he must never allow the despatch of information to jeopardise his other activities or his security. Nor should vague deductions be made, though reliable indications of future moves and negative information are of value.

The questionnaire she was provided microfilm copies of was particularly interesting, revealing not only the extent of the Allies' existing knowledge of Germany's latest weaponry, but also their very serious concerns about its use.

1.   Information is required as to the methods at present in use for transporting component parts of the flying bombs, its launching trolley, and the materials used for fuelling the bomb and providing rocket propulsion, to the depots where it is stored prior to use.

2.   The bomb may be transported in one piece (without planes), in which case the length would be 22 ft. and the diameter about 3 ft. alternatively the war-head may be transported separately; it is a truncated cone of length 47 ins.,

minimum diameter 28 ins., and maximum diameter 33 ins. The forward end is rounded and the base hollow.

It is required to know if the above parts can be identified as travelling by road or rail, if they are completely crated or merely protected by a skeleton crate, how they are guarded, and if there is any possibility of access during a halt or during marshalling.

3.   The launching trolley with the rocket propulsion unit may be transported separately by road or rail.

We want complete details of the trolley, and if possible, a sketch or photograph.

4.   At some time prior to launching, the bomb is fuelled with petrol and the rocket propulsion unit on the trolley is filled with hydrogen peroxide.

Where is this done? Probably one filling station serves a number of launching sites.

5.   An important constituent of the rocket propulsion fuel is almost certainly hydrogen peroxide. This is stored in 2500 gallon aluminium tanks, which may be above or below ground. The storage tanks are supplied by road or rail. Rail transport may be either (i) by large aluminium tank wagons (length of wagon 60 ft.; tank diameter 8 ft. 6 ins.; tank length 30 ft.) or (ii) by a number (12/14) of small aluminium tanks 4 ft. in diameter and 4 ½ to 5 ft. high, arranged in close contact in a double row.

Is there any evidence of road transport? This may be in carboys of 13 gallons capacity.

In the case of rail transport, we wish to know if there is a wooden floor or other woodwork in the tank wagon construction.

Is there any opportunity of access to the wagons at sidings or marshalling yards?

Is there any opportunity of attacking the wagons by rifle or mortar fire from a distance of say 100 yards?

6.   If any depots, assembly or filling points are located, we want to know what kind of road transport is allowed to enter them.

Are any foreign workers allowed to enter?

Are lorries subjected to careful inspection at the entrance?

Is it possible to approach to say within 100 yards of the boundary fence after dark?

Are there any trees or other means of concealment in the vicinity?

How successful operation IMOGEN was is uncertain. We have to presume she managed to pass on SHAEF's directives to the right contacts, who acted on them appropriately. The only indication was a couple of paragraphs in her file:

There was no time to work on my personal mission owing to the fact that I was 'Courier' for Odette. The majority of the time I didn't know which mission I was working for, but information could be obtained from Odette's report. I travelled considerably in the Ardennes, carrying messages, transmitting sets and bringing the revolvers back to Brussels. I was put in contact with Huguette and did some 'courier' for him. Apart from that, I was in charge of the 'service de protection' for Foxtrot and recruited three people to help us. Two were permanent staff and third part-time. I was part of the 'service de protection' on every occasion and usually transported the soul myself to the house elected. The finding of safe houses was also left to me. I never had any trouble of any kind, except once when I was followed for several hours by a suspicious looking character. I managed to shake him off by taking various trams and wandering around the town. This happened after I had been to rendezvous with C. Lapoivre (operational name unknown).

Help and assistance were given by Mlle Denise Leplat, 19 rue de Anges, Liège and Jean Smets (address unknown) who worked full-time as 'service de protection'. Also Anton Smets who worked part-time. The two sisters Lucy and Jeanne Rouffignon, rue Chants d'Oiseaux, Bruxelles, also helped considerably by letting us transmit from their house and in helping me find other houses to transmit from.

Foot's mention of Elaine being involved in the rescue of Prince Charles was hinted at in an interview she gave after the war in *Histoires*, a documentary on Canvas, one of Belgium's two public TV channels. According to Foot, the prince was on the run from the Gestapo and plagued with sciatica. Unable to travel easily, he had had been in hiding in Sart-Lez-Spa.

My *chef de mission* said that I was to come to Ciney (south-east of Namur) and look after this important gentleman. I met him [there], I thought he was very charming. We used to talk, play ping pong together, we used to go walking in the woods. And once we were away from other people, he would speak to me in English. His English was fluent and we had a lot of fun ... He used to question me about London, and London during the wartime, and what was happening ... I thought he was somebody in the resistance who was very important. So, I was his liaison between London and here, I used to code and decode messages. And we were trying to find a small landing ground so the Lysander could come and fetch him. Because the idea was that we wanted to get him to England ... When eventually we did find a landing ground (Sovet) ... it was already so late in the war. The Allies were arriving so quickly after Normandy, that he decided he didn't want to leave because it was too late. That he wouldn't have time to get out of the plane in London, before getting into another plane back to Belgium. So the mission was dropped.

Additional information was provided by Philippe Connart, who said that Elaine hid in the castle of Walter de Sélys-Longchamp in Halloy, near Ciney. He was an important figure in Group G. Also staying with them was a 'Monsieur Jules Bernard', an English-speaking gentleman who had been educated at Eton and Dartmouth. He was in hiding from the Germans and was being helped by Baron Robert Goffinet, who once gave a golden guinea to James Cromar, and a few other Comète evaders. Mr Bernard should have been picked up by Lysander from a small private airfield, but the mission was aborted.

When the Prince Regent gave Elaine an award after the war, she only then realised that he was the Prince of Flanders.

Olga Jackson

Searching for information on Olga Jackson, I found an intriguing snippet on the Adam Matthew Publications website's section on SOE's operations in Western Europe:

> EMELIA. Belgium, August 1944, Mrs Olga Jackson, field name Babette, independent propaganda mission for undermining of morale in Brussels, Ghent, Liege, Antwerp, Charleroi; organisation of prostitution circuit aimed at German officers.[7]

Olga's personnel file in the National Archives contains a fascinating story, worth detailing as it shows what other kinds of political intrigues were thought up by the SOE. On the night of 4 August, the same day Elaine was dropped, she too was parachuted into Belgium. Whether they knew each other in Belgium, had trained together at Wanborough and Arisaig, got their parachute wings at Ringway, and attended the Beaulieu 'finishing school' remains unknown. She was born on 6 January 1909, was called Olga Thioux and was a British citizen. Her personnel file mentions nothing of her early life.

For whatever reason, she jumped before her luggage and two companions. Their intended drop zone was supposed to be thirteen and a half kilometres north of Hals, near Ledeberg. Instead, she landed about three kilometres from Pamel, a small village between Ninove and Brussels, and couldn't make contact with the others, two agents, 'Eugénie' and 'Yvonne'. Whether they really were women and whether those were their real names is unknown. The only other reference to them in Olga's file was their mission names, MENAS and CIMBER. Eugénie's MENAS mission was to contact Samoyède II, Freddy Veldekens's propaganda mission, for pre- and post-liberation work, and jamming German wireless installations with the aim of helping the Allies after D-Day in the use of the press, cinema, and radio. She, if Eugénie was female, also had to contact STENTOR. Who or what STENTOR was has yet to come to light. Yvonne's CIMBER mission, if she was female, involved the transmission of microfiche messages.

After hiding her parachute in some bushes, Olga made her way to the capital. With the help of someone she met on the road who was convinced she was a black marketeer, she avoided the checkpoint and arrived at 0700 at her safe house, the home of Madame and Monsieur René de Pot, the Police Brigadier. When she showed him her identity papers he was suspicious, but a personal message following the BBC news convinced him of her credentials. With the help of one of his friends he got her better identity cards, but as this friend was arrested the following day, she had to be quickly provided with others, just in case he talked. Arrangements were made for her to meet M. Schakewitz, the Joint Police Commissioner and Chief Inspector of Police, who listened with interest to her plans. Although he didn't show much enthusiasm for her enterprise, he promised to help. There was no mention of her being reunited with her luggage or companions.

She then went to Liège and met Frans Banneux. Whether he was another police official, government or Resistance member isn't clear, but she made arrangements with him for her safe house in case the Germans found out what she was up to. What else she did while in Liège is not recorded. When she returned to Brussels three days later, she had another meeting with the Chief Inspector and insisted she be introduced to Monsieur Delecourt, the King's Public Prosecutor. While she was waiting, he introduced her to Monsieur de Lobel, the Chief Bailiff, who agreed to help her. He allocated a room in M. Jungelaus' Brussels office and allocated two women to assist her in collecting information on the private and public lives of important German figures stationed in Belgium. Over time they compiled a list which included

General von Falkenhausen Alexander, Dr. Reeder President Eggert, von Harbou Obest. Von Schon, von Graushaar General, Dr Bayer, Bennewitz Hauptbannfuhrer, von Hammerstein Freiherr Lieutenant-General, Dr. Schulze Adolf, Landesgruppenleiter, Dr. Gentzke, von Clear General, Dr. Busch, Gayler, Angelmann Lieutenant-Colonel, Bruns Major General, von Werder, Dr. Mallia, Schmidt, Dr. Griesbauer, Feldberg, Schindlmayer and Moskopf.

The 'independent propaganda' she was involved with was 'to complement the campaign already being waged by the Mandrill organisation'. This was a Political Intelligence Department mission sent into Belgium in 1943 to liaise with the existing CORDIER mission to demoralise support for the Germans and co-ordinate the reception of propaganda in Lille, Liège, and Ghent. Olga's work, it was stressed, was 'in no way connected with espionage and it must be clearly understood that your task is not the collection of military information. By doing so you would be liable not only to jeopardise your own security but also the success of the mission itself'.

The mission included finding every opportunity to tell people of the imminent arrival of the Allies, of their impending liberation and release from the yoke of German oppression. The members of the Belgian Resistance had to be told to wait until they were given instructions by the Allies' High Command. Olga had to recruit and instruct responsible people to help with her work of disseminating rumours and lies about the enemy and about an imminent Allied landing. This included setting up a radio listening centre, typing false stories to be leaked to the media, and narrating them to people she met. Her list of people to meet included those dealing with news broadcasts, editors, radio announcers, technicians and Morse operators. She had instructions as to what action the civilian population had to take following the Allies' arrival, in particular technicians in the gas, electricity, water, rubbish, railway, tramway, and telecommunication industries as well as factory workers, road workers, dockers, mechanics, and miners.

She had to disseminate supposedly police-generated information about the Allies' plans, their estimated troop numbers, predictions of their movements, military equipment, weapons, food stocks, etc. Where possible she, and those supporting her, had to cause delays and obstruct collaboration with the Germans, undermining their and their collaborators' positions by spreading malicious rumours about conflicts between them, denunciations and recriminations, and what those on the side of the Allies might do to them. Detailed notes had to be made of the preparations the Germans were making for the invasion, what demolition work they were undertaking and their troop movements so as to supply it to the Allies when they arrived. Attempts had to be made to warn the Allies as to the Germans' eventual retreat and to try to ensure that Allied supplies were spread over a wide area.

Another task was to undermine the morale of the German troops, to depress them and make them nervous by spreading stories that parts of Germany were being overrun by Allied troops, that German villages were being bombed, and how other German soldiers stationed in Belgium were becoming irritated and exasperated by what they saw as indiscipline.

According to Olga's instructions, she had to find an organiser in Brussels, Liége, Anvers, Ghent, Namur, and Charleroi and provide them with a list of generally high-ranking German military or administrative officials to 'attack'.

It will be necessary to establish the identity of the Belgian and other non-German mistresses kept by German officers and officials and then to determine how many of them can be utilised either because they are good patriots or for other reasons. Those selected should, through suitable outlets, be approached. Tactics at this point will depend entirely upon the type of individual concerned but in order to obtain their co-operation it will not be necessary to use financial or other material inducements. The women thus to be approached will fall roughly into two categories:

(i) those who have a genuine personal affection for their German masters,

(ii) those who from force of circumstances or otherwise find it easier thus to earn their living and whose personal feelings are not to any extent involved.

As regards (i) these may be the most difficult to enlist but having once convinced them good results should be obtained. It may not be necessary to take this category into your confidence provided they are convinced that defeat for Germany means added danger for their protector unless he covers himself. The line to be taken is that they will clearly wish to do the best for their 'friends'. Whether or not an appeal should be made to their patriotism must be left to the consideration of the person contacting them. The '*amie*' must first be thoroughly convinced that Germany has lost the war and her thoughts must be directed to what is to become of her 'friend'. This thought she must discreetly sow in the mind of the officer or official himself, thus inducing him to defer a decision for a few weeks or months? And if he is not killed on one of the fronts what will he find when he gets home, after most of the others? Or will he, realising how things are going, take steps to see that he at least gets back to Germany alive. What is happening to his family with all the foreign workers at home? Who is to protect them if there is an armed uprising in Germany. How is he viewed by his men and the Belgians? Will the latter give him a good character or is he a 'war criminal'? Other German officers are already taking steps for their own protection and the higher the rank the more active has been the urge to anticipate the future.

The subject must be introduced discreetly and not exaggerated and progress judged in the light of the 'protector's' reactions. If it is clear that he has already been thinking along such lines himself, progress can be more rapid. If however, it is patent that the subject cannot be seduced from his duty by such means then he should be induced to exaggerate any weaknesses he may possess, drinking, general self-indulgence, laziness, gambling.

With younger officers, particularly if they are of an adventurous type, it will be necessary to adopt different tactics.

They should be shown that their authority is nearly over and the 'good times' that went with it. They should be encouraged in any vices they may have and led to excesses in self-indulgence. They should similarly be encouraged to neglect their duties and finally if so inclined to desert altogether to some occupation in which there is a future.

It may be desirable to offer financial assistance to this class of woman, though it should not be on a lavish scale.[8]

Ideally, Olga had to recruit loyal and dependable proprietors or tenants of brothels who would pass on instructions to the women employed there. No attempt was to be made to contact German-run brothels, though non-German women employed there could be approached. They didn't have to give their clients any grounds for reprisals but had to ask seemingly innocent questions. Among the tactics suggested was to regretfully emphasise the level of Germany's moral and political decline, the decadence and ruin that menaced it, and the dark future that it faced if the war continued. They had to underline the regret that Germany was committing treason by allying the white race with the yellow peril. During British and American bombing raids, they had to show intense fear and express awe at what potential they had. They were encouraged to spread stories about the enormous damage being done by the bombing in Germany, ask whether a miracle was possible that would stop the progressive destruction of the entire country and enquire how many years they would have to endure. They had to sympathetically ask about the men's wives and families, whether they were evacuees or requisitioned for compulsory labour. They had to show fear about epidemics, venereal disease, and other ailments which were ravaging the country, frequently ask for explanations, and whether it was true that a typhoid epidemic had broken out in a distant region. It was suggested they spread the slogan '*Schluss*' (The End) around, ask what the significance of the griffon was on all the walls and in the toilets, and spread the story of a new flu epidemic coming from the East. They had to remind the Germans of the Spanish flu epidemic after the Great War, which killed about 18 million people, and express doubt whether there was sufficient medicine, clothes and food. They were to reinforce the natural feeling of envy about the number of government members and high officials who had left the country and were living in comfort and safety after having enriched themselves. They had to emphasise the laziness caused by five years of war, ten years of mobilisation, the long hours of work and the difficult living conditions. They had to accentuate the bad feeling there was about fewer imports and the voluntary reductions people were expected to accept. They had to deplore the inevitable hypocrisy caused by such grievances, especially when many of those who were suffering could see important Germans living a good life.

> To incite or assist a German officer to desert requires very careful planning and the seed must be planted very carefully and nourished without apparent intention. However, when an officer has demonstrated his considered intention to desert help should be given him. He will require two essentials, first civilian clothes and second a temporary hide out. Suitable addresses should be given to him and in both cases he should be required to pay for them.

One has to presume that Olga was involved in such arrangements as well as arranging the writing and sending of anonymous letters to officers' wives. These, she was recommended, had to be written on the type of paper that could then be obtained at any stationer's, to have no address and be posted from one of the central post offices. Her advice was that they

> should not normally be written in a threatening vein but rather in the guise of a well-wisher or friend warning her of the misfortune which will befall her or the treatment planned for Germans and their wives. Reference should also be made to the risks run by her husband, of the necessity of his securing employment after the German army had been defeated.

There was also advice on how she could use vice to target those already known to have 'vicious habits, those susceptible to acquire them or those suffering from diseases rendering them particularly susceptible to demoralisation'. The aim was to lower their efficiency and encourage them to neglect their duties. The information in the section on drugs mentioned that drug traffickers who had been arrested in Brussels had been selling opium with a street value of 60,000 francs a kilo. To put this in perspective, Olga was provided with 15,000 francs a month for spending, 10,000 for accommodation, 15,000 for clothes and 3,500 for postage. The opium had been grown in countries which had developed by increasing their production of oil from poppies. It would only be possible for Olga or her contacts to find out who the drug users were through loyal officers, and they would only be able to get hold of drugs via theft from military pharmacies or drug dealers. It was extremely difficult to get hold of products such as cocaine, heroin, and morphine because they had almost disappeared from the marketplace. Offering such 'merchandise' to serious Germans had to be avoided because they would almost certainly inform their superiors, who would make enquiries as to where they had come from. Importantly, they hadn't to let them fall into the hands of the Belgians. The only places where drugs should be on sale were night clubs or other places specialising in such trade. Some individuals, such as pimps, could be supplied with drugs, as long as they would be able to resell them and make a reasonable profit. However, if drugs were offered to the wrong people, they would immediately believe it was 'a truly shocking and dangerous business'.

Doctors, Private V. D. Specialists and Clinics

The co-operation of those of the above known to be patronised by German officers and officials, should be sought. The patient who suffers or believes himself to suffer from V.D. is particularly liable to be demoralised and the object here is to induce doctors to play up to this weakness to the ultimate demoralisation of the subject. Some difficulty may be anticipated as the more serious members of the medical profession are unlikely on moral grounds to co-operate but on the other hand this field covers a number of quacks and near-quacks to whom the same considerations would not supply.

Officers, Olga was told, took great pleasure in drinking alcohol and often broke the rules and paid a lot of money to get hold of it. Drinking spirits that had been fortified was on the increase, but there were cases of adulterated and dangerous spirits. To further the Allies' aims, Olga was encouraged to get hold of spirits of doubtful origin. If they could be supplied only to the Germans it would be perfect, but it was acknowledged that unfortunately that wouldn't be the case.

As regards jealousy, Olga and her contacts were to target those Germans with wives or girlfriends, telling them that the massive increase in foreign workers in Germany was creating a special situation. Olga would be provided with pamphlets and leaflets and given suggested graffiti, conversations, and rumours to get the attention of German soldiers. There weren't very many men left in Germany and those who remained were too old, too young, wounded, or infirm, and had their own wives. It had been a long time for their wives, sisters, and daughters to have been left alone, especially now that there were formidable numbers of foreign men working in Germany, men who had been sent because they were fit and healthy, the very great majority of whom '*sont originaires de races aux facultés beaucoup plus amoureuses que celle des Allemands (Italians, Français, Belges, etc.)*'. The nervousness caused by Allied bombing and the privations experienced must '*relâcher les consciences*'.

CINEMAS, THEATRES, ETC.

It is anticipated that however willing the managers and proprietors of such establishments may be to co-operate the limit within which they will be able to will be very narrow.

Cinema managers will have very little scope in their choice of films, but where they are able to do so they should present those stressing the pleasures of peace and the horror of bombing (civilian populations, enemy); films implying the ultimate liberation of the occupied countries and the return to normal occupation of the inhabitants.

As regard theatres the situation is more difficult. Where possible plays, operas, etc., in which liberation or democratic themes appear should be presented. Tunes, songs, etc., which are identified with similar sentiments should be chosen.

Last war songs, Tipperary, Pack up your Troubles, Over There (?) Décor should be so displayed as fortuitously to represent the Allied and national colours –

without risk of reprisals – reminding the enemy of approaching defeat.

There were instructions on different types of rumours to be spread among the Germans, and the list of those who might help included traffickers and fraudsters, railway employees, waiters in cafés, hairdressers, priests, doctors, members of the Resistance, sales representatives, gossips, people in queues, and a group described as *les filles de vie*.

> The fact is that this kind of woman is frequently in contact with Germans. That they often speak of what's going on in the war is doubtful as it wouldn't be commercial. Moreover, night clubs etc., are frequently under German police surveillance. It's inevitable that with women, and particularly with these kinds of women – many soldiers let themselves go and confide in them. They think of them a bit like comforters. Although many of these women are very patriotic, it is only with great difficulty possible to envisage them being of use. And yet, if a rumour is convincingly presented it will be passed from one Belgian or another who visits these places before the beginning of the evening. In offering a glass (not two, or there'll be financial interest and risks of exaggerated dependency), he will be able to appear the 'Man in the know' and secretly to take these women into his confidence.

There was plenty of money to finance the EMELIA mission. Before leaving England, Olga had been supplied with 248,500 Belgian francs in 100 franc notes, presumably in a money belt. Two 1,000 French franc notes, 100 Spanish peseta notes, and 4,075 US dollars in mixed notes were hidden in a box of talc to be used on her way back to England three months later. A letter, photograph, and two coins were hidden in her nail brush. There were also details of passwords and replies for her rendezvous, including those needed in Spain and Portugal.

Her file refers to her throughout as 'Jenicot', but she had several other cover names. As she had no wireless operator, she had to sign letters to SOE post boxes in Barcelona and Lisbon as 'Zoe'. When she escaped through Spain, she was to be known as 'Irene Thompson'.

In Foot's *SOE in the Low Countries*, he referred to 'Mrs Jackson' but made no mention of prostitution. According to his research, she was born Belgian, had married an English husband and had lived in England since 1935.

> She had a strong, self-confident, humorous personality, and was a junior FANY officer. She joined SOE in March 1944, and was dropped into Belgium on 4/5 August, with an odd mission: though she spoke not a word of German, her task was to introduce herself to as many senior German staff officers as she could, and proceed to rot their morale by explaining to them that Germany had already

lost the war. In the few weeks that turned out to be available to her, she set about her task with such considerable aplomb that she was mentioned in dispatches for courage and enterprise; concrete results were necessarily slight.

Frédérique Dupuich

My research has revealed that another woman agent was Lysandered into Belgium the day after Olga Jackson. Her name was Frédérique Dupuich. There has been no mention of her in any SOE literature. Details of Frédérique's early life have yet to come to light. Born in 1900, she was an English girl, known to some as Miss Richards. During the 1930s, she worked as a company secretary in Brussels but, four months after the German invasion, decided to join the Belgian underground movement. What work she did for them is unknown, but in July the following year, when one of her friends in the Resistance was betrayed to the Germans, she decided to get out. Being interned for the duration of the war was not what she wanted. The Comète escape line had been in operation for some time so, along with ten other Belgians, she was accompanied by Andrée de Jongh, known as 'Dédée'.

> Once they reached the small town of La Corbie near Amiens, on the banks of the River Somme, which formed a line known as Zone Interdite or Prohibited Zone, they had to find a way of crossing the Somme, without being detected, as it was regularly patrolled by the enemy. Most of the men and Miss Richards couldn't swim and therefore, the inner tube of a large tyre was used with Andrée having to make several return trips pushing them across before they could rest and sleep in the farmhouse of a woman named Nenette in the village of Hamelet on the opposite side of the Somme. 'Next time,' Andrée thought, 'we will need the use of a boat.' The following morning the party made their way to Paris and then by the overnight train to Biarritz and the home of Madame Elvire De Greef. A Basque guide was then employed to guide them over the Pyrénées, and to the Spanish side of the border, where they were left to make their own way to San Sebastian. The journey had been a success, or so it was thought until Andrée and Arnold returned to Anglet and learnt that their party had been arrested in Spain and taken back to the border and handed over to the Germans. 'Next time,' Andrée said, 'evaders must be taken direct to the British Consulate in Bilbao.'[9]

According to Frédérique's obituary in the *Dorset Evening Echo*, the soldiers who were taking her to the authorities for questioning stopped at a café where Frédérique was able to slip a note, addressed to the Belgian consul, to the café proprietor. She thought it was his intervention that allowed her out of Miranda Prison after ten days in captivity. From there she made her way to Tangier, where her sister lived, and then managed to get across to Gibraltar.

She reached England in October 1941 and quickly gained employment as the section head of the London-based Political Warfare and Propaganda Department of the Belgium Sürète de l'Etat. There she must have met Airey Neave, the SIS intelligence officer who, in his *Little Cyclone*, described her as 'the plump lady with the panama hat'. Prior to her mission she undertook training, and her commandant's report stated that 'Miss Dewaay', her codename at 'finishing school', was

> well and widely educated, is intelligent and has plenty of practical ability. She is observant and learns quickly and possesses plenty of presence of mind and has imagination.
>
> She is keen and worked hard, displaying good initiative. Her character is strong. She is determined, steady and reliable, but at the same time modest and unassuming.
>
> Her personality is pleasant, she is a good mixer with considerable charm of manner, tact and sociability. She should inspire confidence and is generally liked.
>
> She has good powers of leadership and should do well in any position of trust and responsibility.[10]

In 1944, she volunteered for an important mission in occupied France. Exactly what it entailed has yet to come to light. On 6 August she was said to have been flown in a light plane, thought to have been a Lysander, to France. The records of 138 and 161 Squadrons do not mention specifically the dropping of a female agent. As her name didn't appear in any of the SOE literature, it is possible she was an SIS agent. She spent weeks working in a region where the Germans were harassing the French Maquis. Her work was considered very valuable as, according to her obituary,

> After crossing the lines to find the American 9th Army in Brittany, she returned to England and later enrolled in the First Aid Nursing Yeomanry. She served with them in South East Asia, India, Malaya, Sumatra and Hong Kong.
>
> Miss Dupuich's exploits earned her the King's Medal for Courage, which was presented to her at the War Office by General Montgomery, the *Croix de Guerre avec Palme*, the *Chevalier de l'ordre de Leopold II* for exceptional service rendered to her country, the *Croix des Evades*, the Resistance Medal, the General Service Medal with clasp and the France and Germany campaign medals.

She had been a much-appreciated intelligence officer at PWE (Political Warfare Executive). By January 1944, she had been trained and fully briefed for a mission but, for whatever reason, it was aborted. When she finally went in, she was the head of an important liaison mission, was captured and imprisoned by both the French Resistance and the French authorities, but managed to survive their interrogations. Even at forty-four, she never ceased from trying to reach Paris, eventually crossing the front line at night on her own.

Missions of a Sensitive Nature

Given the sensitive nature of the aforementioned operations of Olga Jackson, understandably very little has emerged in SOE literature. There's evidence that both the OSS and the SIS employed women to seduce their way to obtaining information vital to the Allies' cause. Wilfred Deac tells the story of Amy Pack (née Thorpe), codenamed 'Cynthia', who worked for the SIS.[11] Having charmed naval codes from the Italians, Betty was sent to Washington, where she had an affair with Brousse, a married official at the French embassy. With his connivance, she managed to unlock the safe holding two French code books, and arrange for them to be photographed and returned without the military attaché knowing. The precious ciphers were sent to London within 48 hours of the theft and were used before and during the Allies' invasion of North Africa.

It is acknowledged that lots of valuable information was obtained from German-frequented brothels. Claudia Pulver, the Viennese dressmaker who created suitable attires for female agents, admitted that:

> We also had quite a lot of prostitutes from the brothels of Paris coming in. We made appropriate underwear, very provocative, whatever they needed. They were very important to whoever was in control of them because their clients were a lot of German officers and they got quite a lot of information out of them. They were the ones that came backwards and forwards more often than others, because I think possibly they had to bring their information back personally. We had one who came backwards and forwards ten or twelve times and survived, only to die of a botched abortion after the war, which was quite sad.[12]

As these women were not official SOE agents, it's possible that Hugh Verity and Freddie Clark did not find them in 161 and 138 Squadrons' records. Might they have been sent in by SIS? Such activities are neither confirmed nor denied.

Verity mentions a *fille de joie* in his autobiography but does not indicate whether she was infiltrated or exfiltrated. Numerous surnames with initial letters appear in the appendices of their books, and any number of the names could have belonged to women.

Hugh Davies, an SOE enthusiast, has lectured on the subject of Fifi, the nickname of Noreen Riols, a young lady employed by the SOE to seduce men while they were at Beaulieu. She had joined the Wrens aged seventeen rather than work in a munitions factory, saying that she would look really smart in their lovely hats. Being fluent in French, having studied at the Lycée in London, she was transferred to the SOE in 1941 and sent to Beaulieu to work as a secretary and driver. In an article in the *Daily Mail* about 'Churchill's Secret Spy School', the elderly Noreen reflected that 'Security was very, very tight. It was like being in a very enclosed family ... I knew I had to keep my mouth shut and not ask questions. My mother thought I was working for the Ministry of Agriculture and Fisheries'. Later, she was required to use her seduction techniques to test how easy it was to get information out of the agents. One strategy was for the target to be invited out for a meal in a hotel in Bournemouth by a businessman who brought his secretary along. During the meal the guest was plied with drink until the host excused himself to make a phone call, came back, apologised profusely and said he had to leave. He told his guest to stay and enjoy the rest of the meal, put his room key on the table and money to pay for the bill, and insisted they enjoy the rest of the evening together.

> 'Then it was up to me,' says Noreen. 'The hotel had a balcony overlooking the sea, and if I could get the man out there on a moonlit night that always helped.' In most cases, she insists, the agents didn't talk. 'But if they were very young and far from their country and their families, they might,' she says. If they did, Noreen had to report it.

In David Stafford's *Secret Agent*, he said all the secretaries seemed to know about 'Fifi', the ultimate *agent provocatrice*, gorgeous, enticing and who 'went all the way' (at least for the male trainees). What temptations, if any, were provided for female agents remains a mystery.

Pattinson commented that FANYs were encouraged by the SOE to test the male agents at Wanborough, particularly after they had been plied with drink. There was no distinction in gender in the surveillance of students' alcohol consumption; but only inebriated male students were encouraged to reveal personal details about themselves.

> The use of young women to extract information suggests that the male students were assumed to be heterosexual. It appears that women were not subjected to this test. This is perhaps because it was thought that unlike men who were considered liable to succumb to women's advances, female agents were less likely to be duped by *agents provocateurs* into revealing information. The testing of men only illustrates assumptions about the workings of gender and heterosexuality.

Pru Willoughby, one of the conducting officers, told Pattinson about Christine, one of these *agents provocatrices*:

I was in charge of a very nice girl who was a prostitute. We told this girl, Christine, to go to the pub and try to break this chap down and try to get him into bed. After the week was up, he came back to Baker Street and there was a committee of people to interview him about what had happened during this week and he found to his horror that there was this girl amongst the people. Christine could also detect whether they talked in their sleep and note in which language. Some students, however, outwitted the SOE's ploy to ensnare them. Bob Maloubier recollected his 'blind date' with an attractive woman whom he immediately realised was a plant. When they retired to his bedroom, he confronted her: 'We talked the matter over in my room. Anyway, she said, "Now what are we going to do?" "I'm going to kill you". [Imitates gun and laughs] I said, "You're dead." We talked the matter over. I said, "OK. You can tell the people that employ you that you came up to my room to extort information out of me and I killed you!"'

In Philippe de Vomécourt's *An Army of Amateurs*, his account of his role in the French Resistance, he described being told by a Parisian oculist that heroin had the opposite effect of carrots in that it seriously affected night vision. He arranged for a kilo of the stuff to be sent from London in the diplomatic bag of a neutral military attaché. He then supplied it to the prostitutes in the brothels in Tours which were frequented by German night fighters. It worked, but after a month or so their doctors realised the cause and interrogated the pilots about their habits, their movements, what they ate and drank, and how much they smoked. This led to police raids on the brothels. While some of the women may have been successfully lifted out and flown back to Tempsford, two were arrested and shot. Philippe continued his resistance work elsewhere.

There was another woman said to have been parachuted into France, but of whom little has come to light apart from a paragraph in Jerrard Tickell's *Moon Squadron*. If his story is true, it's quite possible he deliberately changed her name to help her remain anonymous.

Her Worship, the Mayoress of a town in the Bordeaux area ... was the daughter of an English father and a French mother. Under the code name of Chloë, she was parachuted into France to work as a radio operator with Achille, leader of the local Resistance. To explain away her constant association with him, it was agreed that Chloë should pose as Achille's wife. So popular did the couple become, that, with the cordial approval of the Gestapo, Achille was elected Mayor. Here the years that Chloë had spent at an English public school stood her in good stead. To her duties as Mayoress, she brought all the dignity that she had acquired as a prefect at Roedean, playing the part of a civic hostess as to the manner born. She dispensed cake and conversation to the entire satisfaction of the townspeople – and of the Germans. It was sad when she had to go away for a fortnight into some unspecified place in the sunshine because of a persistent cough. She returned, looking sun-burned and much better. She resumed her duties and a small party was given to celebrate her homecoming. An affecting speech was made by the chief of the Gestapo who was quite unaware that, during her absence, Her Worship the Mayoress had attended speech-day at Roedean, caught a one and a half pound trout in the Test and replenished her make-up box in Dover Street, London, W.1.

Another woman that Tickell refers to, not in the SOE records, is Philippe Livry-Level's second daughter, who was described as a British agent. Philippe was a pilot at Tempsford himself, flying on 161 sorties. His wife and daughter were both imprisoned by the Germans and condemned to death. She managed 'by wit of her inherited wit and ingenuity, to escape whatever passport to eternity the Germans had decided for her. She lived to match her father's *Croix de Guerre* with her own'.

Josephine Hamilton

Jelle Hoolveld gave me the names of the two other female agents sent into Holland, Josephine Hamilton and Jos Gemmeke. They were in SOE's 'N' Section, *Bureau Bijzondere Opdrachten*, which translates as Bureau of Special Duties. On 10 August 1944, a month before the Battle of Arnhem, Flight Lieutenant Terence Helfer of 161 Squadron took off from Tempsford at 0018 hours in his Hudson. Despite poor visibility, at 0204 hours he dropped Antonia, and her brother Frank Hamilton, with a container of weapons and two pigeons near Abbekerk, a rural community about five kilometres north of Hoorn and twenty kilometres north-east of Alkmaar. Given the previous disasters, they were dropped blind.

Their personnel files in the National Archives provided fascinating details of their missions. While in training in Britain, Antonia was known as Josephine. In line with the names of games, which 'N' Section was then using for its agents sent into Holland, hers was TIDDLEYWINKS and Frank's was ROWING. In the field, her codename was HEMERIK.[13]

When they arrived at the barn at Gibraltar Farm, they were issued with the equipment listed on the Air Transport form. Antonia's was stamped MOST SECRET and dated 26 July 1944. It gave her height as 1.72 metres and her weight as 125 pounds – information valuable for the issuing officer, who would be able to locate for her the necessary items on the three-foot-wide concrete shelves that ran around the inside of the building. She was given a Colt .32 revolver with fifty rounds of ammunition, a locking knife, a pocket compass, field dressings, a torch with one spare battery and bulb, a pack of Lyons emergency rations, and a flask of cognac. Over her ordinary clothes she had a 'striptease' parachutist's suit; harness; parachute; an old-type helmet; spine, knee and heel pads; ankle bandages; over-boots; and a spade for burying the parachute after she landed. The 'L' pill was not issued but she took four 'B' tablets, Benzedrine, to help keep her awake.

The cover story she was given had to be as close to the truth as possible. Should she be captured and interrogated, she needed to know the story off by heart. The name on her identity card was 'Antonia Wouters', born on 22 May 1910 at Breda. She grew up at Ginnekenweg 8 and was known to everyone as 'Ton'. Her parents, Anton and Hendrika, were both Dutch and their dates of birth were provided. Her father was a wood broker and her mother a housewife. It detailed which schools she went to and that she helped around the house when she left. From October 1930 until summer 1932 she worked as a housekeeper for Mrs van Oerle of Oegstgeesterweg 8 in Lieden, but when her parents decided, for business reasons, to emigrate to America, she went with them. They lived at 444 Central Park West in New York. Mr Wouters engaged in the wood trade with various American businessmen.

Aged only twenty-two when she was in America, 'Ton' did very little work, just lived off her father's earnings. In 1934 she got engaged to Derek van der Linden, but he broke it off in summer 1938. Heartbroken and rather tired of the Americans, she decided to return to Holland. Although her parents were not keen on this, she was an adult and was determined to leave. The SOE had done their homework. They had gone to the trouble of contacting various shipping agencies to get the correct details for the cost of her return tickets from Rotterdam to New York. She sailed on the SS *Volendam* of the Amerika Line in a cabin which cost £69 in 1932 and £65 10s 0d in 1938. The prices for Tourist-class return tickets for the same years were £43 5s 0d and £50 15s 0d, and third-class £33 5s 0d and £38 10s 0d. They even provided all the dates she needed to convince anyone making enquiries about her travel arrangements.

'Ton' went to work at a friend of her father's in Amsterdam, Dr H. J. Damen of Prinsengracht 1019. In return for looking after the house she was paid a little, but her father had given her sufficient funds to be quite comfortably off. She stayed there during the war until she was called up by the *Arbeidsdienst* (Employment Bureau) and ordered to work as a kitchen inspector in the *Oorlogstijd Afdeeling Massa Voedeing* (Wartime Mass Feeding Programme) in Amsterdam. How and when she got to England was not documented.

The relevant documents, a *Legitimatiebewijs Voedselvoorziening in Oorlogstijd* and a Dutch Identity Card, were provided. She had previously been interviewed by an officer regarding the use of neutral post boxes and passwords. Camouflaged in her handbag were a one-time pad, documents for the journey from Holland to France in case of emergency, and a W.O.K. (Worked Out Key) Code.

The Adam Matthew Publications website provides details, her operation, codenamed TIDDLEYWINKS. She had to re-establish propaganda links and send messages to the underground press on behalf of Queen Wilhelmena, but the mission had to be aborted as she broke both her shin and splint bones on landing in a canal. Despite the pain, she managed to hide for a couple of nights until she was discovered by the Dutch Resistance, who took her to Haarlem via Alkmaar, where she was put in hospital under a fake name. The flask of cognac would have come in handy to dull the pain until she got to see a doctor. She stayed with another Dutch SOE agent, Tom Biallosterski, 'Draughts 2', until Frank found her a safe, isolated farmhouse where she survived the rest of the war.

Sibyl Anne Sturrock

The last recorded WAAF I have come across who was parachuted into occupied Europe was sent by the SIS, which may or may not have records of this. As the woman was in the WAAF, Escott included her details in the postscript to *Mission Improbable*, and her story is worth mentioning here. Whether she was flown out of Tempsford, Tangmere, or Harrington was not mentioned, but it is possible she flew from one of these locations as long flights to Algiers did originate from these airfields.

Sibyl Anne Sturrock was born in Berlin in 1921, and as her father worked in the Foreign Office she spent time studying in schools in Hungary, Yugoslavia and Austria. Known as 'Chibi' to her friends, she was fluent in several languages.

Early in the war she moved to England and joined the WAAF in July 1940 and became a sergeant wireless operator employed on direction finding. She was described by Escott as

> a convinced anti-fascist. She quickly found the rules and petty discipline of her life restrictive, being of an independent, outspoken nature, and felt her abilities wasted until SIS, recognising her peculiar talents, had her seconded to its service. At its insistence she was sent for officer training before working at the Yugoslav desk in London and then Bari [in Italy].

Escott provided background of the politics of Yugoslavia, which were as complicated as those in France. In September 1944, Sibyl was parachuted in

> to work on operations, intelligence gathering and building up good relations with the Yugoslavs, under the leadership of her organiser Major John Ennals and their radio operator Eli Zohar. They were attached to the 10th Corps of the partisan General Tito in the partly liberated territory of Moslavina, about 45 km south-east of the Croatian capital of Zagreb, and surrounded by enemy-held

lines of communications.

In the winter snow, at the end of the year, she travelled with the partisans on foot and on horseback as they retreated painfully, step by step into Slavonia. 'Life was very serious and danger a constant companion.' Her willingness to share their hardships and champion their cause made her very popular and helped to establish confidence between the Allied and partisan authorities.

By about March 1945, they had gone back as far as they would go and the Yugoslav army prepared to take the offensive, eventually advancing into Podravina and joining the advancing Red Army of Russia, Sibyl still accompanying them. In May 1945 Zagreb was finally liberated and she took part in the great victory march through the city. Now her part in the war was over and shortly afterwards she left.

In recognition of her work, she was awarded the OBE in 1946.

Jos Gemmeke

Twenty-two-year-old Jos Gemmeke, codenamed 'Sphinx' and also known as 'Els von Dalen', had been active in the Dutch Resistance as a courier, printing and distributing the underground newspaper *Je Maintiendrai*. She did it so well that she looked after several other journals' distribution as well. Later on, she worked as a communications officer, carrying wireless equipment and other goods dropped by 138 Squadron.

In October 1944, despite being shot at by British planes as she cycled south out of occupied Holland, Jos managed to charm a *Feldwebel* into allowing her to cross the River Waal into Belgium. There, she delivered important papers and microfilm hidden in her powder compact and shoulder pads to the headquarters of Prince Bernard in The Hague. They were destined for the Dutch Secret Service in London. The prince arranged for a plane, a green Dakota, to fly Jos to England where, once she had been debriefed, she started specialist training for the SOE. In Foot's book, he quoted her officers describing her as 'a very level and cool-headed young woman, completely unemotional, very reserved and very determined'. She passed her parachute training at Ringway, was considered outstanding while at Beaulieu, and was awarded a commission in the FANY.

After being flown out of Tempsford, she was dropped at Nieuwkoop on 10 March 1945. Although she was injured parachuting from a low altitude, she managed to complete her mission. She kept as souvenirs her pistol, a bottle of strong drink that she drank to mitigate the impact of her jump, and the belt that held the 100,000 guilders she had brought for the Resistance movement. Her mission was to follow the Allied advance into Germany, under the guise of a secretary to a businessman, and work with Dutch labourers in German factories at sabotage and slowdowns. As relations between the two countries had broken down by then, her mission was aborted, but not before she sent back awful accounts of foreign workers' treatment. She survived the war to be appointed the chairwoman of the *Vereniging Ridders in de Militaire Willemsorde* (Society for Knights in the Military Order of William).

Carpetbaggers' Women

Bowman[14] mentioned two other women who were flown by Carpetbagger pilots from Harrington. Douglas D. Walker, a pilot who arrived in January 1945, recalled in his memoirs being part of Sergeant Swartz's crew.

I was in the waist of the Liberator preparing for the mission while I awaited the arrival of the Joe. The generator was running, so I had a dim light to work by. I looked up as the Joe stepped into the aircraft. I nodded to him, not paying too much attention, as I was busy arranging the static lines.

An OSS Colonel stepped in behind and walked over to me. 'Sergeant', he said, 'Take good care of your Joe tonight – she is a special cargo.' I turned to look and she had removed her helmet, unveiling a casket of blonde hair down to her shoulders, I smiled at her in welcome and told the colonel, 'Don't worry, we'll deliver her in good condition.'

He then told me that she understood only French and German and that her mother and father in France had been killed by the Nazis – the reason she had volunteered to be dropped into Germany, Seems we were dropping her into the Bavarian Alps region to determine if Hitler was really setting up a 'last ditch' stronghold in the so-called mountain redoubt, to hold out against the Allied armies.

After we took off, I made her as comfortable as I could – as comfortable as could be managed in a draughty, unheated bomber on a cold night in January.

With my fractured French and her equally disjointed English, it was difficult, but we managed to communicate so that I could at least keep her mind occupied until the time came for her to jump into Germany.

I'll never forget the sight of that pretty, brave girl, as she sat in the Joe Hole awaiting my signal to jump into the night! Here we were, flying in pitch darkness over enemy territory at 2,000 ft and she had the courage to parachute into enemy skies, not knowing what fate awaited her below! I wished her '*Bon Chance*' as she jumped and she answered with a smile – '*Merci Mon Ami*'.

The tail-gunner, Ralph Schiller, reported that her parachute had opened and 'we flew back to England and safety – leaving a very brave woman behind in a very unsafe place! We never learned what happened to her, but we all agreed that she was one of the bravest people we had ever met!'

Lieutenant John L. Moore, a navigator in the carpetbagger outfit, also fondly recalls one female Joe. 'I briefed the crew, captained by Lieutenant West, which dropped her over south-central France. She was a little thing, 5 ft 2 or 3 in and about 105 lb. How many stone would that be? Beautiful in spite of her Second Lieutenant uniform. Some of the Joes wore British or American uniform so if caught in their 'chutes they would have a part of a cover story. I doubt if the uniforms helped them live long if caught. Hope she lived through the mess.'

During World War Two thousands of agents were parachuted into occupied Europe, and many were female. SOE for instance dispatched 10,000 men and 3,200 women agents and operatives into Europe during the war.

Pattinson commented that these figures are often cited when speaking about the total numbers of men and women who served in SOE. The 3,200 refers to the FANYs mainly, who were employed as wireless operators, coders, secretaries, etc., in Britain, Italy, North Africa and the Far East, and to a lesser extent to civilians (who worked in Baker Street and as seamstresses in The Thatched Barn, for example) rather than operational agents. So the sentence is highly misleading.

Sometimes there was some comic relief, even for the Carpetbaggers. One crew returned from a mission and told the story about a female French agent they were carrying.

She was slow getting to the Joe-hole because of the heavy gear she was wearing and was not allowed to jump, as the reception light went out before she was ready. She sulked on the way back until nature put her under pressure. She was directed to the 'relief tube' in the airplane's rear section. The dispatcher gallantly turned his back while the girl struggled with her zipped up man's flying suit, in an effort to use the tube that was, unfortunately, designed for the male's anatomy. Finally, the girl burst into laughter, and when the dispatcher turned around, she demonstrated to him in rapid-fire French and gestures that her personal 'operation' had not been completely successful. She was considerably dampened below the waist (but not in spirits) ...

Another time a radio operator reported that as the aircraft crossed over a target without making the planned drop, he heard a woman's voice on the ground S-phone yelling in a cockney accent. 'For Christ's sake, come back 'ere: Turn around and come back!'[15]

David Oliver quotes Roy Buckingham, who was posted to 138 Squadron in June 1944.

On one occasion we had to bring our 'Joe', a young lady, back with us to the forward base at Kinloss in Scotland after the 'Joe' hatch had frozen solid over a DZ in Denmark.

It was my duty with Bill Clarkson, the dispatcher, to make sure that no one talked to the agent while we were away from the base. We had to stick close to her even in bed – we were all fully clothed – and when she went to the toilet, the door remained unlocked. We were standing outside the women's toilet when a senior WAAF officer wanted to go in. We barred her way and she demanded to speak to our commanding officer. We gave her the number and when she got through, her face went bright red when he told her in no uncertain terms that she should leave us to do our duty.[16]

Who she was, what her mission was, and whether she went on a subsequent trip remains a mystery.

The Women's Motivation

Of the fifty female SOE agents sent into France, fifteen were caught by the Germans. Only three survived. The French captured three others, two of whom escaped. One died of meningitis, and another had an embolism in the field. Although I have found evidence of over sixty women sent into occupied Europe, the exact number remains unknown.

The motivation for many of these women to undergo specialist training and be sent into enemy-occupied territory knowing about the possibility of arrest, torture, and potential execution, was not the love that Sebastian Faulks' heroine, Charlotte Gray, had for her missing RAF pilot downed somewhere in France. According to Vera Atkins, it was their loathing of Nazi ideology, a love of freedom, and a desire to make an individual contribution to the liberation of France, Belgium, and Holland. They were messengers of hope to the Resistance.

Selwyn Jepson, who recruited the women for SOE, stated that the agents had many different motives for joining:

...there were those seeking escape or relief from domestic pressure. An unhappy marriage, loss of a loved one that might be assuaged by devotion to a cause; perhaps the loss had been through the war simply to carry on where the dead had to stop. Above and beyond these personal motives one has to remember the basic fact that of all stimuli, war is the strongest, enough to deny self in a common need to defeat the enemy.[17]

In an interview recording at the Imperial War Museum, Atkins said:

I've always found personally that being a woman has great advantages if you know how to play the thing right and I believe that all the girls, the women who went out, had the same feeling. They were not as suspect as men, they had very subtle minds when it came to talking their way out of situations, they had many more cover stories to deliver than most men and they performed extremely well. Also they're very conscientious – I'm not saying men are not. They were wonderful radio operators and very cool and courageous.[18]

Elizabeth Nicholas's research led her to be quite critical of the SOE. According to Vera, the women sent to France by 'F' Section were mostly in their early twenties, telephonists, shop assistants and clerks. Most had lived in simple, modest accommodation. Some spoke imperfect French and, after only a few weeks of training, 'were sent to pit themselves against German counter-espionage services manned by men of the utmost shrewdness, highly-trained, with many years of experience in that field'. The men in London who controlled them she described as 'amateurs'.

There were some involved on the British side and many on the French who suggested that the British government sacrificed the lives of many of its British and French agents and sub-agents as part of a grand deception scheme. Its details are outlined in Kramer's *Flames in the Field*. There are many in Holland and Belgium of the same opinion. They argue that, as part of Churchill's agreement with Stalin, a plan was created to distract Hitler from the Eastern Front by pretending an Allied invasion in the Pas de Calais was planned for the summer or autumn of 1943. The intensified provision of agents, arms, ammunition and supplies to the Resistance and their increased sabotage activity in the north of France was part of the scheme.

One female agent interviewed by Pattinson detailed some of her experiences in Normandy and asked to remain anonymous. Not long after D-Day, and with the American army advancing towards Paris, she and her organiser drove back and forth across the lines. Her mission was to provide the Americans with intelligence about the German military disposition. At one point, the car was ambushed and fired on. She admitted that she survived by trying to be nice with the enemy.

> You just react to the moment and think. I'll get by alright with a nice smile. I just sort of smiled and waved to them. All the time. Women could get by with a smile and do things that men couldn't and no matter what you had hidden in your handbag or your bicycle bag, if you had a nice smile, you know, just give them a little wink. It just happened constantly, all the time. So I got away with it. It becomes sort of second nature ... You did that [flirted] automatically. Absolutely. That was just par for the course. Just sort of went into the role automatically, just quite naturally.

On one occasion, the car she was travelling in was stopped and she was forced out. Her papers were hidden in her girdle.

> I heard this marching behind me and I turned around and there were these two guys so I just smiled at them and went on my way and they followed me in and

they raped me. One held me down. My first instinct was to put up a fight and then I thought no, I can't. I've got these papers. If I put up a fight, they're going to overpower me and then they'll probably strip me and we'd be in a worse mess than we are already in. I've just got to let them do it and get on with it ... Anyway, it was quite an experience! But they didn't get my papers! [laughs]

Three survivors interviewed by Pattinson described being badly beaten. Testimonies of locally recruited French Resistance workers note that some women had electric currents run through their nipples, electrodes inserted into their vaginas, their nails extracted, their breasts severed, and some were raped by guards, sometimes in front of their male colleagues.

The horror of being robbed of one's dignity after having been stripped, shaved, and being given shapeless prison clothing and a number was mentioned by many survivors. Lillian Kremer, who researched the Jewish survivors of the Holocaust, said that women were shamed and terrified by SS men who made lewd remarks and obscene suggestions and poked, pinched, and mauled them in the course of delousing procedures and searches for hidden valuables in oral, rectal, and vaginal cavities.

Prisoners were forbidden to exchange their camp clothing, to dress well, to wear make-up, to style their hair – they were, in a word, de-feminised. Many had to cope with diarrhoea, cystitis, malnutrition, excessive exercise and lack of sanitary products. These problems, in addition to maltreatment, often led to the cessation of menstruation. Tania Szabó reported that 'those for whom periods continued, through intentional lack of hygienic material to prevent the menses flowing down the legs of the women ... they suffered great distress and humiliation'. Some were worried that bromide had been put into their soup to stop them from having children.

One poignant account was given by Geneviève de Gaulle, a captured member of the French Resistance, who was celebrating her birthday. She had been given a birthday cake made from compressed breadcrumbs, which had been kneaded together with several spoonfuls of a molasses-like substance they called 'jam' or 'jelly'. Twenty-four twigs were used as candles and leaves picked from the banks of the nearby swamp decorated the edges.[19]

What I found interesting in the accounts of all these women is that there were very few records of them taking advantage of their 'L' pills, the cyanide capsules they were to use *in extremis*. It could well have been that they were convinced that, if they kept to their cover story, they would be able to bluff their way through, even survive the torture. In Marcus Binney's *The Women who Lived for Danger*, he beautifully summed up the role of the SOE women:

In an organisation that recruited numerous outstandingly brave and resourceful men, who repeatedly carried out the most hazardous missions in enemy-occupied Europe, constantly facing the threat of betrayal, arrest and torture by the Gestapo, these women were to show corresponding valour, determination and powers of endurance, serving alone or in small groups. Without hesitation, they risked their lives on an often daily basis. For this they had no previous military or professional training, as many of the men had. They had to be alert, quick-witted, calm and unruffled while constantly acting a part. Women had never had such a role to play before, yet again and again they surprised their comrades with their astonishing mastery of clandestine life.

The Tempsford crews were probably completely ignorant of the women's missions. They were not supposed to know. They undoubtedly heard on the grapevine, or sometimes first-hand, what happened to their colleagues if they crash-landed and survived. If they were very lucky, they themselves might be rescued by the Resistance and sent down the escape line back to Britain. However, there was always the chance of being captured and imprisoned. As prisoners of war, they knew they would be reasonably well treated until the end of the war. However, they probably guessed what happened to captured agents, especially women. Of course, the details of what happened to the women referred to above only came to light well after the war ended.

Yet another woman said to have been sent into France has recently come to light. Friends of the deceased Madge Frith Wilkinson (née Crabtree) believe she was an SOE agent in France and have been trying to find out information about her. Born on 4 February 1921 in Rochdale, she was fluent in French and Spanish and was thought to have been recruited into SOE when she was about twenty. She would have been married at this time but may have used her maiden name of Crabtree or her mother's maiden name of Frith. They did not know her codename. From the few details she gave them, they believe that she was sent out in a submarine to Gibraltar and then made her way up through Spain, across the Pyrénées and into France. The work she did there was largely a mystery to them, but they believe that she was involved in sabotage and returning intelligence to HQ in London. As there are no records of her in the SOE files, it is possible she was employed by the SIS.

Pattinson's investigations revealed that two female agents were arrested at checkpoints while travelling in cars loaded with weapons. One was arrested when she visited her network's wireless operator following a transmission that allowed the Abwehr to locate the operator's position. Five agents were arrested at safe houses under German surveillance. Two were arrested following delation, denunciation by acquaintances hoping for at least a 10,000-franc reward. Another was trapped by a German agent impersonating a new recruit to her network.

Two female wireless operators were captured by their sets having been located by *gonios*, the detection vans. One was denounced by a jealous wife who believed the agent was having an affair with her husband. Another was captured following a young member of her network revealing under torture the address of a safe house they didn't think she would be using. One was caught in a Gestapo raid on a landing field when they were trying to capture someone else, and another was captured immediately on landing by a German reception committee. All told, seventeen were arrested and incarcerated in French prisons. Blanche Charlet managed to escape from Castres along with fifty-three other inmates on 16 September 1943, and Mary Herbert was released after two months because of lack of evidence.

Many of them were said to have feigned ignorance and confessed to being gullible when interrogated. An SOE report in the National Archives notes that:

> A woman agent 'admitted' to having been engaged in subversive activity, but said she had gone into it with her eyes closed and, at first, had no idea of what she was doing. Later, when she did realise she was afraid to give it up. In this way, she was able to represent herself as having been locally recruited, when, in fact, she was a parachuted agent.[20]

In Pattinson's 2006 article, '"Playing the daft lassie with them": Gender, Captivity and the Special Operations Executive', she noted that many played on stereotypically feminine traits, such as foolishness, innocence, lack of common sense, anxiousness and timidity.

Along with the 104 arrested male agents, fifteen women agents were deported from France to concentration camps. Seven were executed shortly after arrival; the others suffered months of incarceration, some in solitary confinement. Three were injected with phenol at Natzweiler concentration camp. Four were shot at Dachau. Three were shot at Ravensbrück, one died in the gas chamber there, and another died of starvation and typhus at Belsen while awaiting repatriation. Only three women and twenty-three men managed to return from the camps.

Baroness Crawley's Debate in the House of Lords

On 6 June 2011, Baroness Crawley started a debate in the British House of Lords in an attempt to persuade the government to commemorate the SOE women sent into France.

> The women concerned were recruited to serve in occupied France. They acted variously as couriers, wireless operators and saboteurs. They found places for planes to land, bringing more agents and supplies. They established safe houses and worked with Resistance movements to disrupt the occupation and clear the

path for the allied advance.

Those women did these things, given wartime pressures, after a very brief period of training. Apparently, they had each been told when recruited that there was only a 50 per cent chance of personal survival – yet, to their eternal credit, off they went. Some had been born in France, some in Britain, a couple in Ireland and some still further afield. Some were Jewish, some convent-educated, one Muslim. Some were already mothers, some just out of their teens; some shop assistants, some journalists, some wives; some were rather poor. In France, they often had to travel hundreds of miles by bike and train, protected only by forged papers, and as they went about their frequently exhausting work they were under constant danger of arrest by the Gestapo. Some were even exposed to betrayal by double agents and turncoats.

The story of what happened to some of those women is often unreadable and, in 21st-century Britain, is perhaps too easily under-remembered. A number were captured in France, horribly brutalised and sent to camps in Germany. There, the torment was often sustained over weeks and months on starvation diets, the women crammed in unsanitary and overcrowded huts with disease rampant. Four of them were killed in Natzweiler by being injected – scarcely credible as it is – with disinfectant. A number, once worked and beaten to a standstill, were shot and hanged at Dachau and Ravensbrück.[21]

Many speeches followed, honouring the women involved, not just those sent into France. This book will help keep alive their memories.

Postscript

In 1983 Josephine Butler published her autobiography entitled *Churchill's Secret Agent*. Code name 'Jay Bee', she claimed that she was the only woman in Churchill's top-secret 'Circle of 12' elite spies. With a photographic memory, impeccable French, karate training and a look-alike cousin who could double for her, Jay Bee claimed to have carried out more than fifty missions in enemy-occupied France. Her sang-froid on missions fraught with danger and importance; her stories of German ruthlessness and atrocity and Gallic tenacity and courage makes compelling reading but her name does not appear in SOE literature, nor is there a personnel file on her in the National Archives. Whilst she may have worked for the SIS, their agents were dropped and picked up by the Special Duties Squadrons. As neither Clarke nor Verity mentions her, one suspects the story to be fictitious.

The Anonymous Belgian Blonde

Philip Johns, the head of SOE's Belgian section, in his wartime memoirs *Within Two Cloaks* provided details some of the agents he sent in. There was no mention of Elaine, Olga or Frédérique but he stated that:

> Another name I have forgotten (and would not mention even if I remembered) was that of a young and exceptionally attractive Belgian girl, with long blonde hair, a beautiful slim figure, intensely blue eyes, and last but not least highly intelligent. Her husband or fiancé had been arrested by the Gestapo, taken to Germany where he was tortured in one of the notorious concentration camps and then hanged as a spy. The girl herself had escaped to England and volunteered to join SOE for eventual parachuting into her country, her personal objective being to revenge her husband or fiance's execution. After the usual training period, she was dropped into Belgium on a mission to proceed independently into Brussels, and then patronise the bars and hotels most frequented by German officers. She was to associate with the latter, offering her services in bed if necessary, and then arrange for these Germans to be beaten up and put out of action for a long time by one of the Resistance groups' assassination squads. Some of her victims were liquidated by meeting with 'fatal accidents'. Apart from her successes in the field, she was also able from time to time to relay to us important military intelligence resulting from the 'pillow indiscretions' of her clients. (Johns, P. *Within Two Cloaks*, William Kimber, (1979), p.161)

Details of who she was, whether she underwent SOE training, when she was infiltrated and the success of her mission have yet to come to light.

Notes

1 Sending Women into Occupied Europe
1. Jepson, S. (1986), [9331], Imperial War Museum, SA.
2. Escott, B. (1991), *Mission Improbable: A Salute to the RAF Women of SOE in Wartime France*.
3. *Sunday Express*, 11 March 1945.
4. Howarth (1980), p. 33.
5. http://www.docstoc.com/docs/71981970/NOTES-ON-SOE.

2 First Contact with the Resistance: May 1941 to November 1942
1. Buckmaster, M. (1946–7), 'They went by Parachute', *Chambers' Journal*.
2. http://www.64-baker-street.org/agents – accessed October 2008.
3. Interview held in the Imperial War Museum, quoted in Pattinson, J. (2007) *Behind Enemy Lines*.
4. www.plan-sussex-1944.net/anglais/pdf/infiltrations_into_france.pdf; Clark, *Agents by Moonlight*; Verity, *We Landed by Moonlight*.
5. TNA HS 9/77/1.
6. http://entertainment.timesonline.co.uk/tol/arts_and_entertainment/film/article4060466.ece.
7. http://www.timesonline.co.uk/tol/news/uk/article5887620.ece.
8. Buckmaster (1946–7).
9. http://www.spartacus.schoolnet.co.uk/SOEborrel.htm.
10. http://www.christopherlong.co.uk/pub/rafes.html.
11. Ibid.
12. Ibid.
13. Kramer (1995), *Flames in the Field*.
14. www.spartacus.schoolnet.co.uk/SOEborrel.htm.
15. More details of Andrée and the other women sent to Belgium can be found in my book *Return to Belgium*.
16. Hallowes (Churchill), O. 9478/3; 31578/3 IWMSA.
17. Jepson, S. (1986), [9331] IWMSA.
18. Hallowes (Churchill), O. 9478/3; 31578/3.
19. Tickell, (1949) *Odette*.
20. Hallowes (Churchill), O. 9478/3; 31578/3.
21. http://etheses.whiterose.ac.uk/1751/1/Ethesis_FINAL.pdf.
22. King's College Library, London: GB99 KCLMA Baynham.

3 Sabotage Operations Begin in Earnest: January 1943 to October 1943
1. Buckmaster (1946–7).
2. TNA HS 9/1452/8.
3. Ibid.
4. www.spartacus.schoolnet.co.uk/SOEProsper.htm.

5. Pawley, *In Obedience to Instructions*; www.plan-sussex-1944.net/anglais/pdf/infiltrations_into_france.pdf.
6. TNA HS 9/140/7; Verity, op.cit.p.297
7. http://www.noormemorial.org/noor.php.
8. Jepson, S. (1986) [9331] IWMSA.
9. Baseden, Y. 6373/2 IWM.
10. TNA HS 9/836/5.
11. http://www.scrapbookpages.com/Natzweiler/SOEagents2.html.
12. http://www.noormemorial.org.
13. Rée, H. 13064, IWM.
14. www.timesonline.co.uk/tol/comment/obituaries/article3752092.ece.
15. Cormeau, Y. 7385/9; 31572/1 IWM.
16. www.timesonline.co.uk/tol/comment/obituaries/article3752092.ece.
17. www.nigelperrin.com/yolandebeekman.htm.
18. Buckmaster (1946–7).
19. Ibid.
20. Cornioley, C. P. 8689/2; 10447/3 IWM.
21. Buckmaster (1946–7).
22. www.timesonline.co.uk/tol/news/uk/article3656045.ece
23. Cornioley, C. P. 8689/2; 10447/3 IWM.
24. Buckmaster (1946–7).
25. Ibid.
26. Gleeson, pp. 53–4.
27. http://soe_french.tripod.com; Gleeson, p. 54.
28. Rochester, *Full Moon to France*.
29. Howarth (1980).

4 Mass Arrests & Torture of SOE Female Agents, January 1944 to D-Day

1. http://www.ww2escapelines.co.uk.
2. http://soe_french.tripod.com.
3. http://memoresist.org.
4. Walters (1946).
5. TNA HS 9/339/2.
6. Ibid.
7. Ibid.
8. TNA HS 9/1407.
9. TNA HS 9/339/2.
10. Starr, G. R. 24613 IWM.
11. http://soe_french.tripod.com.
12. Kramer, *Flames in the Field*; http://www.conscript-heroes.com.
13. Report dated January 1944, quoted in *The Independent*, 29 October 2010.
14. http://www.telegraph.co.uk/news/obituaries/military-obituaries/special-forces obituaries/8009812/Eileen-Nearne.html.
15. TNA HS 9/1089/2.
16. Buckmaster (1946–7).
17. www.guardian.co.uk/uk/2010/oct/13/eileen-nearne-obituary.
18. TNA HS 9/1089/2.
19. TNA HS 9/1089/2.
20. Buckmaster (1946–7).
21. TNA HS 9/1089/2.
22. TNA HS 9/1089/2.
23. http://www.nigelperrin.com/denisebloch.htm.
24. http://www.jewishvirtuallibrary.org/jsource/ww2/sugar2.html.
25. http://soe_french.tripod.com.
26. Baseden, Y. 6373/2 IWM.
27. Gleeson, pp. 9–10.
28. TNA HS 9/457/6.

29. TNA HS 9/339/2.

30. http://www.64-baker-street.org/agents – accessed October 2008.

31. A. Hoffman, 'Judith Pearson delivers a talk on Spy Virginia Hall', *The Trinity Tripod*, 4 April 2006.

32. http://www.smithsonianmag.com/history-archaeology/hall.html.

33. Escott, *Mission Impossible*, p.33.

34. www.plan-sussex-1944.net/anglais/pdf/infiltrations_into_france.pdf.

35. TNA HS 6/585.

36. R. Mackness (1988), *Oradour: Massacre and Aftermath*.

37. Stevenson, W., *Spymistress*, p. 289.

38. http://www.violette-szabo-museum.co.uk.

39. www.jewishvirtuallibrary.org/jsource/ww2/sugar2.html.

40. Ibid.

41. Witherington, P. 8689/2; 10447/3 IWM.

42. TNA HS 9/339/2.

43. *Guardian*, 8 August 2011.

44. http://www.army.mil.nz/at-a-glance/news/army-news/400/pw.htm.

45. http://peek-01.livejournal.com/27044.html.

46. http://www.army.mil.nz/at-a-glance/news/army-news/400/pw.htm.

47. TNA HS6/587.

48. http://peek-01.livejournal.com/27044.html.

49. Foot (1999).

50. http://www.harrowtimes.co.uk/news/579480.from_the_typewriter_to_blazing_sten_gun/.

5 Operations to Support D-Day, 6 June to March 1945

1. Howarth, *Undercover: The Men and Women of the Special Operations Executive*.

2. Ibid.

3. Pawley, *In Obedience to Instructions*.

4. http://www.wordiq.com/definition/Christine_Granville.

5. McCall (1980).

6. TNA HS 6/112.

7. http://www.adam-matthew-publications.co.uk.

8. TNA HS 6/84.

9. http://cometeline.blogspot.com.

10. TNA HS 9/460/3.

11. http://www.historynet.com/amy-elizabeth-thorpe-wwiis-mata-hari.htm.

12. Quoted in Miller, *Behind the Lines*.

13. TNA HS 6/767; see also the author's *Return to Holland* (2009).

14. Bowman (1988).

15. Fish, *They Flew By Night*.

16. Oliver, *Airborne Espionage*.

17. Masson, *Christine*, p. 47.

18. Atkins, V. 9551/3; 12302/1; 23237/3; 31590/3; 31592/3; 31586/3 IWM.

19. http://www.seanet.com/~raines/conflicts.htm.

20. TNA HS 7/66.

21. http://www.memorialgrove.org.uk/SOE%20Women.pdf.

Bibliography

Books

Aubenas, J. Van Rokeghem, S. & Vercheral-Vervoort, J. (2006), *Des Femmes dans l'Histoire de Belgique, depuis 1830*, Editions Luc Pire.

Aubrac, L. (1993), *Outwitting the Gestapo*, University of Nebraska Press.

Basu, S. (2006), *Spy Princess: The Life of Noor Inayat Khan*, Sutton Publishing.

Le Bataillon de Guerrilla de l'Armagnac 158 R.I., AITI, 2002.

Binney, M. (2002), *The Women who Lived for Danger*, Hodder and Stoughton.

Binney, M. (2005), *Secret War Heroes: Men of the Special Operations Executive*, Hodder & Stoughton, London.

Body, R. B. (2003), *Taking the Wings of the Morning*, Serendipity.

Body, R., Ensminger, T., Kippax, S., Portier, D., Soulier, D. & Tillet, P. (2008), *Tentative of History of In/Exfiltrations into/from France during WWII from 1941 to 1945 (Parachutes, Plane & Sea Landings)*.

Bohec, J. (1999), *La Plastiqueuse à bicyclette*, Le Félin.

Bowman, M. W. (1988), *The Bedford Triangle – US Undercover Operations from England in World War Two*, Patrick Stephens.

Braddon, R. (1956), *Nancy Wake*, Cassell.

Buckmaster, M. (1952), *Specially Employed*, Batchworth.

Buckmaster, M. (1958), *They Fought Alone*, Odhams Press.

Butler, E. (1963), *Amateur Agent*, Harrap.

Butler, J. (1983), *Churchill's Secret Agent*, Blaketon-Hall.

Churchill, P. (1952), *Of Their Own Choice*, Hodder & Stoughton.

Churchill, P. (1954), *Duel of Wits*, Hodder & Stoughton.

Churchill, P. (1954), *Spirit in the Cage*, Hodder & Stoughton.

Clark, F. (1999), *Agents by Moonlight*, Tempus.

Collins Weitz, M. (1998), *Sisters of the Resistance*, John Wiley.

Cookridge, E. H. (1965), *They Came from the Sky*, Heinemann.

Crowdy, T. (2007), *French Resistance Fighters: France's Secret Army*, Osprey Publishing.

Crowdy, T. (2008), *SOE Agent: Churchill's Secret Warriors*, Osprey Publishing.

De Vomécourt, P. (1959), *An Army of Amateurs*, Doubleday.

Escott, B. (1991), *Mission Improbable: A Salute to the RAF Women of SOE in Wartime France*, Sparkford: Patrick Stephens Limited.

Escott, B. (2011), *The Heroines of SOE: F Section, Britain's Secret Women in France*, The History Press

Faulks, S. (1999), *Charlotte Gray*, Vintage.

Fish, R. (1990), *They Flew By Night: Memories of the 801st/492nd Bombardment Group as told to Col. Robert W. Fish*, privately published.

Fitzsimons, P. (2002), *Nancy Wake: The Inspiring Story of One of the War's Greatest Heroines*, HarperCollins.

Foot, M. R. D. (1999), *SOE: The Special Operations Executive 1940–1946*, Pimlico.

Foot, M. R. D. (2001), *SOE in the Low Countries*, St Ermin's Press.

Foot, M. R. D. (2004), *SOE in France*, Frank Cass.

Fourcade, M. (1973), *Noah's Ark*, George Allen & Unwin.

Fraser-Smith, C. (1991), *The Secret War of Charles Fraser-Smith*, Paternoster Press.

Griffiths, F. (1981), *Winged Hours*, William Kimber & Co. Ltd.

Heidegger, M. (1962), *Being and Time*, Blackwell.

Helm, S. (2006), *A Life in Secrets: The Story of Vera Atkins and the Lost Agents of SOE*, Abacus.

Heslop, R. (1970), *Xavier*, Hart-Davis.

Howarth, P. (1980), *Undercover: The Men and Women of the Special Operations Executive*, Routledge & Kegan Paul.

Hudson, S. (2003), *Undercover Operator: An SOE agent's Experiences in France and the Far East*, Pen and Sword.

Johns, P. (1979), *Within Two Cloaks*, William Kimber.

Jones, L. (1990), *A Quiet Courage*, Bantam Press.

King, S. (1989), *'Jacqueline': Pioneer Heroine of the Resistance*, Arms and Armour.

Kremer, L. (1999), *Women's Holocaust Writing: Memory and Imagination*, Nebraska Press.

Kramer, R. (1995), *Flames in the Field*, Michael Joseph.

Lynch, D. M. (2007), 'The Labor Branch of the Office of Strategic Services: An Academic Study from a Public History Perspective', MA Thesis, University of Indiana.

Mackness, R. (1988), *Oradour: Massacre and Aftermath*, Bloomsbury.

Marks, L. (1998), *Between Silk and Cyanide*, The Free Press, New York.

Masson, M. (1975), *A Search for Christine Granville*, Hamish Hamilton.

McCall, G. (1981), *Flight Most Secret*, William Kimber and Co. Ltd, London.

McKenzie, W. (2002) *The Secret History of the SOE*, Little, Brown.

Miller, Russell (2002), *Behind the Lines: The Oral History of Special Operations in World War Two*, Jonathan Cape.

Minney, R. J. (1956), *Carve Her Name with Pride*, Newnes.

Mulley, C. (2012), *The Spy Who Loved: The Secrets and Lies of Christine Granville*, Macmillan.

Neave, A. (1954), *Little Cyclone*, Hodder & Stoughton.

Neave, A. (1969), *Saturday at MI9*, Hodder & Stoughton.

Nicholas, E. (1958), *Death Be Not Proud*, Cresset Press.

Nicholson, M. (1995), *What Did You Do In The War, Mummy?*, Chatto & Windus.

O'Connor, B. (2009), *Return to Belgium*, private publication.

O'Connor, B. (2009), *Return to Holland*, Lulu Publishing.

Oliver, D. (2005), *Airborne Espionage: International Special Duties Operations in the World Wars*, The History Press.

Olsen, O. R. (1952), *Two Eggs on My Plate*, Allen & Unwin.

O'Sullivan, D. (1997), 'Dealing With the Devil: The Anglo-Soviet Parachute Agents (Operation "Pickaxe")', *Journal of Intelligence History*, vol. 4, no. 2, Winter 2004, pp. 33–65.

O'Sullivan, D. (2010), *Dealing With the Devil: Anglo-Soviet Intelligence During the Second World War*, Peter Lang Publishing, New York.

Ottaway, S. (2002), *Violette Szabó*, Pen and Sword.

Overton-Fuller, J. (1971), *Noor-un-nisa Inayat Khan (Madeleine)*, East-West Publications Fonds N.V., Rotterdam.

Pattinson, J. (2007), *Behind Enemy Lines: Gender, Passing and the Special Operations Executive in the Second World War*, Manchester University Press.

Pattinson, J. (2008), '"Turning a Pretty Girl into a Killer": Women, Violence and Clandestine Operations during the Second World War', in Throsby, K. & Alexander, F. (eds) *Gender and Interpersonal Violence*, Palgrave, Macmillan.

Pawley, M. (1999), *In Obedience to Instructions: FANY with the SOE in the Med*, Leo Cooper.

Pearson, J. (2005), *Wolves at the Door: The True Story of America's Greatest Female Spy*, The Lyons Press.

Peden, M. (1988), *A Thousand Shall Fall*, Stoddart, Toronto.

Persico, J. E. (1979), *Piercing the Reich: The Penetration of Nazi Germany by American Secret Agents during World War II*, The Viking Press, New York.

Poirier, J. (1995), *The Giraffe Has a Long Neck*, Leo Cooper.

Potten, C. (1986), *7 x 7 x 90: The Story of a Stirling Bomber and its Crew*, Gandy and Potten.

Rake, D. (1968), *Rake's Progress*, Frewin.

Rigden, D. (2004), *SOE Syllabus*, Secret History Files.

Ringlesbach, D. (2005), *OSS: Stories That Can Now Be Told*, Authorhous.

Rochester, D. (1978), *Full Moon to France*, Robert Hale.

Rossiter, M. (1985), *Women in the Resistance*, Greenwood Press.

Ryder, S. (1986), *Child of My Love*, Collins Harvill.

Saward, J. (2006), *The Grand Prix Saboteurs: The Grand Prix Drivers who Became British Secret Agents During World War II*, Morienval Press.

Stevenson, W. (2007), *Spymistress: the life of Vera Atkins the greatest female agent of World War II*, Arcade Publishing.

Szabó, T. (2007), *Young, Brave and Beautiful: The Missions of Special Operations Executive Agent Lieutenant Violette Szabó, George Cross, Croix de Guerre avec Etoile de Bronze*, Channel Island Publishing.

Tickell, J. (1949), *Odette*, Chapman & Hall.

Tickell, J. (1956), *Moon Squadrons*, Allan Wingate Ltd.

Turner, D., (2006) *Station XII: Aston House – SOE's Secret Centre*, The History Press.

Valentine, Ian (2006) *Station 43: Audley End House and SOE's Polish Section*, Sutton Publishing.

Verity, H. (1978) *We Landed by Moonlight*, Ian Allan Ltd.

Vigurs, K. (September 2011), The women agents of the Special Operations Executive F section – wartime realities and post war representations. PhD, University of Leeds.

Vinen, R. (2006), *The Unfree French: Life under Occupation*, Penguin.

Vomécourt, P. de (1961), *An Army of Amateurs*, Doubleday, New York.

Walters, A. (1946), *Moondrop to Gascony*, Macmillan.

Walters, A. (2009), *Moondrop to Gascony*, Moho Books, Wiltshire .

Wake, N. (1985), *The White Mouse: The Autobiography of the Woman the Gestapo Called the White Mouse*, Macmillan, Melbourne.

Ward, I. (1955), *F.A.N.Y. Invicta*, Hutchinson & Co.

Willis, S. & Holliss, B. (1987), *Military Airfields in the British Isles 1939–1945*, Enthusiasts Publications.

Wynne, J. B. (1961), *No Drums, No Trumpets: The Story of Mary Lindell*, Arthur Baker Ltd.

Yarnold, P. (2009), *Wanborough Manor: School for Secret Agents*, Hopfield Publications, Puttenham.

Newspapers and Periodicals

Baltimore Jewish Times, Berg, L., 'Story of an Anti-Nazi Spy', 2 June 2006.

Bedfordshire Times and Standard, 'King and Queen Visit RAF Station', 12 November 1943.

Chambers' Journal, Buckmaster, M. (1946–47), 'They Went by Parachute'.

Daily Graphic, 'First British Woman GC: Fought Gun Battle Alone with the Gestapo', 18 December 1946.

Daily Telegraph, Grice, E., 'Return of the White Mouse', 7 June 1994.

The Economist, 'Nancy Wake, saboteur and special agent, died on August 7th, aged 98' 13 August 2011.

Guardian, Foot, M., 'Wartime secret agent and survivor of hard labour at Ravensbrück', 30 October 2010.

Guardian, 'Nancy Wake obituary', 8 August 2011.

Harrow Times, Ramos, C., 'From the typewriter to blazing Sten gun', 20 March 2005.

Hunts Post, Thomas, G., 'Hunts Was a Nerve Centre of Allied Espionage', 23 December 1954.

Independent, 'Revealed: The story of the spy who led the French Resistance' 1 April 2008.

Independent, Judd, Terri, 'The scatterbrained spy who helped win the war', 29 October 2010.

Independent, 'WW2 resistance hero Nancy Wake dies', 8 August 2011.

London Gazette, Citation for Violette Szabó's GC, 17 December 1946.

Pattinson, J. (2006), '"Playing the daft lassie with them": Gender, Captivity and the Special Operations Executive during the Second World War', *European Review of History*, vol. 13, no. 2, pp. 271–92.

The Seattle Times, 'Nancy Wake Famed WWII Agent', 11 August 2011.

Sun, 'Nancy's Heroes', 23 August 2010.

Rodin, S. 'Mrs Smith: Train-wrecker, spy and Nazi-killer' (1948), held at FANY HQ.
Sunday Express, Simpson, W., 'WAAF girls parachuted into France', 11 March 1945.
Sunday Express, Baseden, Y., 'The Tremendous Things that Happened to a Quiet Little English Secretary: Secret Mission', 9 March 1952.
Sunday Times, 'An MP Paid to Put Paid to Hitler – Before the War', 15 December 1946.
Miami Herald, Florida, 'Marguerite Petitjean Bassett, 78', 5 Aug 1999.
The Times, Violette Szabó, Yvonne Cormeau and Kay Gimpel's obituaries.
The Trinity Tripod, Hoffman, A., 'Judith Pearson Delivers a Talk on Spy Virginia Hall', 4 April 2006.

Documents in the National Archives
HS 9/10/2 Personnel file, Françoise (aka Françine) Agazarian.
HS 9/140/6 Personnel file, Julienne Aisner.
HS 9/77/1 Personnel file, Lise de Baissac.
HS 9/114/2 Personnel file, Yolande Beekman.
HS 9/165/8 Personnel file, Denise Bloch.
HS 9/183 Personnel file, Andrée Borrel.
HS 9/56/7 Personnel file, Sonya Butt.
HS 9/250/2 Personnel file, Muriel Byck.
HS 9/298/6 Personnel file, Blanche Charlet.
HS 9/1654 Personnel file, Madeleine Damerment.
HS 9/460/3; HO 405/10578 Personnel file, Frédérique Dupuich.
HS 9/457/6 Personnel file, Yvonne Fontaine.
HS 6/762 Personnel file, Jos Gemmeke.
HS 9/612 Personnel file, Christine Granville.
HS 9/647/4 Personnel file, Virginia Hall.
HS 6/767 Personnel file, Josephine Hamilton.
HS 6/84 Personnel file, Olga Jackson.
HS 9/815/3 Personnel file, Ginette Jullian.
HS 9/836/5 Personnel file, Noor Inayat Khan.
HS 9/849/7 Personnel file, Marguerite Knight.
HS 9/895/6 Personnel file, Madeleine Lavigne.
HS 9/908/1 Personnel file, Cécile Lefort.
HS 9/910/3 Personnel file, Vera Leigh.
HS 9/888/9 Personnel file, Phyllis 'Pippa' Latour.
HS 6/112 Personnel file Elaine Madden.
HS 9/1089/2 Personnel file Eileen Nearne.
HS 9/1089/4 Personnel file Jacqueline Nearne.
HS 9/1427/1 Personnel file, Maureen 'Paddy' O'Sullivan.
HS 9/1176/1 Personnel file, Marguerite Petitjean.
HS 9/1196 Personnel file Eliane Plewman.
HS /9 392/4 Personnel file, Danielle Reddé.
HS 9/1250/1 Personnel file, Elizabeth Devereaux Rochester.
HS 9/1287/6 Personnel file, Diana Rowden.
HS 9/1289/7 Personnel file, Yvonne Rudellat.
HS 9/648/4 Personnel file, Odette Sansom.
HS 9/1435 Personnel file, Violette Szabó.
HS 9/1452/8 Beatrice 'Trix' Terwindt.
HS 9/1545 Personnel file, Nancy Wake.
HS 9/339/2 Personnel file, Anne-Marie Walters.
HS 9/1424/7 Personnel file, Odette Wilen.
HS 9/356 Personnel File, Cecile 'Pearl' Witherington.

Documents in the Imperial War Museum
Vera Atkins 9551/3; 12302/1; 23237/3; 31590/3; 31592/3; 31586/3; Air ministry document, 27 July 1946.
Yvonne Baseden 6373/2.

Odette Brown 26370/5.
Yvonne Cormeau 7385/9; 31572/1.
Cecile Pearl Cornioley 8689/2; 10447/3.
Jos Gemmeke Mulder 18153/6.
Odette Hallowes (Churchill) 9478/3; 31578/3.
Hidayat Khan (Inayat's brother) 14991/3.
Harry Rée 13064.
Elizabeth Small 29894/2; 29894/7.

Documents in King's College Library
GB99 KCLMA, *'Never Volunteer' Said My Dad*, Derrick Baynham's undated memoirs.

Films and Television
Carve Her Name with Pride, directed by Lewis Gilbert, 1958.
Churchill's Secret Army, Channel 4, 28 January – 11 February 2000.
Female Agents, Revolver Films, 2008.
Histoires, Canvas documentary on Elaine Madden, 17 April 2004.
Moonstrike, BBC TV series, March 1963.
Now the Story Can Be Told, RAF film at Hendon Air Museum, 1944 .
Odette, Wilcox-Neale film directed by Herbert Wilcox, 1950.
Secret Agent: The True Story of Violette Szabó, BBC Midlands documentary by Howard Tuck, 19 September 2002.
Secret Memories, BBC 2 Timewatch (1997), documentary by Jonathan Lewis.
Wish Me Luck, London Weekend Television, 1988–89.

Websites
http://en.doew.braintrust.at/db_gestapo_4446.html.
http://members.iinet.net.au/~gduncan/women.html.
http://www.adam-matthew-publications.co.uk/digital_guides/special_operations_executive_series_1_parts_1_to_5/SOE-Summary-of-Operations-in-Western-Europe.aspx.
http://www.ajex.org.uk.
http://www.bbc.co.uk/ww2peopleswar/stories/55/a6575655.shtml.
http://www.bbc.co.uk/ww2peopleswar/stories/17/a4437317.shtml.
http://www.bbc.co.uk/ww2peopleswar/stories/53/a9010153.shtml.
http://www.bbc.co.uk/ww2peopleswar/stories/66/a4055366.shtml.
http://www.bbc.co.uk/ww2peopleswar/stories/09/a8765409.shtml.
http://www.bbc.co.uk/ww2peopleswar/timeline/factfiles/nonflash/a6649932.shtm.
http://camouflage.osu.edu/leigh.html.
http://www.christopherlong.co.uk/pub/rafes.html.
http://www.cometeline.org.
http://cometeline.blogspot.com/.
http://www.conscript-heroes.com/ResistanceTernoisENG.html.
http://www.creativeboom.co.uk/leeds/2010/03/17/vera-leigh-soe-secret-agent/.
http://www.dailymail.co.uk/femail/article-1274379/School-sabotage-How-arson-bridge-blowing-silent-killing-curriculum-Churchills-school-secret-agents.html?ito=feeds-newsxml#ixzzonQC16Ggl.
http://www.dailymail.co.uk/femail/article-1313039/Charlotte-Gray-revealed-The-Truth-British-Heroine-died-forgotten.htm.
http://www.deols-tourisme.fr.
http://www.deborahjackson.net/childrensnovels/timemeddlersundercover/specialoperationsexecutive.html.
http://www.destentor.nl/regio/deventer/3514561/NIOD-geinteresseerd-in-brief-Trix-Terwindt.ece.
http://en.wikipedia.org/wiki/El%C5%BCbieta_Zawacka.
http://en.wikipedia.org.wike/Virginia_Hall.
http://entertainment.timesonline.co.uk/tol/arts_and_entertainment/film/article4060466.ece).
http://www.escapelines.com.
http://etheses.whiterose.ac.uk/1751/1/Ethesis_FINAL.pdf.

http://www.fondspascaldecroos.org/uploads/documentenbank/fcc3fab138fbdcecfc01632f1e2f679.pdf.

http://www.francaislibres.net/liste/fiche.php?index=96827.

http://www.guardian.co.uk/uk/2010/oct/13/eileen-nearne-obituary.

http://www.geocities.com/uksteve.geo/blunhistory2.html.

http://www.hagalil.com/archiv/2004/07/meisel.htm.

http://harpet.free.fr/creation/hist/08_06.jpg.

http://harringtonmuseum.org.uk/HistoryTempsford.htm.

http://herve.larroque.free.fr/pauline_uk.htm.

http://www.independent.ie/unsorted/features/the-mystery-of-irelands-lethally-seductive-spy-314346.html.

http://members.iinet.net.au/~gduncan/women.html.

http://img.over-blog.com/300x235/2/45/42/71/philippe-8/femmme1.jpg.

http://www.informarn.nl/temasholanda/VivirenHolanda/holo40505_resistencia.html.

http://www.jewishvirtuallibrary.org/jsource//ww2/sugar2.html.

http://www.juppkappius.de.

http://www.nigelperrin.com/denisebloch.htm.

http://www.nytimes.com/2010/09/22/world/europe/22nearne.html.

http://philippepoisson-hotmail.com.over-blog.com/article-alix-d-unienville-agent-du-s-o-e-reporter-hotesse-de-l-air-43696302.html.

http://www.plan-sussex-1944.net.

http://www.praats.be/zero.htm.

http://www.scrapbookpages.com/Natzweiler/SOEagents2.html.

http://www.seanet.com/~raines/conflicts.htm.

http://www.smithsonianmag.com/history-archaeology/hall.html.

http://soe_french.tripod.com.

http://www.specialforcesroh.com.

http://www.telegraph.co.uk/news/obituaries/military-obituaries/special-forces-obituaries/8009812/Eileen-Nearne.html.

http://www.tempsford-squadrons.info/Funniesv2p2.htm.

http://www.thememoryproject.com/VeteranAssets/Artifact/Thumb_Large/acw.jpg.

http://www.thompsononename.org.uk/pdf/SOE.pdf.

http://www.timesonline.co.uk/tol/comment/obituaries/article3752092.ece.

http://www.timesonline.co.uk/tol/comment/obituaries/article3686759.ece.

http://www.timesonline.co.uk/tol/news/uk/article5887620.ece.

http://www.usnews.com/usnews/culture/articles/030127/27heyday.hall.htm.

http://www.wartimememories.co.uk/airfieldstempsford.html#Whitford.

http://www.ww2awards.com/person/341.

http://members.aol.com/HLarroque/pauline.htm.

http://www.plan-sussex-1944.net/anglais/pdf/infiltrations_into_france.pdf.

http://www.buchenwald-dora.fr/4documentation/rp2/2res/3hist/06/03/02his.htm.

http://philippepoisson-hotmail.com.over-blog.com/article—jeanne-bohec-la-plastiqueuse-a-bicyclette—38321016.html.

http://www.adam-matthew-publications.co.uk/digital_guides/special_operations_executive_series_1_parts_1_to_5/SOE-Summary-of-Operations-in-Western-Europe.aspx.

http://www.historynet.com/amy-elizabeth-thorpe-wwiis-mata-hari.htm.

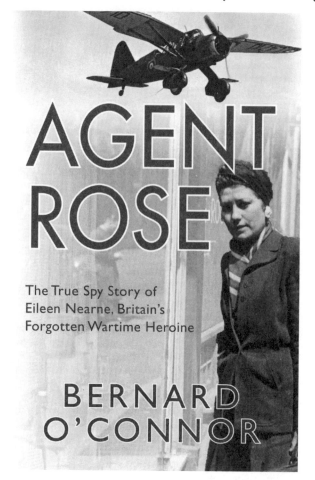

Index